THE DEAD SEA SCROLLS

Hebrew, Aramaic, and Greek Texts
with English Translations

Volume 4A
Pseudepigraphic and Non-Masoretic Psalms and Prayers

The Princeton Theological Seminary Dead Sea Scrolls Project
Editor: James H. Charlesworth

Graphic Concordance
to the Dead Sea Scrolls
Tübingen/Louisville 1991

The Dead Sea Scrolls
Hebrew, Aramaic, and Greek Texts with English Translations

1: Rule of the Community and Related Documents

2: Damascus Document, War Scroll, and Related Documents

3: Damascus Document Fragments,
More Precepts of the Torah, and Related Documents

4A: Pseudepigraphic and Non-Masoretic Psalms and Prayers

4B: Angelic Liturgy: Songs of the Sabbath Sacrifices

5: Thanksgiving Hymns and Related Documents

6: Targum on Job, Pesharim, and Related Documents

7: Temple Scroll and Related Documents

8: Genesis Apocryphon, New Jerusalem, and Related Documents

9: Copper Scroll, Greek Fragments, and Miscellanea

10: Biblical Apocrypha and Pseudepigrapha

Lexical Concordance to the Dead Sea Scrolls

The Dead Sea Scrolls

Hebrew, Aramaic, and Greek Texts with English Translations

Volume 4A

Pseudepigraphic and Non-Masoretic Psalms and Prayers

edited by

JAMES H. CHARLESWORTH

and

HENRY W. L. RIETZ, ASSISTANT EDITOR

with

P. W. FLINT, D. T. OLSON, J. A. SANDERS, E. M. SCHULLER, and R. E. WHITAKER

MOHR SIEBECK · TÜBINGEN
WESTMINSTER JOHN KNOX PRESS · LOUISVILLE

Distributors

for the United States and Canada   *for Europe*

Westminster John Knox Press   *Mohr Siebeck*
100 Witherspoon Street   *Wilhelmstr. 18, Postfach 2040*
Louisville, Kentucky 40202-1396   *D-72010 Tübingen*
USA   *Germany*

All other countries are served by both publishers.

Die Deutsche Bibliothek – CIP-Einheitsaufnahme

The *Dead Sea scrolls:* Hebrew, Aramaic, and Greek texts with English translation; [the Princeton Theological Seminary Dead Sea scrolls project] / ed. by James H. Charlesworth and Henry W. L. Rietz with P. W. Flint ... – Tübingen: Mohr; Louisville: Westminster John Knox Press
Vol. 4A. Pseudepigraphic and non-masoretic psalms and prayers. – 1997
   ISBN 3-16-146649-7

Library of Congress Cataloging-in-Publication Data

Dead Sea Scrolls. Selections.
   The Dead Sea Scrolls : Hebrew, Aramaic, and Greek texts with English translations / edited by James H. Charlesworth
   with P. W. Flint ... et al.
          p.   cm. – (Princeton Theological Seminary Dead Sea scrolls project)
   Contents: v. 1. The Rule of the community and related documents. v.2. Damascus document, War scroll, and related documents.
   v.4A. Pseudepigraphic and non-masoretic psalms and prayers.
   ISBN 0-664-21994-2 (v. 1)
   ISBN 0-664-22037-1 (v. 2)
   ISBN 0-664-22060-6 (v. 4A)
   1. Dead Sea Scrolls—Criticism, interpretation, etc.
I. Charlesworth, James H.   II. Dead Sea Scrolls. English. 1997.
III. Title.   IV. Series.
BM487.A3   1997
296.1'55—dc20   93-34036

© 1997 by J. C. B. Mohr (Paul Siebeck)
P.O. Box 2040, D-72010 Tübingen

Printed by Gulde-Druck in Tübingen on acid free stock paper;
bound by Heinrich Koch in Tübingen.

Table of Contents

The Princeton Theological Seminary Dead Sea Scrolls Project
List of Contributors

JAMES F. ARMSTRONG
Princeton Theological Seminary,
Princeton, New Jersey

JOSEPH M. BAUMGARTEN
Baltimore Hebrew College,
Baltimore, Maryland

CRAIG D. BOWMAN
Pepperdine University,
Malibu, California

GEORGE J. BROOKE
University of Manchester,
Manchester, England

MAGEN BROSHI
Shrine of the Book (Emeritus),
Jerusalem, Israel

JAMES H. CHARLESWORTH
Princeton Theological Seminary,
Princeton, New Jersey

JOHN J. COLLINS
University of Chicago,
Chicago, Illinois

FRANK M. CROSS, JR.
Harvard University (Emeritus),
Cambridge, Massachusetts

MICHAEL T. DAVIS
Princeton Theological Seminary,
Princeton, New Jersey

DEVORAH DIMANT
University of Haifa,
Haifa, Israel

JEAN DUHAIME
Université de Montréal,
Montreal, Quebec, Canada

JULIE A. DUNCAN
Garrett-Evangelical Theological
Seminary,
Evanston, Illinois

ELDON J. EPP
Case Western Reserve University,
Cleveland, Ohio

JOSEPH A. FITZMYER
Catholic University of America
(Emeritus),
Washington, D.C.

PETER W. FLINT
Dead Sea Scrolls Institute,
Langley, British Columbia, Canada

DAVID N. FREEDMAN
University of Michigan,
Ann Arbor, Michigan

MAURYA P. HORGAN
The Scriptorium,
Denver, Colorado

EPHRAIM ISAAC
Institute of Semitic Studies,
Princeton, New Jersey

LOREN L. JOHNS
Bluffton College,
Bluffton, Ohio

DONALD H. JUEL
Princeton Theological Seminary,
Princeton, New Jersey

PAUL J. KOBELSKI
The Scriptorium,
Denver, Colorado

ROBERT A. KUGLER
Gonzaga University,
Spokane, Wasthington

HERMANN LICHTENBERGER
University of Tübingen,
Tübingen, Germany

P. KYLE McCARTER, JR.
Johns Hopkins University,
Baltimore, Maryland

DORON MENDELS
Hebrew University,
Jerusalem, Israel

JACOB MILGROM
University of California,
Berkeley, California

JAMES MUELLER
University of Florida,
Gainesville, Florida

ROLAND E. MURPHY, O. CARM.
Duke University (Emeritus),
Durham, North Carolina

CAROL A. NEWSOM
Emory University,
Atlanta, Georgia

YOSEF OFER
Hebrew University
Jerusalem, Israel

DENNIS T. OLSON
Princeton Theological Seminary,
Princeton, New Jersey

STEPHEN J. PFANN
The Center for the Study of Early
Christianity,
Jerusalem, Israel

ELISHA QIMRON
Ben Gurion University of the Negev,
Beer-Sheva, Israel

HENRY W. L. RIETZ
Princeton Theological Seminary,
Princeton, New Jersey

J. J. M. ROBERTS
Princeton Theological Seminary,
Princeton, New Jersey

JAMES A. SANDERS
Ancient Biblical Manuscript Center,
Claremont, California

LAWRENCE H. SCHIFFMAN
New York University,
New York, New York

EILEEN M. SCHULLER
McMaster University,
Hamilton, Ontario, Canada

DANIEL R. SCHWARTZ
Hebrew University,
Jerusalem, Israel

ALAN F. SEGAL
Barnard College,
New York, New York

SCOTT R. A. STARBUCK
Princeton Theological Seminary,
Princeton, New Jersey

BRENT A. STRAWN
Princeton Theological Seminary,
Princeton, New Jersey

LOREN T. STUCKENBRUCK
University of Durham,
Durham, England

SHEMARYAHU TALMON
Hebrew University (Emeritus),
Jerusalem, Israel

EMANUEL TOV
Hebrew University,
Jerusalem, Israel

JOSEPH TRAFTON
Western Kentucky University,
Bowling Green, Kentucky

EUGENE ULRICH
University of Notre Dame,
Notre Dame, Indiana

JAMES C. VANDERKAM
University of Notre Dame,
Notre Dame, Indiana

MOSHE WEINFELD
Hebrew University,
Jerusalem, Israel

RICHARD E. WHITAKER
Princeton Theological Seminary,
Princeton, New Jersey

SIDNIE A. WHITE CRAWFORD
University of Nebraska-Lincoln,
Lincoln, Nebraska

ADELA YARBRO COLLINS
University of Chicago,
Chicago, Illinois

ADA YARDENI
Hebrew University,
Jerusalem, Israel

BRUCE ZUCKERMAN
University of Southern California,
Los Angeles, California

Preface

The Princeton Theological Seminary Dead Sea Scrolls Project was launched in 1985; since then the Project has benefited from scholarly societies, libraries, museums, foundations, and philanthropists. The Computer Committee, the Board of Editorial Advisors, the Editor's assistants, and especially the subeditors have labored to make this series the critical and comprehensive edition of the non-biblical Dead Sea Scrolls, with texts, English translations, and introductions.

Societies, Libraries, and Museums. Many people assume that the Dead Sea Scrolls are preserved primarily in the Shrine of the Book and the Rockefeller Museum. Almost all of the Dead Sea Scrolls may be found in these two locations, but they are also preserved in other places. The Editor is appreciative to each institution which (or individual who) preserves Scrolls and fragments of the Dead Sea Scrolls or the *Damascus Document* and has made them available for study and imaging. The Editor also is grateful to the institutions and individuals who have provided improved photographs or digital images of the Scrolls. The project is indebted to the following:

The ASOR Ancient Manuscript Committee,
The Israel Department of Antiquities and Museums,
The Shrine of the Book,
The Rockefeller Museum,
The Museum of the Studium Biblicum Franciscanum, Jerusalem,
The Antiquities Department of the Hashemite Kingdom of Jordan,
The Bibliothèque Nationale,
The University of Cambridge Library,
The Musée Terre Sainte, Paris,
The Ancient Biblical Manuscript Center,
Florida Southern College,
The West Semitic Research Project,
Kodansha Ltd.,
The Huntington Library, and
Archbishop Mar Athanasius Y. Samuel.

For this volume, the Very Reverend John Meno provided the Editor with access to the fragments of 1Q34[bis]. Keith T. Knox of the Xerox Corporation and Robert H. Johnston and Roger L. Easton, Jr., of the Rochester Institute of Technology provided the Editor with digital images of the fragments of 1Q34[bis].

Foundations and Philanthropists. The Project has received funding and support from numerous sources. Its success has been made possible by funding from the Foundation on Judaism and Christian Origins, the Institute for Semitic Studies, the Henry Luce Foundation, the Edith C. Blum Foundation, Inc., and especially Princeton Theological Seminary. Special appreciation is also expressed to Frances M. and Wilbur H. Friedman, and Irma Lou Wilcox for their generous support.

Computer Committee, Board of Editorial Advisors, and Assistants. When the Project began, a special Computer Committee was formed. It recommended that the Project work with the IBYCUS Computer System and develop software for the preparation of Semitic texts with appropriate sigla in order to present both on screen and hardcopy the exotic forms found in the Dead Sea Scrolls. Professor James F. Armstrong served as chair of the Committee. The other members were D. Packard, R. E. Whitaker, J. J. M. Roberts, and the Editor. The Dead Sea Scrolls Project is grateful to Professor Roberts and the Princeton Theological Seminary Hebrew Dictionary Project for use of a spare IBYCUS Computer System.

The Editor has been guided by a Board of Editorial Advisors. These are F. M. Cross, J. A. Sanders, D. N. Freedman, and S. Talmon. J. Strugnell offered valuable advice and insight. The Board advised the Editor of documents which should be included in early volumes, as well as those which should not be published presently due to the state of research on these unpublished fragments. The Board, *inter alia*, also suggested scholars who should be chosen as subeditors.

The fourth volume of texts and translations (the third to be published) has been prepared thanks to the labors of gifted assistants, namely M. Ellen Anderson, Casey D. Elledge, and Lidija Novakovic. Worthy of special thanks are four assistants who labored indefatigably. Michael A. Daise, Michael T. Davis, John B. F. Miller, and Brent A. Strawn helped organize research and assisted in editing the contributions. Henry W. L. Rietz served as assistant editor for volume four; he helped the Editor double check all translations and assure the consistent rendering of technical terms. Professor Loren L. Johns provided technical support for the PC Computer System on which the English material was prepared using Nota Bene 4.5. J. P. Kang provided additional exotic characters for the Hebrew texts using Fontographer 4.1.3. Professor Richard E. Whitaker was in charge of the final preparation and printing of all Hebrew texts. The Project is indebted to each of these individuals.

Subeditors. The Project is dependent on the expertise and cooperation of the specialists who prepared the critical texts and translations. The two main criteria employed in selecting a scholar for this work are proven expertise in Qumran research, especially on the document to be assigned, and demonstrated skill with English. Fortunately, virtually everyone invited accepted the invitation. The team of subeditors is from the U.S.A., Canada, Germany, Great Britain, and Israel (see the List of Contributors).

For this volume, permission has been granted by E. J. Brill to include the Syriac texts of Psalms 151, 154, and 155 from W. Baars, ed., "Apocryphal Psalms," in *The Old Testament in Syriac* vol. 4, part 6 (Leiden, 1972) pp. 2−4, 7−10. Permission has also been granted by Vandenhoeck and Ruprecht to include portions of the Greek texts of Psalm 151 from A. Rahlfs, ed., *Septuaginta,* vol. 10 *Psalmi cum Odis* (Göttingen, 1931) pp. 339−40 and Sirach 51 from J. Ziegler, ed., *Septuaginta,* vol. 12, 2 *Sapientia Iesu Filii Sirach* (Göttingen, 1965) pp. 364−68.

Princeton Theological Seminary. Most importantly, the Project is indebted to Dr. Thomas W. Gillespie, President of PTS, who in the mid-eighties saw the unusual significance of preparing a critical text and translation of all the non-biblical Dead Sea Scrolls. The Board of Trustees of Princeton Theological Seminary has officially endorsed and supported the Project. The launching of the Project and its success are directly related to the full support of the Board.

Finally a personal note: The dedication of all concerned was encouraging. The enthusiasm of the subeditors, and especially the dedicated assistants, helped me in ways that are known only to editors of massive and seemingly impossible projects. Georg Siebeck and his staff – and their commitment to making this Project an example of state-of-the-art publishing – have been a special blessing. The cooperation of the editorial staff of Westminster John Knox Press is deeply appreciated. To all mentioned above, and to many others, I am both indebted and grateful.

James H. Charlesworth
July 4, 1997
Princeton Theological Seminary
Princeton, N. J.

Foreword

(with Signa and Sigla)

The Princeton Theological Seminary Dead Sea Scrolls Project was established to make available the first comprehensive edition of texts, translations, and introductions to all the Dead Sea Scrolls that are not copies of biblical books (that is, documents collected in the *Biblia Hebraica*). Hence, the documents composed at Qumran, as well as the Jewish writings composed elsewhere but found in the eleven Qumran caves, are collected in this series. Volume 10 in the series is devoted to Qumran versions of documents considered to be part of the biblical Apocrypha and Pseudepigrapha.

All Qumran sectarian documents are translated so that technical terms are rendered in the same manner (see the Consistency Chart following the Foreword). On the one hand, the Editor and his staff (in consultation with the Board of Advisors) had to decide how to translate *termini technici*; for example, we voted against "the Teacher of Righteousness," in favor of "the Righteous Teacher,"[1] and against *Yaḥad* in favor of "Community." On the other hand, words or phrases with more than one meaning had to be translated consistently, yet with some variety, so as to reflect the literary context or social setting.

Obviously, each introduction must be tailored both for the corpus and for the idiosyncracies of the Scroll under consideration. When the Scroll is extensive, introductions can be organized according to an accepted pattern and a recognized order. For the convenience of the reader the guidelines for introductions may be summarized as follows:

Texts. The contributor presents all textual evidence for the document in light of the present state of research.

Original Language. The scholar discusses the language of composition.

Date. After assessing the date of the earliest witness to a document, the subeditor discusses the probable date of composition.

Provenience. Not all of the documents found in the Qumran Caves were composed at Qumran. Some were composed there; but others were written elsewhere in Palestine (in Jerusalem or perhaps somewhere in Galilee), and perhaps derive from documents (not merely traditions) that took initial shape in Babylon or elsewhere. In light of these insights the specialist discusses the provenience of the document.

History. This section attempts to discern the history or historical episodes reflected in the scroll.

Theology. The expert discusses the major theological ideas and symbols in the writing.

Relation to the Hebrew Bible. The contributor assesses how, if at all, the document is related to the *Biblia Hebraica* (and perhaps to the versions of it extant before 70 C.E.).

Relation to Other Jewish Writings. The scholar discusses possible links to other Jewish writings, especially the *Books of Enoch*, *Jubilees*, and the earliest portions of the *Testaments of the Twelve Patriarchs*. The specialist also reflects on how the document helps us reconstruct Early Judaism (or types of Judaism during the period of the Second Temple).

Relation to the New Testament. The specialist discusses the significant ties with the documents collected into the New Testament and with the figures (like John the Baptist), symbolic language, or world view mentioned or preserved in these documents. Finally, the contributor presents an assessment of how the document may affect the reconstruction of Christian Origins.

Working with the Editor and his assistants, the subeditors reproduce as accurately as possible the texts of the manuscripts. Contributors use the best available photographs. When necessary, the manuscripts are rephotographed or digitized for their use. Whenever feasible, the contributors consult the actual manuscripts. Initial, medial, and final forms of consonants in anomalous positions are reproduced in the transcription precisely as seen. The following signa, sigla, and script are employed in the transcriptions of texts:

א̇	=	essentially certain reading of a damaged character[2]
א̊	=	uncertain reading of a damaged character
°	=	illegible character
א̤ ,א̈ ,א̣	=	deletion by a scribe[3]
אשר-אין	=	deletion by a scribe
ל/ר, ל/רא	=	supralinear correction by a scribe
( )	=	emendation proposed by subeditor (used only in the composite texts)
[ ]	=	lacuna
בני א[ו]ר]	=	restoration of lacuna

---

[1] The *môrēh haṣ-ṣedeq* was not one who taught "righteousness"; he was the right teacher to whom God had revealed all mysteries (cf. 1QpHab 7.4–5).

[2] The dot added by a subeditor is always above the character.

[3] A scribe's use of a single dot over a character is indicated in a footnote to distinguish it from the sign for an essentially certain reading of damaged character.

⟦ ⟧	=	join between fragments
( )	=	area of erasure
(העם)	=	area of erasure with legible character or characters
→	=	separating mark supplied by scribe in margin
ו֜, ֜ו	=	a *waw* which could be a *yodh* (or a *yodh* a *waw*)
VAC, VACAT	=	uninscribed surface[4]
✢	=	end of line mark supplied by scribe in margin of CD
𐤉𐤄𐤅𐤄		Palaeo-Hebrew script for יהוה
𐤀𐤋		Palaeo-Hebrew script for אל
𐤀𐤋𐤄𐤉𐤌		Palaeo-Hebrew script for אלוהים
𐤀𐤋𐤉		Palaeo-Hebrew script for אלי
✘		Ligature (only in CD) signifying אל
. . . .		Signifies יהוה
✕		Palaeo-Hebrew ת

Only obvious restorations of lacunae are attempted in the text and are circumscribed by brackets [ ]. These restorations are based on comparisons with similar passages in the Qumran corpus; the *GC* serves as our guide. When appropriate, restorations of passages from the Hebrew Bible are made according to the Aleppo Codex, Codex Leningradensis, or the Masoretic Text;

this practice is most evident in the *Pesharim*. In the case of documents which are attested in multiple manuscript witnesses, a critical apparatus is employed.[5] Whenever possible, each manuscript witness is presented separately with its own critical apparatus or textual notes. In exceptional instances, a composite text is reconstructed from the fragments of various manuscript witnesses; this method is obvious in the composite text of the *Angelic Liturgy* in volume 4B.

Finally, the translators present in English the literal *meaning* of the Hebrew, Aramaic, or Greek. They avoid free idiomatic renderings. The following signs are employed in the translations:

[. . .]	=	lacuna[6]
Sons of Li[ght . . .]	=	restoration of lacuna
(God)	=	additional words necessary for meaningful English
°	=	illegible consonant
(vacat)	=	uninscribed surface

Italics are used to transliterate consonants or forms that are not translatable.[7]

J. H. Charlesworth
Princeton Theological Seminary

---

[4] This term is demanded by the ambiguity of many fragments. To avoid the intrusiveness of a Latin term in a Semitic (or Greek) manuscript, we use vacat sparingly. Aligning the text so as to clarify an uninscribed surface, especially when the line is indented, serves the intended purpose without intruding editorially into the transcription.

[5] Underlined footnote numbers indicate significant textual variants.

[6] Elipses indicate various lengths.

[7] Transliterations of Hebrew characters are according to the Society of Biblical Literature's "Handbook for Editors and Authors." Since *śîn* and *šîn* are not distinct forms in the manuscripts, both are rendered as š in the translation. However, they may be distinguished in the notes. When relevant, vocalizations appear in the notes following the conventions of the Society of Biblical Literature.

Consistency Chart

The PTS Dead Sea Scrolls Project primarily intends to present an improved critical text — with an *apparatus criticus* where appropriate and possible — to all the non-biblical documents found in the eleven Qumran caves (that means all the documents not collected within the *Biblia Hebraica*). The translation provided is dependent on the text and is an aid to comprehending it; hence, it is as literal as good English will allow. Notes to the translation indicate other possible renderings, clarify how a word or phrase has been previously translated, or draw attention to a variant reading in another copy of the document.

Two principles have been followed so as to present a faithful and coherent translation. First, the meaning of a word must be discerned within its context; that is, within the cluster of contiguous words, and within the flow of the document (or a section of it). Previously, translations of Qumran Hebrew were prepared in light of Biblical Hebrew; now, however, the subeditors have decades of experience in reading and translating Qumran Hebrew in over 600 documents. Second, technical terms must be translated uniformly and consistently throughout the extensive corpus. The following list of terms clarify the decisions obtained from the Editor's dialogues with the subeditors and with the Board of Editorial Advisors (words in parentheses indicate examples of how the word or words have been translated in non-technical contexts).

אביונים	Poor Ones
אודכה אדוני כי	I thank you, O Lord, because
איש הכזב	the Man of the Lie
אלים	divine beings
אסף	gather
ארץ	earth, land
בינה	discernment
בית קודש	House of Holiness
בליעל	Belial
בני אהרון	Sons of Aaron
בני אור	Sons of Light
בני אמת	Sons of Truth
בני השחר	Sons of Dawn
בני חושך	Sons of Darkness
בני צדוק	Sons of Zadok
בני צדק	Sons of Righteousness
גורל	lot
דביר	inner room
דעת	knowledge
הדרך	the Way, the way
חוק	statute, boundary; (assigned)
חטא	sin
חכמה	wisdom
חסד	mercy
טובים	Good Ones
יום הכפורים	Day of Atonement
יום המשפט	Day of Judgment
יום נקם	Day of Vengeance
היחד	the Community; (community, common, each other, together, one, unity)
יעד	be summoned; (appointed)
הכוהן הרשע	the Wicked Priest
הכתיאים	the Kittim
מבקר	Examiner
מועד	appointed time, holy day, season; (meeting, feast, festival)
מורה הצדק	Righteous Teacher
מטע	planting
מטיף הכזב	Spouter of the Lie
מעין	fountain
מעשים	works; (workmanship)
מצוותיו	his ordinances
מקור	spring; (discharge — 1QM 7.6)
משכיל	Master
משפט	judgment, precept; (justice)
נגלות	revealed, revealed (laws)
נפש	soul, being; (life, human being, self)
נצר	shoot
נקמה	(time of) vengeance
סוד	foundation, assembly, principle
עדה	congregation, Congregation
עול	deceit
עון	iniquity
עצה	counsel, the council, the Council
העת, עת	time, the Endtime; (now, age, continually)
פקיד	Overseer
צדקות, צדק	righteous, righteous deeds
צדיקים	Righteous Ones
קדושי קדושים	Most Holy Ones
קדושים	Holy Ones
קהל	assemble, assembly
קץ	Endtime, end, time
רוח קודש	Holy Spirit; (holy spirit)
הרבים	the Many
רז	mystery
תבל	world
תורה	Torah
תירוש	new wine

תכון	norm, measure	תעודה	fixed times, convocation, distinction; (testimony, instruction)
תמים, תם	perfect, perfectly; (perfection, continually, always, every, complete)		
תמימים	Perfect Ones		J. H. Charlesworth

Abbreviations

Modern Publications

AASOR	*Annual of the American Schools of Oriental Research*
AB	Anchor Bible
ABD	Freedman, D. N., ed. *The Anchor Bible Dictionary*, 6 vols. New York, 1992.
Abegg and Wacholder, PEUPDSS	Abegg, M. G. and B.-Z. Wacholder eds. *A Preliminary Edition of the Unpublished Dead Sea Scrolls,* 4 vols. Washington, D. C., 1991–96.
ABRL	Anchor Bible Reference Library
AcOr	*Acta orientalia*
AGAJU	Arbeiten zur Geschichte des antiken Judentums und des Urchristentums
AHDSS	Schiffman, L. H., ed. *Archaeology and History in the Dead Sea Scrolls: The New York University Conference in Memory of Yigael Yadin.* JSOT/ASOR Monograph Series 2; JSPS 8; Sheffield, 1990.
AJSL	*American Journal of Semitic Languages and Literatures*
ALBO	Analecta lovaniensia biblica et orientalia
ANRW	Haase, W., and H. Temporini, eds. *Aufstieg und Niedergang der römischen Welt.* Berlin, New York, 1979–.
ANTI	Arbeiten zum Neuen Testament und Judentum
AO	Analecta Orientalia
AOT	Altorientalische Texte zum Alten Testament
APAT	Kautzsch, E., ed. *Die Apokryphen und Pseudepigraphen des Alten Testaments*, 2 vols. Tübingen , 1900.
APOT	Charles, R. H., ed. *The Apocrypha and Pseudepigrapha of the Old Testament in English*, 2 vols. Oxford, 1913.
ASOR	American Schools of Oriental Research
ATR	*Anglican Theological Review*
BA	*Biblical Archaeologist*
BAGD	Bauer, W., W. F. Arndt, and F. W. Gingrich. *A Greek-English-Lexicon of the New Testament and Other Early Christian Literature*, 2nd ed., rev. and aug. F. W. Gingrich and F. W. Danker. Chicago, 1979.
BAR	*Biblical Archaeology Review*
BASOR	*Bulletin of the American Schools of Oriental Research*
BASORSS	*Bulletin of the American Schools of Oriental Research* Supplementary Studies
BHS	*Biblia Hebraica Stuttgartensia*
Bib	Biblica
BibOr	Biblica et orientalia
BIOSCS	*Bulletin of the International Organization for the Septuagint and Cognate Studies*
BDB	Brown, F., S. R. Driver, and C. A. Briggs, eds. *A Hebrew and English Lexicon of the Old Testament.* Oxford, 1907.
BETL	Bibliotheca Ephemeridum Theologicarum Lovaniensium, Paris and Leuven
BJRL	*Bulletin of the John Rylands Library*
BJRULM	*Bulletin of the John Rylands University Library of Manchester*
BN	Catalogue général des livres imprimés de la bibliothèque nationale
BR	*Biblical Research*
BWANT	Beiträge zur Wissenschaft vom Alten und Neuen Testament
BZ	*Biblische Zeitschrift*
BZAW	*Beihefte zur ZAW*
BZNW	*Beihefte zur ZNW*
BZRG	Beihefte der Zeitschrift für Religions- und Geistesgeschichte
Carmignac, Règle	Carmignac, J. *La Règle de la Guerre des Fils de Lumière contre les Fils e Ténèbres.* Paris, 1958.
CBQ	*Catholic Biblical Quarterly*
CBQMS	Catholic Biblical Quarterly Monograph Series
CCWJCW	Cambridge Commentaries on Writings of the Jewish and Christian World 200 BC to AD 200
CIJ	Frey, J. B., ed. *Corpvs inscriptionvm ivdaicarvm.* Vatican City, 1936–52.
CIS	*Corpus inscriptionum semiticarum.* Paris, 1881.
COR	Christian Origins Library
CPJ	Tcherikover, A., ed. *Corpus papyrorum Judicarum,* 3 vols. Cambridge, MA, 1957–64.
CRB	Cahiers de la Revue biblique
CRINT	Compendia Rerum Iudaicarum ad Novum Testamentum
Cross, AL	Cross, F. M. *The Ancient Library of Qumran and Modern Biblical Studies,* 3rd ed. Minneapolis, 1995.
Cross, "Dating"	Cross, F. M. "Excursus on the Dating of the Copper Document," DJD 3; pp. 217–21.
Cross, "Development"	Cross, F. M. "The Development of the Jewish Scripts," in *The Bible and The Ancient Near East: Essays in Honor of William Foxwell*

	Albright, ed. G. E. Wright. Garden City, New York, 1961; pp. 133–202.
CTSRIR	College Theological Society Resources in Religion
DBSup	*Dictionnaire de la Bible, Supplément*
DCH	Clines, D. J. A., ed. *Dictionary of Classical Hebrew,* 3 vols. Sheffield, 1993-96.
Delcor, *Ancien*	Delcor, M. *Religion d'Israel et proche orient ancien.* Leiden, 1976.
Delcor, *Hymnes*	Delcor, M. *Les Hymnes de Qumrân (Hodayot).* Paris, 1962.
de Vaux, *Archaeology*	de Vaux, R. *Archaeology and the Dead Sea Scrolls,* rev. ed. in an English translation. London, 1973.
DISO	Jean, C.-F. and J. Hoftijzer, eds. *Dictionnaire des inscriptions sémitiques de l'ouest.* Leiden, 1965.
DJD	Discoveries in the Judaean Desert
DNWSI	Hoftijzer, J. and K. Jongeling, eds. *Dictionary of North West Semitic Inscriptions,* 2 vols. Leiden, 1995
DSD	*Dead Sea Discoveries*
DSPS	Sanders, J. A. *Dead Sea Psalm Scroll.* Ithaca, 1967.
Dupont-Sommer, *EE*	Dupont-Sommer, A. *Les Écrits Esséniens découverts près de la Mer Morte,* 4th ed. Bibliothèque historique; Paris, 1980.
EcInt	Dupont-Sommer, A., M. Philonenko, et al., eds. *La Bible ecrits intertestamentaires.* [Paris] 1987.
EncBibl	Encyclopaedia Biblica, Jerusalem
EncJud	Wigoder, Geoffrey, ed. *The Encyclopedia of Judaism.* New York and London, 1989.
ETL	*Ephemerides theologicae lovanienses*
EvT	*Evangelische Theologie*
ExpT	*Expository Times*
Fitzmyer, *Apocryphon*	Fitzmyer, J. A. *The Genesis Apocryphon of Qumran Cave I.* Rome, 1966.
Fitzmyer, *Tools*	Fitzmyer, J. A. *The Dead Sea Scrolls: Major Publications and Tools for Study,* rev. ed. SBLRBS 20; Atlanta, 1990.
FRLANT	Forschungen zur Religion und Literatur des Alten und Neuen Testaments
Gaster, *DSS*	Gaster, T. H. *The Dead Sea Scriptures : In English Translation with Introduction and Notes,* 3rd ed. New York, 1976.
GC	Charlesworth, J. H., et al., eds. *Graphic Concordance to the Dead Sea Scrolls.* Tübingen and Louisville, 1991.
GKC	Kautzsch, E., ed. *Gesenius' Hebrew Grammar,* 2nd ed., rev., A. E. Cowley. Oxford, 1910.
GNMM	*Good News for Modern Man*
HALAT	Koehler, L., and W. Baumgartner, eds. *Hebräisches und aramäisches Lexikon zum Alten Testament,* 2 vols. Leiden 1967–95.
HAR	*Hebrew Annual Review*
HAT	Handbuch zum Alten Testament
HDR	Harvard Dissertations in Religion
Hen	*Henoch*
Hengel, *JudHell*	Hengel, M. *Judaism and Hellenism: Studies in their Encounter in Palestine during the Early Hellenistic Period,* 2 vols., trans. J. Bowden. Philadelphia, 1974.
HNT	Handbuch zum Neuen Testament
Horgan, *Pesharim*	Horgan, M. P. *Pesharim: Qumrân Interpretations of Biblical Books.* CBQMS 8; Washington, D.C., 1979.
HSCPh	Harvard Studies in Classical Philology
HSM	Harvard Semitic Monographs
HSS	Harvard Semitic Studies
HTR	*Harvard Theological Review*
HTS	Harvard Theological Studies
HUCA	*Hebrew Union College Annual*
IDB	Buttrick, G. A., ed. *Interpreter's Dictionary of the Bible,* 5 vols. Nashville, 1962.
IDBS	Crim, K., et al., eds. *The Interpreter's Dictionary of the Bible, Supplementary Volume.* Nashville, Tennessee, 1976.
IEJ	*Israel Exploration Journal*
JAAR	*Journal of the American Academy of Religion*
JANES	*Journal of the Ancient Near Eastern Society of Columbia Univeristy*
JAOS	*Journal of the America Oriental Society*
Jastrow, *Dictionary*	Jastrow, M. *A Dictionary of the Targumim, the Talmud Babli and Yerushalmi, and the Midrashic Literature,* 2 vols. New York, 1950, reprinted in Israel.
JB	*Jerusalem Bible*
JBL	*Journal of Biblical Literature*
JDS	Charlesworth, J. H., ed. *John and the Dead Sea Scrolls.* COR; New York, 1990.
JDSer	Judean Desert Series
JDSS	Charlesworth, J. H., et al. *Jesus and the Dead Sea Scrolls.* ABRL; New York, 1992.
Jeremias, *Lehrer*	Jeremias, G. *Der Lehrer der Gerechtigkeit.* SUNT 2; Göttingen, 1963.
JJS	*Journal of Jewish Studies*
JNES	*Journal of Near Eastern Studies*
JNSL	*Journal of Northwest Semitic Languages*
Joüon-Muraoka, *Grammar*	Joüon, P. and T. Muraoka. *A Grammar of Biblical Hebrew,* 2 vols. Subsidia Biblica 14. Rome, 1991.
JR	*Journal of Religion*
JSHRZ	Jüdische Schriften aus hellenistisch römischer Zeit. Gütersloh, 1973–.
JSJ	*Journal for the Study of Judaism*
JSNT	*Journal for the Study of the New Testament*
JSOT	*Journal for the Study of the Old Testament*
JSP	*Journal for the Study of the Pseudepigrapha*
JSPS	Journal for the Study of the Pseudepigrapha Supplement Series
JSS	*Journal of Semitic Studies*
JSSR	*Journal for the Scientific Study of Religion*
JThC	*Journal for Theology and the Church*
JTS	*Journal of Theological Studies*

KB	Koehler, L. and W. Baumgartner, *Lexicon in Veteris Testamenti Libros* and *Supplementum.* Leiden, 1985.
Knibb, *Qumran*	Knibb, M. A. *The Qumran Community.* CCWJCW 2; Cambridge, 1987.
Lampe	Lampe, G. W. H., ed. *A Patristic Greek Lexicon.* Oxford, 1961.
Leaney, *Rule*	Leaney, A. R. C. *The Rule of the Community and Its Meaning.* NTL; London, 1966.
LibCong	Sussmann, A. and R. Peled, eds. *Scrolls from the Dead Sea: An Exhibition of Scrolls and Archaeological Artifacts from the Collections of the Israel Antiquities Authority.* Washington, 1993.
Licht, *RS*	Licht, J. *The Rule Scroll: A Scroll from the Wilderness of Judea.* Jerusalem, 1965. [Hebrew]
Licht, *TS*	Licht, J. *The Thanksgiving Scroll.* Jerusalem, 1957. [Hebrew]
Lichtenberger, *Menschenbild*	Lichtenberger, H. *Studien zum Menschenbild in Texten der Qumrangemeinde.* SUNT 15; Göttingen, 1980.
Lohse, *Texte*	Lohse, E., ed. *Die Texte aus Qumran.* Darmstadt, 1981.
LSJM	Liddell, H. G. and R. Scott. *A Greek-English Lexicon,* 9th ed., rev. H. S. Jones and R. McKenzie. Oxford, 1940 with a Supplement of 1968.
Maier/Schubert, *Qumran*	Maier, J. and K. Schubert. *Die Qumran-Essener.* Uni-Taschenbücher 224; Munich, 1982.
Milik, *Books*	Milik, J. T. with M. Black. *The Books of Enoch: Aramaic Fragments of Qumrân Cave 4.* Oxford, 1976.
MNTC	Moffatt New Testament Commentary
MQ	Moraldi, L., ed. *I Manoscritti di Qumrân.* Turin, 1971.
NEAEHL	Stern, E., ed. *New Encyclopedia of Archaeological Excavations in the Holy Land,* 4 vols. New York, 1993.
NEB	*New English Bible*
Newsom, *Songs*	Newsom, C. *Songs of the Sabbath Sacrifice: A Critical Edition.* HSS 27; Atlanta, 1985.
NHS	Nag Hammadi Studies
NovT	*Novum Testamentum*
NRSV	*New Revised Standard Version*
NRT	*Nouvelle Revue Théologique*
NTL	New Testament Library
NTS	*New Testament Studies*
OEANE	Meyers, E., ed. *The Oxford Encyclopedia of Archaeology in the Near East,* 5 vols. Oxford, 1997.
Of Scribes	Attridge, H. W., J. J. Collins, T. H. Tobin, eds. *Of Scribes and Scrolls: Studies on the Hebrew Bible, Intertestamental Judaism, and Christian Origins.* CTSRIR 5; Lanham, Maryland, 1990.
OTP	Charlesworth, J. H., ed. *The Old Testament Pseudepigrapha,* 2 vols. New York, 1983, 1985.
OTS	Oudtestamentische Studiën
PDS	Murphy-O'Connor, J. and J. H. Charlesworth, eds. *Paul and the Dead Sea Scrolls.* COR; New York, 1990.
PEQ	*Palestine Exploration Quarterly*
Pouilly, *Règle*	Pouilly, J. *La Règle de la Communauté de Qumrân.* CRB 17; Paris, 1976.
PTSDSSP	Princeton Theological Seminary Dead Sea Scrolls Project
Qimron, *HDSS*	Qimron, E. *The Hebrew of the Dead Sea Scrolls.* HSS 29; Atlanta, 1986.
Qumrân	Delcor, M., ed. *Qumrân: Sa piété, sa théologie et son milieu.* BETL 46; Paris and Leuven, 1978.
Qumran	Grözinger, K. E. et al., eds. *Qumran.* Wege der Forschung 410; Darmstadt, 1981.
Rabin, *QumSt*	Rabin, C. *Qumran Studies.* New York, 1957.
Rabin, *ZadDoc*	Rabin, C. *The Zadokite Documents,* 2nd rev. ed. Oxford, 1958.
RB	*Revue biblique*
Reed, *Catalogue*	Reed, S. A. and M. J. Lundberg with M. B. Phelps, eds. *The Dead Sea Scrolls Catalogue: Documents, Photographs and Museum Inventory Numbers.* SBLRBS 32; Atlanta, 1994.
Reed, *Inventory*	Reed, S. A. and M. J. Lundberg, *Dead Sea Scroll Inventory Project: Lists of Documents, Photographs and Museum Plates.* Claremont, 1993.
ReScRel	*Recherches de Science Religieuse*
RGG	*Die Religion in Geschichte und Gegenwart*
RQ	*Revue de Qumran*
RSV	*Revised Standard Version*
SAOC	Studies in Ancient Oriental Civilization
SBL	Society of Biblical Literature
SBLDS	Society of Biblical Literature Dissertation Series
SBLMS	Society of Biblical Literature Monograph Series
SBLRBS	Society of Biblical Literature Resources for Biblical Study
SBT	Studies in Biblical Theology
ScEs	*Science et Esprit*
Schuller, *PsPsalms*	Schuller, E. M. *Non-Canonical Psalms from Qumran: A Pseudepigraphic Collection.* HSS 28; Atlanta, 1986.
Schürer, *HJP*	Schürer, E. *The History of the Jewish People in the Age of Jesus Christ.* Rev. ed. by G. Vermes, F. Millar, and M. Goodman, 3 vols. Edinburgh, 1973–87.
ScrHie	Scripta Hierosolymitana
SCS	Septuagint and Cognate Studies
SEA	*Svensk exegetisk Årsbok*
Sekine, *DSS*	Sekine, M., ed. *The Dead Sea Scrolls.* Tokyo, 1979.
Sem	*Semitica*
ShaTalmon	Fishbane, M. and E. Tov, eds. *"Sha'arei Talmon" Studies in the Bible, Qumran, and the Ancient Near East Presented to Shemaryahu Talmon.* Winona Lake, Indiana, 1992.

SJLA	Studies in Judaism in Late Antiquity
SJT	*Scottish Journal of Theology*
SNT	Stendahl, K., ed. *The Scrolls and the New Testament*. New introduction by J. H. Charlesworth; COR; New York, 1992.
SNTS MS	*Studiorum Novi Testamenti Societas* Monograph Series
Sokoloff, *Dictionary*	Sokoloff, M. *A Dictionary of Jewish Palestinian Aramaic of the Byzantine Period*. Dictionaries of Talmud, Midrash and Targum 2; Ramat-Gan, 1990.
Sokoloff, *Targum*	Sokoloff, M. *The Targum to Job from Qumrân Cave XI*. Ramat-Gan, 1974.
ST	*Studia Theologica*
STDJ	Studies on the Texts of the Desert of Judah
StNT	*Studien zum Neuen Testament*
SUNT	Studien zur Umwelt des Neuen Testaments
SVTP	Studia in Veteris Testamenti Pseudepigrapha
Talmon, *King*	Talmon, S. *King, Cult and Calendar in Ancient Israel*. Jerusalem, 1986.
Talmon, *World*	Talmon, S. *The World of Qumran from Within*. Jerusalem, 1989.
TANAKH	*TANAKH: A New Translation of the Holy Scriptures According to the Traditional Hebrew Text*. Philadelphia, New York and Jerusalem, 5746, 1985.
TAPA	Transactions and Proceedings, American Philological Association.
TDNT	Kittel, G. and G. Friedrich, eds. *Theological Dictionary of the New Testament*, 10 vols., trans. G. W. Bromiley. Grand Rapids, Michigan and London, 1964–76.
TDOT	Botterweck, G. J. and H. Ringgren, eds. *Theological Dictionary of the Old Testament*, 6 vols., trans. D. E. Green. Grand Rapids, Michigan, 1974–.
TdQ	Carmignac, J., P. Guilbert, É. Cothenet and H. Lignée. *Les textes de Qumran traduits et annotés*, 2 vols. Paris, 1961, 1963.
Thesaurus Syriacus	Payne Smith, R. *Thesaurus Syriacus*, 2 vols. Oxford, 1879–1901; reprinted Hildesheim, 1981.
ThRu	*Theologische Rundschau*
TLZ	*Theologische Literaturzeitung*
Tov, *Companion Volume*	Tov, E. with S. J. Pfann, eds. *Companion Volume to the Dead Sea Scrolls Microfiche Edition*, 2nd rev. ed. Leiden, 1995.
Tov, *Microfiche*	Tov, E., ed. *The Dead Sea Scrolls on Microfiche*. Leiden, 1993.
TWNT	Kittel, G. and G. Friedrich, eds. *Theologisches Wörterbuch zum Neuen Testament*, 10 vols. Stuttgart, 1932–1979.
TZ	*Theologische Zeitschrift*
USQR	*Union Seminary Quarterly Review*
VC	*Vigiliae christianae*
Vermes, *DSS*	Vermes, G. *The Dead Sea Scrolls in English*, 4th ed. London and New York, 1995.
VT	*Vetus Testamentum*

Wernberg-Møller, *Manual*	Wernberg-Møller, P. *The Manual of Discipline: Translated and Annotated with an Introduction*. STDJ; Leiden, 1957.
Wise, *Temple*	Wise, M. O. *A Critical Study of the Temple Scroll from Qumrân Cave 11*. SAOC 49; Chicago, 1990.
WMANT	Wissenschaftliche Monographien zum Alten und Neuen Testament.
WO	Waltke, B. K. and M. O'Connor. *An Introduction to Biblical Hebrew Syntax*. Winona Lake, Indiana, 1990.
WUNT	Wissenschaftliche Untersuchungen zum Neuen Testament
WZ Leipzig	Wissenschaftliche Zeitschrift der Karl-Marx-Universität Leipzig
Yadin, *Message*	Yadin, Y. *The Message of the Scrolls*. New introduction by J. H. Charlesworth; COR; New York, 1992.
Yadin, *Temple*	Yadin, Y. *The Temple Scroll*, 2 vols. Jerusalem, 1983.
ZAW	*Zeitschrift für die alttestamentliche Wissenschaft*
ZKT	*Zeitschrift für katholische Theologie*
ZNW	*Zeitschrift für die neutestamentliche Wissenschaft*
ZTK	*Zeitschrift für Theologie und Kirche*

Additional Abbreviations

ab.	above
add.	added/addition
alt.	alternative
appar.	apparently
assump.	assumption
beg.	beginning
betw.	between
BH	Biblical Hebrew
bl.	below
bot.	bottom
c.	circa
cf.	compare
ch., chs.	chapter, chapters
cit.	citation
col., cols.	column, columns
cons.	consistent
Cop.	Coptic
corr.	corrected/correction/correctly
cpr.	corruption
d.leather	defect in the leather
del.	deletion/deleted
diff.	different/differ
eras.	erasure/erased
ET	English translation
Eth.	Ethiopic
excl.	excluding/excluded
extd.	extended
frg., frgs.	fragment, fragments

Gk.	Greek		**Ancient Documents**	
HB	Hebrew Bible			
Heb.	Hebrew		Bible and Apocrypha	
impf.	imperfect			
impv.	imperative		Gen	Genesis
incons.	inconsistent		Ex	Exodus
init.	initially		Lev	Leviticus
(in mg.)	letter or word written in the margin		Num	Numbers
inter.	interlinear		Deut	Deuteronomy
l., ll.	line, lines		Josh	Joshua
Lat.	Latin		Judg	Judges
lt.	left		Ruth	Ruth
lit.	literally		1Sam	1 Samuel
ltr., ltrs.	letter, letters		2Sam	2 Samuel
LXX	Septuagint		1Kgs	1 Kings
mg.	margin		2Kgs	2 Kings
MH	Mishnaic Hebrew		1Chr	1 Chronicles
MS, MSS	Manuscript, Manuscripts		2Chr	2 Chronicles
msg.	missing		Ezra	Ezra
MT	Masoretic Text		Neh	Nehemiah
n., nn.	note, notes		Esth	Esther
NT	New Testament		Job	Job
OG	Old Greek		Ps(s)	Psalms
orig.	original/originally		Prov	Proverbs
OT	Old Testament		Eccl, Qoh	Ecclesiastes, Qohelet
p., pp.	page, pages		Song	Song of Songs
part.	participle		Isa	Isaiah
pass.	passive		Jer	Jeremiah
pf.	perfect		Lam	Lamentations
pl.	plural		Ezek	Ezekiel
Pl., Pls.	plate, plates		Dan	Daniel
poss.	possible/possibly		Hos	Hosea
prob.	probably		Joel	Joel
prps.	perhaps		Amos	Amos
pt., pts.	part, parts		Obad	Obadiah
QH	Qumran Hebrew		Jonah	Jonah
rdg., rdgs.	reading, readings		Micah	Micah
recop.	recopying		Nah	Nahum
repet.	repetition		Hab	Habakkuk
rest.	restoration		Zeph	Zephaniah
rt.	right		Hag	Haggai
sg.	singular		Zech	Zechariah
sim.	similar		Mal	Malachi
sp.	space		2Ezra	2 Ezra
supral.	supralinear		Tob	Tobit
synt.	syntactically		Jdt	Judith
Syr.	Syriac		AddEsth	Additions to Esther
vert.	vertical		WisSol	Wisdom of Solomon
vs., vss.	verse, verses		Sir	Sirach
writ.	writing/written		1Bar	1 Baruch
			LetJer	Letter of Jeremiah
			PrAzar	Prayer of Azariah
			Sus	Susanna
			Bel	Bel and the Dragon
			1Mac	1 Maccabees
			2Mac	2 Maccabees
			Mt	Matthew
			Mk	Mark

Lk	Luke
Jn	John
Acts	Acts
Rom	Romans
1Cor	1 Corinthians
2Cor	2 Corinthians
Gal	Galatians
Eph	Ephesians
Phil	Philippians
Col	Colossians
1Thes	1 Thessalonians
2Thes	2 Thessalonians
1Tim	1 Timothy
2Tim	2 Timothy
Tit	Titus
Phlm	Philemon
Heb	Hebrews
Jas	James
1Pet	1 Peter
2Pet	2 Peter
1Jn	1 John
2Jn	2 John
3Jn	3 John
Jude	Jude
Rev	Revelation

Pseudepigrapha

All abbreviations are according to *OTP*.

Philo

Abr	*De Abrahamo*
Cher	*De Cherubim*
Conf	*De Confusione Linguarum*
Ebr	*De Ebrietate*
Flacc	*In Flaccum*
Gaium	*De Legatione ad Gaium*
Heres	*Quis Rerum divinarum Heres*

Migr	*De Migratione Abrahami*
Mut	*De Mutatione Nominum*
Op	*De Opificio Mundi*
Post	*De Posteritate Caini*
Praem	*De Praemiis et Poenis*
Quaes Ex I—II	*Quaestiones et Solutiones in Exodus I—II*
Quod Det	*Quod Deterius Potiori insidiari solet*
Quod Deus	*Quod Deus immutabilis sit*
Sacr	*De Sacrificiis Abelis et Caini*
Somn I—II	*De Somniis I—II*
Spec Leg I—IV	*De Specialibus Legibus I—IV*
Virt	*De Virtutibus*
Vita Mos I—II	*De Vita Mosis I—II*

Josephus

Ant	*Jewish Antiquities*
Apion	*Against Apion*
Life	*Life of Josephus*
War	*Jewish Wars*

Rabbinics

ARN	Abot de-Rabbi Nathan
b.	Babylonian Talmud (before a rabbinic text)
Ber	Berakot
GenR	Bere' sit Rabbah
Ḥag	Ḥagigah
m.	Mishnah (before a rabbinic text)
Meg	Megillah
Sanh	Sanhedrin
SifDeut	Sifre Deuteronomy
Sot.	Sotah
t.	Tosephta (before a rabbinic text)
TK	Lieberman, S., ed. *Tosefta Kifshutah*. New York, 1955—.
TargPsJon	Targum Pseudo-Jonathan
y.	Jerusalem Talmud (before a rabbinic text)

General Introduction

James H. Charlesworth

Scholars as well as those who are not research specialists on the Dead Sea Scrolls might appreciate a brief introduction to this collection. The following introduction thus attempts to summarize the position of most Qumran experts. Many of the thoughts mentioned now will be developed in the introductions to the documents in this corpus; they will be supported in various ways in the texts, translations, and footnotes.

The Dead Sea Scrolls have revolutionized scholars' understanding of Early Judaism (Second Temple Judaism) and Early Christianity (Christian Origins). Prior to their discovery, scholars tended to reconstruct pre-70 Judaism in terms of the opening of *Aboth*, according to which Moses received Torah from Sinai, committed it to Joshua, he to the elders, the elders to the prophets, and the prophets to the men of the so-called Great Synagogue. Three things were imperative: be deliberate in judgment, train many disciples, and *construct a fence around Torah*. Accordingly, Early Judaism was considered to be monolithic, orthodox, and isolated ("fenced-off") from the rest of the world. This depiction of Early Judaism was constructed out of improper analyses of the Mishnah, the New Testament, and Josephus.

Since the discovery of the Dead Sea Scrolls in 1947, and their subsequent intensive study beginning in the early fifties, scholars have come to affirm that this reconstruction does not reflect the complexities of Judaism before the destruction of the Temple in 70 C.E. Now, we know — thanks to exhaustive research on the transmission of the tractates in the Mishnah — that the Mishnah was shaped by post-70 Jewish concerns, and was codified by Judah the Prince around 200 C.E. It thus embodies the struggle of Hillel's group of Pharisaism first against the Zealots of 66–70 (the first Jewish revolt against Rome) and then against the zealous warriors who from 132–135 C.E. followed Simon Bar Kosiba (whom Akiba probably hailed as the "Messiah"). Hillel's followers (the House of Hillel) also had to struggle for self-identification and survival against the "Christians" (who made apocalyptic and increasingly exclusivistic claims about their Messiah, Jesus of Nazareth). Further, the Hillelites had to struggle over the meaning of Torah against their fellow Pharisees, notably the followers of Shammai. The Mishnah (and the later Tosephta and Talmudim) nevertheless preserve early traditions and thus provide valuable information regarding religious life in pre-70 Judaism, especially in the Temple cult. Rabbinic literature, therefore, should be read as an edited record of Early Judaism.

The New Testament was another main source for reconstructing the Judaism of Jesus' day. Today, however, scholars have been forced to admit that passages preserved in this canon of scripture are sometimes anti-Jewish (or anti-Semitic), and received their present shape because of many social pressures and needs, including the struggle for self-definition against other Jewish groups. Hence, Paul and the authors of Matthew and John, for example, do not present us with reliable records of what Judaism was like when Hillel was a Rabbi and Jesus was an eschatological prophet from Galilee. Rather, the New Testament documents represent the attempts of some Jews (and also a few Gentiles) to establish and convert others to their own proclamations. Many of the sayings of Jesus preserved in the canon, therefore, reflect the polemical ambience of the period from circa 30 (the date of Jesus' crucifixion) to 100 C.E. (the probable date of the latest gospel, the Gospel of John). The New Testament does provide invaluable data regarding the life and teachings of Jesus, as well as life in Galilee and in Jerusalem when the Temple was the economic and religious center for millions of Jews living in the Hellenistic world. The New Testament gospels, however, are not biographies of Jesus, and the New Testament documents, with the exception of Paul's authentic letters, reached their definitive form after 70, perhaps decades later, and often in places far removed from ancient Palestine.

Finally, before 1947 many specialists considered Josephus to be a reliable and unbiased historian of Jewish thought and history prior to 100 C.E. It was commonly accepted by almost all that he correctly depicted the Judaism of Hillel's and Jesus' time as quadrifurcated into four "sects" like the Greek philosophical schools: Pharisees (the dominant sect), the Sadducees, the Essenes, and the Zealots. Now scholars widely affirm that Josephus' report is biased and at times unrepresentative. There were not "four sects"; and they were not modeled after the Greeks. There were certainly more than 12 groups, and it is unwise (without careful definition) simply to continue to use the sociologically loaded term "sect." Josephus, however, is a reliable source regarding the topography of ancient Palestine, the mood of Palestinian Jews before the War of 66–70, the causes of this revolt, the movement and success of Roman troops, and the general concerns and fears of Jews. Even so, he surely shaped his presentation of Judaism, especially Jewish thought, to win the admiration of his Roman readers, especially the Roman establishment and the Emperor, who paid him an annual stipend.

Now, thanks to the discovery of the Dead Sea Scrolls, we have Jewish documents that are not in any way altered by thoughts, redactions, or additions that date after 68 C.E., the year when the Qumran Community was burned by Roman soldiers. All the Dead Sea Scrolls antedate 68 (with the exception of the *Copper*

Scroll). They were once held and studied by Jews contemporaneous with Hillel and Jesus. Some of the Jewish documents found in the Qumran caves were composed by Jews who lived in the Qumran Community from circa 150 B.C.E. to 68 C.E. Other documents were composed elsewhere and were brought to the Community. Some of them (e.g. *1En*) contain traditions that may be so early as the third, or even fourth, century B.C.E.

Established scholars around the world affirm the indispensability of archaeology and palaeography (which is not simply an art but is also a science which can date a document within plus or minus 50 years). Using these methods scholars can demonstrate that the Qumran Community is where some of the Dead Sea Scrolls were composed and studied. The Dead Sea Scrolls contain allusions to past history; hence, it is possible to reconstruct the origins of the Qumranites. They were priests who left the Temple around 150 B.C.E. because of factions within the priestly circles in Jerusalem. They went into the wilderness of Judaea and found at Qumran an abandoned Israelite ruin, perhaps an old border fort. They built a crude dwelling at this site. Later, the group became a Community and Qumran was considerably expanded. There were many incentives for the move from the Temple to the wilderness: the corruption of the Temple cult by priests who compromised Torah in face of Greek influences from Syria, the conviction that the Righteous Teacher (probably of the lineage of Aaron and Zadok, King David's high priest) alone had been given special powers and revelations by God, the allegiance to a different lunar-solar calendar, the profession of halakot different from the priestly establishment (cf. 4QMMT), and the clarion words of Isaiah 40:3, which were interpreted to mean that they were to heed the Voice and prepare *in the wilderness* the way of the Lord.

Over the next two hundred years converts came from many of the Jewish groups (probably also including the precursors of the Sadducees and Pharisees). After a period of initiation lasting at least two years the novitiates became full members of the Community. The Community existed until the spring of 68 C.E. At that time the Roman legions, under the direction of Vespasian (the future emperor of Rome), had just conquered the last holdouts in Galilee and, before moving up to Jerusalem, quelled all resistance in the environs of Jericho. Qumran is less than 15 kilometers or 10 miles south of Jericho.

Today, most experts recognize that the Qumran library was not a genizah or a depository of scrolls that belonged to only one group of Jews. Rather, experts affirm that the eleven caves – especially Cave IV – preserved documents from a variety of Jewish groups and consituted an early Jewish library. In this Jewish library were preserved all the books of the TANAK or "Old Testament" (with the exception that Esther has not been recognized among the tiny fragments), some of the Apocrypha (esp. *Tobit*) and the Pseudepigrapha (esp. the *Books of Enoch* and *Jubilees*), writings peculiar to and composed at the Qumran Community (notably 1QS, 1QSa, 1QSb, 1QH, 1QM and the Pesharim), and documents written elsewhere by other related groups or subgroups (viz. *Prayer of Joseph, Second Ezekiel, Copper Scroll*).

This ancient library contained early Jewish writings of different genres. Hence, the corpus of this series is divided into the following categories: Rules, Hymns, Liturgies, Targumim, Commentaries, Qumran Apocryphal Works, Miscellanea, and Biblical Apocrypha and Pseudepigrapha.

One final caveat: as early Jewish writings must not be interpreted as if they represent a normative system, so Qumran ideas must not be pressed into a unified system. The documents in this corpus demonstrate many competing ordinances regarding purification and cleansing, different types of calendars (variations of the lunar-solar calendar), and contrasting rules (the *Rule of the Community* was clearly a late "vulgate" text that incorporates different documents with various textual histories – a theory confirmed by the fragments of the document preserved in Cave IV). Most of these clashing concepts, explanations, exhortations, and rules existed at Qumran, if not simultaneously, then at least during the extended history of its existence from 150 B.C.E. to 68 C.E. Therefore it is prudent to speak not about Qumran theology, but about "theologies" at Qumran.

Qumranites seemed to refer to themselves as "the Poor Ones," members of "the Way," the "Sons of Righteousness," "the Most Holy Ones," and notably the "Sons of Light." All others – including Jews and especially the ruling priests in the Temple – were the "Sons of Darkness" and the "Sons of Perversity." As the Qumranites developed their special ordinances, cosmic speculations, and rules they were influenced by the TANAK or Old Testament (especially Isaiah, Deuteronomy, and the Psalms), some so-called extracanonical works (like the *Books of Enoch* and *Jubilees*), and previously hitherto-unknown writings (notably the *Moses Apocryphon*, the *Psalms of Joshua, Pseudo-Ezekiel*, and more "Davidic" Psalms).

The Dead Sea Scrolls present data that are essential for any reconstruction of Early Judaism and Early Christianity. They disclose a variety of creative issues, perspectives, and concerns that were current in many Jewish circles before the destruction of 70 C.E. Most important among these are innovative prescriptions and provisions for ritual purification, the impossibility of obtaining forgiveness except through God's "mercy," speculations on the nature of the human and the origin of evil in the world, and the presence and efficaciousness of good angels. Probably unique to Qumran – at least in terms of development – are the following concepts: The cosmic dualism centered in the opposition between the Angel of Light and the demonic power of the evil angels, notably Belial, who is probably identical (in some scrolls) with the Angel of Darkness; the development of the concept of the Holy Spirit from God (which obviously influenced the development of Christian proclamations and social identity); the cosmic hymnic celebrations at twilight (in the evening for protection from the darkness, and in the morning participating in the bringing of light [the sun] back to God's created order); the clarifications of the importance of the lunar-solar calendar with the special feast days, the weeks, the Sabbaths, the months, and the yearly celebration (perhaps the Day of Atonement); the descriptions of the heavens above filled with angels chanting praises to God (the Creator); the eschatological expectations for God's visitation (the Day of Judgment); and the joyous time when the Messiahs of Aaron and Israel will appear.

The Qumran Community was in existence during the time of

Jesus' ministry; but there is no reference to him or to any of his disciples. There is no reason to be surprised by this fact. There were many groups within Early Judaism, and the Dead Sea Scrolls do not mention any known first-century Rabbi or Jewish leader. It is not the alleged direct influence from the Dead Sea Scrolls upon any New Testament document that is significant (with the probable exception of the Gospel of John which seems to be influenced by the thoughts preserved in a unique way in the Dead Sea Scrolls). What is paradigmatically important is this internationally acknowledged insight: The Dead Sea Scrolls reveal ideas once considered unique to "Christianity" and this discovery proves that Early Christianity was for many years one of the groups (probably a sect) within Judaism. Now, the milieu — the intellectual and social matrix — of earliest Christianity is coming into view. The importance of the Dead Sea Scrolls, however, must always remain firmly grounded in the invaluable and precious insights preserved in them. They were once held, studied, and revered by Jews who lived in an erudite and deeply religious Community that eked out an existence on the western shores of the Dead Sea, waiting for the fulfillment of God's promises.

Qumran Pseudepigraphic Psalms

(4Q380 and 4Q381)

Eileen M. Schuller

Introduction

1. Contents

4Q380 and 4Q381 were published for the first time in 1986.[1] Although there is no overlap of material in the two manuscripts and although they are written by different hands, similarity in the type of material found in each suggests at least that we are dealing with different parts of a single collection of psalms. Hence they are treated together in this introduction, although it is recognized that it is impossible to establish with certainty whether these fragments are from a single collection or from two different collections of psalms.

4Q380 and 4Q381 contain psalms that are similar in style, vocabulary, and theme to many of the biblical psalms. One psalm speaks about Zion (4Q380 frg. 1), others about creation (4Q381 frg. 1; 4Q380 frg. 7, col. 2). Many exhibit aspects of penitential psalms or lamentations (4Q381 frgs. 15, 24, 31, 33, 45) though with hymnic elements (4Q381 frg. 15, ll. 4−7). One group of fragments (4Q381 frgs. 69, 76−77) is more like elevated prose, and strongly Deuteronomistic in language and content. A number have superscriptions attributing the psalm to a biblical figure, including the Man of God (4Q381 frg. 24, l. 4), a king of Judah (name missing in the lacuna, 4Q381 frg. 31, l. 4), Manasseh (4Q381 frg. 33, l. 8), and Obadiah (4Q380 frg. 1, 2.8). The biblical term *selāh* appears at the end of two psalms and can possibly be reconstructed at the conclusion of five others.[2] None of these psalms appears in a canonical Psalter (Masoretic or Greek), nor is any known from any other ancient source. In what remains of these two manuscripts, there is no evidence that any of the psalms of the Hebrew Bible were included in these two scrolls.[3]

2. Text

4Q381 consists of approximately one hundred fragments, and 4Q380 of seven fragments. Many of these are extremely small and offer only isolated letters; the largest fragments preserve between six and sixteen partial lines. No line is preserved in its entirety. There is clear evidence for parts of at least twelve distinct psalms in 4Q381, and at least three in 4Q380; but the collection(s) was probably considerably larger. The scribes left a line or a portion of a line blank between psalms. With one possible exception (4Q380 frg. 4, l. 1), new psalms are not indented. In general, the physical arrangement of the manuscript falls within standard scribal practice for writing biblical psalm manuscripts.

3. Original Language and Date

The original language of the psalms is Hebrew. Although theoretically these psalms could have been composed in the pre-exilic period, a number of linguistic features belong to Late Biblical Hebrew and Qumran Hebrew.[4] Attempts to date the

---

[1] E. M. Schuller, *Non-Canonical Psalms from Qumran: A Pseudepigraphic Collection* (HSS 28; Atlanta, 1986). See also E. M. Schuller, "4Q380 and 4Q381: Non-Canonical Psalms from Qumran," in *The Dead Sea Scrolls: Forty Years of Research,* edited by D. Dimant and U. Rappaport (STDJ 10; Leiden, 1992) pp. 90−100 and DJD 11. Additional comment on these texts has been mainly in terms of surveys of newly published material (the most extensive by F. García Martínez, "Estudios Qumranicos 1975−1985: Panorama Critico (V)," *Estudios Bíblicos* 47 [1989] 93−101), and book reviews (e.g., J. M. Baumgarten, *JBL* 108 [1989] 748−50; F. García Martínez, *JSJ* 20 [1989] 110−15; J. C. VanderKam, *CBQ* 50 [1988] 335−36; G. Vermes, *JJS* 40 [1989] 115−16).

[2] It occurs at 4Q381 frg. 24, l. 3 and frg. 33, l. 6; possibly at 4Q381 frg. 15, l. 11; frg. 21, l. 2; frg. 31, ll. 3, 9; frg. 69, l. 10.

[3] This, of course, does not preclude the fact that biblical psalms could have been part of these texts. In 4Q380 only a few scattered fragments of the total manuscript have survived, and in 4Q381 we seem to have only the final sheet of a longer manuscript. For a reconstruction of the placement of most of these fragments as the final sheet of the manuscript, see the proposal of H. Stegemann, "Appendix A," in Schuller, *Non-Canonical Psalms*, pp. 267−83.

[4] For a full list and discussion of linguistic features, see Schuller, *Non-Canonical Psalms*, pp. 46−52.

language more precisely are limited by the traditional and standard nature of much psalmic language in general, plus the fact that the author(s) of these psalms made such extensive use of biblicizing phraseology.

It is difficult to propose a date for the composition of these psalms any more precisely than a general designation of the Persian and Early Hellenistic period. The copies of the text which we have in 4Q380 and 4Q381 are both written in a Middle to Late Hasmonaean hand. There are virtually no references to contemporary political or historical events, or even polemical thrusts (at least that can be recognized as such). The piety is very general and standard. One aspect that might point to a relatively early date of composition is the absence of any explicit reference to the afterlife.

4. Provenience

It is difficult to be precise about the provenience of these psalms. There is little evidence to point toward their composition within the Qumran community; none of the distinctive ideology or theology of the sectarian community is found here. Where some vocabulary which is associated with Qumran occasionally appears (words such as יחד, גורל, פתאים), the words are used very much in their traditional biblical sense. The tetragrammaton appears frequently (some eleven times) both in quotation of biblical texts and in free composition (but is not written in palaeo-Hebrew or by four dots).[5] Thus, perhaps it is best to situate the composition of these psalms very broadly within mainstream Second Temple Judaism.

5. Relation to the Hebrew Bible

As in much of the psalmody of the Second Temple period, there is considerable dependence upon and reuse of earlier biblical material, especially of the biblical psalms; however, there is actually considerable variety in how scripture is used. One group of psalms, (4Q381 frgs. 15, 24; 4Q380 frg. 1, col. 1) seems to "quote" major segments of material (from five to ten consecutive cola) from biblical psalms, but there is always considerable vari-

ation from the MT or any other recognized version.[6] In another group of psalms, there is not such explicit reuse of the biblical text, but rather a convergence of shared language with a specific text which is more than coincidence[7] (e.g., the relationship of 4Q381 frg. 31, ll. 1—2 and Ps 9; 4Q381 frg. 31 ll. 5—9 and Ps 69; or 4Q381 frgs. 48 and 50 and Ps 76). Other psalms make surprisingly little direct use of scripture.

It is difficult to speak with surety about the exact nature or purpose of this collection of psalms. The superscriptions which link a psalm to a specific individual (e.g., 4Q381 frg. 33, l. 8 "Prayer of Manasseh, king of Judah, when the king of Assyria imprisoned him") may be secondary additions.[8] If 4Q381 is an independent work, it could be a collection of royal psalms; that is, psalms of Manasseh (4Q381 frg. 33, l. 8), of an unnamed king of Judah, perhaps Hezekiah (4Q381 frg. 31, l. 4), and of the Man of God, i.e., David (4Q381 frg. 24, l. 4).[9] 4Q380 would then be a separate collection of psalms of non-kingly figures such as Obadiah (either the prophet or the steward of the house of Ahab, 4Q380 frg. 1, 2.8).[10] However, if 4Q380 and 381 are a single collection, the whole work can be seen as a non-Davidic collection,[11] perhaps even as a supplement to the biblical psalter which, in the Second Temple period, was more and more attributed in its entirety to David.[12]

The discovery of 4Q380 and 4Q381 in the library at Qumran is yet another indication that the composition of psalmody in the post-exilic period was much more extensive than what is preserved in the canonical psalter.[13] Although these manuscripts are unfortunately fragmentary, they provide welcome insights into Second Temple prayer and piety.

6. Relation to Other Writings[14]

These psalms share many features with the hundreds of psalms that antedate the destruction of the Temple in 70 C.E. For example, the refrain "Who can utter the name of Yahweh and (who) can proclaim all [his] praise? Yahweh [remem]bered it . . ." (4Q380 Frg. 1, 1.7—9) is paralleled in other psalms that were composed shortly before the second century B.C.E. Note especially Psalm 151:3:

---

[5] The avoidance of the tetragrammaton in sectarian compositions has been frequently discussed; see especially, H. Stegemann, "Religionsgeschichtliche Erwägungen zu den Gottesbezeichnungen in den Qumrantexten," in *Qumrân: sa piété, sa théologie et son milieu*, edited by M. Delcor (BETL 46; Paris, 1978) pp. 195—217.

[6] That is, variations in word order within a colon, or variations and omissions in the order of cola, changes in syntax and person, and omission of words.

[7] That is, verbal links of short phrases and specific vocabulary, or the same word used in a different context.

[8] This is usually considered the case with the superscriptions in the biblical psalter and in other compositions such as the *Psalms of Solomon*.

[9] 4Q381 frg. 15 may also be a royal psalm if משיחך in l. 7 is interpreted as "your anointed"; see the discussion of various

ways of reading this phrase in Schuller, *Non-Canonical Psalms*, pp. 101—2.

[10] In the only other psalm in 4Q380 with a title, the leather breaks immediately after "Praise of" (4Q380 frg. 4, l. 1).

[11] The phrase "Man of God" may denote Moses (compare Ps 90), a prophetic figure (as in 1Kgs), or simply be a more general designation (cf. the title of Ps 102).

[12] Mk 12:35—37; Acts 2:25, 34, and 4:25; 11Q13 2.10 (11QMelch); 11Q5 27.2—11; 4Q397 frgs. 14—21 line 10 (4QMMT).

[13] As attested also by the non-canonical psalms in 11Q5, 4Q88, 11Q11, the *Thanksgiving Hymns*, the *Psalms of Solomon*, the *Prayer of Manasseh*, other documents in *OTP* 2, and in vols. 4 and 5 of the present series.

[14] This paragraph was added by the Editor.

For who can proclaim and who can bespeak
and who can recount the works of the Lord?
Everything God has seen, ... [15]

The same refrain is picked up again in the earliest Christian
hymnbook, *Odes of Solomon* 26:8–11:

Who can write the odes of the Lord,
or who can read them?
Or who can train himself for life,
so that he himself may be saved?
Or who can press upon the Most High,
so that he would recite from his mouth?
Who can interpret the wonders of the Lord?
Though he who interprets should perish,
yet that which was interpreted will remain. [16]

7. Selected Bibliography

Schuller, E. M. *Non-Canonical Psalms from Qumran: A Pseud-epigraphic Collection*. HSS 28; Atlanta, 1986.

Schuller, E. M. "4Q380 and 4Q381: Non-Canonical Psalms from Qumran." In *The Dead Sea Scrolls: Forty Years of Research,* edited by D. Dimant and U. Rappaport. STDJ 10; Leiden, 1992, pp. 90–100.

Schuller, E. M. DJD 11.

Tov, E. *The Dead Sea Scrolls on Microfiche.* Leiden, 1993 [4Q380: PAM 43.194, 43.362, 41.506, 42.806, 42.035, 41.854, 41.775; IAA 190442; RS 9; 4Q381: PAM 43.226, 43.225, 43.227, 43.224, 42.826, 42.808, 42.806, 42.445, 42.247, 42.246, 41.974, 41.966, 41.939, 41.916, 41.911, 41.903, 41.891, 41.860, 41.853, 41.791, 41.712, 41.694, 41.639, 41.636, 41.412, 41.411, 41.410, 41.409, 41.400, 41.372, 41.347, 41.282, 40.962, 40.592, 40.580; IAA 190443–190447, 190455–190456; RS 9].

---

[15] J.A. Sanders in this volume (11Q5 28.7).   [16] Charlesworth in *OTP* 2.759.

Qumran Pseudepigraphic Psalms
4Q380

Frg. 1, Col. 1
(A Zion Psalm)

1	° ° [
2	ירו]שלם היא
3	יה]וֹה' מעולם ועד]
4	[עולם²]קדשׁים
5	[כי שׁ]ם יהוֹה נקרא עליה
6	[וכבדוֹ] נראה על ירושלם
7	[ו]ציון³ מי ימלל אֹת שם
8	יהוה וישמעו כל תהלתֹ]וֹי'
9	[זכ]רֹוֹ יהוה ברצנו ויפקדֹהֹו
10	לֹהֹראות בטֹוב
11	[בח]יֹרֹיֹו לֹשֹ]מח בשמחת גוי]ן⁵

Frg. 1, Col. 2

1	[י]עשה לכם אֹדם אֹ]	
2	כי הוא זה שמרו אמֹ]ריו	
3	אשר לכל ב]נֹ]יֹ' ישראל [	לא]
4	תושעך ידֹך כי כֹח אֹלֹהֹ]יך	
5	עושה טוב]ה]⁷ ושנאי רעים עדֹ] מתי	
6	תחפצו לעשו]ת רעה פן יוֹבֹדֹ⁸ עוֹ]ל]	
7	↲ VACAT	

("Praise of Obadiah")

8	תהלה לעבדיה אֹלוֹהֹ °°]
9	אמת בה וֹחסדוֹ °°]

---

1 Perhaps restore [העיר בחר יה]וֹה; cf. 1Kgs 14:21, 1Chr 12:13.
2 Restoration based on the formulaic expression; cf. 1Chr 16:36, 29:10; Ps 41:14, 103:17, 106:48.
3 Or [ב]ציוׁן; since the right hand margin is quite irregular, there may have been no letter before the צ.
4 Cf. MT Ps 106:2: מי ימלל גבורות יהוה ישמיע כל־תהלתו.

5 Cf. MT Ps 106:4-5ab: זכרני יהוה ברצון עמך פקדני בישועתך. לראות בטובת בחיריך לשמח בשמחת גויך.
6 Letter abraded; there is no physical break in the leather.
7 There is no physical break in the leather. Possibly no letter after ב, just an unusually large space between words.
8 Read יואבד.

Qumran Pseudepigraphic Psalms
4Q380

Frg. 1, Col. 1
(A Zion Psalm)

1 [...]°°

2 [... Jeru]salem this (is)

3 [... Yah]weh [....][1] From everlasting to

4 [everlasting...] Holy Ones.[2]

5 [For the na]me of Yahweh is invoked upon it,

6 [and his glory] is seen upon Jerusalem

7 [and] Zion. Who can utter the name of

8 Yahweh and (who) can proclaim[3] all [his] praise?

9 Yahweh [remem]bered it[4] with his favor and visited it

10 to show the prosperity of

11 his [cho]sen ones, to glad[den (it) with the gladness of his nation.]

Frg. 1, Col. 2

1 [will][5] a person[6] do for you? '°[....]

2 For this is the one [whose] wor[ds] they kept [...]

3 which (are) to all the chi[ld]ren of Israel.[7] [...]

4 Your hand will [not] save you but the strength of [your] God,

5 who does good and hates the evil ones. How [long]

6 will you delight to d[o] evil lest the deceit[ful] perish.

7 (vacat)

("Praise of Obadiah")

8 Praise of Obadiah. God °°[...]

9 truth in it and his mercy °°[...]

---

[1] Perhaps restore "[the city Yah]weh [chose.]"
[2] Possibly referring to angels.
[3] For the alternation of a singular and plural verb after מי, cf. Ps 107:43.
[4] Or "him." The suffix here and in the following lines can refer

either to Jerusalem (occasionally treated as masculine) or to the one who utters the divine name and praise.
[5] The previous word was probably "what."
[6] Heb. אדם.
[7] Lit. "sons of Israel."

Frg. 2

1	[̊]
2	[וגבעות ה̊רים ̊]
3	[ב]ן יֺוסדו כל י̊חרדו[
4	וקותיהם[ממצ̇ הם בצר יהוה] אל ויזעקו
5	̊[̊ יהוה יֻחנן סֹ̇ד[ח]ל̊] כי יצילם⁹
6	[לאיש¹¹]
7	[ל ̊]

Frg. 3

1	[תמי̊ יד לויתן ת̊]
2	[ישח̇ח̇ק̇ ך̇]
3	[ל̊]

Frg. 4

1	[ל תהלה]
2	[ב̇ תמאסו]
3	[ל̇ החכים]
4	[̊ ̊ וה̊]

⁹ Restorations in lines 4-5 based on MT Ps 107:6: ויצעקו
אל־יהוה בצר להם ממצוקותיהם יצילם.

¹⁰ The first trace of ink could also be an interlinear letter.
¹¹ Or איש ל[.

Frg. 2

   1 [. . .]°[. . .]

   2 [. . .]° mountains and hills [. . .]

   3 [. . .] all who are founded on it will tremble [. . .]

   4 [and they will cry to] Yahweh in their distress, from [their] diffic[ulties]

   5 [he will deliver them.   For] to the [mer]ciful Yahweh is gracious °°[. . .]

   6 [. . .] to the man [. . .]

   7 [. . .] °*l*[. . .]

Frg. 3

   1 [. . .]*t* Leviathan, hand of *tmy*°[. . .]

   2 [. . .]*q* he will play[. . .]

   3 [. . .]*l*[. . .]

Frg. 4

   1 Praise of [. . .]

   2 you will reject *b*[. . .]

   3 he made wise *l*[. . .]

   4 and *h*°°[. . .]

Frg. 5

1   [˚]

2   [בֿסתר ממנו יה]

3   [˚ מֿה ימישו ומה]

Frg. 6

1   [˚˚ ע כֿי נֿחֿל]

2   [ואת חכֿמֿתֿו ואת דֿעֿתֿ]ו

3   [לֿ]

Frg. 7, Col. 1
(A Penitential Psalm)

1   [ ]

2   אשם אֿתֿ [˚]

3   ¹²למֿה ביומצרה [˚]

4   [יוֹם] [לֿ]

Frg. 7, Col. 2
(A Creation Psalm)

1   [˚]

2   י]תֿבונן בגבוֹרֿתֿ חכֿמֿ[ה

3   ויבדלהו מאפלה ואוֹר[ן

4   [לֿ] לֿ [לֿ] [˚˚˚]

---

¹² Read ביום צרה.

Frg. 5

1 [...]°[...]

2 [...] in secret from him *yh*[...]

3 [...] what will they feel[8] and what °[...]

Frg. 6

1 [...] he inherited because ᶜ°°[...]

2 [...] and his wisdom and [his] knowledge [...]

3 [...]*l*[...]

Frg. 7, Col. 1
(A Penitential Psalm)

1 [...]

2 [...]° sin offering

3 [...]°*lmh* in the day of distress

4 [...]*l*[...]*ywm*[9]

Frg. 7, Col. 2
(A Creation Psalm)

1 [...]°[....]

2 [H]e will ponder the strength of wisdo[m....]

3 And he divided it from darkness,[10] and light [...]

4 [...] °°°[...]*l*[...]*l l*[...]

---

8 Or "take away."

9 Possibly "day."

10 Or "gloominess." The Heb. is מאפלה (cf. "Hymn to the Creator" [11Q5 26.11]), not חושך (as in Gen 1:4) [Ed.].

4Q381

Frg. 1
(A Creation Psalm)

1   [הגדתי ונפלאתו אשיחה והיא תהיה לי למורה משפט

2   פי ולפתאים ויבינו ולאין לב ידעון   יהוה כמה גב]ור

3   נפלאות   הוא בימ֗י¹ עשה שמים וארץ ובדבר פיו [

4   ואפ֗יקים   ש֗ך² אור ותׄזׄה³ אגמים וכל בלעה וי֯֯רׄי֯ ל֗[

5   לילה זׄכׄבׄ[בי]ם֗ וכסילים ויׄה֗יׄר ֯מׄ֗ לאׄ[

6   עץ וכל פר֗]י כר]ם֗ וכל תבואות שדה ולפי דבריו ֯֯כׄל [

7   את א[שתו]⁵ וברוחו העמידם למשל בכל אלה באדמה ובכל [

8   [לח]דש ב[ח]ׄדש למועד במועד ליום ביום לאכל פריה תׄנובבׄ[

9   [֯ ֯ ֯]   ֯ [   ]   ֯ ועוף וׄכל אׄשר להם לאכל חׄלׄבׄי֯ כל וגם[

10   [מ֗ש בׄהם וכל צבאיו ומלא]ן֗כיו   ר֗[

11   [֯] ֯ [ ] ֯ לעבד לאדם ולשרתו זׄה֗[

12   [֯ ֯ ל֯ ֯]

Frg. 4	*Frg. 3*	*Frg. 2*
1 [בׄינות לׄי [	1 מ]עׄלׄלׄיׄה ויׄכׄר֯ ֯ ֯ [	1 [מׄו]
2 [לל ֯ ֯ ֯ ֯]	2 [֯ ֯ ל ֯ ֯ ֯]	2 [ל]

Frg. 8	*Frg. 7*	*Frg. 6*⁶
1 [מׄ]	1 [֯ ֯ מׄ]	1 [מׄ֯י יגׄ]
2 [֯ יעמדׄו בׄ]	2 [י ֯ [ ]תׄו בכל]	2 [֯ ה בנהרׄי]ם
3 [֯ ֯ לׄיׄ]	3 [ל֯ ֯ [ ]לׄ ֯]	3 [ל]

Frg. 9

1   בח[

2   עלי[

3   [֯ ֯

---

¹ Read ביומ֗י.
² There are no traces of a letter before ש ; the space between words is slightly larger than usual.
³ Read אורותיה. A bad place in the leather apparently led the scribe to break אורותיה into two words.
⁴ Perhaps ויאמר.
⁵ Or א[דם], although this may be too brief.
⁶ Fragment 5 is now joined with fragment 14.

4Q381

Frg. 1
(A Creation Psalm)

1 I proclaim, and I meditate on his wonders, and this will become for me instruction. Judgment[1] [...]

2 my mouth, and to the simple and they will discern, and to those without understanding[2] (and) they will know. Yahweh,[3] how mig[hty...]

3 wonders. He, by an oath,[4] made (the) heavens and earth, and by the word of his mouth [...]

4 and watercourses. He shut up its rivers, pools and every eddy, and he $y°°r$[5] $l°$[...]

5 night, and st[ar]s and constellations, and he made (them) shine $°mr\ l'w$[...]

6 tree(s) and every fru[it of the vi]ne and all the produce of the field. And according to his words $°°°kl$ [...]

7 with [his] w[ife.][6] And by his breath[7] he made them stand, to rule over all these on the ground and over all [...]

8 [mo]nth by [mo]nth, festival by festival, day by day, to eat its fruit (which) it makes flourish [...]

9 [...]$°°°$[...]$°$ and birds and all which is theirs for food, the choicest of all,[8] and also [...]

10 [...]$mš$ in them and all his hosts and [his] ang[els...]$r°$[...]

11 [...] $°$[...]$°$ to serve humanity and to minister to it[9] and h[...]

12 [...]$°°l°°$[...]

Frg. 2

1 [...]mw[...]

2 [...]l[...]

Frg. 3

1 [...] her [d]eeds and $ykr°°$[...]

2 [...]$°°l$ $°°°°°$[...]

Frg. 4

1 [...] $bynwt$[10] to me [...]

2 [...]$ll°°m$ $°°$[...]

Frg. 6

1 [...]$mny\ yg$[...]

2 [...]$°h$ in river[s...]

3 [...]l[...]

Frg. 7

1 [...]$°°m$ [...]

2 [...]$y\ °$[...]tw in all[...]

3 [...]$l°°$ [...]$l°°$[...]

Frg. 8

1 [...]m[...]

2 [...]$°$ they will stand b[...]

3 [...]$°°°$ $ly°°$[...]

Frg. 9

1 $bḥ°$[...]

2 $°ly°$[...]

3 $°°$[...]

---

1 Or "and this will become for me a just teacher/teacher of judgment."

2 Lit. "to those without heart."

3 Or "and they will know Yahweh."

4 The translation understands ביומי to be a form of the Aramaic root ימי; also possible is some form of "day."

5 Perhaps "and he said."

6 Or "with A[dam]."

7 Or "And by his spirit."

8 Or "and all which is theirs, to eat the choicest of all."

9 Or "for a servant to Adam and to minister to him."

10 Possibly "houses."

Frgs. 10 and 11[7]

1   [לוא ̊]

2   [̇מ השחיתו כי בעיניו זרע]

3   [̇ה בפעם ולא ̊ הוא רחמון]

4   [כה]   [̊ל ̊ ̊עם ל]   [ל עם]

5   [וא תחתיה בשאול] ̊ [   ] ̊ויו [

6   [ ] ̊ ̊ [ ] לן[[

Frg. 12

1   [א ̊ם ̊]

Frg. 13

1   [̊ו נאצת ̊מא[10] ומא בעלת[9] ̊מא ̊]

2   [בני תדע הלוא תכיר הלוא שנך ̊]

3   [אתה לוא[ ]לן[   ] ̊ ̊ ̊ ̊ ̊ [

---

7 These two fragments can be joined tentatively on the basis of
   line 3 where the letters ה פעם are shared. Fragment 11
   supplies the left hand portion of lines 3-6.

8 Read מה.
9 Read בחלת.
10 Read מה.

12

Frgs. 10 and 11

1 [...]° not [...]

2 [...] and evil in his eyes, for they corrupted *m*°[...]

3 [...] compassionate is he, and not once *h*°[...]

4 [...]*l* with °°*l*°[...]*kh* [...]

5 [...] and he *w*°[...]° in the depths of Sheol and ᾿[...]

6 [...]*l*[...]°°[...]

Frg. 12

1 [...]°*m* ᾿[...]

Frg. 13

1 [...]°. What did you abhor, and what did you reject and °°[...]

2 [...] your [...]°*šn*. Will you not recognize, will you not know th[at...]

3 [...]°°° °°[...]*l* [...] not you [...]

Frgs. 14 and 5[11]
(A Psalm about Nature)

] ̊ [	1
[̊ים עננים עבים שלׄג ‖ ‖]וׄבׄרׄד וכל ̊ ‖	2
]הׄו ואין לעבׄוׄר פׄיהו ארבע רׄוחות בׄש]מים	3
[̊ ̊ ̊ ̊ לאׄיׄן ̊ ̊ [ ]]לׄן	4

Frg. 15

[̊ לבבי תשיב וׄ]ן	1
פנה אלי וחנני תנה עזך לעבדך]והושע לבן אמתך עשה עמׄי	2
[אות לטובה ויראו שנאי ויבשו כי אתה א]לׄהי עזרת לי[12] ואערכה לך אלהי	3
אתה[13] משל בגא]ות הים ואתה תשבח גליו[14] אתה	4
[דכאת כחלל רהב בזרע עזך פזרת איביך[15] תבל ו]מׄלאה אתה [י]סדתם לך[16] זרע עם	5
[גבורה תעז ידך תרום ימינך[17] מי בשחק יערך לך] אלהי ומי בבני האילים[18] ובכל	6
כי אתה]תׄפארת הדו ואני משיחך אתבננתׄי	7
כי	
אוד]ךׄ הודעתי[19] והשכיל[20] כי השכלתני	8
[כי בשמך אלהי נקרא ואל ישועתך	9
[̊ ו]בׄמׄעיל ילבשוה וכסוׄתׄ	10
[̊]לׄןׄ[21]	11

---

[11] Frgs. 14 and 5 can be joined on the basis of line 3 in which the letters חות בשׁ are shared. Fragment 5 also supplies the left hand portion of line 2.

[12] Restorations in lines 2-3 are based upon the MT of Ps 86:16-17 which is used extensively in this section: פנה אלי וחנני תנה־עזך לעבדך והושיעה לבן־אמתך עשה־עמי אות לטובה ויראו שנאי ויבשו כי־אתה יהוה עזרתני ונחמתני.

[13] Restorations in lines 4-7 are based upon the MT of Ps 89:10, 11, 12, 14, 7, 8 which is used extensively in this section.

[14] Cf. MT Ps 89:10: אתה מושל בגאות הים בשוא גליו אתה תשבחם.

[15] Cf. MT Ps 89:11: אתה דכאת כחלל רהב בזרוע עזך פזרת אויביך.

[16] Cf. MT Ps 89:12: לך שמים אף־לך ארץ תבל ומלאה אתה יסדתם.

[17] Cf. MT Ps 89:14: לך זרוע עם־גבורה תעז ידך תרום ימינך.

[18] Cf. MT Ps 89:7: כי מי בשחק יערך ליהוה ידמה ליהוה בבני אלים.

[19] Read הודעתני.

[20] Read ואשכיל.

[21] Perhaps reconstruct]לׄ[ה.

Frgs. 14 and 5
(A Psalm about Nature)

1 [...]°[...]

2 [...]°*ym* cloud masses, rain clouds, snow [...] and hail and all °[...]

3 [...]*hw* and not to transgress his command.[11] Four winds in the he[avens ...]

4 [...]°°°° without °°°[...]*l*[...]

Frg. 15

1 [...]° you will turn my heart and *y*[...]

2 [.... Turn to me and be gracious to me; give your strength to your servant] and save the son of your handmaiden.[12] Show me[13]

3 [a sign for good, that those who hate me may see and be put to shame, for you,] my [G]od, have helped me, and I lay (my case) before you, my God.

4 [... you rule over the hei]ghts of the sea, and you still its waves.   You

5 [crushed Rahab like a carcass; you scattered your enemies with your strong arm.   The world and] its fullness you [fo]unded; you have an arm of

6 [strength.   Strong is your hand, high is your right hand.   Who in the sky is to be compared to you,] my God and who among the sons of the gods, and among all

7 [... for you are] the beauty of its majesty.   And I, your anointed, have understood[14]

8 [... I will make] you [kn]own, because you instructed me,[15] and I will teach[16] because you taught me

9 [...] for we will call[17] on your name, my God, and for your salvation

10 [...]° and like a robe they will put it on, and a covering

11 [...]° *l*[...][18]

---

[11] Lit. "his mouth," or "his speech" [Ed.].

[12] Cf. Ps 86:16c. Or "the son of your truth"; cf. 1QH 6.29–30. See also 4Q381 frgs. 33 and 35 line 5.

[13] Lit. "Make for me."

[14] Or "As for me, I have gained understanding from your discourse."

[15] Translating הודעתני, the נ omitted by haplography.

[16] This translation presumes a confusion of gutterals so that ואשכיל = והשכיל; otherwise lit. "he taught."

[17] Or "it is called by your name, my God."

[18] Perhaps restore "[...] Sela[h ...]," which would indicate the end of the psalm.

Frg. 16

1]ה֯ארצות כי חמ֯[

2]°°[ ]°לשמ֯י֯ע֯[

Frg. 17

1]ת֯ °°° ת ל֯ר֯אשי֯ [

2]ב֯הדר תשזף על יהודה וי֯[

3 א]להי באפך תבלעם ותא]כלם אש[22]

4]ל֯[ ]ל[

Frg. 18

1]נ֯א[

2]מבר֯[

3]ב֯ על יד֯[

4]לת כבוד [

5]°לאי֯ן [

Frg. 19, Col. 1

1]בני֯ך֯ ב֯י֯ מ֯ן֯

2]מ֯שפטיך

3]° מעזי ובשחקי֯ך֯

4] פז֯ ותתן לי

5]מ֯לכותך לעבדך

6]נאצו

7]°ל[

Frg. 19, Col. 2

3 אל֯ה֯י֯[

]°

4 ויע֯נ֯[[23]

5 ומה א֯[

6 כי עש[

Frg. 20

1]°°נ֯י ל֯י ה֯[

2]חקתיך֯ [

3]°ך לי֯ וא֯[

4]°° °°°[

Frg. 21

1]°°[

2]ב סלה [

Frg. 22

1]ת֯ב֯אר[

2]ר֯ ירו֯[

22 Restored according to the MT of Ps 21:10: תשיתמו כתנור אש לעת פניך יהוה באפו יבלעם ותאכלם אש.

23 A ן has been corrected by a scribe to another letter. There are traces of an interlinear correction at the very edge of the fragment.

Frg. 16

1 [...] the lands because *ḥm*[...]

2 [...]° °°[...]° to proclaim [...]

Frg. 17

1 [...]*t* °°°*t* to my head [...]

2 [...] in splendor you will look upon Judah and *y*[...]

3 [...] my [G]od in your wrath you will swallow them, and [fire] will de[vour them...]

4 [...]*l*[...]*l*[...]

Frg. 18

1 [...]*n*ʾ[...]

2 [...]*mbr*[...]

3 [...]*b* upon the hand of [...]

4 [...]*lt* glory [...]

5 [...]° without [...]

Frg. 19, Col. 1

1 [...] your sons in me from

2 [...] your judgments

3 [...]° my refuge, and in your skies

4 [...] pure gold, and you will give me

5 [...] your kingdom to your servant

6 [...] they spurned

7 [...]°*l*[...]

Frg. 19, Col. 2

3 my God [...]

4 and *yʿn*[...]

5 and what ʾ[...]

6 because ʿ*š*[...]

Frg. 20

1 [...]°°*ny* to me *h*[...]

2 [...] your statutes [...]

3 [...] your [...]° to me and ʾ[...]

4 [...]°° °°°[...]

Frg. 21

1 [...]° °[...]

2 [...]*b*. Selah. [...]

Frg. 22

1 [...] you will explain [...]

2 [...]*r yr*[...]

Frg. 23

1   [ס̇]

2   [̊ לחדרי]

Frg. 24[24]

1   [̊ ש̊ ̊]   [̊ כם̇]

2   ולשני כג̇מ̇ר ̊ ̊ ̊ ואין מכבה עד י[ן

3   עד לכלה סלה   ]

("Praise of the Man of God")

4   תהלה לאיש ה̇אל[הי]ם̇ יהוה אלהים̇[

5   גאל ליהודה מכל צ̇ר ומאפ̇רים ̊[

6   דור ויהללהו בח̇יניו[25] ויאמרו קום א̇[להי   [א̇ג̇]

7   שמך ישעי סלעי ומצודתי ומפלט̇[י[26]   [ב̇יום א[ידי[27]

8   אקרא ליה̇ו̇ה̇ ויענני אלהי עזרתי[[שנאי ויאמר]

9   [לעם ואני ש̇[כי̇ן[ה̊ ̊]   שועתי ל[פ̇ניו באזניו תבוא̇[28]

10   וק̇ו̇לי מהיכלו ישמע ות̇ר̊ע̊ש הארץ [ותגעש   ת̊ כי חר̇ה̇ לו[29] עלה

11   באפ̇ו עשן[30]   [כלי[31] ̊ ̊ ̊ [̊] ̊ ̊]   [ם̇ השכיל ̇ ̇ שכל

12   [VACAT

Frg. 27   *Frg. 26*   *Frg. 25*

1   [̊]   1   [פ̇תנים ותנ̇ינים   1   [̊ ̊]

2   [ש ויב̇]   2   [ל ̊ ̊]   2   [ה ב̇]

Frg. 28

1   [לפניו ז̇[ב]ג̇ח̇ל̇י אש י̇פזר̇ו̇]

2   [̊ אלי̇ה̇ם ויהמם וי̇ ̊]

3   [מ̇קוה לאיביך יכרתו]

4   [̊ ̊ ם̇ ̊ ̊ ̊ ̊ ̊]

---

24   There is stitching to the right of the right column.

25   Read בחוניו.

26   Cf. MT Ps 18:3: יהוה סלעי ומצודתי ומפלטי אלי צורי אחסה־בו מגני וקרן־ישעי משגבי.

27   Lines 7-11 are restored on the basis of the MT of Ps 18:2, 7, 8, 9 which is used extensively in this section, and which also provides the basis for placing fragment 24B to the left of 24A.

28   Cf. MT Ps 18:7: בצר־לי אקרא יהוה ואל־אלהי אשוע ישמע מהיכלו קולי ושועתי לפניו תבוא באזניו.

29   Cf. MT Ps 18:8: ותגעש ותרעש הארץ ומוסדי הרים ירגזו ויתגעשו כי חרה לו.

30   Cf. MT Ps 18:9: עלה עשן באפו ואש־מפיו תאכל גחלים בערו ממנו.

31   A small piece of leather at this point was originally folded back and stuck on the reverse of the fragment; although it is definitely attached here, the exact alignment is not certain.

Frg. 23

1 [...]*m*[...]

2 [...] to the rooms of °[...]

Frg. 24

1 °°*š*°°[...]*ykm* °[...]

2 And my tongue like a coal[19] °°° and no one can quench (it) until *y*[...]

3 completely. Selah. (vacat) [...]

("Praise of the Man of God")

4 Praise of the Man of G[o]d. Yahweh God [...]

5 he has redeemed[20] Judah from all distress, and from Ephraim °[...]

6 [generation. And his tested ones[21] will praise him, and say, "Rise up [my] G[od...]'*g*[...]

7 your name (is) my salvation. My rock, my fortress, and [my] deliverer [...] On the day of [my] ca[lamity...]

8 I will call to Yahweh, and my God will answer me. My help[22] [...] those who hate me. And he will say [...]

9 because [...] *h*°°*ṣ*[...]*l*ʿ*m*. And I *š*[... my cry be]fore him comes to his ears

10 and [my] voi[ce from his temple he will hear. And] the earth reel[ed and rocked ...] °*t* for he was angry. There went up

11 in [his] nostril(s) [smoke...]°[...]° °°*kl* [...]*m*. He taught, and instruction[23]

12 [...] (vacat)

Frg. 25

1 [...]°° [...]

2 [...]°*h b*°[...]

Frg. 26

1 [...] asps and ser[pents...]

2 [...]*l*°°[...]

Frg. 27

1 [...]°[...]

2 [...]*š* and *yb*[...]

Frg. 28

1 [...] before him. And [with] coals of fire[24] he will scatter [...]

2 [...]° to them. And he will rout them and *y*°[...]

3 [...] hope for your enemies. They will be cut off [...]

4 [...]°°°*m* °°°° °°[...]

---

[19] Or "and my tongue is like the completion of."

[20] Or the imperative "redeem" or a participle "redeemer."

[21] Or "his expert ones/experienced ones" (reading בחוניו); there is some evidence that this root could interchange with בחר, thus "his chosen ones."

[22] Or "the God of my help will answer me."

[23] Or "let him surely teach" or "let him teach instruction."

[24] Alternative restoration: "and [like] coals of fire."

Frg. 29

1] °בתו א[

2]וישלח מלאכיו וי°°[

יאבדו

3 מנש]מת רוח אפך כל בש[ר

4]אלהי תשלח ידך [

5]°°°°°°°°°°°°[

Frg. 30

1]חרן[

2]שמה°[

Frg. 31[32]

1] ברשת זו טמ[נו]°° [ ]°°° [ ]° אזמרה[33] ל[יהו]ה[ ]ני ע°[ ]ב°[

2]אשיח בנפלאתיך כי אל [ ] לפניך תש[ ] תושיעני ותעלני מאהלי מות ות[ ]° לנפי כל [

3 כ]ל דרכו תבואינא[34] אל עו°[ ]במקם[35] קדש[סלה] VACAT

4 [תפלה ל מ]לך יהודה שמע אל[הי]°שיך °°מ°ת עזי[ ]°תך אספרה נגד יראיך [ ]°°°°[ ]עמדי °°[

5 מח]שבתיך מי יבין להמא[36] כי רבו צררי נגדך אתה ידעתם ולשנאי נפשי לנגד ע[יני]ך כפיתה כי אחיה[

6 לא]תכחד עוני לידעי בינה ואתה להם תשחט אלהי ישעי צפנים ימי עמדי ומה יעשה אנוש הנני ואיככה

7 תגיר]לחכי עלידי[37] חרב ביום עברה האמרים פענה שרגו עטרת ראשי כי אדר נציב כבודם ועידם[38]

8]לם שפתי שאלה ס[ ]°° [ ]°°° ° מספר החי[י]ם[ ]מפחדי יתמו [ו]צררי יכלו ואין[[ ]]°°כ°°[[ ]]ן[39]

9]נני שיר ותוד[ה]כל עמך לג[סלה] [ ] [[ ]]

10] [

[32] Fragment 32 contains no writing, but the crumpled state of the leather and the dark color suggests that it comes from near frg. 31.

[33] Possibly אומרה.

[34] Probably an orthographic variant of תבואינה; cf. להמא in line 5.

[35] If the correct reading, the ק has perhaps been corrected from a ו.

[36] Probably an orthographic variant of להמה; cf. תבואינא.

[37] Read על ידי.

[38] Read ועדים.

[39] The join here of the fragment with the reading]°°כ°°[is less than certain.

Frg. 29

1 [. . .]°*btw* ʾ[. . .]

2 [. . .] and he will send his angels and *y*°°[. . .]

3 [. . . at the bl]ast of the breath of your nostril(s) all fle[sh] shall perish [. . .]

4 [. . .] my God you will send your hand [. . .]

5 [. . .]°° °°° °° °° °°[. . .]

Frg. 30

1 [. . .]*ḥr*[. . .]

2 [. . .]*šmh*°[. . .]

Frg. 31

1 [. . .] in the net which [they] hi[de]°°[. . .]°°°[. . .]°. I will sing-praise[25] to [Yahwe]h [. . .]*ny* ʿ°[. . .]*b*°[. . .]

2 [. . .] I will ponder your wonders, for to [. . .] before you. You will *š*[. . . .] You will save me, and bring me up from the tents of death. And you will [. . .]° to the heights of all [. . .]

3 [. . . . A]ll its way(s) will come[26] to ʿ*w*°[. . .] in a holy place. [Selah.] (vacat)

4 [Prayer of . . . ki]ng of Judah. Hear [my] Go[d . . .]° *šyk* °°*m*°*t* my strength [. . .]°*tk*. I will recount[27] before those who fear you [. . .]°°°°[. . .] with me °°[. . .]

5 [. . .] your [tho]ughts, who can discern them?[28] For my foes are many before you. You have humiliated them,[29] and those who hate my life[30] you have overturned before your e[yes]. For I will live[31] [. . .]

6 [. . .] you will [not] hide the iniquities of those who know discernment,[32] but you will slaughter them. God of my salvation, the days of my existence are fixed.[33] And what can be done?[34] Here I am, weak and how

7 [. . . . You will deliver over] those who wait for me (by) the sword; on the day of wrath, those who say *p*ʿ*nh*. They have woven a wreath (for) my head. For the magnificence of *nṣyb* (is) their glory, and their ornamentation

8 [. . .]*lm* my lips a question *s*[. . .]°°[. . .]°°°° from the book of li[f]e[35] [. . .] those who terrify me will cease, [and] my enemies will perish, and no °°*k*°°*n*

9 [. . .]*nny* a song and a thanksgiv[ing . . .]*kl* with you[36] *lg*[. . . . Selah . . . .] (vacat) [. . .] (vacat)[. . .]

10 [. . .] (vacat) [. . .]

---

25 Alternate reading: "I will say."

26 There are many possibilities, especially given that תבואינא is such an unusual form. Perhaps "a]ll its way(s) will bring." Or the subject of the verb could be any feminine plural noun "[. . .] will come to [a]ll its way(s)." "All its way(s)" could end the previous colon; then "you will bring it."

27 "I will recount" could be the conclusion of the preceding colon.

28 Or, dividing slightly differently, "your [tho]ughts, who can discern them for they are many."

29 Or "you have known them."

30 Or "my soul."

31 Or "I will declare," "I will preserve [my life]."

32 Or "Do not hide my iniquities from those who know discernment." Or "my iniquity was not hidden from those who know discernment."

33 Or "hidden are my days with me."

34 Or "And what can a person do?"

35 Or "the number of the li[vi]ng."

36 Or "your people."

Frgs. 33 and 35[40]
(A Penitential Psalm)

1	‏[ת ‏יْכלוْ ‏יْתْ[‏]‏°ْ ° [	‏]ושْרْיْת לוْיْ ‏יْמצא לْהْ [
2	על שמיْ]ם ‏לْזْמה יהוה ואלהْני	ואתה תשיתני לעתות ולמْישْ[ی[42]
3	ת[שْי]‏מْنْ ותהי לי תכחתך לْ]שמחה	ונתהלל בגברתך כי אין חקרْ[
4	‏[לْכْלْنْיْ[ ]ואתה אלהי תשלח רْוْןْחْ[43] ‏וْ]תתן רחמיך	עלם ולרממך כי פשעי רבו ממני זْ[
5	אْ[רْ]ננה[ ]ואגילה בך נגד יראْי]ך כי [תשפט	לבן אמתך וחסדיך לעבד קْרْב לך וْהْ[
6	‏[ ]‏°ْ [ ] לכה סלה VACAT	עבדיך בצדקך וכחْסْדْיْך [ ]לْהציל אצْ°
7	‏]	‏[[	‏]]

(A "Prayer of Manasseh")

8	‏[לْ] ‏]‏קْרוב ישעי לנגד עיניך מה] ‏[לْ]	תפלה למנשה מלך יהודה בכלו אתו מלך אשור [א]לْהْ[[י
9	משْמْחْתْ[44] עוד ולא תْרْאה בטוב נפשי כי [ ] ‏יْ גْלْז ואْ[[	לישע פניך אקוה ואני אכחש לפניך על חْ]טْא[ی כי הْגْדْלْ]ت רחמיך ‏]ואני הרביתי אשמה וכן א]כْרת
10	‏הْ] זْא הרימני למעלה על גْוْی [	משْמْחْת[44] עוד ולא תْרْאה בטוב נפשי כי [ ] ‏יْ גْלْז ואْ[[
11	‏]לي [	ואני לאזכרתيْ[45] ‏[במקו]ם ‏לْ[נْ]דْשْך] לْאْ עْבْדْתْ[یْך

Frg. 37

1	‏]יْدْ[46]
2	‏]מכל
3	‏]בסרי
4	‏]לْ[

Frg. 36

1	‏]נْפלתْ[
2	‏]ואזْ[
3	‏]‏لْ° [

Frg. 34

1	‏[ואْ°]
2	‏[לْוْ°]
3	‏[לْ]

---

40 Fragment 33 comprises two pieces, 33A on the right and 33B on the left. Fragment 35 has been joined to the right of 33B at lines 4-6. The handwriting between lines 1-6 and 8-11 is probably by the same scribe, who seems to have taken a break at the vacat and used a new stylus. [JHC]

41 Read לוא.

42 Or read and restore למْוْع[רים or למْوْע[קה or למْוْع[ים, although the ע is more problematic than ש.

43 Or perhaps read and restore ‏רْוْ[רי]‏رْ.

44 The scribe may have initially written משמת and then converted the ת to ח and added a final ת.

45 Read לא זכרתיך.

46 The lines here must have been very close together, or perhaps these traces are from interlinear letters.

Frgs. 33 and 35
(A Penitential Psalm)

1 [...] and he will not find a remnant for it [...]°°*t* they will perish *yt*[...]

2 And you will set for me³⁷ times, and *lmyš*³⁸[... above the heaven]s, rise up, Yahweh, and [my] God, [....]

3 And we will glory in your might, for unsearchable [... you] will s[e]t me. And may your reproach become for me everlasting [joy,]

4 and for your exaltation. For (my) transgressions are too many for me, and °[...]*lklny*. But you, my God, will send your spir[it] and [you will give your compassions]

5 to the son of your handmaiden,³⁹ and your mercies to the servant near to you. And *h*[...I] will cry out in joy, and I will rejoice in you before those who fe[ar you]. For [you will judge]

6 your servants in your righteousness, and according to your mercies [...] to deliver '*ṣ*[...]°[...] to you. Selah. (vacat)

7 (vacat) [...] (vacat) [...]

(A "Prayer of Manasseh")

8 Prayer of Manasseh, king of Judah, when the king of Assyria imprisoned him. [... my G]od,[...] near, my salvation is before your eyes,⁴⁰ what [...]*l*[...]

9 I wait for your saving presence, and I cringe before you because of my s[in]s. For [you] have magnified [your compassions,]⁴¹ but I have multiplied wrongdoing. And so I [will be cut off]

10 from eternal joy, and my soul will not behold (what is) good.⁴² For [...]*y* they went into exile, and '[...h]e exalted me on high, over a nation⁴³ [....]

11 And I did not remember you [in your] h[oly plac]e, [I] did not serve [you...]*ly* [...]

Frg. 34

1 [...] and '° [...]
2 [...]°*rw* [...]
3 [...]*l* [...]

Frg. 36

1 [...] you fell [...]
2 [...] and then [...]
3 [...]°*l*°[...]

Frg. 37

1 [...] hand
2 [...] from all
3 [...] among the stubborn ones of
4 [...]*l*[...]

---

³⁷ Or "for us," as in line 3. The suffix also may be a direct object: "you will set me / us / it."

³⁸ Alternate restoration: "you will set me/us for times and for festiv[als" or "for afflic[tion."

³⁹ Cf. Ps 86:16c. Or "the son of your truth"; cf. 1QH 6.29—30. See also 4Q381 frg. 15 line 2.

⁴⁰ The colon can be divided in a number of different ways, i.e., "near is my salvation; before your eyes what [...]."

⁴¹ Many alternate restorations are possible here; the phrase could be first person, and negative, e.g., "for [I] have magnified [myself against Yahweh]" (cf. Jer 48:26).

⁴² Or "you will not look upon the good of my soul."

⁴³ Or "h]e removed me totally; upon a nation [...]."

	Frg. 40		Frg. 39		Frg. 38
1	[נע הש̇ן]	1	[ ]° יכנע̇ו [	1	[ ]° [ ] ° [
2	[הנקלי]ם̇	2	[יבש̇ו]	2	[° פלאות ה̇ן]
3	[ות̇ש̇°]			3	[שלמתי]
4	[ ]°[			4	[צע]

	Frg. 43		Frg. 42		Frg. 41
1	[ת̇ג̇ע̇ש̇]	1	ת]ל̇מד בני̇ך̇]	1	[ ]°°°[
2	[מני וי°]	2	[להושיע לע̇]	2	[עלה בעת]
		3	[ ]°°[	3	[ ]°°° בי̇]
				4	[ל̇א]

Frg. 44

1 [ת̇]°[
2 [כ̇]ל ארץ זו הגברת [בה
3 ל[קוי̇ך ומצי̇ל לבטוחים̇] בך
4 [תשכילה בז̇ כי אין כמ̇]וך
5 [ל̇א] [ ]°°[

Frg. 45[47]

1 זאבי̇נ̇א̇ ו̇א̇י̇ן̇ מבין אשכ̇יל ולז̇ °[ ]°°[ ]   [י ואפחד ממך ואטהר
2 מתעבות הכרתי ואתן נפשי להכנע מלפנ̇[י]ך   [הרבו פשעה ועלי יזמו
3 להסגירני ואני בך בטחתי [ל̇א]   [ ]°[ ]   [לא]
4 ואל תתנני במשפט עמך אלהי [
5 מתיעצים עלי פתחו לשן שק̇[ר
6 לי מעשי ש̇ °°[ ]°°°°[
7 לה̇ °°°°°[

---

47 Fragment 45 comprises two pieces, 45A on the right and 45B on the left.

Frg. 38

1 [...]°[...]°[...]

2 [...]° wonders *h*[...]

3 [...] I requited [...]

4 [...]*ṣ*ᶜ [...]

Frg. 39

1 [...]° they will humble [...]

2 [...] they will be ashamed [...]

Frg. 40

1 [...]*n*ᶜ *hš*[...]

2 [...] the base one[s...]

3 [...] and you will *š*°[...]

4 [...]°[...]

Frg. 41

1 [...]°°° °[...]

2 [...] he went up in the time of [...]

3 [...]°°° in me [...]

4 [...]*l*[...]

Frg. 42

1 [... you will] teach your sons [...]

2 [...] to save *l*ᶜ[...]

3 [...]°° [...]

Frg. 43

1 [...] it will shake [...]

2 [...]*mny* and *y*°[...]

Frg. 44

1 [...]° *t*[...]

2 [...] for a land [in] which you acted mightily [...]

3 [...to] those who wait for you, and a deliverer to those who trust [in you...]

4 [...] you will teach her it,[44] for there is none like [you]

5 [...]*l*[...]°°[...]

Frg. 45[45]

1 and I will discern, and the one who does not discern I will teach, and to him[46] °[...]°°[...]*y* and I will be in awe of you, and I will purify myself[47]

2 from abominations (which) I knew,[48] and I will allow my soul to be humble before [you...] they multiplied transgression;[49] and they conspire against me

3 to shut me up. But as for me, I trust in you [...]*l*[...]°[...]*l*[...]

4 and do not set me in judgment with you, my God, [....]

5 Those who conspire against me have loosed a deceit[ful] tongue [....]

6 To me works of *š*°°[...]°°° °°[...]

7 to *h*°° °°[...]

---

[44] Or "she will consider it/me," reading the verb as a third person with an expanded ה.

[45] There are some features of wording and content which suggest that this psalm could be a continuation of a "Prayer of Manasseh," 4Q381 frg. 33.

[46] Or "and I discern, but there is no instructor, I teach, but not [...]."

[47] Or "I will be clean."

[48] Or "the abominations (which) I cut down."

[49] Or "her/its transgression."

Frg. 46[48]

		1
עלי]]		

1   עלי]]

2   ר]ֹב חסדיך]]   [ֹב ול]]   [°°] וחתנתן לי קרן]
           49°°

3   [ֹתֹו בך ואשֹ°]]   כ]סילים חקיך והֹודך ותפארת]ך

4   וכעננים יפרשו על פ]ני הארץ   [ֹת לאבתֹינא יפֹוצו50 לרב עד אן]°ֹיֹ וֹן]עֹת

5   לוא יעז אנוש ולא ירום]]   וב]חנת כל ובחרים כמנחת תטהר לפניך ושנאי]ם

6   כנדה תזנזחי51 ורוח סוערת]]   מ]עלֹילם52 ויראיך לפניך תמיד קרנים קרנים

7   ברזל לנגח בה רבים ֹנגֹחֹו]]   קוה ופרסותם תשים נחשה ופשעיֹם כדמן

8   עלפני אֹדמה ירמסו וֹ°°]]   ינדפו מ]לפֹנֹי ֹבֹ°] בם וֹרֹוחך °°] °ֹלֹה

9   [ ]°ֹוֹאֹש בעוֹרֹ]ת   [ ]°ֹ°[ ]°ֹ[לֹ]° [ ]°°[לֹ[

Frg. 47

1   ]ֹם אלהי כי רחמון וחנון אתה]

2   ]מֹוֹרֹ ֹהֹ °° ֹואהלך באמתך ל]

3   ]מֹבינֹיך ואשכילה]

4   [53VACAT   ]

---

48 Fragment 46 comprises two pieces, 46A on the right and 46B on the left.

49 The faint traces of interlinear letters are impossible to decipher.

50 Or יפֹרֹצו.

51 Read תזניח.

52 Perhaps עלֹולם], a phonetic writing of עלעול; cf. Sir 43:17.

53 Since there is sufficient leather to expect traces of letters from line 4, a vacat is probable.

Frg. 46

1 [...] against me [...]

2 your [abun]dant mercies [...]*b* and *l*[...]°° and a horn will be given to me.[50] [...]

3 [...]° *tw* in you and I will *š*°[...f]ools your statutes. And your majesty and [your] beauty [...]

4 and like clouds they will be spread over the fa[ce of the earth...]°*t l' btyn'* they will be dispersed in great number[51] until '[...]°°*ny* and [...]'*t.*

5 People will not prevail and will not rise [... and] you will [t]est all. And chosen ones, like offerings, you will declare pure before you. And hated one[s]

6 like impurity you will reject.[52] And a stormy wind [...] their [de]ed.[53] But those who fear you are before you always. (Their) horns (are) horns of

7 iron[54] with which to gore many. And they will gore [...] a line. And you will make their hoofs bronze, and transgressors like dung

8 will be trampled upon the face of the ground. And °°[...] they will be driven[55] [from] before *b*°°[...] in them. And your spirit °°[...]°*lh*

9 [...]° and a bla[zing] fire [...]° °[...]°*l*[...]°°[...]*l*

Frg. 47

1 [...]*m* my God. For compassionate and gracious (are) you [...]

2 [...]*mwr ḥ*°°° and I will walk in your truth *l*[...]

3 [...] those who discern you, and I will teach [...]

4 [...] (vacat) [...]

---

[50] Or "you will give me a horn."

[51] Alternate reading: "they will increase greatly."

[52] Taking תזנזח as an error for תזניח from the root זנח, "reject." It could also be from זנח, "to stink": "And hated one[s] like נדה you will declare foul."

[53] Or "their whirlwind."

[54] Cf. Mic 4:13, also 1QSb 5.26–27.

[55] Or "they will drive."

Frg. 48

1   [ֹו ֹל ֹ]

2   [ֹ בֹניך מן]

3   והצליחני ברוח פינך

4   בי יראיך ולבחן שֹ[ן

5   וישבֹוֹ[54] ממבטחן

6   ברכֹי ואני אדלג כאֹי[ן ל

7   ונודעה אלהים ביהו[דה[55]

8   קדשך ותשבר אֹ[ן

9   אבירי]לב נמגו כל [אנשי חיל[56]

10   [עֹבֹדֹ]

Frg. 49

1   [ֹכֹאֹ]

2   [ֹ הבינו ותהי לכם]

3   [ֹ ֹ ל ֹ ל ֹ ל ֹ]

Frg. 50

1   [וֹטוֹמֹי נכֹלֹ]

2   [לֹכֹל ורשעים יֹכבֹו[57]

3   [לֹפניו יזכרו כי נורֹא אתֹה ֹ][58]

4   [ארץ יֹרה ובשקטה[59] במקֹום [אלהים למשפט[60]

5   [ֹ ֹ מֹ וֹנודך][61]

6   [אל ֹ]

Frg. 53, Col. 1		*Frg. 52*		*Frg. 51*	
[על	1	[ֹעֹלֹ ֹ]	1	[ֹת זֹאגֹ]	1
קֹים [ֹ	2	[בשֹובתֹם]	2	[ֹתני קֹ]	2
[גדלות	3	[וירדו]	3	[ֹ ֹ]	3
א[יֹן כח	4				

54   There is evidence of erasure and rewriting of the penultimate letter but it is difficult to reconstruct the stages. The interlinear כ is added by the same hand.

55   Lines 7-9 are dependent on Ps 76:2, 6; cf. MT Ps 76:2: נודע ביהודה אלהים בישראל גדול שמו. The first part of the line seems to have been left blank because of a defect in the leather.

56   Cf. MT Ps 76:6: אשתוללו אבירי לב נמו שנתם ולא־מצאו כל־אנשי־חיל ידיהם.

57   Or restore יֹכבֹ[שו.

58   Cf. MT Ps 76:8: אתה נורא אתה ומי־יעמד לפניך מאז אפך.

59   Cf. MT Ps 76:9: משמים השמעת דין ארץ יראה ושקטה.

60   Restored on basis of Ps 76:8-11 which is reused here in lines 3-5; cf. MT Ps 76:10: בקום־למשפט אלהים להושיע כל־ענוי־ארץ סלה.

61   Cf. MT Ps 76:11: כי־חמת אדם תודך שארית חמת תחגר.

Frg. 48

1 [...]° and *l*°[...]

2 [...] your sons from °[....]

3 And make me prosper by the breath of [your] mouth [...]

4 in me those who fear you.   And to test *š*[...]

5 and they will lie down in trust [...]

6 my knee(s).   And I will leap like a de[er....]

7 And God is known in Ju[dah...]

8 your holiness.   And you will break ʾ°[...]

9 [stout of] heart.   All [men of valor] melted [...]

10 [...] servant [...]

Frg. 49

1 [...]*k*ʾ°[...]

2 [...]° they discern, and let it be to you [...]

3 [...]°° °*l*° *l*°*l*°[...]

Frg. 50

1 [...] *wswmy nkl*°[...]

2 [...] to all.   And wicked ones will be extingui[shed ...][56]

3 [...] before it they will be remembered.   For you are awe-inspiring °[...]

4 [...] land.   And it feared,[57] and in its quietness, when [God] rose [for judgment...]

5 [...]°°*m* and we will thank you [...]

6 [...] to °[...]

Frg. 51

1 [...]*t y*ʾ*g*°[...]

2 [...]°*tny q*[...]

3 [...]° °[...]

Frg. 52

1 [...]°ᵉ*l*°[...]

2 [...] in their returning [...]

3 [...] and they went down [...]

Frg. 53, Col. 1

1 [...] upon

2 [...]°*qym*

3 [...] great things

4 [... n]o strength

---

[56] Alternative restoration: "will tramp[le down ...]."

[57] The translation assumes that this line is a reworking of Ps 76:9—10.

	Frg. 55		*Frg. 54*		*Frg. 53, Col. 2*
1	[֯ עד֯]	1	[ר֯]	3	מא֯ן
2	[זרע בא]	2	[נ֯ז]	4	ו֯[

	Frg. 58		*Frg. 57*		*Frg. 56*
1	[ו֯ו֯]	1	[עד֯י]	1	[במ֯ין]
2	[בות ֯]	2	[ב֯שר ֯]	2	[עד ש֯]
		3	[° ° ° ° ° °]		

	Frg. 61		*Frg. 60*		*Frg. 59*
1	[ה֯ז מספר]	1	[מצ]	1	[מחק]
2	[֯ לן]ל֯ן[	2	[לן]	2	[מ֯ן]

	Frg. 64		*Frg. 63*		*Frg. 62*
1	[א֯ן]	1	[ה֯ל ֯]	1	[הסתר֯ן]

	Frg. 67		*Frg. 66*		*Frg. 65*
1	[ו֯ א֯]ן	1	[֯ י כ֯]	1	[֯]
2	[ב֯ר֯]ן	2	[ין֯]	2	[֯ גיא]ן

Frg. 68

1 [הן]
2 [֯ בן]

Frg. 69[62]

1 [לכם כי ת֯ן]   [לם בראותו כי התעיבו עמי [הא]ר֯ץ[63]
2 היתה]כל הארץ לנדת טמאה בנדתי[64] טמאה והפלא מראשונה
3 נ]זעץ אל לבו להשמידם מעליה ולעשות עליה עם
4 [ב֯כם וינתם[65] לכם ברוחו נביאים להשכיל וללמד אתכם
   [֯ כם מן שמים ירד וידברעמכם[66] להשכיל אתכם ולהשיב ממעשי ישבי[67]
5 נתן ח]לים תורות ומצות בברית העמיד ביד֯] משה[

---

62 Frg. 69 seems closely related to frg. 77 and may follow directly upon it (see Schuller, *Non-Canonical Psalms*, pp. 225-26).
63 There is a spot of ink after the ע; the final word was possibly הארצות.
64 Or בנדת.

65 Read ויתנם or ויתנם.
66 Read וידבר עמכם. See Plate for lack of word division; possibly the scribe was concerned about spacing.
67 The interlinear addition seems to be a correction of a mechanical scribal error by the same hand.

Frg. 53, Col. 2

1 *m*ʾ[…]

2 *w*°[…]

Frg. 54

1 […]°*k* […]

2 […]*nw* […]

Frg. 55

1 […]ʿ*k* °[…]

2 […]arm *b*ʾ[…]

Frg. 56

1 […]*bmy*[…]

2 […]ʿ*d š*[…]

Frg. 57

1 […]ʿ*dy* […]

2 […]flesh °[…]

3 […] °°°°° […]

Frg. 58

1 […]° *w*°[…]

2 […]°*bwt* […]

Frg. 59

1 […]*mḥq*[…]

2 […]from[…]

Frg. 60

1 […] *mṣ*[…]

2 […]*l*[…]

Frg. 61

1 […]*ḥy* number[58] […]

2 […]°*l*[…]*l*[…]

Frg. 62

1 […] he hid […]

Frg. 63

1 […]*ḥl* °[…]

Frg. 64

1 […]°°[…]

Frg. 65

1 […]°[…]

2 […]°*gy*ʾ[…]

Frg. 66

1 […]°*y k*[…]

2 […]*yn*[…]

Frg. 67

1 […]*w* ʾ°[…]

2 […]*br*°[…]

Frg. 68

1 […]*h*[…]

2 […]°*bw*[…]

Frg. 69

1 […]*lkm* because *t*°[…]*lm*.   When he saw that the people of [the la]nd acted abominably

2 […] all the land [became] unclean defilement in unclean defilement.   And wonderfully from the beginning

3 […] he [to]ok counsel with himself[59] to destroy them from upon it, and to make upon it a people

4 […]*bkm*, and he gave[60] to you by his spirit prophets to instruct and to teach you (. . . .)

5a […]°*km* from heaven he came down, and he spoke with you to instruct you, and to turn (you) away from the works of the inhabitants of (. . . .)

5 [He gave sta]tutes, laws, and ordinances by the covenant (which) he established through [Moses]°°°

---

[58] Or "from the book."

[59] Lit. "with his heart." Note that אל is the preposition.

[60] The verb in Hebrew (וינתם) suffers from either metathesis (for ויתנם) or haplography (for וינתנם).

6   [ויא ‬ ‬ ‬ישו שבו על הארץ אז תטהר ויא ‬ ‬]

7   [‬ואם 68לוא תהיו אם בכם להשכיל]

8   ל‬
     [‬וא ולהנכר‬ ‬ לכם כרת ברית ולהפיר‬ ‬]

9   [‬מעלא פיהו 69דבריו ולהמיר רשעה על]

10   [לן]   [‬ ‬]

Frg. 72		Frg. 71		Frg. 70	
[‬די ‬ ‬]	1	[חקן]	1	[כתוב לכ‬ם ‬]	1
[‬ל ‬]	2	[‬ ‬]	2	[‬ ‬ ‬ ‬]	2

Frg. 75		Frg. 74		Frg. 73	
[חרבת ‬ ‬]	1	[הלוא]	1	[ח ע‬]	1
[‬עוף ואנשי‬ם]	2	[ואהיה]	2	[‬ ‬ ‬]	2
[יכנעו ול‬ן]	3	[לן]	3		

Frgs. 76–77 [70]

1   [אלי חיות ועוף הקבצון]

2   [‬ם לבני אדם כיצר מחשב]ות לבם

3   [היתה ההוה ע‬ן]

4   ר[שף 71 זכלה ואין ח‬ן]קר

5   ישרא[ל עם סגלתו]

6   [‬ק ‬]   [ ]   [ ]

7   עד]ת קדוש קדושים גורל מלך מלכים ‬[ ]

8   [‬ ‬ דברי ותשכילו לחכמה מפי תצא ותבינ‬ו 72]ן

9   יש‬
     [ושפט אמת ועד נאמן אם בכם כח להשיבנו ‬]

---

68 Read לו.
69 Read דברי.
70 The two fragments have been joined tentatively on the basis of matching edges and the lines of folding, but there is no

overlap of letters to make the join certain. Fragment 76 supplies lines 1–5; fragment 77 supplies lines 6–16.
71 Or נ]שף.
72 Or ותכונ]ה.

6 [...]*yšw* dwell upon the land.   Then it will be purified[61] and he will ʾ°°[...]

7 [...] to consider among yourselves, if you will be his or if [...]

8 [...] and to break the covenant (which) he cut with you, and to act as a stranger, and not [...]

9 [...] against wickedness, and to change the words of his mouth[62] *mᶜlʾ* [...]

10 [...]°°[...]*l*[...]

Frg. 70

1 [...]° written to yo[u ...]

2 [...]°°° °[...]

Frg. 71

1 [...] *ḥq*[...]

2 [...]°°[...]

Frg. 72

1 [...]°*y wy*°[...]

2 [...]°*lᵓ*[...]

Frg. 73

1 [...]*ḥ* ᶜ°[...]

2 [...]°°°[...]

Frg. 74

1 [...] is it not [...]

2 [...] and I will be [...]

3 [...]*l*[...]

Frg. 75

1 [...] the ruin of °°[...]

2 [...]° birds and me[n ...]

3 [...] they will be humbled, and *l*[...]

Frgs. 76—77

1 [...] to me, beasts and birds, be gathered [...]

2 [...]*m* to humans,[63] according to the inclination of the thought[s of their heart(s) ...]

3 [...] was destruction[64] ᶜ[...]

4 [... fl]ame[65] and destruction and unse[archable ...]

5 [... Israe]l a people his treasure [...]

6 [...]°*ṣ*. (vacat) [...] (vacat) [...]

7 [... congrega]tion of the Most Holy Ones, lot of the king of kings °[...]

8 [...]°° my word(s), and you will pay attention to the wisdom (which) goes forth from my mouth, and you will disce[rn ...][66]

9 [...] and a true judge and a faithful witness.   Do you have strength to answer him[67] °[...]

---

[61] Or "they returned to the land; then it was purified."

[62] Reading the Hebrew as an error for דברי פיהו.

[63] Lit. "sons of Adam" or "sons of humanity."

[64] Or read a participle: הויה "was," "is."

[65] Alternative restoration: "[twi]light."

[66] Alternative restoration: "the wisdom which goes forth from my mouth and the understanding."

[67] Or "to restore him."

10   לשמﹾﹾﹾﻴﻉ מי בכם ישיב דבר ויעמד בהתוכח עﹾמו]

11   כﹾי רﹾבים שפטיכם ואין מספר לעﹾדיכם כי אם]

12   ﹾיﹾ יהוה ישב במשפטיכם לשפט אמת ואין עולﹾה]

13   רﹾוﹾחיו לעשות בכם משפטי אמת היש בינה תלמדﹾוﹾ]

14   אﹾדﹾני האדונים גבור ונפלא ואין כמהו הוא בחר בכﹾם]

15   מעמים רﹾ]בﹾים ומגויים גדולים להיות לואﹾ[73] לעם למשל בכלﹾ]

16   שמﹾ]ﹾים וארץ ולעליון על כל גוי הארץ ולהﹾשﹾ]

Frg. 78

1   [ﹾﹾﹾ]

2   [ﹾ ניﹾו באﹾﻑﹾ וחמה ﹾ]

3   [ר חרבות ורמﹾחﹾיﹾﹾﹾ]

4   [הם זﹾﻇﹾﻥ ﹾﹾ ﻠﻛﹾ]

5   [ﹾ דﹾשנם שנתﹾ]

6   [זﹾ זﹾרותה האﹾ]רץ

Frg. 79

1   [ﹾﹾﹾ]

2   [[74]   זקן לוא יחננﹾ] עﹾלﹾ]

3   אﹾ]שמה ועמי יאשמו יחד עﹾמﹾהם הﹾ]

4   לﹾ]אﹾ ﹾישפט עולה כי נדחתי ﹾﹾﹾ]

5   [ﹾ ת תעואת להשכיל לﹾ]

6   אﹾ]להי אﹾל תעזﹾבﹾ]ני

Frg. 82		*Frg. 81*		*Frg. 80*	
[ﹾאﹾﹾﹾ]	1	[ﹾﹾﹾﹾ]	1	[לﹾשכיל אליﹾ]	1
		[עﹾת בﹾﹾﹾ]	2	[לﹾכﹾ]	2

---

[73] **Read** לו.
[74] The uninscribed section results from the scribe's avoidance of a small circular patch of damaged leather.

10 [...] to proclaim.   Who among you will reply a word, and (who) will stand in controversy wi[th him...][68]

11 [...] for many are those who judge you, and there is no number to those who witness against you.   But if [...]

12 [...]°*y* Yahweh will sit in judgment with you, to judge truly and without deceit [...]

13 [...] his spirits, to render you true judgments.   Is there discernment (which) you may learn[69] [...]

14 [...] Lord of lords, mighty, and wonderful, and there is no one like him.   He chose yo[u]

15 [from m]any [peoples] and from great nations to be his people, to rule over all [...]

16 [... hea]vens and earth, and as most high over every nation of the earth, and to *hš*°[...]

Frg. 78

1 [...]°°°[...]

2 [...]°*nyw* with wrath and anger °[...]

3 [...]*r* swords and spears [...]

4 [...]*hm wṣ*[...]°° *hk*°[...]

5 [...] their fatness *šnt*[...]

6 [...]*w* and the la[nd] was saturated [...]

Frg. 79

1 [...]° °°[...]

2 [...] they do not honor an old man [...] upon [...]

3 [wr]ongdoing.   And my people will do wrong together with them *h*[...]

4 He will [no]t judge deceitfully, for I was banished °°°[...]

5 [...]°*t* errors[70] to instruct *l*[...]

6 my [G]od, do not abandon [me...]

Frg. 80

1 [...] to instruct me [...]

2 [...]*lk*[...]

Frg. 81

1 [...]°° °°[...]

2 [...]*ᶜt b*°°°[...]

Frg. 82

1 [...]°° ᵓ°[...]

---

[68] The line can be divided and reconstructed slightly differently, with the question ending after "reply"; thus: "and he will stand in controversy wi[th you]."

[69] Or "you may teach."

[70] Apparently from the root תעה; cf. תעות in 1QS 3.21; 1QH 2.14; 4.12, 16, 20.

Frg. 83
1 [ ]י ֯[
2 י(ה) קדם]
3 [֯רתך אלהני

Frg. 84
1 [עם יה]
2 [ותשמ]ע ֯
3 [ד צדק]

Frg. 85
1 [רי הבן]
2 ה]חרש ושועתי הקשב[
3 [הם ומרמה בלבבם]
4 [˚˚˚˚˚˚˚]

Frg. 86
1 [מי חוק]
2 [ים יהוה א] ֯
3 [ובזרע עזך]
4 [הו]דך והדר[ן
5 [ני זיש]
6 [מצוות]

Frg. 87
1 [בו וא]
2 [ומ] ֯

Frg. 88
1 [ולדכ]

Frg. 89
1 [ר א]
2 [ ]

Frg. 90
1 [עב]

Frg. 91[75]
1 [נת]
2 [להין]

Frg. 92
1 [ודבר]
2 [ ]

Frg. 93
1 [זו אבתי במעשי ד]
2 [ל ˚˚˚˚˚˚]

Frg. 94
1 [לכל אל בן]
2 [אתה לשנת]

Frg. 95
1 [ני יבילן]
2 [˚˚]

Frg. 96
1 [תם פיהם]
2 [עליך]
3 [לא]

Frg. 97
1 [תם ˚]
2 [ני כי כל]
3 [מאש]
4 [˚˚]

75 Fragments 91-102 are lost; the transcriptions are based on photographs.

Frg. 83

1 [...]°*ny* [...]

2 [...]*y* before [...]

3 [...] your[...]°*rt* [my] God [...]

Frg. 84

1 [...] people *yh*°[...]

2 [...]° and you will he[ar...]

3 [...]°*d* righteousness [...]

Frg. 85

1 [...]*ry* discern [...]

2 [... be s]ilent and attend to my cry [...]

3 [...]°*hm* and treachery in their heart [...]

4 [...]°°°° °°°°[...]

Frg. 86

1 [...]*my* statute [...]

2 [...]°*ym* Yahweh ʾ[...]

3 [...] and with the arm of your strength [...]

4 [...] your [maje]sty and [your] splendor [...]

5 [...]*nny* and he will *š*°[...]

6 [...] ordinances [...]

Frg. 87

1 [...]*bw w*ʾ[...]

2 [...] *wm*[...]

Frg. 88

1 [...]*wdk*[...]

Frg. 89

1 [...]*r* ʾ°[...]

2 [...]°[...]

Frg. 90

1 [...]ʿ*b*°°[...]

Frg. 91

1 [...]°*nt* [...]

2 [...]*lhyz*[...]

Frg. 92

1 [...] he will speak [...]

2 [...]° [...]

Frg. 93

1 [...]*w* my fathers in works of *d*°[...]

2 [...]*l*°° °°°°[...]

Frg. 94

1 [...] to all ʾ*l*° *b*[...]

2 [...] you *lšnh*[...]

Frg. 95

1 [...]*ny ykyl*[...]

2 [...]°° °[...]

Frg. 96

1 [...]*tm* their mouth

2 [...] upon you

3 [...] not

Frg. 97

1 [...]*tm* °[...]

2 [...]*ny* because all [...]

3 [...] and from fire [...]

4 [...]°°°[...]

Frg. 100   *Frg. 99*   *Frg. 98*

1   ] ֿ ֿ [1   [הל]   1   [ראֹ]
2   [ֿהלֿ ֿע]   2   [ֿל]   2   [ֿוכֹ ז]
                                                 3   [ֿ ל]

Frg. 103[76]   *Frg. 102*   *Frg. 101*

1   [ֿם]   1   [ֿויכֹ ֿ]   1   [ֿבכ ֿה ֿ]
2   [בכל ויחי]   2   [ֿ ביד ו]   2   [ֿ ֿ ֿיכ]
3   [ל ל ל]   3   [ֿל ֿ]

Frg. 106   *Frg. 105*   *Frg. 104*

1   [אֹי ֿ ו ֿ]   1   [ושֹ ע]   1   [ם]
2   [ומ]

Frg. 109   *Frg. 108*   *Frg. 107*

1   [ֿא]   1   [א ֿ ֿ ֿ]   1   [ֿד]
                                                 2   [ֿ ֿ]

                                                 Frg. 110

                                                 1   [ֿ ֿ ֿ]

---

[76] Fragments 103-110 were lost before they were photographed. The transcriptions are taken from the notes of J. Strugnell.

Some of these fragments may now be joined to other fragments of 4Q381.

Frg. 98

1 [...]*rʾw*[...]
2 [...]*y* and *k*°[...]
3 [...]*l*°[...]

Frg. 99

1 [...]*lh*[...]
2 [...]*l*°[...]

Frg. 100

1 [...]°°[...]
2 [...]*ʿ°lh* °[...]

Frg. 101

1 [...]°*h kb*°[...]
2 [...]*ky*°°*l*°°[...]

Frg. 102

1 [...]° and he *k*[...]
2 [...]*n* in the hand °[...]
3 [...]°*l* [...]

Frg. 103

1 [...]*m* [...]
2 [...]and he will live in all[...]
3 [...]*l l*[...]

Frg. 104

1 [...]*m*[...]

Frg. 105

1 [...]*ʿ šw*°[...]

Frg. 106

1 [...]°*w yʾ*[...]
2 [...]*wm*[...]

Frg. 107

1 [...]°*d*[...]
2 [...]°°[...]

Frg. 108

1 [...]°°°ʾ[...]

Frg. 109

1 [...]°ʾ[...]

Frg. 110

1 [...]°°°[...]

A Form of Psalm 89

(4Q236 = 4QPs89)

PETER W. FLINT

Introduction

1. Description and Contents

4Q236 (4QPs89) is one of the most unusual Psalms manuscripts to be found at Qumran, and was preliminarily published by J. T. Milik in 1966.[1] Measuring some 6.0 cm high and 4.5 cm wide, this single fragment has been aptly described by Patrick Skehan as a "battered and isolated bit."[2] It preserves parts of Psalm 89, written in prose format and in an arrangement that is otherwise unattested: verses 20–22, 26, 23, 27–28, 31. Both the PAM photographs and the transcription below provide several indications that many letters have been squeezed together: spaces are not always left between words; four of the eight lines have endings that crowd the left-hand margin; letters are written supralinearly above lines 5, 6, and 7; a word is written below line 1; and the text runs very close to the holes for stitching on the left margin.[3]

2. Original Language and Linguistic Features

The original language is Hebrew. The orthography, which is unusual and difficult to categorize, has been classified as "archaic,"[4] and seems to display Aramaic influence.[5] The use of medial letters in final position is consistent for Kaph (ל[בחריכ, it occurs only in line 1), and usual for Mem (עמ, line 2; בימ, line 5; אמ, line 8; but note תכנכמ, line 4). For Nun the final form is used in final position throughout the manuscript.[6]

3. Date and Provenience

Palaeographical analysis indicates that 4Q236 was copied in the Hasmonaean period,[7] which makes it one of the earliest Psalms scrolls; only 4QPs[a] (4Q83) may be older.[8] While there are no

---

[1] J. T. Milik, "Fragment d'une source du Psautier (4QPs89) et fragments des Jubilés, du Document de Damas, d'un phylactère dans la Grotte 4 de Qumrân," *RB* 73 (1966) 94–104; Pl. I. Some of Milik's conclusions were reached in dialogue with John Strugnell, who examined the fragment under ultraviolet light in 1965. The manuscript is currently being prepared by P. W. Flint and E. Ulrich for the series *Discoveries in the Judaean Desert* (Oxford).

[2] P. W. Skehan, "Gleanings from Psalm Texts from Qumrân," in *Mélanges bibliques et orientaux en l'honneur de M. Henri Cazelles*, edited by A. Caquot and M. Delcor (AOAT 212; Neukirchen-Vluyn, 1981) p. 439.

[3] To account for this crowding of letters, Skehan suggests that the fragment is the blank guard sheet from a scroll already in use now turned upside down and used for jotting down a text chosen at random (in *Mélanges*, p. 441).

[4] Milik, *RB* 73 (1966) 97–98 and *passim*; cf. van der Ploeg, "Le sens et un problème textuel du Ps LXXXIX," in *Mélanges bibliques et orientaux en l'honneur de M. Henri Cazelles*,

edited by A. Caquot and M. Delcor (AOAT 212; Neukirchen-Vluyn, 1981) p. 477.

[5] Note especially the use of מן עם and מן שמן in unassimilated form; אואב for אויב; and את for אתה (cf. Skehan, in *Mélanges*, pp. 441–42).

[6] The statement presumes that a letter was originally written at the end of line 7, where the leather is now abraided.

[7] Milik suggests a date of between 175 and 125 B.C.E. (*RB* 73 [1966] 95, 102). However, van der Ploeg dates the manuscript substantially later, to the second half of the first century B.C.E. (van der Ploeg, in *Mélanges*, p. 475).

[8] 4QPs[a] was copied in the mid-2nd century B.C.E. (P. W. Skehan, "Littérature de Qumran–A. Textes bibliques," *Supplément au Dictionnaire de la Bible* [1973–81] 9/10.815–16; P. W. Flint, "The Psalters at Qumran and the Book of Psalms" [Ph.D. dissertation, University of Notre Dame, 1992] p. 40; P. W. Flint, *The Dead Sea Psalms Scrolls and the Book of Psalms* [STDJ 17; Leiden, 1997] p. 33).

firm indications of the date or provenience of composition, this form of Psalm 89 is probably much earlier than the Qumran Community.

4. Relation to the Hebrew Bible

4Q236 is one of only two Psalms manuscripts from Qumran and other Judaean sites to preserve part of Psalm 89,[9] and the only scroll that contains these specific verses: 20–22, 26, 23, 27–28, and 31. Obviously at variance with the Masoretic Psalter, the composition has been variously evaluated as part of a source for the Psalter,[10] as a "practice page written from memory,"[11] or as possibly belonging to a libretto of messianic testimonia.[12] I agree with the first position: 4Q236 preserves one of the sources of Psalm 89, or is a very early form of this Psalm.

4Q236 differs substantially from the Masoretic form of this Psalm; specific details are provided in the notes to the synoptic comparison of the two texts. One significant variation is found in line 7, where only verse 27a appears in 4Q236. Another is evident in lines 4–5, where the emphasis is on David's hand which will establish and strengthen the people.[13] This contrasts with the Masoretic Text, where it is God's hand that will remain with David, and God's arm that will strengthen him. The collation of variants provided in the notes makes it clear that the MT and LXX are almost always in agreement against 4Q236. In line 6, however, the preserved reading for verse 23 seems to agree substantially with the LXX text for this verse.[14]

5. Presentation of the Document

Since the relationship of this composition to Psalm 89 in the Masoretic Text is of central importance, two different transcrip-

tions are given on the following pages. The first presents the text as it appears on the leather and the three available photographs (PAM 40.620, 41.438, 43.399).[15] The second transcription gives the text of 4Q236 in one column alongside the corresponding verses from the MT (*BHS*) in a second column. The facing page contains the English translations of these two columns, with the second column of the English generally corresponding to the *NRSV*.

6. Selected Bibliography

Flint, P. W. *The Psalters at Qumran and the Book of Psalms*. Ph.D. dissertation, University of Notre Dame, 1992, pp. 44, 223.

Flint, P. W. *The Dead Sea Psalms and the Book of Psalms*. STDJ 17; Leiden, 1997, p. 38.

Glessmer, U. "Das Textwachstum von Ps 89 und ein Qumran-fragment," *Biblische Notizen* 65 (1992) 55–73.

Milik, J. T. "Fragment d'une source du Psaultier (4QPs89) et fragments des Jubilés, du Document de Damas, d'un phylac-tère dans la Grotte 4 de Qumran," *RB* 73 (1966) 94–106, esp. 94–104; Pl. I.

Ploeg, J. P. M. van der. "Le sens et un problème textuel du Ps LXXXIX." In *Mélanges bibliques et orientaux en l'honneur de M. Henri Cazelles*, edited by A. Caquot and M. Delcor. AOAT 212; Neukirchen-Vluyn, 1981, pp. 471–81.

Skehan, P. W. "Littérature de Qumran–A. Textes bibliques." *Supplément au Dictionnaire de la Bible* (1973–81) 9/10.806–22, esp. 813–17.

Skehan, P. W. "Gleanings from Psalm Texts from Qumrân." In *Mélanges bibliques et orientaux en l'honneur de M. Henri Cazelles*, edited by A. Caquot and M. Delcor. AOAT 212; Neukirchen-Vluyn, 1981, pp. 439–52, esp. pp. 439–45.

---

[9] The other is 4QPs[e] (4Q87), which preserves Ps 89:44–48, 50–53.

[10] This is the view of Milik, as the title of his article indicates.

[11] Skehan regards this piece as "secondary to the canonical Psalm" (in *Mélanges*, p. 439). While recognizing that the scribe is under Aramaic influence, Skehan believes that he was not "checked by a written prototype." Thus the scribe's

failure to use final Mem in some words is due to "simple ineptitude" (in *Mélanges*, p. 441).

[12] Van der Ploeg, in *Mélanges*, pp. 475, 481.

[13] The second verb is restored in line 5; see the synoptic texts.

[14] See the notes to line 6 for details.

[15] Thanks are extended to the Israel Antiquities Authority for affording access to these photographs.

A Form of Psalm 89
(4Q236 = 4QPs89)

4Q236 (= 4QPs89)

ל[ב]חריכ׳ תא̇מר² שת³ עו̇]זר⁴ על[⁵
ג̇[בור[⁶   1

ב[חר⁷ מן עם⁸ מצתי̇ן[⁹   2

[מן שמן¹⁰ קדשי   3

אש[ר̇¹¹ שמ̇ן̇¹² ידו¹³ תכנכם¹⁴   4
ת

ו[ש̇מתי בים ידו¹⁵ בנהר̇¹⁶   5
ו̇

[אואב¹⁷ ובן על¹⁸ לענות̇¹⁹   6
ו̇

א[ב̇י את²⁰ אני²¹ בכור אתנו̇[²²   7
ו̇

[אר̇ץ̇ אם יעזבו   8

---

1 MT (similarly LXX): לחסידיך (cf. Ps 132:9, 16); cf. MT Ps 89:4: כרתי ברית לבחירי. Note the use of the medial כ at the end of the first word in 4Q236 line 1.

2 MT (similarly LXX): ותאמר.

3 MT: שויתי; the text of 4Q236 may be an orthographic difference under the influence of Aramaic.

4 MT (similarly LXX): עזר.

5 The first line is written in smaller letters than the following ones, and is crowded into the available space. This indicates that the thin and irregular blank leather above the writing was most likely the top of the fragment.

6 The trace of ג on the left edge of the fragment is due to the scribe's attempt to squeeze in גבור.

7 MT (similarly LXX): בחור. The ר seems to have been written over an original י.

8 In this MS medial מ is generally used in final position (cf. בים in line 5; אם in line 8); but note תכנכם in line 4.

9 MT: מצאתי; the difference is orthographic.

10 MT (similarly LXX): בשמן.

11 Traces of the ר in אשר are just visible on the right edge of the leather.

12 After originally writing שמן, an inadvertent repetition from the previous line, the scribe corrected the text by placing dots above and below this word.

13 MT (similarly LXX): ידי. The reading ידו (thus Skehan) seems preferable to ידי (Milik), since the head of the third letter seems more like ו than י when compared with ו and י elsewhere on the fragment.

14 MT: תכון עמו; LXX: συναντιλήμψεται αὐτῷ.

15 MT (similarly LXX): ידו.

16 Read בנהרת; MT (similarly LXX): ובנהרות.

17 MT (similarly LXX): אואב בו; the difference between אואב and אויב is orthographic (cf. 4Q88 frg. 10 line 11: אואבים).

18 MT: עולה; it is difficult to tell whether the difference is orthographic in this MS.

19 MT: לא יעננו; cf. LXX and 2Sam 7:10: ולא יסיפו בני עולה לענותו. This word is very difficult to read, but appears to be an infinitival form. The letter which runs up against the stitching seems to be ת (thus Skehan) rather than ה (Milik).

20 MT: אתה אלי וצור ישועתי; it is difficult to determine whether the difference between את and אתה is merely orthographic.

21 MT (similarly LXX): אף אני.

22 MT: אתנהו. The supralinear ו is medial in form, which indicates that it was not the final letter in the word (cf. מן in line 2; מן שמן in line 3; ובן in line 6). The letter ו seems to have been written at the end of the line, where the leather is now abraded.

A Form of Psalm 89
(4Q236 = 4QPs89)

4Q236 (= 4QPs89)

1 [. . . to] your chosen ones[1] you will say:[2] "I have laid[3] a hel[per[4] upon (one who is)] mi[ghty,][5]

2 [. . .one cho]sen from (the) people.   I have found [. . .]

3 [. . .] from[6] my holy oil

4 [. . . .]   His hand[7] shall establish you;[8]

5 [. . . .   And] I will set (his) hand[9] on the sea, on the rivers[10]

6 [. . .] (the) enemy and the wicked[11] oppress him.[12]

7 [. . .] 'You[13] are my [Fa]ther.'[14]   I[15] will make him[16] the firstborn,

8 [. . .] (the) earth.   If they forsake

[1] MT: "your faithful ones."

[2] MT: "and you said."

[3] The context demands a first person verb; Milik suggests שתי. The unusual form שת may be a result of Aramaic influence.

[4] 4Q236 has the participle where MT has a noun and reads "help." The admissability of נֶזֶר ("crown") as a preferable reading (cf. *BHS* note 20ᵇ) need not concern us here.

[5] The first line was inserted in the top margin of the fragment, apparently to provide a setting for the passage as a whole; thus the reading "mi[ghty]" is misplaced (see the interlinear correction between lines 1 and 2).

[6] The partitive use of מן with שמן to denote anointing with oil is possible but is not common usage.

[7] Lit. "[Whos]e hand." The order of verses in this MS (22, 26, 23, 27–28) indicates that the reference is to the hand of David, not God's hand as in MT.

[8] In accordance with the sense of the passage as a whole, David's hand will establish (כון=*Hip'il*) God's chosen ones, whereas in MT God's hand will remain (כון=*Nip'al* with עם) with David.

[9] MT: "his hand" (with suffix).

[10] MT: "and on the rivers." In 4Q236 the scribe originally wrote "on the river" (בנהר), and then inserted ת above the line due to lack of writing space.

[11] Lit. "son of wickedness." The form על is difficult; according to Skehan, the form עֲוֶל should be understood (cf. MT: עולה, "wickedness"). While this scribe uses ו for an internal vowel letter (אואב in line 6; בכור in line 7), here it seems to be omitted when used as a consonant.

[12] 4Q236 has a *Piel* infinitive, so literally "to oppress him." MT has a *Piel* future third person singular and thus reads "he shall not oppress him."

[13] The form את seems due to Aramaic influence.

[14] MT reads further "my God, and the Rock of my salvation."

[15] MT reads "Also I."

[16] The scribe wrote the second נ above the line, apparently because of the lack of space.

4Q236 compared with the Masoretic Text of Psalm 89

Masoretic Text of Psalm 89 (rearranged)	*4Q236*
[20] אז דברת בחזון לחסידיך ותאמר	[1] [בחזון ל]ב̇חריכ תאמר
שויתי עזר על גבור	שת עו]ז̇ר על] ג̇[בור]
הרימותי בחור מעם	[2] [הרימותי ב]ח̇ר מן עם
[21] מצאתי דוד עבדי	[3] מצתי̇]ן̇ דוד עבדי]
בשמן קדשי משחתיו	[4] מן שמן קדש̇י[משחתיו]
[22] אשר ידי תכון עמו	[אש]ר̇ (שמן) ידו תכ̇נכם
אף זרועי תאמצנו	[5] [ותאמצכם]23
[26] ושמתי בים ידו	[6] [ו]ש̇מתי בים יד
ובנהרות ימינו	בנהרת̇[ימין]24
[23] לא ישא אויב בו	[לא יוסיפ̇]25 אואב[
ובן עולה לא יעננו	ובן על לענות̇ו̇
[27] הוא יקראני אבי אתה	[7]]יקראני26 א[ב̇י את
אלי וצור ישועתי	
[28] אף אני בכור אתנהו	אני בכור את̇ננו
עליון למלכי ארץ	[8] [עלין למלכי] אר̇ץ̇
[31] אם יעזבו בניו תורתי	א̇ם יעזבו]

23 The longer reading found in both MT and LXX (אף זרועי תאמצנו) is not possible because of spacing.

24 ימין is reconstructed without a suffix (MT [similarly LXX]: ימינו) on the analogy of יד earlier in the verse (MT [similarly LXX]: ידו).

25 לא יוסיף is reconstructed with reference to the infinitive לענותו later in the verse, as well as to LXX (οὐ προσθήσει τοῦ κακῶσαι αὐτόν = לא יוסיף לענותו).

26 MT (similarly LXX): הוא יקראני; spacing shows that the beginning of 4Q236 is shorter.

4Q236 compared with the Masoretic Text of Psalm 89[17]

4Q236

(1)[In a vision[18] to] your chosen ones you will say:

"I have laid a hel[per upon (one who is)] mi[ghty,]
(2)[I have exalted one cho]sen from (the) people.

I have found (3)[my servant David;]
from my holy oil (4)[I have anointed him.]

His hand shall establish you;
(5)[and will strengthen you.][19]

20[And] I will set (his) hand on the sea,
[(his) right hand][21] on the rivers.

(6)22[No longer shall][23] (the) enemy
and the wicked[24] oppress him.

(7)25[He shall cry to me,] 'You are my [Fa]ther.'

I will make him the firstborn,
(8)[the highest of the kings of] (the) earth.

26If they forsake [. . . ."]

Masoretic Text of Psalm 89 (rearranged)

(20)Then you spoke in a vision to your faithful ones,
and said:

"I have laid help upon (one who is) mighty,
I have exalted one chosen from the people.

(21)I have found my servant David;
with my holy oil I have anointed him;

(22)my hand shall remain with him;
my arm also shall strengthen him.

(26)And I will set his hand on the sea,
and his right hand on the rivers.

(23)(The) enemy shall not deceive him,
and the wicked[27] shall not oppress him.

(27)He shall cry to me, 'You are my Father,
my God, and the Rock of my salvation!'

(28)Also I will make him the firstborn,
the highest of the kings of (the) earth.

(31)If his children forsake my law . . . ."

---

17 Superscripted numbers in parentheses indicate line numbers for 4Q236 and verse numbers for the MT, respectively. For this Psalm the versification of the MT and Christian English translations differs by one verse (MT verse 20 equals Christian English translations verse 19, etc.). In the LXX this is Psalm 88 and the versification follows MT.

18 Due to the need for space, the scribe is more likely to have provided בחזון than אז דברת (= MT), since תאמר later in the line provides the necessary verb of speaking.

19 The context requires the second person plural object suffix, with "his hand" acting as subject for both verbs in the verse. In MT "my arm" serves as a separate subject for the second verb.

20 Note the difference in verse order from MT.

21 The restoration lacks the suffix (cf. MT "his right hand") on the basis of יד earlier in the line.

22 Note the difference in verse order from MT.

23 The reconstructed words לא יוסיף (literally, "he shall not continue") seem most appropriate in view of the infinitival phrase at the end of the verse, as well as the LXX ("he will no longer oppress him"). According to Skehan, the text for line 6 is in fact a harmonizing borrowing from 2Sam 7:10 ("No longer shall wicked men oppress them"). MT reads "he shall not deceive."

24 Lit. "son of wickedness."

25 Note the difference in verse order from MT.

26 Note the difference in verse order from MT.

27 Lit. "son of wickedness."

Prayers for Festivals

(1Q34–1Q34[bis]; 4Q507–509)

J. H. CHARLESWORTH and D. T. OLSON[1]

Introduction

1. Contents

The manuscript witnesses of the *Prayers for Festivals* from Qumran Cave 4 (4Q507–509) are extremely fragmentary, and are often difficult to reconstruct. We are aided, fortunately, by the more complete text of the "Prayer for the Day of Atonement" in 1Q34–1Q34[bis] which duplicates parts of 4Q509, and contains motifs closely related to elements found within 4Q507 and 4Q508. 1Q34–1Q34[bis] and 4Q507–509 probably represent four copies of the same document. Two of the festivals most clearly associated with the *Prayers for Festivals* are the Day of Atonement and Shavuot (the Day of First Fruits).[2] M. Baillet has suggested several plausible connections between the *Prayers for Festivals* and other Jewish festivals, including the New Year, Tabernacles, the Offering of the Barley Harvest, and the Second Passover.[3] Baillet seems to be correct in assuming the *Prayers for Festivals* originally specified the prayers to be recited throughout the Jewish liturgical calendar.

The major Jewish festivals are the following: Pesah (Passover) in the spring was a commemoration of the Exodus from Egypt. Shavuot (Pentecost, Feast of Weeks, or Day of First Fruits) followed 50 days later and was originally a celebration of the wheat harvest (Deut 16:9–11), but before the first century C.E. it had become a festival for celebrating the Giving of the Torah and Covenant at Sinai. Sukkot (Tabernacles or Feast of Booths) in autumn just before the rainy season was originally the main harvest celebration (Exod 23:16), but by the first century C.E. it had obtained the added commemoration of the wandering in the wilderness before the Conquest. These three festivals constituted the three pilgrimages to Jerusalem demanded of every Jewish male (Shalosh Regalim [Deut 16:16–17, Exod 23:14]).

During the Second Temple period, Judaean Jews could easily attend the Temple for each of these celebrations; those living in Galilee might attend once a year (usually at Passover). Diasporic Jews might make a pilgrimage once in their life. For example, we know that Philo of Alexandria made at least one pilgrimage to Jerusalem. If Passover was the most popular or greatest festival, Sukkot was the main festival in Jerusalem and especially in the Temple (see m.Sukkah). It was preceded by two high holy days, Rosh Hashanah (New Year) on the first day of the month of Tishri and Yom Kippur (Day of Atonement) on the tenth day.

1Q34–1Q34[bis] is a fragmentary text that refers to several festivals. Fragments 1–3 col. 1 may refer to Sukkot because of the allusions to dew and the earth (appropriate for the main harvest), and the concluding reference to the Day of Atonement. Rosh Hashanah may be reflected in the reference to "the solstitial point" (frgs. 1–3 1.5). Fragments 3–5 col. 2 refers to a festival that mentions the giving of the covenant; it may thus be related to Shavuot (Pentecost).

Writing is visible on three of the fragments of 4Q507. Fragment 1 is a communal confession of sin. Fragments 2 and 3 contain a blessing formula which praises the deity; "Blessed (be) the Lord" (for the reconstructed text, see frg. 2 line 2 and frg. 3 line 1). Fragment 3 has a doxological double "Amen" which apparently signals the conclusion of a prayer of praise.

The forty-three fragments of 4Q508 contain several probable references to festivals in the Jewish ritual calendar. Baillet associates fragments 1, 3, 7, 30, and 39–41 with the Day of Atonement on the basis of similarities to 1Q34–1Q34[bis] which is explicitly linked to the Atonement festival. References to "the festival of your compassions" and "a festival of fasting" (frg. 2

---

[1] Charlesworth is responsible for 1Q34–1Q34[bis]; Olson is responsible for 4Q507–509. They are grateful to Craig Bowman whose unpublished paper, "A Theological Analysis of the Prayers from Qumran: the Prayers for the Festivals (4Q507–509)," provided helpful insights and bibliography in the preparation of the introduction. Charlesworth is indebted to the Very Rev. J. Meno for access to the manuscript of 1Q34[bis] and to R. Johnston and R. Easton of Rochester Institute of Technology, and K. Knox of Xerox Corporation for new digital images of 1Q34[bis].

[2] The Day of Atonement is explicitly mentioned in 1Q34–1Q34[bis] frgs. 1–3 1.9. The phrase "Day of Atonement" is not extant in 4Q507–509 even though these manuscripts do preserve references to atonement and sin. The feast for Shavuot, or the Day of First Fruits, is specifically mentioned in 4Q509 frgs. 131–132 2.5.

[3] See Baillet's discussion of the *Prayers for Festivals* in DJD 7, pp. 175–215.

lines 2–3) as well as the occurrence of "atone" (frg. 7 line 1) and "to atone" (frg. 30 line 1) support Baillet's contention. With less certainty, Baillet posits possible associations with other festivals. Fragment 2 may be a conclusion to a prayer for the New Year Festival. Fragments 22–23 line 3 contains the phrase "the [pr]oduce of our land for wav[ing]," which suggests the Festival of the Barley Harvest. The Festival of the New Moon may be in the background in fragment 32. Some less specific references to festivals, such as "festivals of glory and of holine[ss]" (frg. 13 line 2), are difficult to identify.[4] A strong emphasis on the covenant relationship between God and the Community permeates the prayers as does an emphasis on the holiness of God. Confession of sin is evident in fragments 3, 5, 39, and 41; the motif of atonement is evident in fragments 7 and 30. Fragment 20 contains a doxological double "Amen," which marks the conclusion of a prayer. The specific mention of "offerings," "sacrifice," and "contribu[tions]" (frgs. 9 line 1, 15 line 1, 17 line 1), as well as the reference to "his covenant" (frg. 4 line 2), probably relates to Shavuot (Pentecost). Fragment 13 line 3 enumerates a triad of offerings which are frequently mentioned in the Hebrew Bible: "gr[ain,] new wine, and olive oil."[5]

The prayers in the three-hundred thirteen fragments of 4Q509 provide only tantilizing glimpses into early Jewish liturgical and festival life at Qumran. Fragments 1–7 may be linked to Rosh Hashanah (New Year Festival) in light of fragment 3 line 7 with its reference to "the festivals of green vegetation." Since fragments 3 lines 2–9 and 97–98 line 1 duplicate portions of 1Q34–1Q34^{bis} which are expressly associated with Yom Kippur (Atonement Festival), these fragments may well be part of the liturgy for the Day of Atonement. This association is strengthened by the presence of the phrase "you have atoned" (frg. 54 line 2). Fragments 131–132, which refer to "first fruits" and "free-will offerings" tied to the land, suggest connections with Shavuot, the Day of First Fruits (frgs. 131–132 2.5–11). It is difficult to align clearly many of the fragments with one of the major festivals; note the truncated passages such as "[A pra]yer for the festival of [...]" (frgs. 10–11 2.8).

B. Nitzan analyzes the structure of the individual prayers of the *Prayers for Festivals* and finds them to be fairly regular and similar to the *Words of the Lights* (4Q504–506).[6] Each prayer contains a heading specifying the time of the prayer ("Prayer for the festival of ..."). The prayers begin by petitioning God to remember ("Remember, O Lord, ...") followed by a series of historical remembrances and petitions which form the body of the prayer. The prayers close with a blessing ("Blessed be the Lord who... us...") followed by a congregational response ("Amen. Amen"). Divisions between the prayers are often indicated by a vacat.

2. Texts

Prayers for Festivals is extant in four different copies (1Q34–1Q34^{bis}, 4Q507–509).

4Q509 is the earliest copy of the collection of *Prayers for Festivals*. It is written in a late Hasmonaean script from circa 70 B.C.E. The collection consists of 313 fragments which were originally published by Baillet.[7] The arrangement of some of the fragments was facilitated by the fact that identifiable portions of the sixth exemplar of the *War Scroll* (4Q496) were found on the backside of fragments 1–119. Moreover, the third exemplar of the *Words of the Lights* (4Q506) was inscribed on the back of fragments 131–82. The remaining fragments have script only on one side and thus their arrangement is often difficult to reconstruct. Indeed, fragments 225–313 may contain pieces which actually belong to 4Q515 (=4Q163).[8]

1Q34–1Q34^{bis} comprise five fragments from the same manuscript. Milik first published a single fragment (1Q34)[9] to which Trever associated the other four (1Q34^{bis}).[10] The script is on lined leather and frequently similar to 4QSam^a (4Q51); it is an early Herodian book hand to be dated circa 50–25 B.C.E.[11]

4Q507 consists of only four fragments and is the least preserved manuscript of the *Prayers for Festivals*. The text was arranged by J. Starcky, and the first critical edition of the prayers appeared in the work by Baillet.[12] Baillet was also the first to situate this material in the collection of *Prayers for Festivals* because of similarities to 1Q34–1Q34^{bis} and 4Q508–509.[13] J. Strugnell related the style or form of these prayers to the prayers in 1QH, but he acknowledged that no similarity of content was evident between the two collections.[14] The Hebrew script of 4Q507 is Herodian and dates to the early first century C.E.[15]

4Q508 was also first published by Baillet, and consists of 43 fragments. Its Herodian script dates from the same period of the early first century C.E. as 4Q507.[16]

---

[4] Baillet, DJD 7, p. 177.

[5] Baillet, DJD 7, p. 181. The triad of "grain, new wine, and olive oil" offerings are mentioned together in several biblical texts; examples include: Num 8:12; Deut 12:17, 14:23, 18:4; Neh 10:40; 13:5, 12; 2Chr 31:5.

[6] See B. Nitzan, *Qumran Prayer and Religious Poetry* (STDJ 12; Leiden, 1994) esp. the summary on p. 71.

[7] Baillet, DJD 7, pp. 184–215.

[8] Baillet, DJD 7, pp. 184–85.

[9] J. T. Milik, "Recueil de prières liturgiques (1Q34)," DJD 1, p. 136; Pl. XXXI.

[10] J. C. Trever, "Completion of the Publication of Some Fragments From Qumran Cave I," *RQ* 19 (1965) 323–36, Pls. 1–7; cf. Milik, "Recueil de prières liturgiques (1Q34^{bis})," DJD 1, pp. 152–55.

[11] Distinctive consonants are א (as in 4QDeut^c [4Q30] and 4QSam^a [4Q51]), ב and ד (as in 4QSam^a), ע (as in 4QSam^a), and ר (as in 4QDeut^c).

[12] Baillet, DJD 7, pp. 175–77.

[13] Baillet, DJD 7, p. 175.

[14] J. Strugnell, "Le Travail d'edition: des Fragments Manuscripts de Qumran," *RB* 63 (1956) 54.

[15] Baillet, DJD 7, p. 177.

[16] Baillet, DJD 7, p. 177.

3. Date and Original Language

As evidenced by the earliest manuscript, 4Q509, the *Prayers for the Festivals* was composed sometime before 70 B.C.E. Since the *Prayers* probably originated within the Qumran Community, the earliest possible date is around the middle of the second century B.C.E. There is no reason to doubt that the original language of this document was Hebrew.

4. Provenience

The collection of *Prayers for Festivals* was probably not brought to Qumran, but rather was most likely composed there.[17] Numerous technical words and self-designations are likely Qumranic; note for example the following: "the lot of the Right[eo]us" (1Q34—1Q34[bis] frgs. 1—3 1.2) and "the Righteous Ones" (1Q34—1Q34[bis] frgs. 1—3 1.3). Especially significant for understanding this important collection of prayers are the group's self-understandings: their opponents, "the huma[n] seed," (1Q34—1Q34[bis] frgs. 3—5 2.4; cf. 4Q509 frgs. 97—98 1.2) have not discerned "your great strength" (1Q34—1Q34[bis] frgs. 3—5 2.5), and so God "rejected them" (1Q34—1Q34[bis] frgs. 3—5 2.5). The Qumranites are those whom God "chose" (1Q34—1Q34[bis] frgs. 3—5 2.6), and are singled out "for holiness" (1Q34—1Q34[bis] frgs. 3—5 2.7), because God "remembered" the "covenant" (1Q34—1Q34[bis] frgs. 3—5 2.6); that is, God established the Qumran Community (cf. 1QS 1—2). They are "the poor and ne[edy]" (1Q34—1Q34[bis] frgs. 3—5 2.9) as in 1QH.[18]

The Qumran Community looks at others, probably the "wicked" in Israel and the "evil" priests in Jerusalem, and considers them "our tormentors" (1Q34—1Q34[bis] frgs. 1—3 1.6). They perceive themselves to be "blessed" (1Q34—1Q34[bis] frgs. 1—3 1.7) and God's elect (4Q508 frg. 4 line 2). Those who "know the disciplines of glory" (1Q34—1Q34[bis] frgs. 3—5 2.8), probably the statutes and laws explained in 1QS, and participate in "the eternal ascents" (1Q34—1Q34[bis] frgs. 3—5 2.8, cf. ShirShab), possibly the renewal at Qumran (1QS 5.20—24), are without doubt the members of the Community. A possible apocalyptic note is sounded in 4Q508 fragment 2 line 4: "but you know the things hidden and the thing[s] revea[led." This line is partially repeated in 4Q509 fragment 212 line 1 and reflects a motif

common in Qumran literature.[19] The references to "the lot of the Right[eo]us" and "the wicked ones" (1Q34—1Q34[bis] frgs. 1—3 1.2) probably represent Qumran technical terms, and reflect the predestinarian belief of the Qumran Community. The dualism here between the righteous and the wicked is reminiscent of some passages in the *Psalms of Solomon*; but it is more in line with the absolute dualism developed in 1QS 3 and 4. As in 1QS 4 the wicked ones will not endure the coming judgment.

5. Theology

Significant in this document are the prayers for "the solstitial point" (1Q34—1Q34[bis] frgs. 1—3 1.5) which is probably the beginning of the year or Rosh Hashanah. Also note the reference to the sun in 1Q34—1Q34[bis] fragments 3—5 2.2: "the gre[at] light for the festival of the[...]." Ten days after Rosh Hashanah, Jews (then and today) celebrate Yom Kippur, "the Day of Atonement" (10 Tishri). It is highly significant, therefore, that the beginning of a prayer to be recited on the Day of Atonement is preserved; note 1Q34—1Q34[bis] fragments 1—3 1.9: "A prayer for the Day of Atonement." It begins with the exhortation for the Lord to remember; unfortunately, the rest of the prayer in this column is lost. Most likely "the Day of Atonement" is "the day of the fast" mentioned in CD MS A 6.19. This celebration was probably the most important time for the members of the Community.

As is well known from the study of the *Habakkuk Pesher*,[20] the time for the celebration of Yom Kippur at Qumran was according to a calendar different from the one used by the ruling priests living in Jerusalem. The Qumranites celebrated according to a calendar that was not lunar, but solar or lunar-solar (more than one calendar is known to be important according to the Qumran Scrolls).[21] When the Qumranites were resting, celebrating their calculated time for the celebration of the Day of Atonement, "the Wicked Priest" came from Jerusalem and persecuted the Qumran group, especially its founder, "the Righteous Teacher" (see 1QpHab 11.1—8).

Some of these prayers may also have been associated with the Covenant Festival at Qumran. Many of the prayers stress the remembrance and renewal of the covenant along with the confession of covenant unfaithfulness: "we have forgotten yo[ur]

---

[17] C. Newsom has expressed some doubt about Qumran authorship of the *Prayers for Festivals*, raising the issue that this document reflects different calendrical assumptions than those associated with Qumran, and that separating the covenant "from all the peoples" might indicate Israel as a whole. See C. Newsom, "'Sectually Explicit' Literature from Qumran," in *The Hebrew Bible and its Interpreters*, ed. W.H. Propp, et al. (Biblical and Judaic Studies from the University of California, San Diego, vol. 1; Winona Lake, 1990) pp. 167—87. Newsom thinks that the language, while suggestive, does not point "clearly to Qumran authorship" (p. 177).

[18] See esp. 1QH 2.34, 5.14.

[19] On Qumran and the relationship to apocalyptic thought, see J. H. Charlesworth, "A Critical Comparison of the 'Dualism'

in 1QS 3:13—4:26 and the 'Dualism' Contained in the Gospel of John," in *JDS*, pp. 76—106 and J. Gammie, "Spatial and Ethical Dualism in Jewish Wisdom and Apocalyptic Literature," *JBL* 93 (1974) 356—85.

[20] See especially the judicious comments published by S. Talmon in "Yom Hakippurim in the Habakkuk Scroll," in *The World of Qumran from Within: Collected Studies* (Jerusalem and Leiden, 1989) pp. 186—99 (originally published in *Biblica* 32 [1951] 549—63).

[21] Among other studies one of the most important is S. Talmon's "The Calendar of the Covenanters of the Judean Desert," in *The World of Qumran*, pp. 147—85 (originally published in *Scripta Hierosolymitana* 4 [1958] 162—99). Also see Talmon, *King*, esp. pp. 165—201.

covenant" (4Q509 frg. 18 line 2). The Qumran covenant festival which is outlined in the *Rule of the Community* (1QS 2.19–25) may be a helpful backdrop for understanding some of the prayers in 4Q509. [22] This covenant renewal context is further indicated by the polarities which make up the structure of the prayers: judgment and salvation, affliction and compassion, blessings and curses, iniquity and forgiveness, impurity and holiness, unfaithfulness and atonement. Running throughout the negative recitals of past unfaithfulness is an overarching tone of joy, gladness, and praise in light of the faithfulness and love of God who forgives and triumphs over the enemies of God's chosen people.

Two additional aspects require comment as one examines the *Prayers for Festivals*. One aspect is the function of the doxological double "Amen" which appears in several of the fragments (4Q507 frg. 3 line 2; 4Q508 frg. 20 line 1; and 4Q509 frg. 4 line 5, frgs. 131–132 2.3). The double "Amen" appears only five times in the Hebrew Bible while it occurs fourteen times in the extant liturgical fragments of Qumran. The double "Amen" marks the conclusion to three of the five divisions of the book of Psalms as it appears in the Masoretic Text. Thus, the Amen formula could have a literary function in marking the end of written collections of prayers (Ps 41:14; 72:19; 89:53). However, the double "Amen" could also function as an actual liturgical response in a festival liturgy as in Neh. 8:6: "And Ezra blessed Yahweh, the great God; and all the people answered, 'Amen, Amen,' lifting up their hands." This dual function as both literary marker and actual liturgical practice likely applies to the use of the double "Amen" formula in the Qumran Community (see esp. 1QS). Given the formula's limited use in the Hebrew Bible and its extensive use in Early Judaism and Early Christianity, the Qumran material provides an important link in tracing its increased use in liturgical practice and texts in that era. [23]

A second aspect suggested by the *Prayers for Festivals* is the relationship of prayers and sacrifices in the festival liturgies of Qumran. It is generally agreed that there is no evidence for actual physical sacrifice at Qumran, and yet the *Prayers for Festivals* apparently continue to affirm the value and validity of religious sacrifice. This has led scholars to conclude that the practice of prayer had in part replaced the sacrificial system, at least for those sacrifices associated with the Temple at Jerusalem. [24] However, the frequent mention of offerings in the *Prayers for Festivals* may indicate that the prayers were accompanied by rituals of non-animal offerings or sacrifices such as meal offerings including "grain, new wine, and oil." Hence, sacrifice may not have been totally replaced by prayer; ritual action and sacrifice may have accompanied prayer as a means of atonement and expiation. Attention to purity rituals, obedience to the commandments, keeping the festivals, and the experience of confession and forgiveness were other aspects of the process of communal and individual atonement. [25] Worship, seeking forgiveness, offerings, and obedience were part of the larger dynamic of liturgy and prayer in the Qumran Community.

6. Selected Bibliography

Nitzan, B. *Qumran Prayer and Religious Poetry*. STDJ 12; Leiden, 1994.

1Q34–1Q34^{bis}

Carmignac, J. "Le recueil de prières liturgiues de la Grotte 1 (I Q 34 et 34 *bis*)," *RQ* 4 (1963) 271–76.
Milik, J. T. "Recueil de prières liturgiques (1Q34, 1Q34^{bis})," DJD 1, pp. 136, 152–55; and Pl. XXXI.
Tov, E. *The Dead Sea Scrolls on Microfiche*. Leiden, 1993 [PAM 40.537].
Trever, J. C. "Completion of the Publication of Some Fragments from Qumran Cave I," *RQ* 5 (1965) 323–36; and Pl. IV.

4Q507–509

Baillet, M. "Prières pour les fêtes (4Q507)," DJD 7, pp. 175–77; and Pl. XXVIII.
Baillet, M. "Prières pour les fêtes (4Q508)," DJD 7, pp. 177–84; and Pl. LIV.
Baillet, M. "Prières pour les fêtes (4Q509)," DJD 7, pp. 184–215; and Pls. IX, XI, XIII, XV, XVII, XIX, XXI, XXII.
Tov, E. *The Dead Sea Scrolls on Microfiche*. Leiden, 1993 [4Q507: PAM 43.617; 41.349, 893, 894; 42.511, 933. 4Q508: PAM 43.621; 40.975; 41.286, 375, 477, 480, 942, 950; 42.057, 441. 4Q509: PAM 42.058, 060, 062, 064, 068, 069, 455, 488, 497, 837; 43.634–41, 644, 646, 648–51, 653, 655–57, 659, 855, 857, 859, 861, 864; 40.629, 635, 974, 980; 41.988, 991; 42.067, 071, 072].

---

[22] See Charlesworth in PTSDSSP 1, and Knibb, *Qumran*, pp. 88–90.

[23] On the use of the Amen formula in the synagogue (m.Berakot 5.4; 8.8) and in the early church (1 Cor 14:16), see E. Schürer, *The History of the Jewish People in the Age of Jesus Christ*, rev. ed. (Edinburgh, 1979) vol. 2, p. 450, n. 108; and Jepsen, "'mn" *TDOT*, vol. I, p. 321.

[24] L. H. Schiffman, "The Dead Sea Scrolls and the Early History of Jewish Liturgy," in *The Synagogue in Late Antiquity*, edited by L. I. Levine (Pittsburgh, 1987) p. 42. Although the verb "to sacrifice" does occur in 4Q508 frg. 15 line 1, this

isolated occurrence should not be misunderstood as evidence of a literal sacrifice at Qumran. M. Knibb notes with respect to 1QS 8–9 that "despite some uncertainties of translation these words seem to constitute a clear statement that prayer and right behavior would take the place of sacrifice as the means of effecting atonement" (*Qumran*, p. 138). See also S. Talmon, "The Emergence of Institutionalized Prayer in Israel," in *The World of Qumran*, pp. 200–43.

[25] For example, 1QS 3.4–12 and 9.3–5 suggest that the offering of the lips according to the Torah replaces the flesh and fat of burnt offerings as an acceptable means of expiation.

1Q34–1Q34^{bis}

Frgs. 1–3, Col. 1[1]

] ˚˚[וֹצוֹ]ה [	1
] ˚˚ בגורל צדֹ[י]ק ולרשעים גֹ[ו]רֹלֹ	2
] ˚ בעצמותם חרפה לכֹל בשר וצדיקים	3
]דֹשן בעֹדֹי שמים ותנובֹת ארץ לחֹ]ין[ת³ מֹועד שלומ]נו² [	4
בין¹ צ]דֹיק לרשע ונתתה¹ רשעים [לכֹ]וֹפרנו ובֹ]וג[דֹים⁷ נפֹ]שוֹתינו¹ לתקופֹה [למועד [	5
]כֹלה בכל מעינו ואנו נודה לשֹמֹך⁸ לעולם⁹]כֹרביבים עלי[הארץ במוֹעֹד	6
]כֹי לזאת בראתנו וזה אשֹ]רינו ומהל[לך¹³ ברוד¹⁴ לדור ודור¹⁰ ברוך אדניי¹¹ אֹ]שֹר [[שמחֹנ]ו¹² [	7
VACAT [[ ]] VACAT	8
¹⁶] [[תפלה ליום כפורים זכוֹ]ר א[ד]וני אֹ]ת¹⁵	9
]רֹ[ ]לֹ[ ]לֹ[ ]לֹ[	10

---

[1] The beginning of lines 4–10 are supplied by frg. 2 (= Trever, Pl. IVd); the end of the lines are supplied by frg. 3 (= Trever, Pl. IVc). The middle of lines 4–7 are supplied by frg. 1 (DJD 1; cf. Trever, Pl. IV); portions of the ש and ר of אשר in line 7 are present on frgs. 1 and 2. The join of frgs. 1 and 2 with 3 is indicated by the quotation of Psalm 79:13 in lines 6-7 (Carmignac, *RQ* 4 [1963] 271-76). It is not possible to determine with certainty the width of the lacuna between frgs. 1 + 2, and 3.

[2] 4Q509 frg. 3 line 2: תֹה מֹועֹדֹ שלומֹנֹוֹ].

[3] Probably plural, not singular construct.

[4] The ש should not be confused with a ר, although the upper part of it looks very much like a Herodian ר.

[5] The לרשע demands something like בין before צ]דֹיק; cf. 1QH 7.12, CD 20.20-21, and especially 4Q508 frg. 1 line 1.

[6] 4Q508 frg. 1 line 1: אֹ בין צדיק לרשע ונתֹה].

[7] Carmignac:]ֹים; Milik: וֹב]דֹים;]בוצר.

[8] 4Q508 frg. 1 line 2:]בֹכול מעינו ואנו נודה ל]כֹ.

[9] After lines 6 and 7 there is space denoting the left margin of a

column, which is picked up by the writing on the right edge of col. 2, especially lines 6 & 7 (note the renumbering in the present edition).

[10] Probably a quotation of Psalm 79:13: נודה לך לעולם לדר ודר (Carmignac, *RQ* 4 [1963] 271-76). Note the significant variant לשמר.

[11] Defective spelling for אדוני. Cf. 4Q507 frg. 2 line 2, frg. 3 line 1; 4Q509 frg. 206 line 1.

[12] Cf. 4Q509 frg. 3 lines 8-9: פֹלא] תֹיכה לדור ודו[ ]ר אדונֹיֹ[ ]שר שמחֹ].

[13] Leather is abraded with no physical break; there is room for 8 (or 9) spaces (or letters).

[14] Probably plural, not singular construct.

[15] Cf. 4Q507 frg. 3 line 3: זֹבֹ [; 4Q508 frg. 2 line 2: זכורה אֹ בֹכֹוֹרֹיֹם זכורה 4Q509 frgs. 131-132 2.5: אדוני מועד רֹחמיך אֹ]נֹי מֹוֹעֹד.

[16] Lines 9 and following are blackened; no letters are discernable.

1Q34–1Q34^bis

Frgs. 1–3, Col. 1

1 [...]and he comman[ded...]°°[...]

2 [...]°° in the lot of the Rigth[eo]us¹ but to the wicked ones the l[o]t of

3 [...]° in their bones (which is) a reproach for all flesh, but the Righteous Ones²

4 [...] the festival³ of [our] peace[...] it became plump⁴ due to (the) heavens, and the produce of the earth for livi[n]g (beings)⁵

5 for the festival [...] our [sou]ls for the solstitial point⁶ [...between the right]eous and the wicked.   And you have given the wicked ones and the tre[acher]ous ones [for] our [ra]nsom.

6 The earth at the festi[val...] as dew⁷ upon [...]the annihilation⁸ of⁹ all our tormenters.¹⁰ (So) we give thanks¹¹ to your name for ever

7 (from) generation to generation, blessed be the Lord who causes u[s] to rejoice [...]for that (is why) you created us, and thus [we are] hap[py, and the one who prais]es you is blessed.

8 (vacat) [...] (vacat)

9 A prayer for the Day of Atonement.¹² Rememb[er, O L]ord, t[he...] [...]

10 [...]*l*[...]*l*[...]*d*[...]

---

¹ Because of the singular, not "the lot of the Righteous Ones" (contr. Milik). See וצדיקים in line 3. "Lot" (גורל) is a technical term at Qumran for the predestined status ("lot") of the individual. A person is created to be either in "the lot of God" (1QS 2.2) or "the lot of Belial" (1QS 2.5).

² The thought seems to be that "the wicked ones" will be reproached, but "the Righteous Ones" rewarded as in 1QS 4. In the following lines the author states that the wicked ones will be annihilated, a thought well known from 1QS 4. For the concept of חרפה see 1QS 4.12; 1QH 2.9, 34.

³ Or "appointed time."

⁴ Some plant (or animal) became "fat" in a good sense; contrast Milik: "de prospérer grâce à l'ornement' du ciel ...."

⁵ The earth's produce is for all life, not just "pour les animaux" (Milik).

⁶ Or "turn of the year"; probably a reference to an event in Tishri, perhaps the autumn ingathering of fruits or Rosh Hashanah. Cf. 1QS 10.1, 2, 3, 6.

⁷ Lit. "heavy dew."

⁸ See 1QS 4.21–23, according to which "lying abominations" and "perversity" will cease to exist at the end of time.

⁹ Note the extended use of ב here for the expected ל.

¹⁰ *Pi'el* participle.

¹¹ Recall the *Hodayot* formula: "We thank you, O Lord, for...."

¹² The vacant line preceding these words indicates that line 6 is the beginning of a (or the) prayer for the Day of Atonement (Yom Kippur).

Frgs. 3–5, Col. 2[17]

1   [18]

2   [ה̇ מועד]לׄ [מאור גדׄו]ל גדון

3   [וכולם וחוקיהם לעבׄור ואין [̊] [̊]

4   ידעוך ולא הנחלתו אשר בׄכל [19]האדׄ[ם] זרע הבין ולא תבל בכל וממשלתם [̊]

5   [20] תחפץ לא כי בם ותמאס [ ]הגדול[21]בכוחׄ הבינו ולא מכׄול וירשיעו דברך

6   בׄעׄ[ול]ה̇ [22] ורשע[23] לא יכון לפניׄך ותבחר לך עם בקׄ[ץ] רׄצונך כי זכרת בריתך

7   ותׄ[תנ]ׄם להבדל לך לקודש[24] מכׄול העמים ותחדש בר[י]ׄתך להם במראׄת[25] כבׄ[ו]ד ודברי

8   [רוח] קׄודשׄך במעשי ידׄיך וכתבׄ[26] ימינך להודיעם[ ]יסורי[27] כבוד ומעלׄי עולם

9   [לׄ]ה[ ]ם̊ רׄועה נאמׄן מׄ̊[ ]   נפׄ[ ]ש עני[28] ורׄ[ ]ש והע[ני]מים[29]

---

17 The beginning of lines 6-7 are supplied by frg. 3 (= Trever, Pl. IVc); the end of lines 4-9 are supplied by frg. 5 (= Trever, Pl. IVa); the rest are from frg. 4 (= Trever, Pl. IVb).

18 The lines are renumbered, because frg. 3 col. 1 indicates the height of the columns.

19 4Q509 frgs. 97-98 1.2: .[זׄ[ ][וׄ]הׄאׄדׄם

20 Perhaps restore לעשות on the basis of 4Q509 frgs. 97-98 1.3. The phrase is not found among the published DSS, but see the biblical phrases in which עשה appears with דבר.

21 4Q509 frgs. 97-98 1.4: .[בכוחכה]יׄנו

22 4Q509 frgs. 97-98 1.5: .[בׄעׄולה]

23 The scribe, apparently under the influence of the frequently

written רשעים (see 2.5), wrote ים and then erased the two consonants; hence the space here is not to indicate a new section. Milik expressed the opinion that the leather was defective at this spot.

24 4Q509 frgs. 97-98 1.7: .[לקׄוׄדש]כׄה

25 4Q509 frgs. 97-98 1.8: .[במראׄת]להם תכה

26 4Q509 frgs. 97-98 1.9: .[וכתבׄ]ידיכה פׄעׄשי

27 See 1QS 3.6; 6.26.

28 See 1QH 1.36; 2.34; 5.13, 14.

29 There is room for a maximum of 5 spaces (or letters); for the restoration see נפש עני ורש in 1QH 2.34 and 5.14 (cf. CD 6.21, 14.14), and העמים above in line 7.

Frgs. 3–5, Col. 2

1 [...]

2 [...]the gre[at] light for the festival of the[...][13]

3 [...]°[...]° and there is nothing to transgress[14] their statutes,[15] and all of them[...]

4 [...]° and their dominion (is) on all the world.   But the huma[n] seed has not had discernment in all he inherited.[16] And they have not known you

5 [...][17] your word; but they acted wickedly against all.[18] And they did not discern your great strength.[19] And you rejected them for you do not delight

6 in de[ce]it.   And wickedness shall not endure before you.   But you chose for yourself a people at the time of your pleasure, because you remembered your covenant.

7 And you [designed][20] them to single out[21] for yourself for holiness from all the peoples.   And you renewed[22] your cove[na]nt[23] with them by a vision of glo[r]y and the words of

8 your Holy [Spirit][24] by the works of your hands.[25] And your right (hand) wrote so that they could know the disciplines of glory[26] and the eternal ascents[27]

9 [...]for [th]em a faithful shepherd[28] *m*°[... the sou]l of the poor[29] and ne[edy.[30] And the peo]ples

---

[13] See 1QS 10.1–5.

[14] The meaning is more Qumranic and Mishnaic than biblical. The idea that nothing transgresses (or disobeys) God's laws for the universe is found in the apocalypses (see *1En*) and later hymns (see *OdesSol*).

[15] I.e. God's decrees (or commands) for them.

[16] The reference is to the beginning of Genesis, according to which God gives the human authority over the earth; note especially also 1QS 3.17–18: "And he (God) created the human (אנוש) for the dominion of the world ...." The author of 1QS continues by stressing that Belial now has dominion over the earth, but that his end is coming and assured (see also 1QM).

[17] Perhaps restore "[to do]."

[18] As Milik noted, "all" refers to all God's word. See the preceding "your word." Cf. 1QS 1.13–14.

[19] Cf. Acts 8:10.

[20] Lit. "gave"; but note ל with the infinitive.

[21] Or "separate." The Qumranites — mostly priests or Levites — looked back at their explusion from the Temple and conceived of their separation as God's gracious act to separate them from the wicked of Israel whom they regarded as "perverse men." The Qumranians considered themselves to be God's special and elect ones. See 1QS 5.1–2, 10; 8.11, 13; 9.5–6, 9, 14, 20–21; CD 6.14–15; 7.3–4.

[22] For the claim that God "renewed" the covenant with the elect, the Qumranites, so that God may "raise up the kingdom of his people for eve[r]," see esp. 1QSb 5.21, and also 1QSb 3.26. CD 6.2–21 presents the concept in significant detail. For the Qumran claim that the present eschatological age was "the time of renewal" see 1QS 4.25.

[23] The concept of "covenant" is pervasive among the Qumran writings. The members of the Community saw themselves as enjoying God's "new covenant." See esp.CD 6.19. This idea is important for a better understanding of the background of earliest Christianity.

[24] As is well known the stress on "the Holy Spirit" is one of the unique features in Qumran theology.

[25] The Qumranites probably celebrated this prayer as they thought about themselves as the only elect of God. It has become clear that these prayers were composed by the Qumranites and not brought to the Community from elsewhere.

[26] Probably the rules described in 1QS (see esp.3.1, 6.26).

[27] The Qumranians met (probably during the Day of Atonement ceremony) to be promoted (or demoted); the ascent had an apocalyptic dimension since the movement was from early holiness to heavenly angelic status (and being).

[28] Cf. Ps 23.

[29] Heb. עני; a technical term used by the Qumranites to refer to themselves (see esp.1QH 5.13; cf. CD 6.21, 14.14).

[30] Another self-designation of the Qumranites; for the phrase "the soul of the poor and the needy" (נפש עני ורש) see 1QH 2.34, 5.14.

4Q507

Frg. 1

1   [ ]ֹמת ˚ ˚ ˚ ˚ [ ] ˚יֹה] ˚ינוֹ ˚ ˚ [

2   ואנו בעולה מרחם ומשדים בֹאֹ[

3   ֹועד היותנו צעדינו עם נדה יֹבֹ[

Frg. 2

1   [כול הֹ]

2   בֹ]רֹוך אדוני' [

3   [   ]

4   ֹי   כֹ[

Frg. 3[2]

1   ]כֹהֹ[בֹ]רֹוך אֹדֹ[וֹ]ני'[3]

2   דוֹ]רֹוֹתֹי' עולֹם אמן אמֹן[

3   [זלֹ]ורה אדוני'[5]

---

[1] Cf. 1Q34 frgs. 1-3 1.7.
[2] Frg. 4 contains no visible letters.
[3] Cf. 1Q34 frgs. 1-3 1.7.

[4] Cf. 1QH 1.18, 6.11; 4Q504 frg. 7 1.3, and frg. 8 1.11; 4Q252 frg. 1 1.4.
[5] Cf. 1Q34 frgs. 1-3 1.9; 4Q508 frg. 2 line 2; 4Q509 frgs. 131-132 2.5.

4Q507

Frg. 1

1 [. . .]*mt* °°°°° [. . .]°*yh*[. . .]°*y* us °°[. . . .]

2 But we in deceit from the womb and from the breasts in ʾ[. . .]

3 and while[1] we are, our steps (are) with impurity *yb*[. . .]

Frg. 2

1 [. . .] all *h*[. . .]

2 [. . . . Bl]essed be the Lord [. . .]

3 [. . . .] (vacat) [. . .]

4 [. . .]*y k*[. . .]

Frg. 3

1 [. . .]*kh*[. . . . Bl]essed be the Lo[rd . . .]

2 [. . . gene]rations forever. Amen. Amen. [. . .]

3 [. . . .] Rem[ember, O Lord, . . .]

---

[1] Or "and as long as."

4Q508

Frg. 1

1   ]ת̊ בין צדיק לרשע ונתת̊ן̇ה[1]

2   ]ב̊כול מעינו ואנו נודה ל[ש]מ̊כ̊ן̇ה[2]

3   א]ש̊ר נשיב לכ̊ה̊ [

Frg. 2

1   ] ושכנ̊ת̊ה̊ בתוכנו̊ן̇ [

2   ]ם̊ זכורה אדוני מועד[3] ר̊חמיך ועת ש̊ו̊ב[

3   ]ותקימם עלינו מועד תענית חוק עו̇[לם

4   ]ו̊אתה ידעתה ה̊נסתרו̊ת̊י̊ ו̊ה̊נ̊ג̊ל̊[נ]ות[4]

5   י]ד̊עת יצרנו מ̊[

6   ]ו̇ ו̊ש̊ו̊כבנו ת̇ת̊[

Frg. 3

1   א̊] ה̊רשע̊נו [

2   ]ו̊מ̊ר̊בם̊ ו̊[ת̊]קם לנוח [

3   ליצ]ח̊ק וליעקוב אמנ̊[תך

4   ]°[ ]ה̊ ז̊כ̊ר̊ת̊ה קצי̊ן[

Frg. 4

1   ]ה̊[ ]בנותיה השוממות̊[

2   ] אשר בחר בנו ובריתו [

3   ]ל̊[

---

[1] 1Q34 frgs. 1-3 1.5: ד̊יק לרשע ונתתה[.   ]

[2] 1Q34 frgs. 1-3 1.6: ל̊ה בכל מעינו ואנו נודה לש̊מ̊ך̊[.   ]

[3] 4Q509 frgs. 131-132 2.5: ב̊כ̊ו̊ר̊ו̊ם̊ זכורה א̊[ ]נ̊י̊ מ̊ו̊ע̊ד̊; cf. 1Q34 frgs. 1-3 1.9: א̊[רוני] זכ̊ו̊]ר תפלה ליום כפורים.

[4] 4Q509 frg. 212 line 1: הנסתרו̊[.

4Q508

Frg. 1

1 [. . .]*t* between the righteous and the wicked.   And you have give[n . . .]

2 [. . .] of all our tormentors.   (So) we give thanks to yo[ur na]me [. . .]

3 [. . . wh]ich we returned to you [. . .]

Frg. 2

1 [. . .] and you will dwell in our midst [. . .]

2 [. . .]*m*.   Remember, O Lord, the festival of your compassions and the time of return [. . .]

3 [. . .] and you have established them[1] for us (as) a festival of fasting, a statute forev[er . . .]

4 [. . .] but you know the things hidden and the thing[s] revea[led . . .]

5 [. . .] you [k]now our inclination[2] *m*[. . .]

6 [. . .]*w* and (when) we lie down you *t*[. . .]

Frg. 3

1 [. . .]' we have been guilty[3] [. . .]

2 [. . .] and because of their multitude.   [And] you established with Noah [. . .]

3 [. . . to Is]aac and to Jacob [your] pledge [. . .]

4 [. . .]°[. . .]*h* remember the times of[. . .]

Frg. 4

1 [. . .]*h* [. . .] her desolate daughters [. . .]

2 [. . .] who has chosen us, and his covenant [. . .]

3 [. . .]*l*[. . .]

---

[1] The scribal correction reads "it."

[2] Or "thought."

[3] Or "wicked."

Frg. 5

1 [ ]תֹנו ואתה[

2 [חֹטתנֹ]ו

Frg. 6

1 [ ]שֹגֹגֹ[

2 [לֹ]

Frg. 7

1 [כֹפר עֹ]ל

2 [ ]גמֹ[

Frg. 8

1 [ר אֹ]ר[

Frg. 9

1 [וֹמֹנחוֹתֹ]

2 [לֹ]

Frg. 10

1 [ ]מֹלֹ[

Frg. 11

1 [ ]כֹהֹ וֹלֹ[ ]

2 [לֹ וֹלמֹעֹ]יֹן

Frg. 12

1 [רֹ לֹ]

2 [לֹ]

Frg. 13

1 א]דֹוני כי באהבתכה

2 [מכה במועדי כבוד ולקדֹ]ש

3 [דֹ]גן [תֹירוש ויצהר[5]

Frg. 14

1 אדוֹמֹ]ה

2 אובֹ]

3 [ ]ֹ[ ]

Frg. 15

1 [ ]ולזבוח שוֹ[ן

Frg. 16

1 [תֹו]

2 [לֹ]

Frg. 17

1 [נֹו וֹתֹרֹוֹמֹ]ותינו

2 [לֹ]

Frg. 18

1 [ ]ֹ[ ] [ֹ]

2 [קודש עמכול[6]]

Frg. 19

1 [בֹטֹמֹאֹ]ת

2 [לֹבֹלתי הראֹ]ות

Frg. 20

1 [נֹו אמן אמן]

2 [נֹו לשמח לפניֹ]ן

Frg. 21

1 [מֹוֹ בכֹ]

2 [ובֹזֹיינו ואֹורֹחינו וֹאביוניינוֹ]

3 [ ]ואיֹן[ ]ֹ ֹ בכֹול]ֹ

Frgs. 22–23[7]

1 א]שֹר רחמנו בֹעֹן

2 ר[וֹב רֹ[[ ]]חמיכהֹ]

3 תֹ[בֹואת ארצֹ[[ ]]נו לתנוֹ]פה[8]

---

5 For restoration cf. 2Chr 31:5. Cf. Baillet.

6 Read עם כול.

7 Frg. 22 supplies the beginning of lines 2-3.

8 4Q509 frg. 8 line 4: [צונו לתֹנֹוֹפֹ].

Frg. 5

1 […]*t* us⁴ and you […]

2 […] ou[r] sin […]

Frg. 6

1 […] error […]

2 […]*l*[…]

Frg. 7

1 […] atone fo[r …]

2 […] *gm*[…]

Frg. 8

1 […]*r* ᵓ°[…]

Frg. 9

1 […] and offerings […]

2 […]*l*[…]

Frg. 10

1 […] *mq*[…]

Frg. 11

1 […]° you⁵ and *l*°[…]

2 […]*l* and in order that *y*[…]

Frg. 12

1 […]*r l*[…]

2 […]*l*[…]

Frg. 13

1 [… O L]ord, for in your love

2 […] your […]*m* in festivals of glory and of holine[ss]

3 […] gr[ain,] new wine, and olive oil⁶

Frg. 14

1 re[d …]

2 ᵓ*wb*°[…]

3 […]°[…]

Frg. 15

1 […] and to sacrifice *šw*[…]

Frg. 16

1 […]*tw* […]

2 […]*l*[…]

Frg. 17

1 […] our […] and [our] contribu[tions …]

2 […]*l*[…]

Frg. 18

1 […]°[…]*m*[…]

2 […] holiness with all […]

Frg. 19

1 […] in impuri[ty …]

2 […] not to se[e …]

Frg. 20

1 […] us. Amen. Amen. […]

2 […] us to rejoice before […]

Frg. 21

1 […]*mw* in *k*[…]

2 […] and despised us, our caravans and our Poor Ones °[…]

3 […] and there is no °°° in all °[…]

Frgs. 22–23

1 [… w]ho has compassion upon us in ʿ[…]

2 [… the abun]dance of your compassions […]

3 […] the [pr]oduce of our land for wav[ing …]

---

⁴ Or "our […]*t*."

⁵ Or "you […]°."

⁶ Cf. Deut 14:23.

Frg. 26   *Frg. 25*   *Frg. 24*

Frg. 24

1   °מ]ֿ[ ]°°[ ]
2   ]בֿארתנו ועולי[

Frg. 25

1   קֿוֹדֿ]ש
2   ]לחֿ

Frg. 26

1   ]נֿוֹ[ ]זֿ[
2   ]לֿ

Frg. 27

1   ]תה°[
2   ]לֿ

Frg. 28

1   ]בֿ[
2   ]לֿ

Frg. 29

1   ]ותינו[
2   ]מֿ לֿ[

Frg. 30

1   ]ו לכה לֿכפֿר] על]יוֹ עֿ]ל [כֿוֹלֿ
2   ]מֿלפֿניכה וֿתֿ[ ]אֿרֿץ במועדי
3   [ ]לֿ

Frg. 31

1   ]י מֿיֿו[ ]יֿ[
2   ]לֿ[ ]מ °° [

Frg. 32

1   ]יֿם[ ]יֿ[ ]ים[
2   ]רֿאשי חודשֿ[ים
3   לכ]מֿה לזכֿרֿ]ון
4   ]לֿ

Frg. 33

1   ]אֿוֹת דֿקֿנֿו[
2   ]תֿהֿ[ ]לֿ[

Frg. 34

1   ]יֿאֿ[
2   ]יֿ °[

Frg. 35

1   ]°[

Frg. 36

1   ]בֿרֿדתנֿוֹ[
2   ]לֿ

Frg. 37

1   ]°°[
2   ]יֿוֹל[

Frg. 38

1   ]בֿ[
2   ]מֿ[

Frg. 39

1   ]ואנו חיינו בלב יגון יֿ[
2   ]לוא נאמין בחיינו [
3   ]לֿ

Frg. 40

1   ]אשר נתתה לֿ[ה
2   ]לֿ משנאינֿוֹ ואיכֿ[ה
3   ]פֿ כוֹל [

Frg. 41

1   ] נגד כול חֿטֿאֿתֿנֿוֹ[
2   ]דֿה יומם ולילה[
3   [ ]°°נֿוֹ ולבמ[

Frg. 42

1   [ ]לוא הֿ[
2   ]לֿ[

Frg. 43

1   ]נֿוֹ א[
2   ]°יר°[

Frg. 24

1 [...]°°[...]*m*°[...]

2 [...] you have made clear to us and ‘*wly*[...]

Frg. 25

1 [...] holine[ss...]

2 [...]*lḥ*[...]

Frg. 26

1 [...]*n* [...]*nw*[...]

2 [...]*l*[...]

Frg. 27

1 [...]°*th* [...]

2 [...]*l*[...]

Frg. 28

1 [...]*b*[...]

2 [...] *l*[...]

Frg. 29

1 [...] our [...]*wty* [...]

2 [...]*m l*[...]

Frg. 30

1 [...]*w* to you to atone [for] him f[or] all

2 [...] from before you and *t*[...] land in the festivals of

3 [...] [...]*l*

Frg. 31

1 [...]*y myw*[...]

2 [...]°*m*°[...]*l*[...]

Frg. 32

1 [...]*y* [...]*ym* [...]

2 [...] the beginnings of month[s...]

3 [... for y]ou for a remembra[nce...]

4 [...]*l*[...]

Frg. 33

1 [...]’*wt* we have crushed [...]

2 [...]*th l*°[...]

Frg. 34

1 [...]*y*’[...]

2 [...]*y* °[...]

Frg. 35

1 [...]°[...]

Frg. 36

1 [...] when we went down [...]

2 [...]*l*[...]

Frg. 37

1 [...]°°[...]

2 [...]*ywl*[...]

Frg. 38

1 [...]*b*[...]

2 [...]*m*[...]

Frg. 39

1 [...] but we lived with a heart of sorrow *y*[...]

2 [...] we are not confident in our living [...]

3 [...]*l*[...]

Frg. 40

1 [...] whom you have given to *h*[...]

2 [...]*l* the ones hating us and how [...]

3 [...]*m* all [...]

Frg. 41

1 [...] in the presence of all our sin [...]

2 [...]*dh* day and night [...]

3 [...]°° us and *lbm*[...]

Frg. 42

1 [...] not *h*[...]

2 [...] *l*[...]

Frg. 43

1 [...] us[7] ’[...]

2 [...]°*yr*°[...]

---

[7] Or "our [...]."

4Q509

Frgs. 1–2[1]

1	[כנו]
2	[מ֗ו]
3	[כט]י֗ט חוצות[2]
4	[ש֗ נשפוך ה֗]
5	[ה֗ בקץ ח֗][ ][
6	[לן][ל֗][ ][בן ג֗]
7	[ ][ ][ו֗]
8	[לא תדבר ומ֗ו֗שה֗]
9	[על אשר ים֗ ˚ ˚ ˚ ˚ ˚]
10	[לא ו֗צויתו א֗[שר]
11	[ב֗ עמכה ה֗ב֗]
12	[˚ ˚]

Frg. 3

1	[ואו֗נה ˚ ˚ ˚]
2	[שלומנו֗ מועד֗ ת֗ה][3]
3	[ואספתה֗ מיגוננו֗ נ֗ו]
4	[ק֗][ל֗ ונפוצותינו֗ו]
5	[כש֗ עדתנו על ח]סד֗יכ֗ה֗
6	[ ] [ ]
7	[ו֗ דשא במועדי ש֗ב֗]
8	ר֗ודו֗ לדור ת֗יכה[5]נ[פלא]ו[
9	שמח֗]נו[6] [א]שר אדוני֗ ברו[ך
10	[˚ ˚]

---

1. Frg. 1 supplies portions of lines 1-6 and frg. 2 supplies portions of lines 5-11. In lines 5-6 frg. 1 is situated to the left of frg. 2.
2. For the restoration cf. 1QSb 5.27; 2Sam 22:43; Ps 18:43; Micah 7:10; Zech 9:3.
3. 1Q34 frgs. 1-3 1.4: [מ֗ועד שלום].
4. The lacuna in this line represents a place where the letters are abraded; there is no physical break in the papyrus.
5. The ו is abraded; there is no physical break in the papyrus. For the restoration cf. 4Q509 frgs. 131-32 line 13 and 1QH 1.33-34; 3.23; 6.11; 10.21; etc.
6. Cf. 1Q34 frgs. 1-3 lines 6-7: ואנו נודה לשמ֗ך לעולם לדור ודור . ברוך אדני א[שר שמח֗נ].

4Q509

Frgs. 1–2

1 [. . .]*k* us[1] [. . .]

2 [. . .]*wm* [. . .]

3 [. . .like m]ud of the streets [. . .]

4 [. . .]*h* we pour out *š*[. . .]

5 [. . .] [. . .]*ḥ* us[2] in the end *h*[. . .]

6 [. . .]*n b*[. . .] [. . .]*l*[. . .]*l*[. . .]

7 [. . .]*w* [. . .] [. . .]

8 [. . .] Moses, and you spoke to [. . .]

9 [. . .]°°°° °° in the day which upon [. . .]

10 [. . . wh]ich you commanded him to [. . .]

11 [. . .] you,[3] with you[4] *b*[. . .]

12 [. . .]° °[. . .]

Frg. 3

1 [. . .]°°° and her trouble [. . .]

2 [. . .]*th* the festival of our peace [. . .]

3 [. . .] us[5] from our sorrow, and you gather [. . .]

4 [. . .] and our scattered women *l*[. . .]*q*[. . .]

5 [. . .] your [m]ercies upon our congregation as *š*[. . .]

6 [. . . .] (vacat) [. . .]

7 [. . .]*šb* in the festivals of green vegetation. And [. . .]

8 [. . .] your [w]ondr[o]us deeds (from) generation to genera[tion . . .]

9 [. . . . Bless]ed be the Lord, [w]ho causes [us] to rejoice [. . .]

10 [. . .]°°[. . .]

[1] Or "our [. . .]*k*."
[2] Or "our [. . .]*ḥ*."
[3] Or "your [. . .]."

[4] Or "your people."
[5] Or "our [. . .]."

Frg. 4

1]ׄילו לכול חׄ[

2]עׄולם וישמחנו[ׄ]

3]אׄדׄוׄנׄי הׄמבׄיׄנׄנׄו בׄ[

4]עׄד אמׄן אמן [

5] ׄ [

Frgs. 5—6, Col. 1

4]םׄ

Frgs. 5—6, Col. 2[7]

1]שׄ ׄ ׄ יׄאׄיׄםׄ[

2]הׄ דׄמׄנו בקצׄ[

3 כוׄ]ל בנו לקראׄתנו כוׄ]ל [ׄ]

4]םׄ ידעתה הכוׄל[ ]ׄ ׄ ׄ[ ]בׄ[

5 פלגתה ותגדׄ[ ]ׄ   כ]וׄל האלוׄת[

6]וׄ כאשר דברתׄהׄ[ ]

7]הׄ]נׄ[כ]ה שוכב עם אבׄ[ותיכה[8]

Frg. 7

1]בׄתהוׄמות ובכוׄל [

2 כׄי מעולׄם שנאתה [

3]יׄחיד מׄלפניכה [

4 באׄחרית הׄימים[

5]טׄן קׄשׄאׄ[י]ׄם וׄ[

6]תם להשמר בׄ[

7]לׄ[ ] הׄ[ ] [

---

[7] Frg. 5 supplies portions of 2.1-5; frg. 6 supplies portions of 1.4 and 2.4-7.

[8] Cf. Deut 31:16: הנך שכב עם אבתיך.

Frg. 4

1 [. . .]*ylw* to all *ḥ*°[. . .]

2 [. . .]° forever, and he caused us to rejoice [. . .]

3 [. . .] the Lord, who has made us discern *b*[. . .]

4 [. . .] forever. Amen. Amen. [. . .]

5 [. . .]°[. . .]

Frgs. 5–6, Col. 1

4 [. . .]*m*

Frgs. 5–6, Col. 2

1 [. . .]*š*°° *y'ym*[. . .]

2 [. . .]*h* our blood in the end[6] [. . .]

3 [. . .]° in us to meet us (in) al[l . . .]

4 *b*[. . .]°° °°[. . .]*m* you know all [. . .]

5 you have divided, and you have declared [. . . a]ll the curses [. . .]

6 [. . .] us,[7] as you have said [. . . .]

7 [Be]hold, you are going to lie down with [your] father[s . . .]

Frg. 7

1 [. . .] in the depths and in all [. . .]

2 for from eternity you hated [. . .]

3 [. . .] alone from before you [. . .]

4 in the latter days [. . .]

5 [. . .]*tn qš*'°*m*[8] and [. . .]

6 [. . .]*tm* to be kept *b*[. . .]

7 [. . .]*l*[. . .] *ḥ*°[. . .]

6 Or "in the time [. . .]."

7 Or "our [. . .]."

8 Note the superlinear "*d*."

Frg. 10, Col. 1		*Frg. 9*		*Frg. 8*	
ל[מֹעֹן ֯ ֯	**1**	]ר בֿתֿ[	**1**	] המעשהֿ[	**1**
] וברכתה	**2**	]רחמינו[	**2**	]כה וֹתֿ[	**2**
]מֹה[10] אשר	**3**			] [	**3**
]תֿכֿהֿ	**4**			אר]צֹנו לתֹנוֹפֹ[ה][9]	**4**
]תֿוֹ אֿ[	**5**			קוֹ[	
]כֿ[	**6**			]בֿראשית דֿ[	**5**
[֯]	**7**			מ]אֹוֹד]	**6**
]לֿ[	**8**			]וֹאֹבֿיֹוֹנֹיֹוֹ]	**7**
				מ]מֹשלת נֿבֿ[	**8**
				[֯ ֯]	**9**

Frgs. 12–14 and 75, Col. 1[11]

הֹמנוֹ[[]]דֹחים התועים מבלֹיֹן	**1**	
[מ]בֿליֹ][[]] אוֹמֿץֹ הֹנופלים מבלֹין	**2**	
מבליֹ][[]] מֿבֿיֹן הנשברים מבלֹין	**3**	][וֿ
ב]עוונֹ][[]] [[]]אין רופֿאֿ]	**4**	
מנחמֿ][[]] [[]] נכשלים בפשעיהם[[]]	**5**	][כור
יגון וֹ[[]] [[]]בֿלֿי תתֿרֹֿעֹה אסירי[[]]ם	**6**	][ר

---

[9] 4Q508 frgs. 22-23 line 3: [.בֿוֹאת ארצֿ]נו לתֿנוֹ .

[10] A medial מ followed by ה, but the medial form looks more like a final ם. Perhaps the shape of the letter is caused by the horizontal lines of the papyrus [Ed.].

[11] Frg. 12 supplies the left hand portions of lines 3, 5 and 6.

Frg. 8

1 [. . .] the work [. . .]
2 [. . .]you[9] and *t*[. . .]
3 [. . .] [. . .]
4 [. . .] our [lan]d for wavin[g . . .]
5 [. . .] in the beginning of *d*[. . .][10]
6 [. . . v]ery [. . .]
7 [. . .] and our Poor Ones [. . .]
8 [. . . d]ominion of *nb*[. . .]
9 [. . .]°°[. . .]

Frg. 9

1 [. . .]*r bt*[. . .]
2 [. . .] our compassions [. . .]

Frg. 10, Col. 1

1 [. . . in] order that °°°
2 [. . .] and you will bless
3 [. . .]*mh* who
4 [. . .]*t* you[11]
5 [. . .]*tw* ʾ[. . .]
6 [. . .]*k*[. . .]
7 [. . .] °[. . .]
8 [. . .]*l*[. . .]

Frgs. 12–14 and 75, Col. 1

1 the wandering exiles without [. . .]
2 [wi]thout strength, those who are falling without [. . .]
3 without discernment, those who are being broken without [. . .]*n*
4 [in] iniquity [. . .] there is no one healing [. . .]
5 comforting those who are stumbling in their rebellions [. . .]*kwr*.
6 (In) sorrow and weeping, you are a friend to prisoner[s . . .]*r*

9 Or "your [. . .]."
10 Note the superlinear "*qw*[. . .]."

11 Or "your [. . .]*t*."

Frgs. 10–11, Col. 2[12]

1	[
2	[רח
3	[רעיתה ול֯ב
4	[תכה] [בע
5	[ומלאכיכה]
6	[ונחלתכה נ]
7	[אדוני]
8	[תפ[ל֯ל֯]ה למועד]
9	[יכה אש֯ר]
10	[ים יעד]
11	[ך כול]
12	[לל֯ב ˚˚]

Frg. 16

1	[בכול עצב֯]יתם[13]
2	[ר֯חמהם על ת֯עניתם]
3	[יגון זקנינו ול֯כבד֯]ינו[14]י
4	[נ֯ערים תעתעו בם]
5	[ל]וא הביטו כי א֯]
6	[חכמתנו ˚˚ל˚˚]
7	[ו֯אנו הב֯]

Frg. 15, Col. 2		*Frg. 15, Col. 1*		*Frg. 12, Col. 2*	
[	1	[שכה	1	[˚ [	1
[	2	[ה	2	[נדע	2
[א	3	[בות	3	[כי נ	3
[	4	[ם	4	[עשיתה	4
[	5	[ש את	5	[אותכ]ה	5
				[וש֯]	6

---

12   Frg. 10 supplies portions of lines 2-7; frg. 11 supplies portions of lines 7-12.

13   The restoration of the third person plural suffix is based on תעניתם in the next line.

14   The restoration of the plural with the second person suffix is based on the preceding זקנינו.

Frgs. 10–11, Col. 2

1 [...]

2 *rḥ*[...]

3 you have been a shepherd and *b*[...]

4 in your ʿ[...]*t* [...]

5 and your angels [...]

6 and your inheritance *n*[...]

7 the Lord [....]

8 [A pra]yer for the festival of [...]

9 [...] your[...]*y* wh[o...]

10 [...]*ym yʿd*[...]

11 [...]*k* all [...]

12 [...]°° *lk*[...]

Frg. 16

1 [...] in all [their] trouble[s...]

2 [...] has compassion upon them because of their fasting[12]

3 [...] the sorrow of our elders and [our] honored one[s...]

4 [...] young lads made fun of them

5 [...] they did [n]ot consider that ʾ[...]

6 [...] our wisdom °°*l*°°

7 [...] and we *hb*°[...]

Frg. 12, Col. 2

1 [...]°[...]

2 *ndʿ*[...]

3 because *n*[...]

4 you mad[e...]

5 yo[u...]

6 and *š*[...]

Frg. 15, Col. 1

1 [...] your [...]*š*

2 [...]*h*

3 [...]*bwt*

4 [...]*m*

5 [...]*š* the

Frg.15, Col. 2

1 [...]

2 [...]

3 ʾ[...]

4 [...]

5 [...]

---

[12] Or "affliction."

Frg. 17

1   [ודׄתׄםׄ כיא]

2   ר]חמנו מעולם[

3   ]ה מעולם [

4   ] לתבואת [

5   [אׄשׄרׄ בׄשׄ]

Frg. 18

1   [מׄי עד ולׄנׄוׄ בושׄ]ת

2   [שכחנו בריתׄכׄ]ה

3   א]דוני אשר[

4   [חׄ]

Frg. 21	*Frg. 20*	*Frg. 19*
1 [° ° ° °]	1 [°]	1 [°]
2 [ב לפניכה]	2 [רׄ]	2 [° וׄתׄ]
	3 [נׄוׄגׄ]	
	4 [רׄ]	

Frg. 23, Col. 2	*Frg. 23, Col. 1*	*Frg. 22*
1 [בׄא]	1 [זׄ]	1 [הׄ [ ]
2 [ברוך]	2 [לׄמׄחׄשׄבׄ]¹⁵ תׄוׄ	2 [וׄ עמכׄה]
3 [לׄ]		3 י]תׄיצבוׄ [ ]
		4 [ולהללׄ]

Frg. 26	*Frg. 25*	*Frg. 24*
1 [ישרא]ל	1 [זכׄ]¹⁶	1 [עׄוׄלׄמׄי]
2 [מאׄהׄ]	2 [לנו °]	2 [יׄשחק]
3 [עׄתׄה]	3 [לׄ]	3 [לכול]

---

¹⁵ Read לׄמׄחׄשׄבׄתׄ.

¹⁶ Probably restore some form of זכר.

Frg. 17

1 [...] their[...]*wd* because [...]

2 [...] he has had [c]ompassion (upon) us from eternity [...]

3 [...]*h* from eternity [...]

4 [...] for produce [...]

5 [...] who *bš*[...]

Frg. 18

1 [...]*my* forever and to us shame [of...]

2 [...] we have forgotten yo[ur] covenant [...]

3 [... L]ord who [...]

4 [...]*ḥ*[...]

Frg. 19

1 [...]°[...]

2 [...]° *wt*[...]

Frg. 20

1 [...] °[...]

2 [...] *r*[...]

3 [...]*nwg*[...]

4 [...]*d*[...]

Frg. 21

1 [...]°°°°[...]

2 [...]*b* before you [...]

Frg. 22

1 [...]*h* [...] [...]

2 [...]*w* your people[13] [...]

3 [... they] have arrived [...]

4 [...] and to praise [...]

Frg. 23, Col. 1

1 [...]*yz*

2 [...] to his[14] plan

Frg. 23, Col. 2

1 *b'*[....]

2 Blessed [...]

3 [...]*l*[...]

Frg. 24

1 [...] forever [...]

2 [...] Isaac[15] [...]

3 [...] to all [...]

Frg. 25

1 [...] *zk*[...]

2 [...] to us °[...]

3 [...]*l*[...]

Frg. 26

1 [...] Israe[l...]

2 [...]*m'yh*[...]

3 [...] now [...]

13 Or "with you."

14 Superlinear scribal correction or addition.

15 For the unusual spelling of "Isaac," see Jer 33:26; Ps 105:9; Amos 7:9, 16.

Frg. 29

1   [בבו]ן [

2   [ל ו]ש[

3   [א ל]ן

Frg. 28

1   [מ]

2   [ה העו]ן

3   [זעק]ת

4   [והתו]ן

5   [הרע]ן

6   [ו]ע[

7   [בו]ן

Frg. 27

1   [אש]

2   [אשר]ן

3   [קוד]ש

Frg. 32

1   [ ]ן [המה ילכו]

2   ולוא[ימותו בטמא]ה

3   ש[מחי רצון במועדי]ן

4   [ ][קודש עם כ]ן

5   [לתו] [כ]ן

Frg. 31

1   [ו]ן

2   [° ° ° ש]ן

3   [קודשכ]ן

4   [וחוקי]ן

5   [כול אש]ן

6   [ ] לנו ותצו[ן]ה

7   [מתה ו]ן

Frg. 30

1   [° °]ן

2   [שר י]ן

3   [הלכה]ן

4   [ש]ן

Frg. 35

1   [° °]ן

2   [אשר]ן

3   [ולם]ן

Frg. 34

1   [מ]

Frg. 33

1   [ו]ן

2   [ה]ן

3   [ל]ן

Frg. 38

1   [°]ן

2   [° ת]ן

3   [וחו]ן

4   [כו]ן

Frg. 37

1   [° ° °]ן

2   [וכול]ן

3   [תכה]ן

Frg. 36

1   [משפח]ה

2   [ה ופ]ן

3   [ל]ן

Frg. 27

1 [. . .] ʾš[. . .]
2 [. . .] who d[. . .]
3 [. . .] holine[ss . . .]

Frg. 28

1 [. . .]m[. . .]
2 [. . .]ḥ hʿz[. . .]
3 [. . .] the cry of [. . .]
4 [. . .] and ḥtw[. . .]
5 [. . .]ḥrʿ[. . .]
6 [. . .] and ʿ[. . .]
7 [. . .]bw[. . .]

Frg. 29

1 [. . .] in bw[. . .]
2 [. . .]l and š[. . .]
3 [. . .]ʾ l[. . .]

Frg. 30

1 [. . .] °°[. . .]
2 [. . .]šr y[. . .]
3 [. . .] she¹⁶ walked [. . .]
4 [. . .]št[. . .]

Frg. 31

1 [. . .]w[. . .]
2 [. . .]°°° š[. . .]
3 [. . .] your holiness [. . .]
4 [. . .] and the statutes of[. . .]
5 [. . .] all which [. . .]
6 [. . .] to us, and you command[ed. . .]
7 [. . .] you have [. . .]m and l[. . .]

Frg. 32

1 [. . .] they will walk [. . .]
2 [. . . and] they will [not] die in uncleann[ess . . .]¹⁷
3 [. . . the j]oys of favor in the festivals of [. . .]
4 [. . .] [. . .] holiness with k[. . .]
5 [. . .]ltw [. . .]q[. . .]

Frg. 33

1 [. . .]w [. . .]
2 [. . .]h [. . .]
3 [. . .]q [. . .]¹⁸

Frg. 34

1 m[. . .]

Frg. 35

1 [. . .]°°[. . .]
2 [. . .] who [. . .]
3 [. . .]wlm [. . .]

Frg. 36

1 [. . .]cla[n. . .]
2 [. . .]h and p[. . .]
3 [. . .]l[. . .]

Frg. 37

1 [. . .]°°°[. . .]
2 [. . .] and in all [. . .]
3 [. . .]t you [. . .]

Frg. 38

1 [. . .]°[. . .]
2 [. . .]t°[. . .]
3 [. . .]wḥw [. . .]
4 [. . .]kw[. . .]

¹⁶ Read "you" with superlinear scribal correction.
¹⁷ Cf. Lev 15:31.
¹⁸ Note the superlinear "y[. . .]."

73

Frg. 39

1 [לזרע]
2 [ולפ']

Frg. 40

1 [המה]
2 [אתמ']
3 [ה]

Frg. 41

1 [א]ז[
2 [והפ'][° ° ° °]
3 [מרפ']

Frg. 42

1 [נו]
2 [דבר']

Frg. 43

1 [שי]ן
2 [ל]

Frg. 44

1 [° ם]
2 י[שרא]ל
3 [ה]

Frg. 45

1 [°]
2 [ה]

Frg. 46

1 [בגויכה]

Frg. 47

1 [לכנו כ]
2 [° ° °]

Frg. 48

1 [כ]
2 [י °]

Frg. 49, Col. 1

2 ה]

Frg. 49, Col. 2

1 לעול]ם
2 VACAT]

Frg. 50

1 [בקולכה]
2 [וחסיד]

Frg. 51

1 [מ]לכותכה[°]
2 [°]ש

Frg. 52

1 [המ]
2 [ם]

Frg. 53

1 [וגם אנו מ]
2 [° ל ותשא °]

Frg. 54

1 [° ° °]
2 [מ]עלת הכפרתה מ[

Frg. 55

1 [°]
2 [חכמתכה]
3 [ב]ראתם ובכוחכה[
4 [ל]נ[ ]ל[ ] [ ]לנ[

Frg. 39
1 [...] to the seed [...]
2 [...] and *lp*°[...]

Frg. 40
1 [...]*hmh* [...]
2 [...]ʾ*tm*[...]
3 [...]*h* [...]

Frg. 41
1 [...]*n* ʾ[...]
2 [...]°°°° [...] and *hp*[...]
3 [...]*mrp*[...]

Frg. 42
1 [...]us[19] [...]
2 [...] word [...]

Frg. 43
1 [...]*šy*[...]
2 [...]*l*[...]

Frg. 44
1 [...]*m* °[...]
2 [... I]srae[l...]
3 [...]*h*[...]

Frg. 45
1 [...]°[...]
2 [...]*h*[...]

Frg. 46
1 [...] in your nation [...]

Frg. 47
1 [...]*lk* us[20] *k*[...]
2 [...]°°°[...]

Frg. 48
1 [...] *k*[...]
2 [...]°*y*[...]

Frg. 49, Col. 1
2 [...]*h*

Frg. 49, Col. 2
1 foreve[r...]
2 (vacat) [...]

Frg. 50
1 [...] with your voice [...]
2 [...] and a pious one [...]

Frg. 51
1 [...]° your kingdom [...]
2 [...]°*š*[...]

Frg. 52
1 [...]*hm*[...]
2 [...]*m*[...]

Frg. 53
1 [...] and also we *m*[...]
2 [...]° and you forgave
   l°[...]

Frg. 54
1 [...]°°°[...]
2 [...] unfaithfulness you have
   atoned *m*[...]

Frg. 55
1 [...]°[...]
2 [...] your wisdom [...]
3 [...] you [c]reated them and in
   your power [...]
4 [...] [...] *l*[...]*l*[...]*l*[...][21]

---

[19] Or "our [...]."
[20] Or "our [...]*lk*."

[21] Note the superlinear "*b*."

Frg. 56

1] ° [
2 [דו ומ̇ידכה]
3] ° ° ° בֿ ° [

Frg. 57

1] ° בֿ ° ° [
2 וגילו[ן]
3 [ס בֿ]

Frg. 58

1] ° [
2] ° [ ] ° ° [
3 [ה מ̇]ן[ס̇]
4 [א ואת̇ °]
   ה̇
5 [ת̇ בבנ̇] ° [ ]
6 [י קוד]ש[°]
7 [אונו יא]° [
8 [גדו̇לים כול א]
9 [ל̇]

Frg. 59

1] ° ° ° [
2 [מצאונו]
3 [° ° ° ה̇]

Frg. 60

1 כ̇[ן

Frg. 61

1 [ם̇]
2 [צ̇]

Frg. 62

1 [א]ר̇צנו ° [

Frg. 63

1 [ו̇]

Frg. 64

1 [° י̇]
2 [° ° ר̇]

Frg. 65

1 [° רב]ן
2 [ל̇]

Frg. 66

1 [°]
2 [ותצ̇]

Frg. 67

1 [אר̇]

Frg. 68

1 כ̇[ן
2 [° °]

Frg. 69

1 [א °]

Frg. 70

1 [ה ב̇]
2 [ל]ל̇[ל]

Frg. 71

1 [ד̇ין]
2 [ש̇ח̇]

Frg. 72

1 [ינו̇]
2 [° נ̇]

Frg. 73

1] ° [
2 [ם̇ עלי]ן
3 [ע̇ולם̇]

Frg. 56

1 [...]°[...]
2 [...]*dw* and from your hand [...]
3 [...]°*b*°°°[...]

Frg. 57

1 °°*b*°[...]
2 and they will rejoice [...]
3 [...]*m b*[...]

Frg. 58

1 [...]°[...]
2 [...]°°[...]°[...]
3 [...]*h* from [...]*m* [...]
4 [...]' and '*t* °[...]
5 [...]*t* in *bn*°[...]°[...]²²
6 [...]*y* holine[ss]°[...]
7 [...] his strength *y*'[...]°[...]
8 [...] great things, all '[...]
9 [...]*l*[...]

Frg. 59

1 [...]°°°[...]
2 [...] they found us [...]
3 [...]°°°*h*[...]

Frg. 60

1 *k*[...]

Frg. 61

1 [...]*m* [...]
2 [...]*ṣ* [...]

Frg. 62

1 [...]our [l]and °[...]

Frg. 63

1 [...]him²³ [...]

Frg. 64

1 [...]*y*°[...]
2 [...] *r* °°[...]

Frg. 65

1 [...]° *rb*[...]
2 [...]*l*[...]

Frg. 66

1 [...]°[...]
2 [...] and *tṣ*[...]

Frg. 67

1 [...]'*r*[...]

Frg. 68

1 [...] *k*[...]
2 [...] °°[...]

Frg. 69

1 [...]'°[...]

Frg. 70

1 [...]*h b*[...]
2 [...]*l*[...]*l*[...]

Frg. 71

1 [...]*dy*[...]
2 [...]*šḥ*[...]

Frg. 72

1 [...]*y* us²⁴ [...]
2 [...]°*n*[...]

Frg. 73

1 [...]°[...]
2 [...]*m* upon *y*[...]
3 [...] forever

---

²² Note the superlinear "*h*."
²³ Or "his [...]."

²⁴ Or "our [...]*y*."

Frg. 77	Frg. 76	Frg. 74
1　] ° [	1　]שׁים[	1　] יׄ[
2　] הׄ [	2　] עב ° [	2　]הׄ כׄ[
3　]לׄ[		

Frg. 80	Frg. 79	Frg. 78
1　] צׄ[	1　]וׄ[	1　]רׄ[
	2　]לׄ[	2　]נׄ[תתה ב[

Frg. 83	Frg. 82	Frg. 81
1　] °° בׄ [	1　] °° [	1　]בׄ[
2　]ואין ל[	2　]נׄפוֹתׄ[	2　]ארׄצׄ[
		3　]מוֹדׄ[
		4　]לׄ[

Frg. 86	Frg. 85	Frg. 84
1　]שלוׄ בנׄ[	1　]תפׄ[	1　]הׄ להׄבׄ[
	2　]סׄלׄ[	2　]לוא מׄל[

Frg. 89	Frg. 88	Frg. 87
1　]יהםׄ[	1　] °°°°° [	1　]תׄוׄחׄלתוׄן[
2　]ל [	2　] °°°°° [	

Frg. 92	Frg. 91	Frg. 90
1　] ° [	1　] הבׄ[ ]הׄ[	1　]בׄ[
2　] °° [		2　] וׄא[
		3　]ל [

Frg. 95	Frg. 94	Frg. 93
1　]ס עׄ[	1　]תׄ[	1　]דׄבׄ[
	2　]הׄוׄ[	2　] [

		Frg. 96
		1　]ל ל[
		2　]ס ז[

Frg. 74
1 [...] *y*[...]
2 [...]*h k*[...]

Frg. 76
1 [...]*šym* [...]
2 [...]° *ʿb*[...]

Frg. 77
1 [...]°[...]
2 [...]*h* [...]
3 [...]*l*[...]

Frg. 78
1 [...]*r*[...]
2 [...] you [g]ave *b*[...]

Frg. 79
1 [...]*w*[...]
2 [...]*l*[...]

Frg. 80
1 [...] *ṣ*[...]

Frg. 81
1 [...]*b*[...]
2 [...] land[...]
3 [...]*mwd*[...]
4 [...]*l*[...]

Frg. 82
1 [...]°°[...]
2 [...]*npwt*[...]

Frg. 83
1 [...]*b* °°[...]
2 [...] and there is not *l*[...]

Frg. 84
1 [...]*h lhb*[...]
2 [...] not *ml*[...]

Frg. 85
1 [...]*tp*[...]
2 [...]*sk*[...]

Frg. 86
1 [...]*šlw bn*[...]

Frg. 87
1 [...] his hope [...]

Frg. 88
1 [...]°°°°[...]
2 [...]°°°°°[...]

Frg. 89
1 [...]*y* their [...]
2 [...] *l*[...]

Frg. 90
1 [...]*b*[...]
2 [...] and ʼ[...]
3 [...]*l* [...]

Frg. 91
1 [...] *hb*[...]*h*[...]

Frg. 92
1 [...]°[...]
2 [...]° °[...]

Frg. 93
1 [...]*dk*[...]
2 [...][...]

Frg. 94
1 [...]*t*[...]
2 [...]*hn*[...]

Frg. 95
1 [...]*m ʿ*[...]

Frg. 96
1 [...]*l l*[...]
2 [...]*m z*[...]

Frgs. 97—98, Col. 1[17]

1	]
2	ולוא הבי]ן ז]רע [הֿאֿדֿם[18]
3	[לעשות (לֿעֿשֿוֿתֿ)
4	ולוא הב]יֿנו בכוחכה
5	לוא תחפ]ץֿ בֿעֿוֿלֿהֿ][19]
6	]]
7	ל]כֿהֿ לקֿוֿדש[20]
8	ברי]תכה להם במראתי[21]
9	[מֿעֿשי ידיכה וכתבֿ[22]

Frg. 99, Col. 2		*Frg. 99, Col. 1*		*Frgs. 97—98, Col. 2*	
]˚[ ]˚[ ]	1	[˚] מוצא חן	1	]˚˚	1
לֿהֿ]	2	]˚[	2	כתֿרֿ צֿדֿ]ק	2
				נזר יֿפֿ]	3
				צדק ל ˚ ˚]	4
				אֿ]ל	5
				]]	6
				]˚	7
				אֿ ˚ ˚ עלֿ יֿכֿ]	8
				יֿ]ן [שֿוֿבֿ]	9
				[ ] ˚˚˚	10

---

17 Frg. 98 columns 1 and 2 supplies portions of lines 1-5; frg. 97 supplies portions of 1ines 7-9.

18 1Q34 frgs. 3-5, 2.4: ולא הבין זרע האֿדֿ].

19 1Q34 frgs. 3-5, 2.5-6: ולא הבינו בכוחך הגדול [ ] וֿתמאס בם. כי לא תחפץ בעֿ]הֿ.

20 1Q34 frgs. 3-5, 2.7: וֿתֿ]ֿם להבדל לך לקודש מכול העמים.

21 1Q34 frgs. 3-5, 2.7: ותחדש בר]תֿך להם במראת כבֿ]ד.

22 1Q34 frgs. 3-5, 2.7-8: ודברי [] קֿוֿדֿשֿך במעשי ידיֿך וכתב ימינך. להודיעם] יסורי כבוד ומעלי עולם.

Frgs. 97–98, Col. 1

1 [...]

2 [.... But] the human se[ed has not had discern]ment

3 [...] to do[25]

4 [.... And] they [did not dis]cern your [great] strength.

5 [... you do not delig]ht in deceit.   [...]

6 [...]

7 [... for] yourself for holiness

8 [...] your [cove]nant with them by a vision of

9 [...] the works of your hands.   And it wrote

Frgs. 97–98, Col. 2

1 [...]°°[...]

2 crowned (with)
righteous[ness...]

3 headband *yp*[...]

4 righteousness *l*°°[...]

5 [...]*l*[...]

6 [...]

7 °[...]

8 °°° *ʿl yk*[...]

9 *y*[...]*šwb*[...]

10 [...]°°°

Frg. 99, Col. 1

1 [...]° finding grace

2 [...]°[...]

Frg. 99, Col. 2

1 [...]°[...]°[...]

2 to her [...]

---

[25] The second לעשות is erased; a scribal correction.

Frg. 100

1]ש̇[
2]כול[
3]ש̊ ˚ ˚[
4]פטכה[

Frg. 101

1]˚[
2]˚ ˚ל ˚[
3]א̊ ˚[
4][

Frg. 102

1]ו̇כ̊[
2]˚ ˚[

Frg. 103

1]ם̊[
2]ה[

Frg. 104

1]˚[
2]מ̇ועד[
3]לה[

Frg. 105

1]ם̊[ל̇
2]לת[

Frg. 106

1]˚יכ[
2]מ̊ ˚[

Frg. 107

1]והש[
2]זרע[

Frg. 108

1]כת̊[
2]כב[

Frg. 109

1]˚[
2]כ ˚[

Frg. 110

1]ם̊[
2]ה̊ יע̊[

Frg. 111

1]ם[
2]˚ ר̇ ˚[

Frg. 112

1]מ̇ר[
2]ע̊ י̊[

Frg. 113

1]ב[
2]ל ˚[

Frg. 114

1]ה̊ ב[
2]ק̊ו̊[

Frg. 115

1]ח̊נ̊ו ה̊[

Frg. 116

1]ד ב̇מע[

Frg. 117

1]˚[
2]מ̇ן ˚ ˚[
3]˚[

Frg. 100

1 […]*š*[…]

2 […] all […]

3 […] *š*°°[…]

4 […]*pṭ* you²⁶ […]

Frg. 101

1 […]°[…]

2 […] °°*l*°[…]

3 […]*°*[…]

4 […] […]

Frg. 102

1 […] and *k*[…]

2 […]°°[…]

Frg. 103

1 […]*m*[…]

2 […]*h*[…]

Frg. 104

1 […]°[…]

2 […] festival […]

3 […] *lh*[…]

Frg. 105

1 […]*m*[…]

2 […]*lt*[…]²⁷

Frg. 106

1 […]°*yk*[…]

2 […]°*m*°[…]

Frg. 107

1 […] and *hš*[…]

2 […] seed […]

Frg. 108

1 […]*kt*[…]

2 […]*kb*[…]

Frg. 109

1 […]°[…]

2 […] *k*°[…]

Frg. 110

1 […]*m* […]

2 […]*h y*ᶜ[…]

Frg. 111

1 […]*m*[…]

2 […]°*r*°[…]

Frg. 112

1 […] *mr*[…]

2 […]*ṣ y*[…]

Frg. 113

1 […]*b*[…]

2 […]*l* °[…]

Frg. 114

1 […]*h b*[…]

2 […] *qw*[…]

Frg. 115

1 […]*ḥ* us²⁸ *h*[…]

Frg. 116

1 […]*d* in *m*ᶜ[…]

Frg. 117

1 […]°[…]

2 […]*mn* °°[…]

3 […]°[…]

²⁶ Or "your […]*pṭ*."
²⁷ Note the superlinear "*d*."

²⁸ Or "our […]*ḥ*."

83

Frgs. 131–132, Col. 1	*Frg. 119*	*Frg. 118*
3] ˚ ˚ [	1 [עש]	1 [ם̇]
4 [בות		
5 [קׄודשׄכ]ה		
6 [לית		
7 [יו		
8 [כׄ]וׄל ירחיׄ		
9 [שׁונו		
10 לשמוׄע] ˚ [		
11 [בכול		
12 [שינו		
13 נפׄ[לׄ]אותיכה[23]		
14 [שלחתנו		
15 [רׄותם		
16 [ראתך		
17 ש]נׄאתה		
18 [היתה		
19 [לפני		
20 [		
21 [לׄ		

23 A scribe has corrected the ת from a כ. For the restoration cf.
4Q509 frg. 3 line 8 and 1QH 1.33, 34; 3.23; 6.11; 10.21; etc.

Frg. 118

1 […]*m* […]

Frg. 119

1 […]ʿ*š*[…]

Frgs. 131−132, Col. 1

3 […]°°[…]

4 […]*bwt*

5 […] yo[ur] holiness

6 […]*lyt*

7 […] his […]*y*

8 [… a]ll the months of

9 […] his tongue

10 […]° to listen

11 […] in all

12 […]*šy* us[29]

13 […] your [wo]ndrous deeds

14 […] you sent us

15 […] their […]*rw*

16 […]*r*ʾ you

17 […] you [h]ate

18 […] she was

19 […] before

20 […]

21 […]*q*

[29] Or "our […]*šy*."

Frgs. 131–132, Col. 2[24]

] ˚ ˚ [	1
] לכ]בֹודכה[25]	2
עֹיו אמן אמֹן][26]	3
] VACAT [	4
[בֹכֹוֹרֹים זכורה אֹ]דו[נֹי מֹוֹעֹד[27]	5
[וֹנדבות רֹצוונכה אשרֹ צויתה]	6
[יֹ]גֹיש לפניכה רשית מעשיֹ]כה	7
לבֹ]]ֹם עלי ארץ להֹיוֹת קֹן	8
[ ] ˚ ˚ [ ]ֹכֹה כי ביֹוֹם []הֹן	9
אֹ[ ]רֹ הקדשתֹן]	10
אֹֹת שגר [	11
צֹ[	12
אֹ[	13
בֹרוֹ[	14
עם נֹֹֹ[	15
קוד]ש	16
בכול [	17
[	18
לֹ[	19
יֹ[	20

Frg. 135		Frg. 134		Frg. 133	
שוֹתֹ]	1	מֹֹם וחיֹקֹ]	1	עֹו לכֹן]	1
וֹ זֹ[	2	[פֹלֹ[ ] לשׁ	2	עֹמוד כֹי לכֹן]	2
וֹ בֹן]	3				
] ˚ [	4				

---

[24] Frg. 131 supplies column 1 and in column 2 the beginning of lines 8, 10, 12-17, and 19-20.

[25] For the restoration cf. 1QH 1.10, 6.10, etc.

[26] For the restoration cf. 4Q507 frg. 3 line 2, 4Q508 frg. 20 line 1, and 4Q509 frg. 4 line 5.

[27] 4Q508 frg. 2 line 2: זכורה אדוני מועד]ֹֹם[; cf. 1Q34 frgs. 1-3 1.9: תפלה ליום כפורים זכו]ֹ רֹוֹני אֹ[.

Frgs. 131–132, Col. 2

1 [...]°°[...]

2 [... for] your [g]lory [...]

3 [...] his [...]ʿ*y*. Amen. Ame[n....]

4 [...] (vacat) [...]

5 [...] first fruits.   Remember, O L[or]d, the festival of

6 [...] and free-will offerings (which are) pleasing to you which you commanded

7 [...pre]sent before you the best of [your] works

8 to *b*[...] them upon (the) land to be *q*[...]

9 [...]°° [...] you[30] for in the day [...]*h*[...]

10 ʾ[...]*r* you have sanctified [...]

11 [...] the offspring of [...]

12 *ṣ*[...]

13 ʾ[...]

14 in *rw*[[31]...]

15 with[32] *nh*[...]

16 holine[ss...]

17 in all [...]

18 [...]

19 *l*[...]

20 *y*[...]

Frg. 133

1 [...]ʿ*w lk*[...]

2 [...] to stand, because to *k*[...]

Frg. 134

1 [...]*m*°*m* and bosom [...]

2 [...] *pl*°[...] *lš*[...]

Frg. 135

1 [...]*šwt*[...]

2 [...]*w z*[...]

3 [...]*w b*[...]

4 [...]° [...]

---

[30] Or "your [...]."

[31] Or restore some form of ברוך.

[32] Or "people."

Frg. 138	*Frg. 137*	*Frg. 136*
1 ‏לם]‏	1 ‏[̊ ̊ם]‏	1 ‏[̊]‏
2 ‏[ה]‏	2 ‏[ליה]‏	2 ‏[שח]‏
3 ‏[נ]‏		3 ‏[ה]‏
4 ‏[̊]‏		4 ‏[מע]‏

Frg. 141	*Frg. 140*	*Frg. 139*
1 ‏[חשב]‏	1 ‏[̊]‏	1 ‏[̊]‏
2 ‏[תו]‏	2 ‏[ש עבודה]‏	2 ‏[ואתה]‏
		3 ‏[והד]‏
		4 ‏[̊ [ ] ̊]‏

Frg. 144	*Frg. 143*	*Frg. 142*
1 ‏[̊ ̊]‏	1 ‏[ה מועד] ̊ ̊ ̊ ̊ [ ]‏	1 ‏[ה]‏
2 ‏[ואתה]‏	2 ‏[ולבער ממנו] ̊ [ ]‏	2 ‏[דב]‏
3 ‏[והה ̊ [ ]‏	3 ‏[את ̊]‏	
	4 ‏[ל א]‏	

Frg. 147	*Frg. 146*	*Frg. 145*
1 ‏[̊ ̊]‏	1 ‏[שתנו]‏	1 ‏[ו ̊]‏
2 ‏[אתה]‏	2 ‏[לאהב]‏	2 ‏[ר]חמיכה]‏
3 ‏[וחו ̊]‏	3 ‏[ך שמכה]‏	3 ‏[̊]‏
4 ‏[ל]מען]‏	4 ‏[ל ̊ להטו]‏	4 ‏[רתנו]‏
5 ‏[נפלאות]‏	5 ‏[ר]שענו ב]‏	5 ‏[̊]‏
6 ‏[̊ ̊]‏	6 ‏[נ]שחתות]‏	
	7 ‏[לקדוש]‏	
	8 ‏[ל]‏	

Frg. 136

1 [. . .]°[. . .]

2 [. . .]*šḥ*[. . .]

3 [. . .]*h* [. . .]

4 [. . .] *m*ᶜ[. . .]

Frg. 137

1 [. . .]°°*m*[. . .]

2 [. . .]*lyh*[. . .]

Frg. 138

1 [. . .]*lm*[. . .]

2 [. . .]*h* [. . .]

3 [. . .]*n* [. . .]

4 [. . .]°[. . .]

Frg. 139

1 [. . .]°[. . .]

2 [. . .] and you [. . .]

3 [. . .] and *hd*[. . .]

4 [. . .]°[. . .]°[. . .]

Frg. 140

1 [. . .]°[. . .]

2 [. . .]*š* service [. . .]

Frg. 141

1 [. . .]devise [. . .]

2 [. . .]*t* him[33] [. . .]

Frg. 142

1 [. . .]*h*[. . .]

2 [. . .]*db*[. . .]

Frg. 143

1 [. . .]°°°°[. . .]*h* festival [. . .]

2 [. . .]° and in order to root out[34] from us[35]

3 [. . .]’*t* °[. . .]

4 [. . .]*l* ’[. . .]

Frg. 144

1 [. . .] °°[. . .]

2 [. . .] and you [. . .]

3 [. . .]° and *ht*[. . .]

Frg. 145

1 [. . .]*w* °[. . .]

2 [. . .] your [co]mpassions [. . .]

3 [. . .]°[. . .]

4 [. . .]you have [. . .]*r* us [. . .]

5 [. . .]°[. . .]

Frg. 146

1 [. . .] you have [. . .]*š* us [. . .]

2 [. . .] to love [. . .]

3 [. . .]*k* your name [. . .]

4 [. . .]*l*° his flame[36] [. . .]

5 [. . .]we have been wicked *b*[. . .]

6 [. . . c]orruptions [. . .]

7 [. . .] for a holy [. . .]

8 [. . .]*l*[. . .]

Frg. 147

1 [. . .]°°[. . .]

2 [. . .] you [. . .]

3 [. . .]*wḥ* him[37] °[. . .]

4 [. . . in] order that [. . .]

5 [. . .] wondrous deeds [. . .]

6 [. . .]°°[. . .]

---

[33] Or "his [. . .]*t*."

[34] Cf. the Syriac for meaning; in Heb. the root בער usually means "to burn up."

[35] Or "from him."

[36] Not "they burn."

[37] Or "his [. . .]*wḥ*."

Frg. 151
1 תֿנון[
2 מביֿתֿ]
3 וֿשֿ ˚ [

Frg. 150
1] ˚ ˚ [
2] ˚ ˚ [
3] ˚ שׁ ˚ [
4] ˚ ˚ [

Frg. 148[28]
1]בֿ ˚ [
2]כֿ כה ˚ [
3]א ושׁובו[
4]וֿאן חרו[

Frg. 154
1]שׁ ˚ [
2] ˚ל[

Frg. 153
1 צרֿ[
2]וֿת ˚[
3] ˚ וֿרֿ ˚ [

Frg. 152
1]ינוֿ[
2] ˚ וֿ סֿ[
3 שֿם[

Frg. 157
1]סֿ ˚ ˚ בֿ ˚ ˚ [
2 שׁועו עיני[
3] [ ]
4]הֿון

Frg. 156
1] אר[
2]ם לב[
3]ל ˚ [

Frg. 155
1]וֿעולמיֿם[
2]קֿ ל ˚ שׁ[

Frg. 160
1] ˚ [
2]ר[אשוֿן
3] ˚ ˚ [

Frg. 159
1] ˚ [
2]קֿ
3]מֿ

Frg. 158
1] ˚ [
2] ˚ הֿ[
3]תֿיח
4]עֿ

Frg. 163
1] ˚ בֿרֿ ˚ [
2]תֿנוֿ [

Frg. 162
1]מים[
2] ˚ יֿק[

Frg. 161
1]רֿינוֿ[
2]י לוא נֿ[
3]אֿחרֿ[

Frg. 167
1] ˚ ˚ [
2]בֿ ˚ [
3]וֿ ˚ [

Frg. 166
1] ˚ ˚ [
2]וֿ[

Frg. 164[29]
1]להֿבֿלֿ[
2]יֿם[

---

28 Frg. 149 no longer exists. [Ed.]

29 Frg. 165 no longer exists. [Ed.]

Frg. 148

1 [...]°*b*[...]

2 [...]° you[38] *k*[...]

3 [...]*šwbw* ʾ[...]

4 [...]*ḥrw* and ʾ[...]

Frg. 150

1 [...]°°[...]

2 [...]°°[...]

3 [...]°*š*°[...]

4 [...]°°[...]

Frg. 151

1 [...]*t* us[39][...]

2 [...] from the house [...]

3 [...]° *wš*[...]

Frg. 152

1 [...]*y* us[40] [...]

2 [...]*m* and °[...]

3 [...]*šm*[...]

Frg. 153

1 [...]*ṣr*[...]

2 [...]*wt* and [...]

3 [...]°*rw*°[...]

Frg. 154

1 [...]°*š*[...]

2 [...]*l*°[...]

Frg. 155

1 [...] and the ages [...]

2 [...]*q l*°*š*[...]

Frg. 156

1 [...]ʾ*r*[...]

2 [...]*m lb*[...]

3 [...]°*l*[...]

Frg. 157

1 [...]°°*b* °°*m*[...]

2 [...]*šwʿw* the eyes of [...]

3 [...] (vacat) [...]

4 [...]*hw*[...]

Frg. 158

1 [...]°[...]

2 [...]*h*°[...]

3 [...]*tyḥ*[...]

4 [...]ʿ[...]

Frg. 159

1 [...]°[...]

2 [...]*q*[...]

3 [...]*m*[...]

Frg. 160

1 [...]°[...]

2 [... f]irst [...]

3 [...]°°[...]

Frg. 161

1 [...] our [...]*ry* [...]

2 [...]*y* not *n*[...]

3 [...]after[...]

Frg. 162

1 [...]*mym* [...]

2 [...]°*yq* [...]

Frg. 163

1 [...]°*br*°[...]

2 [...]*t* us[41] [...]

Frg. 164

1 [...] to *hbl*[...]

2 [...]*ym*[...]

Frg. 166

1 [...]°°[...]

2 [...] and [...]

Frg. 167

1 [...]°°[...]

2 [...]°*b*[...]

3 [...]*w*°[...]

---

[38] Or "your [...]°."
[39] Or "our [...]*t*."
[40] Or "our [...]*y*."
[41] Or "our [...]*t*."

Frg. 170	*Frg. 169*	*Frg. 168*
1 [˚]	1 [˚]	1 [קֿדושׁ]
2 [˚]	2 [אֿין]	
3 [קֿוֿ]		
	.	
Frg. 173	*Frg. 172*	*Frg. 171*
1 [˚]	1 [חֿרן]	1 [לינוֿן]
2 [רֿוֿת]	2 [˚]	
Frg. 176	*Frg. 175*	*Frg. 174*
1 [אֿין]	1 [וֿי בֿ]	1 [˚ תֿ]
2 [וליֿן]	2 [בֿקֿ ˚ ל]	2 [כֿ]
		3 [˚]
Frg. 179	*Frg. 178*	*Frg. 177*
1 [וֿן]	1 [רֿשֿ]	1 [תֿ]
2 [הֿ]	2 [ל ˚]	2 [כֿול רˉ בֿ]
Frg. 182	*Frg. 181*	*Frg. 180*
1 [וֿ אֿ ˚]	1 [עֿהֿ]	1 [תֿ חן]

Frg. 168

1 […] holy […]

Frg. 169

1 […]°[…]
2 […] there is not […]

Frg. 170

1 […]°[…]
2 […]°[…]
3 […]qw[…]

Frg. 171

1 […]ly us […]

Frg. 172

1 […]ḥr[…]
2 […]°[…]

Frg. 173

1 […]°[…]
2 […]rwt […]

Frg. 174

1 […]°t[…]
2 […] k[…]
3 […]°[…]

Frg. 175

1 […]ny b[…]
2 […] in q°l[…]

Frg. 176

1 […] there is not […]
2 […]wly[…]

Frg. 177

1 […]t[…]
2 […] all r°b[…]

Frg. 178

1 […]dš[…]
2 […]l°[…]

Frg. 179

1 […]w[…]
2 […]h […]

Frg. 180

1 […]t ḥ[…]

Frg. 181

1 […]ʿh[…]

Frg. 182

1 […]w ʾ°[…]

Frg. 184, Col. 2	*Frg. 184, Col. 1*	*Frg. 183*
4]°	1 [°°	1 [הגוים]°[
5 א[	2 [את]	2 [ושמה]
6 כ[	3 [ ] לעיני עמכה	3 [ ]°[ ]ן דרן]°
7 ו[	4 [כה ומעשי]	4 [ ]°°ולי]ניה
8 ב[	5 [ה וכול בר°°]	5 [וברוב]ה
9]°	6 [°°]	6 [הדחתו]ן
10]°	7 [בל]	7 [לבני יה]ודה
11]י	8 [ ]°°ו	8 [זואת]ן
	9 [שו]	9 [בא מא]ן]ת[אתן[
	10 [תהו ובכה]	10 [כה]
	11 [רתה]	11 [עלינו]
	12 [מאכל ל]	
	13 י נדה[	

Frg. 187	*Frg. 186*	*Frg. 185*
1 [ה ב]	1 [ב]	1 [ה]
2 [°] אש[	2 [°]	2 ב[
3 [תחרץ]	3 [עם°°]	3 [ ]°
4 [תם]	4 [°א]	4 [°°°°יב]
		5 [ ]°ה

Frg. 190	*Frg. 189*	*Frg. 188*
1 [° ס]	1 [בוד]	1 [את בריתכ]ה
2 [ל לש]	2 [ד ארצנו]	2 [ולוא] מ[
3 [ל]	3 [צלמות ומ]	3 [הרעות האלה ו°°]
	4 [נו כי תניח]	4 ג[מ]ול רעתנו אשר [
	5 ע[ובדכה בא]	
	6 [°]	

Frg. 183

1 [...]° the nations [...]

2 [...] and there [...]

3 [...]*n dr*[...]°[...]

4 [...]*nyh* and *ly*°[...]

5 [...]*h* and in the
abundance of [...]

6 [...] he scattered him in [...]

7 [...] to the sons of Ju[dah...]

8 [...] these *b*[...]

9 [...]*b' m'*[...]⁴²

10 [...] you⁴³ [...]⁴⁴

11 [...] upon us [...]

Frg. 184, Col. 1

1 [...]°°

2 [...]'*t*

3 [...] to the eyes of your people

4 [...]you⁴⁵ and the works of

5 [...]*h* and all *br*°°

6 [...]°°

7 [...]*bl*

8 [...]°*w*

9 [...] his [...]*š*⁴⁶

10 [...] you have [...] him
and he will weep

11 [...] you have [...]*r*

12 [...] feeding for [...]

13 [...]*y* impurity

Frg. 184, Col. 2

4 °[...]

5 '[...]

6 *k*[...]

7 and [...]

8 *b*[...]

9 °[...]

10 °[...]

11 *y*[...]

Frg. 185

1 *t*[...]

2 *b*[...]

3 °[...]

4 *yb*°°°°[...]

5 *t*°[...]

Frg. 186

1 [...]*b*[...]

2 [...]° [...]

3 [...]'*m*°°[...]

4 [...] °'[...]

Frg. 187

1 [...]*h b*[...]

2 [...]° '*š*[...]

3 [...] you will determine [...]

4 [...]*tm*[...]

Frg. 188

1 [...] yo[ur] covenant [...]

2 [...] and not [...]*m*[...]

3 [...] these evil things and °[...]

4 [... ret]ribution of our
wickedness which [...]

Frg. 189

1 [...]*bwd*[...]

2 [...]*d* our land [...]

3 [...] shadow and *m*[...]

4 [...] us,⁴⁷ because you will
give rest [...]

5 [...] your [se]rving in '[...]

6 [...]°[...]

Frg. 190

1 [...]°*m*[...]

2 [...]*l lš*[...]

3 [...]*l*[...]

---

⁴² Note the interlinear "[...]*t*."

⁴³ Or "your [...]."

⁴⁴ Note the interlinear "'*tn*[...]."

⁴⁵ Or "your [...]."

⁴⁶ Or "[...]*š* him." Note the interlinear "*y*."

⁴⁷ Or "our [...]."

Frg. 191

1 [ ] ֺ ֺ [ ]
2 [לפניכֹהֹ]
3 [שמכהֹ]
4 ה[מֹשֹלֹתֹנֹו]
5 [ ] ֺ [ ]

Frg. 192

1 [ ] ֺ יסֹפֹרֹ[ ]
2 [בֹעסים בשֹ]
3 [שֹכה לֹהֹ]
4 [עה בֹ]

Frg. 193

1 [טֹמאֹה]
2 [ֺ כל בֹא]

Frg. 193

1 [בֹ]
2 [תינו תֹרצֹ]   בֺ
3 [כֹה בקרבֹנֹו]

Frg. 195

1 [והֹוסֹי]
2 [יֹינֹו]
3 [ ] ֺ [ ]

Frg. 196

1 [מֹ]
2 [מֹלֹך ֺ]

Frg. 197

1 [תֹה]
2 [ה את]
3 [ ] ֺ ֺ ל]

Frg. 198

1 [ואֹוֹתֹכֹ]
2 [כֹול היֹות בֹ]
3 [תֹצֹדֹק לֹ]

Frg. 199

1 [וֹכֹ]
2 [לֹבֹינֹת]
3 [תֹ שֹ]
4 [חֹק מֹ]

Frg. 200

1 [ ] ֺ [ ]
2 [חֹיתֹימֹ]
3 [ ] ֺ ֺ ל יֹן]

Frg. 201

1 [ ] ֺ [ ]
2 [מֹאֹן כֹ]
3 [ ] ֺ שֹ ֺ [ ]

Frg. 202

1 [ ] ֺ יֹ [ ]
2 [ ] ֺ בֹ]
3 [ ] שֹ ֺ [ ]

Frg. 203

1 [שֹר ֺ]
2 [וֹ אֹוֹ]
3 [ ] ֺ [ ]

Frg. 204

1 [כֹולֹםֹ]
2 [עֹולֹמֹיֹםֹ]
3 [וֹאֹ] ֺ [ ]

Frg. 205

1 ר[שֹעֹהֹ לֹ]
2 ק[ץ הרשעה][30]
3 [ ] ֺ ֺ ֺ בֹאֹ]

Frg. 206

1 [ם ברוך אדונֹי המֹן]
2 [ ]   [ ]

Frg. 207

1 [ ] ֺ [ ]
2 [ ] ֺ דֹוֹ]
3 [הֹ הֹ]

Frg. 208

1 [וֹן]
2 [ ] ֺ [ ]
3 [ ] ֺ [ ]

---

[30] Cf. CD 15.7, 1QpHab 5.8.

Frg. 191

1 […] °°[…]
2 […] before you […]
3 […] your name […]
4 [… yo]u made us to rule […]
5 […]°[…]

Frg. 192

1 […]he will count °[…]
2 […] among the peoples *bš*[…]
3 […]*š* you[48] to *h*[…]
4 […]*ʿh b*[…]

Frg. 193

1 […] impurity […]
2 […]°*kl* he came […]

Frg. 194

1 […]*b* […]
2 […] our […]*ty trṣ*[…][49]
3 […] you[50] in o[ur] midst […]

Frg. 195

1 […] and the silences of […]
2 […]*yynw*[…]
3 […]°[…]

Frg. 196

1 […] *m*[…]
2 […] king °[…]

Frg. 197

1 […]*th* […]
2 […]*h ʾt*[…]
3 […]°°*l*[…]

Frg. 198

1 […]*wʾwtk*[…]
2 […] all which is *b*[…]
3 […] you are righteous to […]

Frg. 199

1 […] and *k*[…]
2 […] for the discernment of […]
3 […]*t š*[…]
4 […]*ḥq m*[…]

Frg. 200

1 […]°[…]
2 […]*ḥytym*[…]
3 […]°°*l y*[…]

Frg. 201

1 […]°[…]
2 […] to refuse *k*[…]
3 […]°*š*°[…]

Frg. 202

1 […]°*y*[…]
2 […]°*b*[…]
3 […]*š*°[…]

Frg. 203

1 […] *šr*°[…]
2 […]*w ʾw*[…]
3 […] °[…]

Frg. 204

1 […] all of them
2 […] ages
3 […]° and ʾ[…]

Frg. 205

1 [… w]ickedness *l*[…]
2 [… ti]me of[51] wickedness […]
3 […]°°° *bʾ*[…]

Frg. 206

1 […]*m*. Blessed be the Lord (who) *hmn*[…]
2 [… .] (vacat) […]

Frg. 207

1 […]°[…]
2 […]°*dw*[…]
3 […]*h h*[…]

Frg. 208

1 […]*w*[…]
2 […]°[…]
3 […]°[…]

---

48 Or "your […]*š*."
49 Note the interlinear "*b*."
50 Or "your […]."
51 Or "e]nd of."

Frg. 209
1 [°° דֿ° °]
2 ם בֿמ[
3 הֿולל[

Frg. 210
1 [וֹ]
2 הֹן]
3 [°]

Frg. 211
1 [ים מֿן]
2 הֿ מ[

Frg. 212
1 הנסתרוֹ]תי 31
2 לֿ]

Frg. 213
1 כֿי לֿכֿהֿ]
2 ותבדילֿנֿו [

Frg. 214
1 [°°]
2 ה אלוהינֿו]
3 לֿלֿ]

Frg. 215
1 [°°°]
2 לטובכה]

Frg. 216
1 [°]
2 [°תֿ]
3 [°רֿ]

Frg. 217
1 חתומים]
2 לֹות °וֹ]

Frg. 218
1 בכול]
2 קֿדֿוש]

Frg. 219
1 [°]
2 והמ°]
3 שֿם]

Frg. 220
1 מֹועדיֿם]
2 לֹן [

Frg. 221
1 ולאלֿ]
2 קֿצֿ]

Frg. 222
1 [ה]
2 [°° ה]

Frg. 223
1 [°]
2 בטֿהֿ [

Frg. 224
1 [לוֹא]
2 הֹםֿ]

Frg. 225
1 וֿענֿשֿיֿן

Frg. 226
1 חֿר יֿב]
2 [°]

Frg. 227
1 [°]
2 שֿ רחמ]

Frg. 228
1 מֿ]
2 בֿפֿיה מֿן]
3 לֿן]

Frg. 229
1 הֿ ניֿתֿ]
2 וֿאמרו [

Frg. 230
1 נֹן °°]
2 ב °° רוֹן]

Frg. 231
1 [°° ע הֿ]
2 [°°]

Frg. 232
1 וב °]
2 הגוֹן]

31 4Q508 frg. 2 line 4:]וֿאתה ידעתה הֿנסתרות וֿהֿנֹגֿלֿ[.

Frg. 209
1 [. . .]°°*k* °°[. . .]
2 [. . .]*m bm*[. . .]
3 [. . .]*hwll* [. . .]

Frg. 210
1 [. . .]*w*[. . .]
2 [. . .]*h*[. . .]
3 [. . .]°[. . .]

Frg. 211
1 [. . .]*ym mr*[. . .]
2 [. . .]*h m*[. . .]

Frg. 212
1 [. . .] the thing[s] hidden [. . .]
2 [. . .]*l*[. . .]

Frg. 213
1 [. . .] because to you [. . .]
2 [. . .] and you separated u[s . . .]

Frg. 214
1 [. . .]°°[. . .]
2 [. . .]*h* our God [. . .]
3 [. . .]*ll*[. . .]

Frg. 215
1 [. . .]°°°[. . .]
2 [. . .] for your good [. . .]

Frg. 216
1 [. . .]°[. . .]
2 [. . .]*t*°[. . .]
3 [. . .]*r*°[. . .]

Frg. 217
1 [. . .] seals [. . .]
2 [. . .]*w*°*lwt* [. . .]

Frg. 218
1 [. . .] in all
2 [. . .] holy

Frg. 219
1 °[. . .]
2 and *hm*°[. . .]
3 there[52] [. . .]

Frg. 220
1 [. . .] festivals [. . .]
2 [. . .] *ly*[. . .]

Frg. 221
1 [. . .]*wl'l*[. . .]
2 [. . .]*qṣ*[. . .]

Frg. 222
1 [. . .] *h*[. . .]
2 [. . .]°*h* [. . .]

Frg. 223
1 [. . .]°[. . .]
2 [. . .] in *ṭh*[. . .]

Frg. 224
1 [. . .] not [. . .]
2 [. . .]*hm* [. . .]

Frg. 225
1 and I will punish [. . .]

Frg. 226
1 [. . .]*ḥr yb*[. . .]
2 [. . .]° [. . .]

Frg. 227
1 [. . .]°[. . .]
2 [. . .]*š* compassion[. . .]

Frg. 228
1 [. . .]*m* [. . .]
2 [. . .] in her mouth from [. . .]
3 [. . .]*l*[. . .]

Frg. 229
1 [. . .]*h nyt*
2 [. . .] and they will say

Frg. 230
1 [. . .]°°° us[53] [. . .]
2 [. . .]*b*°°*rw*[. . .]

Frg. 231
1 [. . .]°ᶜ *h*[. . .]
2 [. . .]°°[. . .]

Frg. 232
1 [. . .]*wb*°[. . .]
2 [. . .] *hgw*[. . .]

---

[52] Or "name."

[53] Or "our [. . .]°°°."

Frg. 235	*Frg. 234*	*Frg. 233*
1] ˚ [	1 [שׄרׄחׄ]	1 [˚כׄ]
2 [אׄתׄ]	2 [אׄוׄקׄ]	2 מ] רׄדׄנו בכחׄ]

Frg. 238	*Frg. 237*	*Frg. 236*
1 [טׄמׄאת]	1 [˚ ˚]	1 [אלׄ]
2 [לן	2 [ונפלאו]ת	2 [נׄו יתן]

Frg. 241	*Frg. 240*	*Frg. 239*
1 [בׄ] ˚ ˚]	1 [אׄ]	1 [שׄים]
2 [כׄיׄםׄ]	2 [אין]	2 [˚]

Frg. 244	*Frg. 243*	*Frg. 242*
1] ˚ [	1 [רׄכׄבׄ]	1 [בׄכליון]
	[שׄ	
2 [אלוהׄ]ים	2 [רׄאׄ]	2 [לׄ] [לׄ]

Frg. 247	*Frg. 246*	*Frg. 245*
1 [םׄ]	1 [בׄא]	1 [˚ [ ] ˚ [
2 [וׄתׄכ]	2 [דׄ ˚]	2 [דׄ וׄ ע]

Frg. 250	*Frg. 249*	*Frg. 248*
1 [אׄת עׄ]	1 [רׄו]	1 [םׄ]
2 [אׄורהׄ]	2 [רׄ]	2 [כׄת ˚]

Frg. 253	*Frg. 252*	*Frg. 251*
1 [בׄנׄ ˚ ˚]	1 [כׄאׄמׄרׄי]	1 [קׄ]
2] ˚ [	2 [דׄ]	2 [לׄ] [בׄה]

Frg. 256	*Frg. 255*	*Frg. 254*
1 [˚ יׄורׄדׄ ˚]	1 [ימׄיׄםׄ]	1 [לׄ]
2 [הׄ כׄ]	2 [לׄ ˚]	2 [יׄל הׄכׄ]

Frg. 259	*Frg. 258*	*Frg. 257*
1 [אל]	1 [וׄאׄ]	1 [דׄ רׄ]
2] ˚ [	2 [אׄת בׄ]	2 [הׄ בם]

Frg. 233

1 [...]*k* °[...]

2 [...] we [rev]olted against you [...]

Frg. 234

1 [...] *šrḥ*[...]

2 [...] *'wq*[...]

Frg. 235

1 [...]°[...]

2 [...] *'t*[...]

Frg. 236

1 [...]*'l*[...]

2 [...]us[54] *yt*[...]

Frg. 237

1 [...]°°[...]

2 [...] and wonder[s...]

Frg. 238

1 [...] impurity of [...]

2 [...]*l*[...]

Frg. 239

1 [...]*šym* [...]

2 [...]°[...]

Frg. 240

1 [...]*t* [...]

2 [...]*'y*[...]

Frg. 241

1 [...]*b*°°[...]

2 [...]*bym*[...]

Frg. 242

1 [...] in destruction [...]

2 [...]*l*[...]*l*[...]

Frg. 243

1 [...] ride [...]

2 [...]*r'*[...][55]

Frg. 244

1 [...]°[...]

2 [...] Go[d ...]

Frg. 245

1 [...]°[...]°[...]

2 [...]*k* and *'*[...]

Frg. 246

1 [...]*b'*[...]

2 [...]*d*°[...]

Frg. 247

1 [...]*m* [...]

2 [...]*wdk*[...]

Frg. 248

1 [...]*m*[...]

2 [...]*kt*°[...]

Frg. 249

1 [...]*rw* [...]

2 [...] *r*[...]

Frg. 250

1 [...] *'t* *'*[...]

2 [...]*'wrh*[...]

Frg. 251

1 [...]*q*

2 [...]*l*[...] *bh*

Frg. 252

1 [...] according to the words of [...]

2 [...]*d* [...]

Frg. 253

1 [...] *b*°*n*°°[...]

2 [...]°[...]

Frg. 254

1 [...]*ṣ*[...]

2 [...]*yl hk*[...]

Frg. 255

1 [...] days [...]

2 [...]°*l*[...]

Frg. 256

1 [...]°*ywrd*°[...]

2 [...]*h k*[...]

Frg. 257

1 [...]*y r*[...]

2 [...]*h bm*[...]

Frg. 258

1 [...] and *'*[...]

2 [...]*'t b*[...]

Frg. 259

1 [...]*'l* [...]

2 [...]°[...]

---

[54] Or "our [...]."

[55] Note the superlinear "[...]*š*."

Frg. 262	*Frg. 261*	*Frg. 260*
1] ֯ [	1]ֹ֯רֹ[	1] ֯ ֯ ֯ [
2] בכֹ[	2] ֯ רֹ [	2]אֹחד[

Frg. 265	*Frg. 264*	*Frg. 263*
	1]עֹ[	1] ֯ת [
1]כן	2] רֹ ֯[	2] ֯יֹ ֯ [

Frg. 268	*Frg. 267*	*Frg. 266*
1]הֹיֹו[	1]שעֹ[	1] ֯רֹות [
2]ל[	2]ס בֹ[	2] ֯ [

Frg. 271	*Frg. 270*	*Frg. 269*
1]שׁ ֯ ֯ ֯ נועֹ[	1]אה בֹ ֯ [	1]וֹא[
2] ֯ []֯ [	2] ֯ [	2] ֯יֹ[

Frg. 274	*Frg. 273*	*Frg. 272*
1]כֹ[	1]מֹוֹ[	1]שׁוֹכֹ ֯ [
2]רֹ[	2]שׁ[	2] ֯ ֯ [

Frg. 277, Col. 1	*Frg. 276*	*Frg. 275*
1]וחתֹם	1] ֯ ֯ [	1 א[פקוד על פרי גֹ]ודל לבב[32]
	2]מכול רעֹ ֯ [	

Frg. 279	*Frg. 278*	*Frg. 277, Col. 2*
1] ֯ בר עבֹוֹדֹ]ה	1] כבוד לֹ[	1 לֹוא קשׁ[

Frg. 282	*Frg. 281*	*Frg. 280*
1]מרוֹ ֯ [	1]וֹנוֹ אֹ ֯[	1]אֹין מנֹהֹ[

Frg. 285	*Frg. 284*	*Frg. 283*
1] אדֹנֹיֹ [	1]שׁלֹום [	1]עֹקרה [

Frg. 288	*Frg. 287*	*Frg. 286*
1]שׁפטֹ וֹ[	1]מולה עֹ[	1]הֹזה ולֹ[

Frg. 291	*Frg. 290*	*Frg. 289*
1] וֹבמֹ[	1]תכם [	1]נו בֹ[

---

[32] The citation from Isa 10:12 with *plene* writing is also found in
the Great Isaiah Scroll from Cave 1 (9:26): אפקוד על פרי גודל לבב.

Frg. 260

1 [...]°°°[...]

2 [...] one [...]

Frg. 261

1 [...]*yr*[...]

2 [...]°*r*[...]

Frg. 262

1 [...]°[...]

2 [...] *bk*[...]

Frg. 263

1 [...]*t* [...]

2 [...]*y*°[...]

Frg. 264

1 [...]ʿ[...]

2 [...]*r*°[...]

Frg. 265

1 *k*[...]

Frg. 266

1 [...]*rwt*°[...]

2 [...]°[...]

Frg. 267

1 [...]*š*ʿ[...]

2 [...]*m b*[...]

Frg. 268

1 [...]*hyw*[...]

2 [...]*l*[...]

Frg. 269

1 [...]*wʾ*[...]

2 [...] *y*[...]

Frg. 270

1 [...]ʾ*h b*°[...]

2 [...]°[...]

Frg. 271

1 [...]*š*°°°*nw*ʿ[...]

2 [...] °[...]°[...]

Frg. 272

1 [...]*šwk*°[...]

2 [...]°°[...]

Frg. 273

1 [...]*mw*[...]

2 [...]*š*[...]

Frg. 274

1 [...]*k*[...]

2 [...]*r*[...]

Frg. 275

1 [...I] will bring judgment upon the fruits of in[solence of heart...]

Frg. 276

1 [...]°°[...]

2 [...] from all evil °[...]

Frg. 277, Col. 1

1 [...]*wḥ* you

Frg. 277, Col. 2

1 not *qš*[...]

Frg. 278

1 [...] glory to [...]

Frg. 279

1 [...]°*br* servi[ce...]

Frg. 280

1 [...] there is not from *nh*[...]

Frg. 281

1 [...]*w* us[56] ʾ°[...]

Frg. 282

1 [...]*mrw*° [...]

Frg. 283

1 [...] barren [...]

Frg. 284

1 [...] peace [...]

Frg. 285

1 [...] Lord [...]

Frg. 286

1 [...] this [...] and *n*[...]

Frg. 287

1 [...] circumcision ʿ[...]

Frg. 288

1 [...]*špṭ* and [...]

Frg. 289

1 [...]us[57] *b*[...]

Frg. 290

1 [...]*tkm* [...]

Frg. 291

1 and *bm* [...]

[56] Or "our [...]*w*."

[57] Or "our [...]."

Frg. 294	*Frg. 293*	*Frg. 292*
1] םׄ לבׄהׄ [	1]לה[	1]יׄחׄ וׄן

Frg. 297	*Frg. 296*	*Frg. 295*
1]הׄעׄ[	1]דרד[	1] מׄעׄוׄלׄ[ם

Frg. 300	*Frg. 299*	*Frg. 298*
1]יׄפר[	1]ם אשׄי[ן	1] ׄ ׄ ם[ ]

Frg. 303	*Frg. 302*	*Frg. 301*
1]מׄאׄ[	1]ה הׄ ׄ[	1] אשׄ[

Frg. 306	*Frg. 305*	*Frg. 304*
1]תׄנׄו[	1] ׄ [	1]יׄ ד[
2] ׄ [	2]וׄ יׄעׄ[	

Frg. 309	*Frg. 308*	*Frg. 307*
1]אׄל [	1]זׄנׄו[	1]טהׄר[
2] ׄ [		

Frg. 312	*Frg. 311*	*Frg. 310*
1] ׄ [	1]כׄוׄ ׄ[	1]פׄ ׄ[
2]מׄוׄ[		

		Frg. 313
		1] בׄ[

Frg. 292

1 [...]*yḥ* and [...]

Frg. 293

1 [...] *lh*[...]

Frg. 294

1 [...]*m* her heart [...]

Frg. 295

1 [...] from eterni[ty...]

Frg. 296

1 [...] way [...]

Frg. 297

1 [...]*hʿ*[...]

Frg. 298

1 [...]*m* °°[...]

Frg. 299

1 [...]*m ʾšy*[...]

Frg. 300

1 [...] he will destroy [...]

Frg. 301

1 [...] *ʾš*[...]

Frg. 302

1 [...]*h h*°[...]

Frg. 303

1 [...]*mʾ*[...]

Frg. 304

1 [...]*y d*[...]

Frg. 305

1 [...]°[...]

2 [...]*r yʿ*[...]

Frg. 306

1 [...]*t* us[58] [...]

2 [...]°[...]

Frg. 307

1 [...] purified [...]

Frg. 308

1 [...]*z* us[59] [...]

Frg. 309

1 [...]*ʾl* [...]

2 [...]°[...]

Frg. 310

1 [...]*p*°[...]

Frg. 311

1 [...]*kw*°[...]

Frg. 312

1 [...]°[...]

2 [...]*mw*[...]

Frg. 313

1 [...] *b*[...]

[58] Or "our [...]*t*."

[59] Or "our [...]*z*."

Words of the Lights

(4Q504−506 = 4QDibHam^a-c)

DENNIS T. OLSON

Introduction

1. Contents

Glimpses into the Community piety of Qumran emerge out of the 182 fragments which make up the psalms in 4Q504−4Q506.[1] The psalms, or prayers, of 4Q504, 4Q505, and 4Q506 were apparently intended for liturgical usage within the setting of a weekly cycle of prayers. As an example, the prayers of 4Q504 reflect certain themes assigned for each day of the week. Thus, the first day of the week remembered the events of creation. The fourth day of the week, Wednesday, was the day of the covenant (4Q504 frg. 3 2.5, 13). Saturday was the day of praise (4Q504 frgs. 1−2 7.4) while the preceding prayers assigned to Friday (4Q504 frgs. 1−2 1.1−7.3) focus on the confession of sin and forgiveness. The fragments in 4Q504−506 are not presented in this edition in the random numerical order originally assigned to them. While often a difficult process, it is possible to reconstruct the sequence in which at least some of the fragments should be ordered. We may begin with 4Q504 which is the most complete of the three collections. Some of its fragments may be arranged in the following order on the basis of their titles, content, and place within the collection when discovered:[2]

Frg. 8 −−−− Title of the collection
Frg. 8 −−−− Beginning of the text. Creation and sin (Sunday?)
Frg. 5 −−−− (Monday? −− found underneath frg. 3)

Frg. 3 Col. 1 −−−− (Tuesday?)
    2.5 −−−− Covenant at Sinai (Wednesday)
Frg. 23
Frg. 21
Frg. 7
Frg. 18
Frg. 45
Frg. 6
Frg. 10
Frg. 4
Frg. 43
Frg. 40
Frgs. 1 and 2 Col. 1−7.2 −−−− (Friday)
    7.4 to the end of the text −−−− (Saturday)
Frgs. 1−2 7.3-end −− Conclusion?

In terms of some of the other fragments in 4Q504, fragment 17 2.5 appears to mark the end of a section with the word "Amen." Fragment 28 probably immediately preceded fragment 29, and fragment 33 immediately preceded fragment 41.

The prayers of 4Q505 are so fragmentary as to defy any clear ordering. However, the prayers in 4Q506 have some parallels to the prayers in 4Q504 and thus the original sequence of some of the fragments may be reconstructed as follows: frg. 124, frg. 157, frg. 129(?), frgs. 125 and 127, frg. 126, frgs. 131−132.

---

[1] M. Baillet's first work on 4Q504 included "Psaumes, hymnes, cantiques et prières dans les manuscrits de Qumrân," in *Le Psautier: Ses orignes. Ses problèmes littéraires. Son influence* (Orientalia et Biblica Lovaniensia 4; Louvain, 1962) pp. 389−405. Baillet first published 4Q504 frgs. 1−2 and frg. 8 with extensive notes in "Un recueil liturgique de Qumrân, grotte 4: 'Les Paroles des Luminaires'," *RB* 68 (1961) 195−250; and Pls. XXIV-XXVIII.
Some changes in readings and other reinterpretations for 4Q504 were suggested by K.G. Kuhn, "Nachträge zur Konkordanz zu den Qumrantexten," *RQ* 4 (1963) 163−234 and by M.R. Lehmann, "A Re-interpretation of 4Q Dibrê ham-

Me'oroth," *RQ* 5 (1964) 106−110. Consult Baillet, "Remarques sur l'édition des Paroles des Luminaires," *RQ* 5 (1964) 23−42. Baillet published the prayers of 4Q504−4Q506 in their entirety in DJD 7, pp. 137−75.

[2] The reconstructions of the original sequence of the fragments presented here have been suggested by Baillet, DJD 7, pp. 138, 170. He is in part dependent on the initial work on this collection by J. Starcky who was responsible for the ordering of frgs. 1−2 and for separating some of the fragments which were found stuck together one on top of the other. Cf. J. Starcky, "Le travail d'édition des fragments manuscrits de Qumrân," *RB* 63 (1956) 66.

B. Nitzan analyzes the structure of the individual prayers of the *Words of the Lights* and finds them to be fairly regular and similar to the *Prayers for Festivals* (1Q34–34bis, 4Q507–9).[3] Each prayer contains a heading specifying the time of the prayer ("Thanksgiving for the day of..."). The prayers begin by petitioning God to remember ("Remember, O Lord, that") followed by a series of historical remembrances and petitions which form the body of the prayer.[4] The prayers close with a blessing ("Blessed be the Lord who... us...") followed by a congregational response ("Amen. Amen."). Divisions between prayers are often indicated by a vacat and, in the case of 4Q504, occasionally by special characters.

2. Date and Provenience

The dates of the three manuscripts are varied. The Hasmonaean script of 4Q504 places it sometime around 150 B.C.E. The script of 4Q505 seems to be from later in the Hasmonaean period, perhaps 70–60 B.C.E. The prayers of 4Q506 are written in a script with some later forms which correspond to those found in post-Herodian ossuaries and which suggest a date sometime in the first century C.E.[5] As to the origins of these prayers, the reader will note that the themes or vocabulary which are peculiar to the Qumran Community are largely absent in this liturgical material.[6] Thus, these prayers may have been inherited from an earlier Jewish community to which the Qumran Community was the spiritual heir.[7] The number of copies, spanning the history of the Community, suggests that the prayers were valued by the Community and probably were used in worship at Qumran.

3. Relation to the Hebrew Bible and Other Jewish Writings

One important issue which arises out of this collection of prayers is the interpretation of the title for the prayers in 4Q504 fragment 8, דברי המאורות. We have literally translated the title as "The Words of the Lights." However, the Hebrew word דברי has a wide semantic range, including "matters" (1Chr 27:1), daily "duties" or "liturgies" (1Chr 16:37; Ezra 3:4), "acts" (2Chr 13:22), or "things" (Isa 42:16). Thus, one might translate the title as "The Liturgies of the Lights" or "The Acts of the Lights."

What then are the "Lights" to which the title refers? One possibility is that the "Lights" refer to the stars which in turn are sometimes identified as symbols of the heavenly angels which are intelligent beings capable of speech. One finds this association of

stars and angels in 4Q511 as well as in *1 Enoch* 86:1, 3; 88:1. Hence, the title may refer to the words of the stars or angels which the Community uses for its own prayers.

More probable, however, is the association of the "words" or "liturgies" to the daily and monthly cycles of "Lights" including the sun, moon, and stars. The Qumran Community sought to adhere closely to the 364-day solar calendar which used the heavenly lights to regulate its liturgies and festivals. In the Priestly account of creation in Genesis 1, the "lights" are created on the fourth day of the week, Wednesday, which in this perspective may be considered the most important day of the week.[8] The importance of the regulation function of the "lights" in Early Judaism is also indicated by the title of the section in *1 Enoch* 72–82, "The Book of the Itinerary of the Luminaries of Heaven" (*1En* 72:1). The title of 4Q504 may then mean "The Liturgies (according to the Cycle of Heavenly) Lights."

Yet another possibility is that the "Lights" refer to the priests who are seen as intermediaries of the heavenly light from God. In Sirach 45:17, the high priest Aaron is depicted as the vehicle of God's light to the people. The *Testament of Levi* attributes this same function to Levi the priest (4:3), and the priest who is to come (18:3–4), both of whom are compared to the sun. The association of priests and light is also found in the sectarian Qumran material itself. In 1QS 2.3, the light of wisdom is part of the blessing of the priests. A sectarian prayer from Qumran requests that God make the priest "a great light for the world" through wisdom, thus enlightening the face of the people (1QSb 4.27). In a different context, a saying attributed to Jesus uses a similar image as he charges his disciples: "You are the light of the world."[9] One of the sources for this image may be the ancient Aaronic blessing in Numbers 6:25 in which the priests are instructed to bless the people using the image of divine light shining upon the people: "The Lord make his face to shine upon you, and be gracious to you." This association of the "Lights" and the function of the priests would suggest an understanding of the title, "Words of the Lights" as "Words/Prayers/Liturgies of the Priests."

Whatever the precise meaning of the superscription "The Words of the Lights," the psalmic prayers of 4Q504, 4Q505, and 4Q506 appear to be daily prayers or liturgies used in weekly cycles which were led by priests from within the Community. The prayers build upon biblical phrases and images and span the range of prayer from confession of sin to praise, from lament of the Community's rebellions to the remembrance of God's covenant faithfulness.

---

[3] See B. Nitzan, *Qumran Prayer and Religious Poetry* (STDJ 12; Leiden, 1994) esp. the summary on p. 71.

[4] See E. G. Chazon's discussion of the progression of the historical remembrances ("*4QDibHam*: Liturgy or Literature?" *RQ* 15 [1991–1992] 447–55).

[5] Baillet, DJD 7, pp. 137, 168, 170.

[6] See Chazon, "Is *Divrei ha-Me'orot* a Sectarian Prayer?" in *The Dead Sea Scrolls: Forty Years of Research,* edited by D. Dimant and U. Rappaport (STDJ 10; Leiden, 1992) pp. 3–17.

[7] Chazon persuasively argues that the collection is shaped by the chronological progression of historical remembrances, and that this structure indicates that the collection in its present form is a unitary composition. See Chazon, *RQ* 15 (1991–1992) 447–55.

[8] A. Jaubert, *La date de la Cena* (Paris, 1957) pp. 24, 26–27, 42–44.

[9] Mt. 5:14. Cf. Baillet, DJD 7, pp. 138–39.

4. Selected Bibliography

Baillet, M. "Paroles des luminaires," DJD 7, pp.137–177; and Pls. XXIII-XXIV, XLIX-LIII.

Chazon, E. G. "Is *Divrei ha-Me'orot* a Sectarian Prayer?" In *The Dead Sea Scrolls: Forty Years of Research*, edited by D. Dimant and U. Rappaport. STDJ 10; Leiden, 1992, pp. 3–17.

Chazon, E. G. "*4QDibHam:* Liturgy or Literature?" *RQ* 15 (1991–2) 447–55.

Nitzan, B. *Qumran Prayer and Religious Poetry*. STDJ 12; Leiden, 1994.

Tov, E. *The Dead Sea Scrolls on Microfiche*. Leiden, 1993 [4Q504; PAM 41.141, 41.463, 41.515, 41.677, 41.951, 42.010, 42.033, 42.184, 42.439, 43.611, 43.612, 43.613, 43.626, 43.630, 43.869; 4Q505: PAM 40.629, 42.060, 42.497, 43.635, 43.653, 43.655, 43.859; 4Q506: PAM 40.628, 40.981, 42.059, 42.061, 42.063, 42.489, 42.498, 43.652, 43.654, 43.656, 43.658, 43.858, 43.860, 43.865].

Words of the Lights
(4Q504)

Frg. 8 back

1   דברי המֿאֿרֿות

Frg. 8 front

זכו]רֿ אד]ו]נֿי [כֿיא מֿעֿמֿ[1

[קֿתנו ואתה חֿי עולֿ]ם   2

[°̊ נפלאות מקדם ונוראוֿתֿ[3

אדם א]בֿיֿנו יצרתה בדמות כבודֿ[4

נ]פֿחֿתה באפו ובינה ודעֿתה[5

ג]ן עדן אשר נטעתהֿ² המשלֿתֿה[6

[ם ולתהלך בארץ כבֿוד אֿ[7

אֿ] שמר ותקם עליו לבלתי סֿ[8

[בֿשֿר הואה ולעפר הֿ³[9

[תֿו ואתה ידֿעתה [10

[לדֿורות עולֿם[11

[אל חי וידכֿהֿ[12

[הֿאדם בדרכֿי[13

[אֿרֿץ   14
ח]מֿס ולשֿפֿוֿ]ך

---

¹ **Cf. MT** Gen 2:7: וייצר יהוה אלהים את־האדם עפר מן־האדמה
ויפח באפיו נשמת חיים ויהי האדם לנפש חיה ;and possibly 4Q7
(4QGen MS g):].וי/ייצר י]°̊ .

² **Cf. MT** Gen 2:8: ויטע יהוה אלהים גן־בעדן מקדם וישם שם
את־האדם אשר יצר.

³ **Cf. MT** Gen 3:19b: כי־עפר אתה ואל־עפר תשוב.

Words of the Lights
(4Q504)

Frg. 8 back

1 The Words of the Lights

Frg. 8 front

1 [. . .   Rememb]er, O L[o]r[d,] that *mᶜm*[. . .]

2 [. . .]*qtnw* and you living forev[er . . .]

3 [. . .]° wonders from ancient time(s) and marvels [. . .]

4 [. . .Adam] our [fa]ther you formed in the image of glory [. . .]

5 [. . .] you [b]lew in his nose and discernment and knowledge [¹ . . .]

6 [. . . gar]den of Eden which you planted.² You made to rule [. . .]

7 [. . .]*m* and to walk about in the land of glory ʾ[. . .]

8 [. . .]ʾ he kept and you imposed upon him not *s*[. . .]

9 [. . .] he (is) flesh and to dust *h*[³. . .]

10 [. . .]*tw* and you knew [. . .]

11 [. . .] to generations forever [. . .]

12 [. . .] living God and your hand [. . .]

13 [. . .] the man in the ways of [. . .]

14 [. . .] earth⁴ [. . .vio]lence and to pour o[ut. . .]

---

¹ Cf. Gen 2:7: "And Yahweh God formed the human [or "Adam"] (from) the dust of the ground and blew in his nose the breath of life, and the human [or "Adam"] became a living soul."

² Cf. Gen 2:8: "And Yahweh God planted a garden eastward in Eden and placed there the human [or "Adam"] whom he had formed."

³ Cf. Gen 3:19b: "for you (are) dust and to dust you shall return."

⁴ Written supralinearly.

Frg. 5, Col. 1

1   ש[למֹנֹיֹכֹה

2   [תֹ עשיתה

3   [שם עולם ולרֹא]וֹתֹ

4   גב[וֹרתכֹה לדורוֹתֹ]

5   [   ]

6   [לֹיכה בשמיֹ]ם ובא[רֹץֹ

7   [דֹם אֹ   [תֹה

8   [תֹועים

Frg. 5, Col. 2

1   בזרעם אחריהֹם לֹ]וֹ

2   קודש עֹומד לפניכֹ]הֹ

3   [זֹ]כֹורֹ אֹדוני כיא שֹ]

4   [   ]ֹ וֹבך נחגה גאל[תנוֹ

5   בֹפשעינו ולתור בֹשֹ]

6   הרעֹ בעיניכה צוֹיתֹ]

7   וכאשר בֹנפשֹ]

8   לביֹנתכה וֹלֹ]

Frg. 3, Col. 1

14   [אֹוֹ

15   [ֹינו

16   [ֹחנו

17   [ֹ ו לעשוֹֹ^ת

18   [בֹֹהֹ

19   [ֹ

---

4 Cf. 4Q506 frg. 124 line 2: .[ריהם לֹ].
5 Cf. 4Q505 frg. 124 line 7: .[קֹרֹוש עומד לפֹנֹ].
6 Cf. 4Q506 frg. 124 line 3: .[זכֹורֹהֹ].

7 Cf. 4Q506 frg. 124 line 4: .[הֹ גאלתֹנֹוֹ].
8 Cf. 4Q506 frg. 124 line 5: .[שֹוֹתֹ הרֹ].
9 Read לעשֹות.

Frg. 5, Col. 1

1 [...] your [g]ifts

2 [...]*t* you did

3 [...] name forever and to s[e]e

4 [...] your [stren]gth to generations [...]

5 [....] [...]

6 [...]*lykh* in the heaven[s and on the e]arth

7 [...]°*dm* '[...]*th*

8 [...] confusions

Frg. 5, Col. 2

1 with their seed after them *l*[...]

2 holiness standing before yo[u....]

3 [Re]member, O Lord, that *š*[...]

4 [...]°*wbk* let us celebrate the festival of [our] redempt[ion...]

5 in our transgressions and to spy out *bš*[...]

6 the evil in your eyes.   You commanded [...]

7 and according to the soul [...]

8 to your discernment and *k*[...]

Frg. 3, Col. 1

14 [...] then

15 [...]°*ynw*

16 [...]°*ḥnw*

17 [...]°*w* to do

18 [...]*b*°*h*

19 [...]°

Frg. 3, Col. 2

1	[מ]
2	[ים בר]וך הא[ל]ה[ניחנו]
3	[אמן]
4	[ ]
5	ביו[ם הרביעי זכור אדוני]
6	[°ליכה יתקדש בכבו]ד
7	עין [ב]עין[¹⁰ נראיתה בקרבנו]
8	[א ודברי קודשך שמע]נו
9	[כ]ה עלפנינו לבלתי נ[°]
10	קו[ד]שכה הגדו[ל]
11	[א]רץ התבו[ן]¹¹
12	[ו]בעבור נאמין [¹²
13	לעולם ותכרות אתנו ברית בחו[ר]רב¹³
14	על כול החו[ק]י[ם והמשפטים הא]לה
15	והטו[ב] [ים וקדושי]ם ו[
16	אשר] [מושה ול°מ] דב[ת]ה
17	בכול] [פ]נים אל פנים או[ת]ו¹⁴
18	כבו]ד [רצית]ו וימצאו]¹⁵
19	[ה]מה בידו¹⁶ לעיני[נ]

Frg. 23

1	[° ק]
2	[פקודי]ה
3	[° °]

---

¹⁰ For formulaic restoration, cf. Num 14:14.
¹¹ 4Q505 frg. 124 line 2: [. °ל הא[.
¹² Cf. 4Q505 frg. 124 line 3: [° ה ובעבו]ר.
¹³ For possible restoration, cf. Deut 5:2.

¹⁴ 4Q506 frgs. 125 and 127 line 2: [. °ים אל פ°נ[ ]ב°רתה ע[°.
¹⁵ 4Q506 frgs. 125 and 127 line 3: [. °רצ°יתו[ ]א°ו ח°ן ב°ע[.
¹⁶ Read בידיו.

Frg. 3, Col. 2

1 [. . .]*m*[. . .]

2 [. . .]*ym*. Blessed is Go[d] who gives us rest [. . .]

3 [. . . .] Amen. (vacat) [. . .]

4 [. . .] [. . .]

5 [. . . on] the fourth [da]y. Remember, O Lord, [. . .]

6 [. . .]°*lykh* he makes himself holy with glory [. . .]

7 [. . .eye] to eye you have been seen in our midst [. . .]

8 [. . .]' and your holy words w[e] have heard [. . .]

9 [. . .] your [. . .] before us so that we do not °[. . .]

10 [. . .] your great [holi]ness [. . .]

11 [. . .] earth *htbw*[. . .]

12 [. . .] and in order that we would believe [. . .]

13 forever. And you have made with us a covenant on Ho[reb. . .]

14 upon all the[se] statu[te]s and precepts [. . .]

15 and the good [. . .]*ym* and Holy Ones and[. . .]

16 who [. . .] Moses and *k*°*m*[. . .]

17 in all [. . .] face to face yo[u] spoke[5] with [him . . .]

18 glor[y. . .] you were pleased with him and they found [. . .]

19 [. . .] they in his hands to our eyes [. . .]

Frg. 23

1 [. . .]°*q*[. . .]

2 [. . .] appointment [. . .]

3 [. . .]° °[. . .]

---

[5] The phrase "yo[u] spoke," which has been added above the
line, refers to God speaking to Moses. The gloss here is in the
main body of the parallel text in 4Q506 frg. 127 line 1.

Frg. 21

1   [אֹ רֹאִינֹוֹ]

2   [רֹגליכֹהֹ]

3   [אֹ לֹוֹא]

Frg. 7

1   את מֹישר תֹהֹ[

2   נפ[לֹאים אשר עשיתֹהֹ

     יִשׁרֹאל

3   לספר דורות עולם [

4   מֹעֹשֹי ידיכה[

5   לכבודכה רֹ [°

      רֹ

6   תקצֹ[17] הֹיֹאה לוא

7   ממכה כוֹל צֹר[

8   ה היאה [°

9   שמתה שימה[18]

      וֹ

10   שׁ ואל תטושנֹ[19]

11   רֹך וברחמיכה[

12   שֹוֹת קדמנו[

13   נשאתה א[שר

14   המרו בֹר אשר[

      ס

15   וימצאוכֹהֹ וֹינכוה[20] [°

16   האמינו רֹ לֹ[ ] [

17   ראו הֹא ר[

18   עינים[ ] לֹ[

19   ב]רֹוֹך

20   [°

---

17 Read תקצֹר.
18 See Aramaic סימא.

19 Read תטושנו.
20 Read וֹינסכוֹה.

Frg. 21

1 [. . .] we saw '[. . .]

2 [. . .] your feet [. . .]

3 [. . .] not '[. . .]

Frg. 7

1 [. . .]*th* straightness '*t*

2 [. . .wond]rous things which you have done

3 [. . .] so that [I]srael[6] will recount (for) eternal generations

4 [. . .] works of your hands

5 [. . .]°*r* to your glory

6 [. . .] she was not shortened

7 [. . .]*ṣr* from you all

8 [. . .]°*h* she

9 [. . .] you have set a treasure

10 [. . .]*š* and do not forsake us

11 [. . .]*rk* and in your compassions

12 [. . .]*šwt* we have met

13 [. . .w]hich you lifted up

14 [. . .]*br* who have shown bitterness

15 [. . .] and they poured it out and they found you

16 [. . .]*r l*[. . .] they trusted

17 [. . .]*r* they saw there

18 [. . .]*l*[. . .] eyes

19 [. . .bl]essed

20 [. . .]°

---

6 The word "[I]srael" has been added above the line.

Frg. 18

1	]הֿנו לֿ]ֿ ֿת ֿ[
2	נ]תֿתה להמה לבֿ[
3	] לראות ואוזנ]ים'[²¹
4	ל[אֿחרון ותשעֿ[
5	]אֿרוֿח בֿ[
6	]רֿ מֿבֿ[

Frg. 45

1	]ֿ ֿ[

---

21 Perhaps an adaptation of Deut 29:3: ולא־נתן יהוה לכם לב   ֿוֿ. [ ]אֿ[ ]עד היום הֿזה (4QDeut MS l):
לדעת ועינים לראות ואזנים לשמע עד היום הזה ;4Q39

Frg. 18

1 [...]*hnw l*[...]°*t*° [...]

2 [...] you have [gi]ven to them a heart [...]

3 [...] to see and ear[s...]⁷

4 [... to] the last and you shut [...]

5 [...] wander in [...]

6 [...]*r mk*[...]

Frg. 45

1 [...]°[...]

---

⁷ Perhaps an adaptation of Deut 29:3: "And Yahweh has not
given to you a heart to know and eyes to see and ears to hear to
this day."

Frg. 6

[דם וכ]	1
[ת ופרי מחשבת אש]	2
[ה להתבונן בכול חוק]י	3
[שר תבואתה להתבו]נן	4
[ור א] [ת בעלילותיכה תמיד]	5
ז[כור נא כיא עמכה כולנו ותשאנו פלא]י[ם]	6
[נשרים ותביאנו אליכה²² וכנשר יעיר קנו]	7
[ירחף יפרוש כנפיו ויקח וישאהו על²³]	8
[[ש]כנו בדד ובגוים לוא נתחשב²⁴ וא]	9
[אתה בקרבנו בעמוד אש וענן ב[²⁵]	10
קוד]שכה הולך לפנינו וכבודכה בתוכ]נו	11
[פני מושה עב]דכה	12
[כיא אתה ה]	13
ונקה	
[ה ולוא תנק]ה²⁶	14
[כיסר איש]	15
[שים וטהור]	16
[אדם וחי בם²⁷ ב]	17
ש[ב]ו[ע]ה אשר נשב[עתה]	18
[ים בפניכה] [ה]	19
[ברוך אדוני]	20
[נחקר גדולות]	21
[רוח כול ח]י	22

---

22 Cf. MT Ex 19:4: אתם ראיתם אשר עשיתי למצרים ואשא אתכם על-כנפי נשרים ואבא אתכם אלי.

23 The scribe first wrote אל, then changed it to על. Cf. Deut 32:11 from which the phrase seems to derive: כנשר יעיר קנו על-גוזליו ירחף יפרש כנפיו יקחהו ישאהו על-אברתו.

24 Cf. MT Num 23:9b: הן-עם לבדד ישכן ובגוים לא יתחשב.

25 Cf. MT Ex 13:21: ויהוה הלך לפניהם יומם בעמוד ענן לנחתם הדרך ולילה בעמוד אש להאיר להם ללכת יומם ולילה; and 4Q14 (4QExod MS c): ר ענן לנחותם [בעמ] [ם] [לפניהם]

שמעו כי- אתה יהוהבקרב MT Num 14:14b: [ ]הדר; ולילה העם הזה אשר-עין בעין נראה אתה יהוה ועננך עמד עלהם ובעמד ענן אתה הלך לפניהם יומם ובעמוד אש לילה; and Ex 14:24.

26 Cf. MT Num 14:18: יהוה ארך אפים ורב-חסד נשא עון ופשע ונקה לא ינקה פקד עון אבות על-בנים על-שלשים ועל-רבעים.

27 Cf. MT Lev 18:5: ושמרתם את-חקתי ואת-משפטי אשר יעשה אתם האדם וחי בהם אני יהוה.

Frg. 6

1 [...]*dm* and *k*[...]

2 [...]*t* and the fruits of the thoughts of '*š*[...]

3 [...]*h* to discern all the statute[s of...]

4 [...]*šr* her produce to disc[ern...]

5 [...]*wr* '[...]*t* in your deeds continually [...]

6 [.... Re]member now that all of us (are) your people, and you have lifted us up (as) wonder[s...]

7 [...] eagles and you brought us to you.[8] And as an eagle stirs up its nest [...]

8 [...] he will hover, he will spread out his wings, and he will take and lift him up upon[9] [...]

9 [...]°[...] we [dw]elt alone and we did not count ourselves among the nations[10] and '[...]

10 [...]° you (were) in our midst in a pillar of fire and a cloud *b*[[11]...]

11 [...] your [holin]ess going before us, and your glory in [our] midst [...]

12 [...] face of Moses [your] serv[ant...]

13 [...] for you *h*[...]

14 [...]*h* and you certainly will not leave unpunish[ed[12]...]

15 [...] as a man disciplines [...]

16 [...]*šym* and pure [...]

17 [...] a person and he will live in them *b*[[13]...]

18 [... o]a[t]h which [you] swo[re...]

19 [...]*ym* in your faces [...]*ḥ*[...]

20 [....] Blessed is the Lord [...]

21 [...] we have explored great (deeds) [...]

22 [...] spirit of every living thing [...]

---

8 Cf. Ex 19:4: "You saw what I did to the Egyptians, and I lifted you up on the wings of eagles and brought you to me."

9 Cf. Deut 32:11: "As an eagle rouses its nest, upon its young it will hover, it will spread out its wings, it will take and lift it upon its feathers."

10 Cf. Num 23:9b: "Behold, a people dwells alone and does not count itself among the nations."

11 Cf. Ex 13:21: "And Yahweh was going before them by day in a pillar of cloud to lead them (along) the way, and by night in a pillar of fire to give them light so that they may go by day and by night;" Num 14:14b: "They have heard that you, O Yahweh, (are) in the midst of this people, where you, O Yahweh, are seen eye to eye, and your cloud stands over them, and in a pillar of cloud you walk before them by day and in a pillar of fire by night;" and Ex 14:24.

12 An infinitive absolute form of the same verb already in the text, "to leave unpunished," has been added above the line. The result is an emphatic form of the verb: "and you will certainly not leave unpunished." The phrase is a frequent biblical idiom with alternate forms which are reflected here in the original and corrected texts. Cf. Exod 20:7: "You shall not lift up the name of Yahweh your God in vain, for Yahweh will not leave unpunished the one lifting up his name in vain;" and Num 14:18: "Yahweh (is) slow (to) anger and abounding (in) mercy, forgiving iniquity and transgression, but he will certainly not leave (it) unpunished, visiting iniquity of the fathers upon the sons, upon the third and upon the fourth (generation)."

13 Cf Lev 18:5: "You shall keep my statutes and my precepts which a person shall do and he will live in them: I (am) Yahweh."

Frg. 10

1　[הגשתנו]

2　[ובתוכנו עו]ן

3　[נראה עלינ]ו

4　[ת̇י̇ה ירא]ן

Frg. 4

1　[ ]°[ ]או[ן

2　[שר רציתה ל]ד̇ורות̇[ן][28]

3　[ארץ ועבודת כול ה]ן[29]

4　כי]א̇ אתה̇ אל הדעות̇[ן][30]ו̇[כ̇ול מחשב̇][31]

5　לפניכ]ה̇ אלה ידענו באשר חנוא̇ת̇[ן][32] ו̇[רוח ק̇]נ̇ודש[33]

6　ואל תז]כ̇ור לנו עוונות רשונים[34] בכול ג̇מולם הר̇[ע][35]

7　[בעורפם][36] אתה פ̇דינו וסלח̇[ן]לעווננו ולח̇[טתנו][37]

8　ק̇י̇כ̇ה תורה̇ אשר צו̇]יתה ב̇]י̇ד מ̇ו̇ש̇]ה

9　[ ]°[ל̇]ן [ ]אשר °° [ ]בכ̇]ו̇[ל]ן

10　[כ̇והנים וגוי קדוש]

11　א[שר בח̇רת מולה עורלת̇][38]

12　[ ]°[ל̇]ן [ ]עוד חזק לבנו ל̇עשות̇]ן

13　ל]לכת בדרכיכה]

14　 אדוני אשר הודי]ע

15　[אמן אמן]

16　[אדוני שם קו̇דשכ̇]ה

---

[28] 4Q506 frgs. 131-132 line 7: ת̇ה ה̇י̇ו̇[.

[29] 4Q506 frgs. 131-132 line 8: ר̇ץ̇ ו̇ע̇]ת̇ה לו ב̇ט̇[.

[30] 4Q506 frgs. 131-132 line 9: ב̇ם כ̇י̇א̇[ת̇ .

[31] 4Q506 frgs. 131-132 lines 9-10: ו̇כ̇ול] ש̇ב̇ת̇ [.

[32] 4Q506 frgs. 131-132 lines 10-11: נ̇י̇כה אלה ידענו[שר] א̇ת̇[.

[33] 4Q506 frgs. 131-132 line 11: ה̇קודש רחמנו [.

[34] Cf. MT Ps 79:8: אל־תזכר־לנו עונת ראשנים מהר יקדמונו רחמיך כי דלונו מאד .

[35] 4Q506 frgs. 131-132 lines 12-13: ל̇ [ ] הרישנים̇ [תזכו] א̇ב̇ו̇ת̇י̇נ̇ו̇ ג̇מ̇ו̇] .

[36] 4Q506 frgs. 131-132 line 13: ש̇ו̇ בעור̇פ̇ם] .

[37] 4Q506 frgs. 131-132 line 14: ט̇תנו] . Cf. MT Ex 34:9: ויאמר אם־נא מצאתי חן בעיניך אדני ילד־נא אדני בקרבנו כי עם־קשה־ערף הוא וסלחת לעוננו ולחטאתנו ונחלתנו .

[38] Cf. MT Deut 10:15-16: רק באבתיך חשק יהוה לאהבה אותם ויבחר בזרעם אחריהם בכם מכל־העמים כיום הזה ; and 4Q39 (4QDeut MS l): א̇ת̇ם̇] . Perhaps עוד in the next line concludes the adaptation of these verses. ומלתם את ערלת לבבכם וערפכם לא תקשו עוד

Frg. 10

1 [...] you have brought us near [...]

2 [...] and in our midst ʿw[...]

3 [...] he appeared upon u[s...]

4 [...]tʿyh yrʾ[...]

Frg. 4

1 [...]°[...]ʾw[...]

2 [...]šr you are pleased [for] generations [...]

3 [...] earth and the service of all h[...]

4 [...becau]se you, the God of knowledge [and] every design [...]

5 [...before yo]u.   These (things) we know because you have been gracious [...]   H[oly] Spirit [...]

6 [...and do not re]member against us the iniquities the ancestors¹⁴ with all their ev[il] conduct [...]

7 [...] in their neck, you redeem us and forgive our iniquity and [our] s[in¹⁵...]

8 [...]qykh Torah which [you] comman[ded] by the hand of Mose[s...]

9 [...]° l[...] who °°[...] in a[l]l [...]

10 [...] priests and a holy nation [...]

11 [...w]hom you chose.   Circumcision of the foreskin of [¹⁶...]

12 [...]° r [...] any longer.   Strengthen our heart to do [...]

13 [...to] walk in your ways [...]

14 [...] Lord who has made know[n...]

15 [...] Amen.   Amen.   (vacat) [...]

16 [...] Lord, yo[ur] holy name [...]

---

¹⁴ Lit. "former ones." Cf. Ps 79:8: "Do not remember against us the iniquities of the former ones; let your compassions come to us quickly for we are exceedingly lowly."

¹⁵ Cf. Ex. 34:9: "And he said, 'If I have found favor in your eyes, let the Lord go, O Lord, in our midst, although this (is) a stiff-necked people, pardon our iniquity and our sin, and take us as your inheritance.'"

¹⁶ Cf. Deut 10:15−16: "Surely Yahweh attached (his) love to your fathers alone, and chose their seed after them, (that is) you, from all the peoples as (it is) this day. Circumcise the foreskin of your heart, and do not stiffen your neck any longer."

17   ˚רֹ למענכה ועֹל דברֹ]יכה [

18   ˚˚ך [ ] [מֹ רב

19   ˚ו פשֹע] [בֹ [

20   את רוֹח]

21   וערֹת מֹוֹדֹה]

22   ם לתפֹש ב]

Frg. 43

1   הֹ] [

Frg. 40

1   ˚מֹ ˚]

2   [ ]˚

Frg. 1, Col. 1

7   אמן אמן]

8   ו נפלאות]

9   ממצרים [

10   מ]דבר

17 [. . .]°*r* for your sake and on account of [your] word[s . . .]

18 [. . .]°°*k* [. . .]*m rb*[. . .]

19 [. . .]°*w* transgression [. . .]*b*[. . .]

20 [. . .]ʾ*t* spirit [. . .]

21 [. . .]*wˁrt* giving thanks [. . .]

22 [. . .]*m* to seize *b*[. . .]

Frg. 43

1 [. . .] *h*[. . .]

Frg. 40

1 [. . .]*mw*°[. . .]

2 [. . .]°[. . .]

Frg. 1, Col. 1

7 [. . .] Amen. Amen.

8 [. . .]*w* wonders

9 [. . .] from Egypt

10 [. . .wi]lderness

Frg. 1, Col. 2

6   [ ]   ̊[ ] ̊[ ] ̊[ ][ת̊יכה]

7   אנא אדׄני עשה נׄא כׄמׄוׄכה כגדול כוׄחׄכׄה אׁשׁ[ר נ]שׁאתׄ[ה]

8   לאבותינו בהמרותם את פיכה[39] ותתאנף בם להשמידׄם ותחס

9   עליהמה באהבׄתכה אותם ולמׄען בריתכׄה כיא כפׄר מׄושה

10   בעד חטאתם[40] ולמען דעת את כוחכה הגׄדול ואת רובׄ חׄסׄדׄכׄ[ה]
                            על כול חטׄ[אתם][41]

11   לדורות עולם ישוב נא אפכה וחמתכה מעׄמכה ישראל וזכרתה

12   אׄת נפלאותיכה אשר עשיתה לעני גוים כיא נׄקרׄ[42] שמכה עלינו

13   [ל̊] [ ]בׄנו בכול לב ובכול נפש ולטעת תורתכה בלבנׄוׄ
                             וׄל̊סור

14   [מ̊]ימין ושמאול כיא תרפאנו משגעון ותמהון

15   בע[וׄוׄנותינו נמכרנו ובפשעינו קרתנו[43]

16   ] והצלתנו מחטוא לכה

17   ] ̊ת̊ ולהביננו לתעודות

18   ]לוׄת̊ אתה עשיתם

19   ]ם̊ וׄפׄעׄולתׄם̊

---

[39] Cf. MT Num 14:19: סלח־נא לעון העם הזה כגדל חסדך וכאשר; and Deut 1:26 (cf. 9:23): נשאתה לעם הזה ממצרים ועד־הנה ולא אביתם לעלת ותמרו את־פי יהוה אלהיכם.

[40] Cf. MT Ex 32:30: ויהי ממחרת ויאמר משה אל־העם אתם חטאתם חטאה גדלה ועתה אעלה אל־יהוה אולי אכפרה בעד חטאתכם; and 4Q22 (4QpaleoExod MS m): [ ]ויהי ממוחרׄתׄ[משה אל ה̊ע̊]חטאה גדׄולה ועתה אעלה אל י̊[ ].

[41] Cf. MT Dan 9:16: אדני ככל־צדקתך ישב־נא אפך וחמתך מעירך ירושלם הר־קדשך כי בחטאינו ובעונות אבתינו ירושלם ועמך לחרפה לכל־סביבתינו; Deut 9:18: ואתנפל לפני יהוה כראשנה ארבעים יום וארבעים לילה לחם לא אכלתי ומים לא שתיתי על כל־חטאתכם אשר חטאתם לעשות הרע בעיני יהוה להכעיסו; and 4Q504 frgs. 1-2 6.11: ישוב נא אפכה וחמתכה ממנו.

[42] Read נׄקרׄא.

[43] קרתנו is defective writing for קראתנו. Cf. קראתי in Isa 50:1-2a, the source from which this line has apparently been adapted; MT: כה אמר יהוה אי זה ספר כריתות אמכם אשר שלחתיה או מי מנושי אשר־מכרתי אתכם לו הן בעונתיכם נמכרתם ובפשעיכם שלחה אמכם מדוע באתי ואין איש קראתי ואין עונה היד קצרה ידי מפדות ואם־אין־בי כח להציל; and 1QIsa MS a: כוה אמר יהוה אי זה ספר כריתות אמכמה אשר שלחתיה או מי מנושי אשר מכרתי אתכמה לו הנה בעוונותיכמה נמכרתמה ובפשעיכמה ש/ו/לחה אמכמה מדוע באתי ואין איש קראתי ואין עונה היד הקצור קצרה ידי מפדות אם אין בי כוח להציל. Note the fuller forms בע[וׄוׄנותינו (4Q504) and בעוונותיכמה (1QIsa MS a) compared to בעונותיכם (MT).

Frg. 1, Col. 2

6 [...]°[...]°°[...]°[...]*tykh*[....]

7 O Lord, act now according to yourself, according to the greatness of your power (by) whic[h] yo[u en]dured

8 our fathers in their rebellions against your word,[17] and you were angry with them to (the point of) destroying them, but you had compassion

9 on them in your love for them, and on account of your covenant when Moses atoned

10 for their sin,[18] and on account of (their) knowledge of your great power and the abundance of yo[ur] mercy

11 for generations forever. Turn back now your anger and your wrath from your people Israel on account of all [their] si[n].[19] And remember

12 your wonders which you did in the eyes of the nations for your name has been placed upon us.

13 [...]*l*[...]*bnw* with all heart and with all soul and to implant your Torah in our heart

14 [...] from the right or the left for you have healed us from madness and blindness[20] and confusion

15 [... because of] our [i]niquities we have been sold but in (spite of) our transgressions you have called us

16 [...] and you have delivered us[21] from sinning against you

17 [...]°*t* and to cause us to discern the testimonies

18 [...]*lwt* you have made them

19 [...]*m* and their deeds

---

[17] Lit. "mouth." Cf. Num 14:19: "Forgive the iniquity of this people according to the greatness of your mercy and according to which you have forgiven this people, from (the time of) the Egyptians and until now;" and Deut 1:26 (cf. 9:23): "And you were not willing to go up and you rebelled against the word of Yahweh, your God."

[18] Cf. Ex 32:30: "On the next day, Moses said to the people, 'You have sinned a great sin. And now I will go up to Yahweh; perhaps I can atone on behalf of your sin.'"

[19] The phrase "on account of all [their] si[n]" has been added above the line. The addition apparently seeks to justify the anger of God as a righteous response to the sin of the people. Cf. Dan 9:16: "O Lord, according to all your righteousness, turn back now your anger and your wrath from your city Jerusalem, your holy mountain, for by our sins and by the iniquities of our fathers Jerusalem and your people (have become) a reproach to all our neighbors;" Deut 9:18: "And I lay prostrate before Yahweh as before, forty days and forty nights; I did not eat bread and I did not drink water on account of all your sin which you sinned by doing evil in the eyes of Yahweh to provoke him;" and 4Q504 frg. 2 6.11: "turn back now your anger and your wrath from us."

[20] A scribe has added "and blindness" above the line. Blindness is one of the series of covenant curses for disobedience derived from Deut 28:28.

[21] Cf. Isa 50:1−2a: "Thus says Yahweh, 'Where then (is) your mother's bill of divorce (with) which I sent her away? Or to which of my creditors did I sell you? No, behold, because of your iniquities you were sold, and because of your transgressions your mother was sent away. Why was there no one (when) I came, and (when) I called there was no one answering? Is my hand shortened (that it cannot) redeem? Do I not have power to deliver?'"

Frgs. 1 and 2, Col. 3 [44]

1　אׄבׄיׄ֯נׄו [45]　　　　　　[ה

2　אׄוׄןׄ [ ] ׄ ׄ [ ] [ ] לׄ[חׄשׄב אׄ]שׄ הן
　　נחשׄבׄ[ו]

3　כׄוׄל הׄגוים כׄאׄ]ׄין נגדכׄהׄ] כׄ]תׄהׄוׄוׄ וׄאׄפׄס לפניׄכׄה [46]

4　רק בשמכה] הזׄ]ׄכׄרנו ולכבודׄכׄה ברתנו [47] ובנים

5　שמתנו לכה לעׄיני כול הגוים כיא קרתה

6　[לׄי]שראל בני בכורי [48] ותיסרנו כיסר איש את
　　רׄ

7　בׄנוׄ [49] ותב(רׄנׄוׄ) [50]　　　　אותנו בשני דורותינו
　　רעים

8　[　　　]חׄוליים ורׄׄעב וצמא ודברׄ וחרב [51]

9　[　　　]מת בריתכה כיא אותנו בחרתה לכה

10　[　　　]הארץ עלכן שפכתה אלינו את חמתכה

11　[　　　]תׄכה בכול חרון אפכה [52] ותדבק בנו

12　[　　] [ ] ׄ [ ] [[וׄתׄיׄׄׄכׄה אשר כתב מושה ועבדיכה

13　הנביאים אשׄ[ר　　　שׄ[לׄחׄתׄהׄ לׄ[נׄקׄרׄ]תׄנו הרעה באחׄרׄיׄׄׄת

14　הימים [53] כיא]

15　ומלכינו כיא]

16　לקחת בנוׄת]

17　וישחיתו בׄהׄ]

18　בריתכה ולׄ]

19　זרעׄ ישראל]

20　תצדק למׄ]

21　וׄתׄ]

---

[44] Frg. 1 supplies the right hand portions of lines 12-21; frg. 2 is placed to the left of 1 and supplies the left hand portions of lines 1-13.

[45] See frg. 1 2.8; perhaps also אׄבׄ]תׄינו, as in frg. 8 back line 4.

[46] Cf. MT Isa 40:17: כל־הגוים כאין נגדו מאפס ותהו נחשבו־לו; and 1QIsa MS a: כול הגואים כאין נגדו וכאפס ותהו נחשבו לו.

[47] Cf. MT Isa 43:7.

[48] Cf. MT Ex 4:22: ואמרת אל־פרעה כה אמר יהוה בני בכרי ישראל.

[49] Cf. MT Deut 8:5: וידעת עם־לבבך כי כאשר ייסר איש את־בנו; and 5Q1 (5QDeut): [תׄ בנו]. ; יהוה אלהיך מיסרכ.

[50] ותברנו was an error in the text which the scribe has corrected to read ותרב by adding a supralinear ר and erasing the three consonants רנו.

[51] Cf. MT Deut 28:48, 59.

[52] Cf. MT Zeph 3:8: לכן הכו־לי נאם־יהוה ליום קומי לעד כי משפטי לאסף גוים לקבצי מלכות לשפך עליהם זעמי כל חרון; and 4Q504 frg. 2 5.4-5: אפי כי באש קנאתי תאכל כל־הארץ שממה על אויביהמה כיׄאׄ [כׄה חמתר וחרׄ/וׄ/ני אפכׄ/ה/ באש קנאתכה להׄהׄחׄריבה.

[53] The text is an adaptation of Deut 31:29 which provides the basis for the reconstruction here: כי ידעתי אחרי מותי כי־השחת תשחתון וסרתם מן־הדרך אשר צויתי אתכם וקראת אתכם הרעה באחרית הימים כי־תעשו את־הרע בעיני יהוה להכעיסו במעשה ידיכם.

Frgs. 1 and 2, Col. 3

1 [our] fathers [...]*h*

2 '*wz*[...]°° [...]°[... to] consider '[...]*š*. Behold

3 all the nations (are) [as no]thing before you, as nothingness and emptiness th[ey] are considered[22] before you.

4 Only your name have we [acknow]ledged, and for your glory you have created us and (as) sons

5 you have established us for yourself before the eyes of all the nations, for you have called

6 [I]srael "my first-born son."[23] And you have disciplined us as a man disciplines

7 his son,[24] and you have made us great[25] in the years of our generations.

8 [...]severe[26] diseases, famine, thirst, pestilence, and sword.

9 [...]*mt* your covenant, for you have chosen us for yourself

10 [...] the earth. Therefore you have poured out toward us your wrath

11 [..]*tkh* in all the heat of your anger.[27] But you clung to us

12 [...]°[...]°[...]*wtykh* which Moses wrote, and your servants

13 the prophets, whe[n] you [s]ent the evil to [befa]ll us in the latter

14 days. For [...]

15 and our kings. For [...]

16 you took sons [...]

17 and they acted corruptly *bḥ*[...]

18 your covenant and *l*[...]

19 the seed of Israel [...]

20 you are righteous *lm*[...]

21 and *t*°[...]

---

[22] A scribe added "th[ey] are considered" above the line, apparently to correct the text toward Isa 40:17 from which this line is adapted. Cf. Isa 40:17: "All the nations (are) as nothing before him, (as) emptiness and nothingness they are considered before him."

[23] Cf. Ex 4:22: "And you shall say to Pharaoh, 'Thus says Yahweh: Israel (is) my chosen son.'"

[24] Cf. Deut 8:5: "And you shall know with your heart that as a man disciplines his son, Yahweh, your God, disciplines you."

[25] By inserting an additional consonant and erasing three other consonants, a scribe has corrected an erroneous reading to "and you have made great."

[26] רעים, "severe," is an adjective modifying "diseases" which has been added above the line. The addition is probably dependent on Deuteronomy, esp. on the form of the list of covenant curses in Deut 28:59.

[27] Cf. Zeph 3:8: "'Thus, wait for me,' says Yahweh, 'for the day (when) I arise as a witness, for my judgment (is) to gather the nations, to assemble kingdoms, to pour out upon them my indignation, all the heat of my anger, for in the fire of my jealousy all the earth will be consumed';" 4Q504 frg 2 5.4−5: "For you have [pou]red out your wrath and the heat of your anger in the fire of your jealousy."

Frg. 2, Col. 4

2   מ֯[ש]כנכה֯]   [מ֯נ֯וחה

3   בירוש[לים   בח]רתה בה מכול הארץ[54](superscript)

4   להיות֯]   [ה֗ שם לעולם כיא אהבתה

5   את ישרׄאׄל מכול העמים ותבחר בשבט

6   יאודה ובריתכה הקימותה לדויד להיות[55](superscript)

7   ל֯רעׄי נגיד על עמכה וישב על כסא ישראל לפניך

8   כול הימים וכול הגוים ראו את כבודכה

9   אשר[56](superscript) נקדשתה בתוך עמכה ישראל ולשמכה

10   הגדול ויביאו[57](superscript) מנחתם כסף וזהב ואבן יקרה

11   עם כ(ו)֗ל חמדת ארצם לכבד את עמכה ואת

12   ציון עיר קודשכה ובית תפארתכה ואין שט֯ן

13   ופגע֯[58](superscript) רע כיאם שלום וברכה ממ֯]

14   ו֯י֯א֯[כ]לו וישבעו ויד֯ש֯נ֯ו֯]59(superscript)
            אש[

15   [   ] ה ו֯ה֯ש֯ל֯]

Frg. 2, Col. 5

1   [ ] [˚] י֯ ירׄ֯ין

2   מ֯ק֯ור מים חיים[60](superscript) א֯ן   [ ]֯[ ]שם

3   ו֯י֯ע֯ב֯ו֯ד֯ו אל נכר באר֯צם[61](superscript) ו֯גם ארצם

4   שממה על אויביהמה כיא֯ן ש[פכה חמתך

5   וחרני[62](superscript) אפכ[63](superscript) באש קנאתכה[64](superscript) לה֯ח֯ריבה

---

54 The original לארץ has been corrected to הארץ.

55 The original לדויד, perhaps the result of dittography, has been corrected to להיות.

56 The original אשב has been corrected to אשר.

57 Probably an error for הביאו.

58 The original ופגר has been corrected to ופגע.

59 Cf. MT Deut 31:20: כי־אביאנו אל־האדמה אשר־נשבעתי לאבתיו זבת חלב ודבש ואכל ושבע ודשן ופנה אל־אלהים אחרים ועבדום ונאצוני והפר את־בריתי.

60 Cf. MT Jer 2:13, 17:13.

61 Cf. MT Jer 5:19.

62 The supralinear ו suggests a correction from וחרני to וחרני.

63 An earlier correction read אפו, "his anger," while a second hand has changed the ו to כ and corrected the text to אפכה, "your anger."

64 Cf. MT Zeph 3:8: לכן חכו־לי נאם־יהוה ליום קומי לעד כי משפטי לאסף גוים לקבצי ממלכות לשפך עליהם זעמי כל חרון אפי כי באש קנאתי תאכל כל־הארץ; and 4Q504 frgs. 1-2 3.10-11: [הארץ עלכן שפכתה אלינו את חמתכה [ ]ה֯כה בכול חרון אפכה.

Frg. 2, Col. 4

2 your dwe[lli]ng place [...] resting place

3 in Jerusa[lem...] you have [chos]en it from all the earth[28]

4 to be [...]*h* there forever. For you loved

5 Israel more than all the peoples, so you chose the tribe of

6 Judah, and your covenant you established with David (so he would) be

7 as a shepherd, a prince over your people. He was seated upon the throne of Israel before you

8 all the days, and all the nations saw your glory

9 (by) which you were honored as holy in the midst of your people Israel; and to your great

10 name they brought their offering: silver and gold and precious stone(s)

11 with all the treasure(s) of their land in order to glorify your people and

12 Zion, your holy city, and your marvelous house. There is no adversary

13 or evil occurrence, but peace and blessing *mm*[...]

14 and they have ea[t]en and they were full and they grew fat[29] [...]

15 [...]*h* and *hšl*[...]'*š*[...][30]

Frg. 2, Col. 5

1 [...]°[...]*y yry*[...]

2 a spring of living waters '[...]°[...]*šm.*

3 They served a foreign god in their land and even their land

4 was made desolate by their enemies. For you have [pou]red out your wrath

5 and the heat of your anger in the fire of your jealousy[31] so that it was made desolate,

[28] The motif of the election of Jerusalem is frequent in the Hebrew Bible, e.g., 1Kgs 8:44, 11:32, 14:21, which has certainly shaped this document.

[29] The sequence of verbs follows the text of Deut 31:20 in which Moses predicts future experiences of disobedience and judgment upon the people. Cf. Deut 31:20: "For (when) I have brought them to the land which I promised their fathers, flowing with milk and honey, and they have eaten and become full and grown fat, they will turn to other gods and serve them, and spurn me and break my covenant."

[30] '*š*[...] is written supralinearly.

[31] Cf. Zeph 3:8: "'Thus, wait for me,' says Yahweh, 'for the day (when) I arise as a witness, for my judgment (is) to gather the nations, to assemble kingdoms, to pour out upon them my indignation, all the heat of my anger, for in the fire of my jealousy all the earth will be consumed';" 4Q504 frg. 2 3.10–11: "Therefore you have poured out toward us your wrath [...]*tkh* in all the heat of your anger."

6   מעובר ומשב בכול זואת לוא מאסתה

7   בזרע יעקוב ולו געלתה את ישראל

8   לכלותם להפר בריתכה אתם כיא אתה

9   אל חי לבדכה ואין זולתכה[65] ותזכור ברית כה

10   אשר הוצאתנו לעיני הגוים[66] ולוא עזבתנו

11   בגוים ותחון את עמכה ישראל בכול

12   [ה]ארצות אשר הדחתם שמה להשיב

13   אל לבבם לשוב עודך ולשמוע בקולכה

14   [כ]כֿוֿל אשר צויתה ביד מושה עבדכה[67]

15   [כי]א יצקתה את רוח קודשכה עלינו

16   [לה]ביא ברכתיכה[68] לנו לפֿקודכה[69] בצר לנו

17   [ולל]חֿש בצקון מוסרכה[70] ונבֿואה בצרות

18   [ונגי]עֿים ונסויים בחמת המצֿיק כיא גם

19   [הו]גֿעֿנֿו בעוונֿנו העבדנו צֿוֿֿר בֿחטֿ[תנו]אל[71]

20   [ולוא]הֿעֿבדתנו להועיל מדרכי[נו בד]רֿך[72]

21   [   ]בֿֿדֿֿ[ ]לוא הֿקשבנו אֿ[ל][73]

---

65 Cf. MT Lev 26:44: פ־גם־זאת בהיותם בארץ איביהם לא־מאסתים
ולא־געלתים לכלתם להפר בריתי אתם כי אני יהוה אלהיהם.

66 Cf. MT Lev 26:45: זכרתי להם ברית ראשנים אשר הוצאתי־אתם
מארץ מצרים לעיני הגוים להית להם לאלהים אני יהוה.

67 Cf. MT Deut 30:1-3.

68 A supralinear gloss adds a ו, substituting full for defective
writing. Cf. MT Isa 44:3c: אצק רוחי על זרעך ;1QIsa MS a:
וֿכן אצק רוחי על זרעכה.

69 לפקודכה corrected to למקודכה.

70 Cf. MT Isa 26:16: יהוה בצר פקדוך צקון לחש מוסרך למו;
and 1QIsa MS a: יהוה בצר פקדוך צקון לחשו מוסריך למו.

71 Cf. MT Isa 43:24b: אך העבדתני בחטאותיך הוגעתני בעונתיך;
and 1QIsa MS a: אך העבדתני בחטאותיכה הוגעתני בעונכה.

72 Cf. MT Isa 48:17: כה־אמר יהוה גאלך קדוש ישראל אני יהוה
אלהיך מלמדך להועיל מדריכך בדרך תלך:a 1QIsa MS;
כוה;
and 1Q8 (1QIsa MS b): אמר יהוה גואלכה קדוש ישראל אני יהוה אלוהיכה מלמדכה
להועיל הדריכה בדרך אשר תלך בה;
כה אמר יהוה גאלך [ ][ם] [מ]ֿדֿר להועיל מדריכך בדרך תלך.

73 Cf. MT Isa 48:18: לוא הקשבת למצותי ויהי כנהר שלומך;
ולוא הקשבתה אל מצותי:a 1QIsa MS; וצדקתך כגלי הים
and 1Q8 (1QIsa MS b): והיה כנהר שלומכה וצדקתך כגלי הים;
ולא הק[ ]הר שלמך וצדקתך כגלי הים. For the
reconstruction see 1QIsa MS a's variant אל מצוותי.

6 (unsuitable) for traveling through or returning.   (But) in all of this, you did not reject

7 the seed of Jacob, and you did not despise Israel

8 to their end to break your covenant with them.   For you

9 (are) a living God, you yourself, and there is none other than you.[32]   And you remembered your covenant[33]

10 so that you brought us out in the eyes of the nations, and you did not forsake us

11 among the nations.[34]   And you were gracious with your people Israel in all

12 [the] lands (to) which you exiled them in order that they might be made to return

13 to their heart and to return again to you and to heed your voice

14 [according to] all which you commanded by the hand of Moses your servant.

15 [Fo]r you have poured out your Holy Spirit upon us

16 [to br]ing your blessings[35] to us in order that we might seek you out in our anguish

17 [and to whisper a p]rayer during the oppression of your discipline.[36]   We came into anguish,

18 [afflict]ions, and trials in the wrath of the oppressor.   For indeed

19 we have wearied God[37] with our iniquity.   We have burdened (the) Rock with [our] si[n.]

20 [But] you did [not] burden us to (our) advantage, guiding [us] in the w[ay...][38]

21 [...]*bh* [...] we have not paid attention t[o[39] ...]

---

[32] Cf. Lev. 26:44: "And yet even (for) that, when they are in the land of their enemies, I will not reject them, and I will not abhor them to destroy them, to break my covenant with them, for I (am) Yahweh their God."

[33] The possessive pronoun "your" has been added above the line to modify "covenant."

[34] Cf. Lev 26:45: "And I will remember for them my covenant (with) the former ones whom I brought out from the land of Egypt before the eyes of the nations to be to them God: I (am) Yahweh."

[35] Cf. Isa 44:3: "For I will pour out water upon the thirsty, and streams upon the dry; I will pour out my spirit upon your seed and my blessing upon your offspring;" cf. also Deut 28:2, Job 29:13, Prov 24:25.

[36] Restoration based on Isa 26:16: "O Yahweh, in anguish they sought you, whispering a prayer (during) oppression, while you were disciplining them."

[37] The direct object, "God," has been added above the line. The phrase is adapted from Isa 43:24: "You have burdened me with your sins; you have wearied me with your iniquities."

[38] Restoration based on Isa 48:17: "Thus says Yahweh, your redeemer, the holy one of Israel, 'I (am) Yahweh your God, teaching you for your advantage, guiding you in the way you (should) walk.'"

[39] Or "if only we had paid attention t[o ...]." Cf. Isa 48:18: "If only you had paid attention to my ordinances, then your peace would have been like a river and your prosperity like the waves of the sea."

Frg. 2, Col. 6

2   ]ך מ[ע]לינו כול פשעינ[ו]י[74] ות[ן]הרנו ﮕ

3   מחטתנו למׄענכה לכה אתה הצדקה[75] כיא   *(אדוני above)*

4   אתה עשיתה את כול אלה ועתה ביום הזה

5   אשר נכנע לבנו רצינו את עוננו ואת עוון

6   אבותינו במעלנו ואשר הלכו[76] בקרי ולוא מאסנו   *(נ above)*

7   בנסׄוייכה ובנגיעיכה לוא געלה נפשנו להפר

8   את בריתכה בכול צרת הׄנׄישנו[77] כיא אתה   *(פ above; אשר השלחתה בנו את אויבינו[78] above)*

9   חזקתה את לבבנו ולמען נספר גבורתכה לדורו   *(ת above)*

10   עולם אנא אדוני כעשותכה נפלאות מעולם ועד

11   עולם ישוב נא אפכה וחמתכה ממנו[79] וראה עׄ[נ]ינו

12   ועמלנו ולחצנו והצילה את עמכה ישר[א]ל[80]

13   הארצות הׄקרובות והרחוקות א[ן

14   שם כול הכתוב בספר החייׄ[ם]

15   לעובדכה ולהודות ל[ן

16   מכול צורריהמׄה[ו][81]   *(ה above)*

17   מכשילים]   *(ה above)*

18   שׄ]

19   לׄ[ן

---

[74] Cf. MT Ezek 18:31.

[75] Cf. MT Dan 9:7a: לך אדני הצדקה.

[76] A supralinear scribal gloss corrects הכלו to הלכו.

[77] תישנו corrected to נׄפׄישנו.

[78] The supralinear continues past col. 6 and into col. 7, causing a pseudo-vacat between lines 9 and 10. This phenomenon is unusual in the Qumran Scrolls [Ed.]

[79] Cf. MT Dan 9:16: דני ככל־צדקתך ישב־נא אפך וחמתך מעירך ירושלם הר־קדשך כי בחטאינו ובעונות אבתינו ועמך ישוב נא אפכה; and 4Q504 frgs. 1-2 2.11: לחרפה לכל־סביבתינו וחמתכה מעׄמכה ישראל

[80] Cf. MT Deut 26:7: ונצעק אל־יהוה אלהי אבתינו וישמע יהוה את־קלנו וירא את־עניו ואת־עמלנו ואת־לחצנו.

[81] צורריהמה is corrected to צורריהמה.

Frg. 2, Col. 6

2 [...]*k* from [u]pon us all ou[r] transgressions and you have [pu]rified us

3 from our sin for your sake.   To you, you (alone) O Lord,[40] (belongs) righteousness.[41]   For

4 you have made all these (things).   And now in this day

5 (in) which our heart is humbled, we have made expiation for our iniquity and for the iniquity of

6 our fathers in our unfaithfulness and in the resistance in which we walked.   But we have not refused

7 your toils and your afflictions.   Our soul has not despaired to the point of breaking

8 your covenant (even) with all the anguish of our soul.   For you, who has sent away our enemies for us,[42]

9 have given courage to our heart, in order that we may recount your mighty deeds for generations[43]

10 forever.   Now, O Lord, according to your wondrous works from of old and until

11 forever, turn back now your anger and your wrath from us.[44]   And see [our] af[fliction][45]

12 and our trouble and our distress and deliver your people Isra[el[46] ...]

13 the lands near and far '[...]

14 the name of everyone who is written in the book of life [...]

15 to serve you and to thank *l*[...][47]

16 from all their tormentors [...][48]

17 the ones who cause to stumble [...]

18 *š*°[...]

19 *l*[...]

---

40 The vocative, "O Lord," has been added here above the line to conform more closely to the biblical source of the phrase in Dan 9:7.

41 Cf. Dan 9:7a: "To you, O Lord, (belongs) righteousness."

42 The interlinear addition ("who has sent away our enemies for us") may be adapted from 1Sam 19:17.

43 A supralinear gloss adds a ת to לדורו and thus corrects "for his generation" to "for generations." Cf. 1QH 6.11.

44 Cf. Dan 9:16: "O Lord, according to all your righteous deeds, turn back now your anger and your wrath from your city Jerusalem, the holy mountain, for by our sins and by the iniquities of our fathers Jerusalem and your people (have become) a reproach to all our neighbors;" Deut 9:18: "And I lay prostrate before Yahweh as before; forty days and forty nights I did not eat bread and I did not drink water on account

of all your sin which you sinned by doing evil in the eyes of Yahweh to provoke him;" and 4Q504 frg. 1 2.11: "Turn back now your anger and your wrath on account of all [their] si[n] from your people Israel."

45 Restored on the basis of the cluster of similar words in Deut 26:7. "And we cried to Yahweh, the God of our fathers, and Yahweh heard our voice and saw our affliction and our trouble and our distress."

46 Deut 26:7: "And we cried to Yahweh, the God of our fathers, and Yahweh heard our voice and saw our affliction and our trouble and our distress."

47 Numerous restorations are possible: "the name," "you," "your name," etc.

48 The verb in the present text is a participial form of צרר, "to bind," "to torment." The scribal gloss substitutes a ר for an ע.

Frg. 2, Col. 7

1   [שׁמֹ] [ ]ֹ [ ]ֹ היהֹ]

2   אשר הצילנו מכול צרה אמֹן]

3   ]

4   הודות ביום השבת ׳ הודֹן]

5   את שם קודשו תמיד בשֹ]

6   כול מלאכים רקיע קודש וֹן]

7   לשמים הארץ וכול מחשבֹיה]

8   רבה ואבדון והמים וֹכֹוֹל אשֹרֹ]

9   כול בריאותיו תמיד לעולמֹ]

10   ]

11   קודשו הרננו לאלי[82] נֹ ֹ ֹ]

12   כבֹוד ולֹ] [ ]ֹ ֹ]

Frg. 2, Col. 3 back

1   [ ]ֹ הֹ [83]

Frg. 2, Col. 7 back

1   נֹדיבֹים]

2   ירומֹמֹו]

3   רֹי כבוֹד]

4   כי כול]

5   ויברא את]

6   מֹוֹרֹ את ֹֹ]

7   אל קוֹדשיהם ֹֹֹֹ]

8   קודשו וֹישא]

9   בריתו וֹישֹב]

10   ל תהליהמֹה]

---

[82] להל corrected to לאל.

[83] Baillet does not supply a photograph of this fragment. This transcription is based on his transcription.

Frg. 2, Col. 7

1 [. . .]*šm*[. . .]°[. . .]° *hyh*[. . .]

2 who has delivered us from all anguish.   Amen.   [. . .]

3 (vacat) [. . .]⁴⁹

4 Thanksgivings for the day of the Sabbath.   Give thanks [. . .]

5 his holy name continually *bš*[. . .]

6 all the angels, holy firmament and [. . .]

7 to the heavens, the earth, and all its intelligent creatures [. . .]

8 great and Abaddon,⁵⁰ and the waters and all which [. . .]

9 all his creatures continually forever [. . . .]

10 (vacat) [. . .]

11 his holiness, they shouted with joy to the God *n*°°[. . .]

12 glory and *l*[. . .]°°°[. . .]

Frg. 2, Col. 3 back

1 [. . .]°*t*[. . .]

Frg. 2, Col. 7 back

1 [. . .] nobles

2 [. . .] they will exalt

3 [. . .]*ry* glory

4 [. . .] because all

5 [. . .] and he created the

6 [. . .]*mwr* ʾ*t*°°

7 [. . .]°°°° unto their holy places⁵¹

8 [. . .] his holiness and he lifted up

9 [. . .] his covenant and he returned

10 [. . .]*l* their praises

---

⁴⁹ Because the leather is not scored with horizontal lines, the vacat is indicated by the space between the lines, but esp. by the beginning of the new section "Thanksgivings for the day of the Sabbath. . . ."

⁵⁰ Abaddon is a poetic name for the nether world. Cf. Ps 88:12, Job 26:6, Prov 15:11, and 1QH 3.19.

⁵¹ Or "God their holy (offerings)."

Fragments whose position cannot be determined

Frg. 9

1 ‏[ב]‎
2 ‏[ובי]ן‎
3 ‏[י]ם טהורי[ם]‎
4 ‏[י]שים ו[ק]‎
5 ‏[ר]צה פרי ל כ°[ן][84]‎
6 ‏מ[שפטיו וי]רי[ם]‎
7 ‏[ת ומני]נו‎

Frg. 11

1 ‏שים]‎
2 ‏ת רצון]‎
3 ‏תה לכפר]‎
4 ‏וצדקה]‎

Frg. 12

1 ‏[ ]°[ ]°[ ]‎
2 ‏[ך אותנ]ו‎
3 ‏[ר הלכנו]‎
4 ‏[מא]‎

Frg. 13

1 ‏[ם]‎
2 ‏[ל מ]‎
3 ‏[ה כיא]‎
4 ‏[ר ד°]‎

Frg. 14

1 ‏[ ] [אות]‎
2 ‏[ו]א‎
3 ‏ב[ר]‎
4 ‏פני]‎
5 ‏ב]‎

Frg. 15, Col. 1

1 ‏[°‎
2 ‏[רו‎

Frg. 15, Col. 2

1 ‏כ[י]ן‎
2 ‏כלי[ן]‎

Frg. 16

1 ‏[ ]°[°]‎
2 ‏[אכל עשב]‎
3 ‏[ ]°[°]‎

Frg. 17, Col. 1

5 ‏[°°‎
6 ‏[י]ם‎

Frg. 17, Col. 2

1 ‏[ ] [א]‎
2 ‏[ ] [ו]מכול‎
3 ‏[א]לינו[85] וישמ[‎
4 ‏בדרכי ה[י]‎
5 ‏ישר אמן [‎
6 ‏[פ]‎

Frg. 19

1 ‏[ם אל תר]‎
2 ‏[למזמו]ר‎
3 ‏[שם תשע]‎

Frg. 20

1 ‏[במצ]‎
2 ‏[תה °‎
3 ‏[ ]°[ ]‎

---

[84] Perhaps read פרי לכ°[.   [85] Or עלינו.

Fragments whose position cannot be determined

Frg. 9

1 [. . .]*b*[. . .]
2 [. . .]*wby*[. . .]
3 [. . .]*ym* purities [. . .]
4 [. . .] they set and *q*[. . .]
5 [. . .]*rṣh* fruits *lk°*[. . .]
6 [. . .] his [ju]dgments and he raised up[. . .]
7 [. . .]*t* and [we] number [. . .]

Frg. 11

1 [. . .]*šym*
2 [. . .]*t* favor
3 [. . .]*th* to atone
4 [. . .] and righteousness

Frg. 12

1 [. . .]°[. . .]°[. . .]
2 [. . .]*k* u[*s* . . .]
3 [. . .]*r* we walked [. . .]
4 [. . .]*m*'[. . .]

Frg. 13

1 [. . .]*m*[. . .]
2 [. . .]*l m*[. . .]
3 [. . .]*h* because [. . .]
4 [. . .]*r d°*[. . .]

Frg. 14

1 [. . .]'*wt*[. . .]
2 and '[. . .]
3 *br*[. . .]
4 face of [. . .]
5 *b*[. . .]

Frg. 15, Col. 1

1 [. . .]°
2 [. . .]*dw*

Frg. 15, Col. 2

1 because [. . .]
2 vessel [. . .]

Frg. 16

1 [. . .]°°[. . .]
2 [. . .] eat an herb
3 [. . .]°°[. . .]

Frg. 17, Col. 1

5 [. . .]°°
6 [. . .]*ym*

Frg. 17, Col. 2

1 [. . .]'[. . .]
2 [. . .] and from all [. . .]
3 [t]o us[52] and *yšm*[. . .]
4 in the ways of *hy*[. . .]
5 straight. Amen. [. . .]
6 °[. . .]

Frg. 19

1 [. . .]*m* not *tr*[. . .]
2 [. . .] to a pruning hook [53] [. . .]
3 [. . .]*šm tš̆ᶜ*[. . .]

Frg. 20

1 [. . .]*bmṣ*[. . .]
2 [. . .]*th°* [. . .]
3 [. . .]° [. . .]

[52] Or "[up]on us."

[53] Or "to sing-praise."

Frg. 22

1]מ[
2]בוק[ ] ̇[
3]אשר גאלה[
4]הארץ כ ̇[

Frg. 24

1]ל בונ[
2]כה ̇ ו[
3]למחשב[
4 ̇]ר[

Frg. 25

1]תים[
2]טמאת[
3]מואדה[
4 ̇]אה[
5]ר[

Frg. 26

1]כו[
2]תכה
3 נפ]לאותיכה
4]גוים
5]בכור
6]את ארצכה
7]להכעיס[ ]ללו[
8]האלות
9]מציתה[[86]

Frg. 27

1]ל מלכ[
2]צל ̇[
3]ל ̇°[
4] °° [

Frg. 28

1]ה [
2]ו [
3]ול [
4]°[

Frg. 29

1]ויעבו[
2]ס בא[
3]בעסו[

Frg. 30

1] ברו[
2]ו בר[
3]ל מו[

Frg. 31

1]ה [
2]אש[
3]ן עמ[

Frg. 32

1]לש[
2]כול[
3]°[

Frg. 33

1]° °[
2]ח גדו[

Frg. 34

1]ונה זכ[
2]ס וכול י[

Frg. 35

1]ר[
2]בכת ̇[

Frg. 36

1]ב
2]א

Frg. 37

1]ה[
2]בע ̇[

---

86 מציתה probably corrected from מציוכה.

Frg. 22

1 [...]*m*[...]

2 [...]°[...]*bwq*[...]

3 [...] who redeemed her [...]

4 [...] the earth *k*°[...]

Frg. 24

1 [...]*l bwn*[...]

2 [...]*kh*° and [...]

3 [...] for considering [...]

4 [...]° *r*[...]

Frg. 25

1 [...]*tym* [...]

2 [...] unclean [...]

3 [...] very [...]

4 [...]'*h*°[...]

5 [...]*r*[...]

Frg. 26

1 [...]*kw*[...]

2 [...]*tkh*

3 [...] your [won]ders

4 [...] nations

5 [...] first-born

6 [...] your land

7 [...] to provoke to anger [...]*ll*[...]

8 [...] curses

9 [...] you drained [...]

Frg. 27

1 [...]*l* king[...]

2 [...]° *ṣl*[...]

3 [...]*k* °°[...]

4 [...] °°[...]

Frg. 28

1 [...] *h* [...]

2 [...]*w* [...]

3 [...]*wl* [...]

4 [...]° [...]

Frg. 29

1 [...] and they grew fat [...]

2 [...]*m b*'[...]

3 [...]*b*ʿ*sw*[...]

Frg. 30

1 [...] *brw*[...]

2 [...]*nw br*[...]

3 [...]*l mw*[...]

Frg. 31

1 [...]*h* [...]

2 [...]'*š*[...]

3 [...]*n* ʿ*m*[...]

Frg. 32

1 [...]*lš*[...]

2 [...] all [...]

3 [...]°[...]

Frg. 33

1 [...]°°[...]

2 [...]*t gdw*[...]

Frg. 34

1 [...] shout of joy *zk*[...]

2 [...]*m* and all *y*[...]

Frg. 35

1 [...]*r*[...]

2 [...]*bkt*°[...]

Frg. 36

1 *b*[...]

2 '[...]

Frg. 37

1 [...]*h*[...]

2 [...]*b*ʿ°[...]

Frg. 41	Frg. 39	Frg. 38
1] ̊צ̊ [	1 [א]	1 [ב̊ו̊א]
	2]חת ל̊]	2 [מ] ̊

Frg. 46	Frg. 44	Frg. 42
1] ̊ [	1] ̊ [	1 [הֿרֿ]

Frg. 49	Frg. 48	Frg. 47
1] ̊ [	1 [מגוי]	1 [כבודנו לֿ]
	2 [לל]	2 [את מנו]

Frg. 38
1 [. . .] come [. . .]
2 [. . .]° *m*[. . .]

Frg. 39
1 [. . .]ˀ[. . .]
2 [. . .]*th l*[. . .]

Frg. 41
1 [. . .]*s̆*°[. . .]

Frg. 42
1 [. . .]*hr*[. . .]

Frg. 44
1 [. . .]°[. . .]

Frg. 46
1 [. . .]°[. . .]

Frg. 47
1 [. . .] our glory to [. . .]
2 [. . .]ˀ*t mnw*[. . .]

Frg. 48
1 [. . .] from a nation of [. . .]
2 [. . .] *ll*[. . .]

Frg. 49
1 [. . .]°[. . .]

4Q505

Frg. 120

1 ‫]תֿ נפשֿ[‬
2 ‫]לבלתין[‬
3 ‫]ֿם לאֿ[‬

Frg. 121

1 ‫מד]רכינו[י‬
2 ‫מצו]ותיכה[‬

Frg. 122

1 ‫]מֿושה עֿבֿ]דכה‬
2 ‫]ֿה נֿקֿם ֿה[‬

Frg. 123

1 ‫] ובגוֿיֿם[‬

Frg. 124

1 ‫] צֿוֿיֿכֿ[‬
2 ‫]ל האֿ]רץ²[‬
3 ‫] ֿ ה ובעבורֿ[³‬
4 ‫]ֿם ותקם לֿנֿ]ו‬
5 ‫] ֿ ֿ ֿ ה אֿ[‬
6 ‫]ולישחק וליעֿ]קוב‬
7 ‫]קֿדוש עומד לֿפֿנֿ]יכהי‬
8 ‫] ֿ ה [‬

Frg. 125

1 ‫]שֿמֿורים זֿכֿ ֿ[‬
2 ‫]ֿה עלבֿתֿינו [‬
3 ‫] לוא חלצכ]ה‬
4 ‫]כֿול הגוֿיֿם [‬

Frg. 126

1 ‫]שֿםֿ ֿ ֿ כה [‬
2 ‫]בנים קראתֿנֿ]ו‬
3 ‫]כה הֿ ֿ ֿ ֿ[‬

Frg. 127

1 ‫] [ ]כֿן בֿ]ן[‬
2 ‫נפלאותיכה[‬
3 ‫התגברתֿה[‬
4 ‫] ֿ כֿ ֿלֿ[‬

Frg. 128

1 ‫]תֿאפקֿ[‬
2 ‫]נֿו בעמֿוֿ]ד‬
3 ‫]לֿבֿרֿתֿהֿ[‬

Frg. 129

1 ‫]ֿה הגדולֿ[‬
2 ‫]אֿשֿרֿ[‬

---

1 Cf. the parallel in 4Q504 frgs. 1-2 5.20.
2 Cf. 4Q504 frg. 3 2.11: ‫]אֿרץ התבֿל[‬.
3 Cf. 4Q504 frg. 3 2.12: ‫]וֿבעבור נאֿיֿן[‬.
4 Cf. 4Q504 frg. 5 2.3: ‫קודש עומד לפניֿכֿ[‬.

4Q505

Frg. 120

1 [...]*t* soul [...]

2 [...] not [...]

3 [...]*m l'h*[...]

Frg. 121

1 [... from] our [w]ays [...]

2 [...] your [ordin]ances [...]

Frg. 122

1 [...] Moses [your] serva[nt...]

2 [...]*h* he took revenge *h*[...]

Frg. 123

1 [...] and among the nations [...]

Frg. 124

1 [...]*ṣwyk*[...]

2 [...]*l* the ea[rth...]

3 [...]°*h* and in order that [...]

4 [...]*m* and you established for u[s...]

5 [...]°°°*h* '[...]

6 [...] and to Isaac and to Ja[cob...]

7 [...] holy standing before [you...]

8 [...]°*h* [...]

Frg. 125

1 [...] watching *zk*°[...]

2 [...]*h* upon our houses [...]

3 [...] he has not delivered yo[u...]

4 [...] all the nations [...]

Frg. 126

1 [...]*šm*°°*kh* [...]

2 [...] sons you have called u[s...]

3 [...]*kh h*°°°°[...]

Frg. 127

1 [...]*kn bd*[...]

2 your wonders [...]

3 you have shown yourself to be mighty [...]

4 [...]°*k*°*l*[...]

Frg. 128

1 [...] you restrained yourself [...]

2 [...] us in a pilla[r...]

3 [...] you spoke [...]

Frg. 129

1 [...]*h* the great [...]

2 [...] who [...]

4Q506

Frg. 124

1　‏[כֹּה כול מֹחֹ]

2　‏אחֹ]ריהם לֹ'‏[1]

3　‏[זכוֹרֹהֹ]‏[2]

4　‏נחג]ֹה גאלתנֹו]‏[3]

5　‏לע]ֹשֹוֹת הרֹ]ע‏[4]

6　‏[לֹ]

Frg. 157

1　‏[˚ ˚]

2　‏[רֹבֹיעֹו]

Frg. 129

1　‏[˚˚]

2　‏א]ֹשֹר צויתֹ]הֹ‏[5]

3　‏[˚]

Frgs. 125 and 127[6]

1　‏[[　　]]

2　‏פנ]ֹים אל פֹנֹי]ֹם דֹ]בֹרתה עמֹ]וֹ‏[7]

3　‏[רֹצֹיתֹוֹ]] וימצ]ֹאוֹ חֹן בעֹ]יניכה‏[8]

4　‏[וֹ כוֹלֹ ˚˚]]

Frg. 126

1　‏[˚] תֹ] [לֹ]

2　‏בע]ֹמוד ענן בֹעֹ]

3　‏[כֹנֹוֹ]

1　Cf. 4Q504 frg. 5 2.1: [לֹ בזרעם אחריהֹם.

2　Cf. 4Q504 frg. 5 2.3: [בֹור אֹדוני כיא שׁ.

3　Cf. 4Q504 frg. 5 2.4: [וֹבך נחגה גאלֹ.

4　Cf. 4Q504 frg. 5 2.7: [הרע בעיניכה צֹוֹֹה.

5　The restoration is based on 4Q504 frgs. 1-2 5.14.

6　Frg. 125 is placed to the right of 127.

7　4Q504 frg. 3 2.17: [פֹנים אל פנים /דֹבֹר] [הֹ' אֹוֹֹה] בכול[.

8　4Q504 frg. 3 2.18: [רֹצֹיתו וימצאוֹ] [כֹבֹוֹ.

4Q506

Frg. 124

1 [. . .] your [. . .] all *mḥ*[. . .]

2 [. . .aft]er them *l*[. . .]

3 [. . .]°. Remember, [. . .]

4 [. . .]let [us celebrate the festival of] our redemption [. . .]

5 [. . .] to [d]o the ev[il . . .]

6 [. . .]*l*[. . .]

Frg. 157

1 [. . .]°°°[. . .]

2 [. . .] fourth [. . .]

Frg. 129

1 [. . .] °°[. . .]

2 [. . .wh]ich yo[u] commanded [. . .]

3 [. . .]°[. . .]

Frgs. 125 and 127

1 [. . .] °°[. . .]

2 [. . .fa]ce to fac[e] you [s]poke with [him . . .]

3 [. . .] you were pleased with him [and they fo]und grace in [your] e[yes . . .]

4 [. . .]*w* all °°[. . .]

Frg. 126

1 [. . .]° *t*°[. . .]*k*°[. . .]

2 [with a pi]llar of cloud *bwʿ*[. . .]

3 [. . .]*knw*[. . .]

Frgs. 131 and 132 [9]

1	[ונ֯תן֯]
2	[אנו ה֯]
3	[אשה]
4	[א֯ ורוח֯ ושי֯]
5	[נ]֯תתה לנו לכ֯ו֯ל֯[ן]
6	[א]ד֯ם נולד ב֯[ן]
7	רצי]תה הי֯ו֯[ן][10]
8	[א]ר֯ץ וע֯[בודת][11]
9	[לב]ב֯ם כיא֯[ן]
10	[מח]שב֯ת [ן][13]
11	[בא]שר חננ[ו]את֯[ן][14]
12	[ואל]תזכו[ר][16]
13	[בכו]ל גמו֯[לם][17]
14	ולח֯]טתנו[19]

Text on left column (131):

7	[[ ]°°]]
8	ה֯]תה לו במ֯[ן]
9	הדעו]]ת֯[12] וכול
10	לפ]]ניכה אלה ידענו
11	ה֯קודש רחמנו[15] [ן]
12	אבו֯ת֯ינ֯ו הרישנים[[
13	ק֯]]שו בעורפם[18]

Fragments whose position cannot be determined

Frg. 134   *Frg. 133*   *Frg. 128*

	Frg. 134		Frg. 133		Frg. 128
1	[ה֯]	**1**	[ ]°[ ]°[ ]	**1**	[ש֯]ר֯[ ]
2	[תח]°[ ]ל֯[ ]ל֯[ ]	**2**	[ותיכה֯]°[ ]°°[ ]		

Frg. 137   *Frg. 136*   *Frg. 135*

	Frg. 137		Frg. 136		Frg. 135
1	[בא]°[ ]	**1**	[ור֯[ ]	**1**	[ר °[ ]
2	[ל֯]°[ ]	**2**	[וד֯[ ]	**2**	[לח֯]
		3	[ ]°[ ]		

Frg. 140   *Frg. 139*   *Frg. 138*

	Frg. 140		Frg. 139		Frg. 138
1	[ ]°[ ]	**1**	[ ]°[ ]°[ ]	**1**	[ם]
2	[ח֯]°[ ]	**2**	[ב֯[ ]	**2**	[מ֯]
		3	[ ]°°[ ]		

[9] Frg. 132 is placed to the left of 131.
[10] 4Q504 frg. 4 line 2: [ר֯ורות֯] [שר רציתה֯].
[11] 4Q504 frg. 4 line 3: [ה֯]ארץ ועבודת כול ה֯].
[12] 4Q504 frg. 4 line 4: [א֯ אתה֯ אל הדעות].
[13] 4Q504 frg. 4 line 4: [כ֯ול מחשב֯].
[14] 4Q504 frg. 4 line 5: [ה֯ אלה ידענו באשר חננא֯ה֯].
[15] 4Q504 frg. 4 line 5: [רוח ק֯].

[16] Cf. MT Ps 79:8 אל־תזכר־לנו עונת ראשנים מהר יקדמונו רחמיך כי דלונו מאד.
[17] 4Q504 frg. 4 line 6: [זכ֯ור לנו עוונות רשונים בכול גמו֯לם הר֯].
[18] 4Q504 frg. 4 line 7: [בעורפם].
[19] 4Q504 frg. 4 line 7: אתה פ֯ד֯ינו וסלח֯[ ]לעווננו ולח. Cf. MT Ex 34:9 ויאמר אם־נא מצאתי חן וסלחת לעוננו ולחטאתנו ונחלתנו.

148

Frgs. 131 and 132

1 [. . .] and *t*[. . .]

2 [. . .]*h* we [. . .]

3 [. . .] woman [. . .]

4 [. . .]*šy* and spirit '[. . .]

5 you [g]ave to us all [. . .]

6 [a pe]rson born in [. . .]

7 [. . .] you [are pleased] *hy*w[. . .] °°[. . .]

8 [. . . ea]rth and the se[rvice of . . .]*th* to him *bt*[. . .]

9 [to] their [he]art because [. . .knowled]ge and every

10 [d]esign [. . . bef]ore you.   These (things) we know

11 [beca]use y[ou have been gracio]us [. . .] Holy [. . . .]   Have compassion on us

12 [and] do [not] rememb[er . . .] our fathers the ancestors[1]

13 [with al]l [their] condu[ct . . . st]iff in their neck

14 [. . . and] our [s]in[2]

Fragments whose position cannot be determined

Frg. 128

1 [. . .]*r*[. . .]*š*[. . .]

Frg. 133

1 [. . .]°[. . .]°[. . .]

2 [. . .]°[. . .]°°*wtykh* [. . .]

Frg. 134

1 [. . .]*h* [. . .]

2 [. . .]*l*[. . .]° *th*[. . .]

Frg. 135

1 [. . .]°*r* [. . .]

2 [. . .]*lt* [. . .]

Frg. 136

1 [. . .]*yr*[. . .]

2 [. . .]*wd*[. . .]

3 [. . .]°[. . .]

Frg. 137

1 [. . .]° *b*' [. . .]

2 [. . .] *l*°[. . .]

Frg. 138

1 [. . .]*m* [. . .]

2 [. . .]*m*[. . .]

Frg. 139

1 [. . .]°[. . .]°[. . .]

2 [. . .]*b* [. . .]

3 [. . .]° °[. . .]

Frg. 140

1 [. . .]°[. . .]

2 [. . .]°*ḥ*[. . .]

---

[1] Lit. "the former ones." Cf. Ps 79:8: "Do not remember against us the iniquities of the former ones; let your compassions come to us quickly for we have been brought exceedingly low."

[2] Cf. Ex 34:9: "And he said, 'If I have found favor in your eyes, let the Lord go, O Lord, in our midst, although this (is) a stiff-necked people, pardon our iniquity and our sin, and take us as your inheritance.'"

Frg. 141

1]°[ ]°[
2]ה̇ ד[

Frg. 142

1]°[
2]ב̇[

Frg. 143

1]°°[
2]° [
3]° ס̇מ]°[
4]°[ ]°[ ]°[

Frg. 144

1]°[
2]ש̇א
3]ל̇[

Frg. 145

1]°[
2]° ל[

Frg. 146

1]ה̇
2 תי]נו
3 אליכה[
4]°

Frg. 147

1]°[
2]ש̇ת]°[
3]ימ̇י[
4]ר̇ו[

Frg. 148

1]ב א̇[
2]עשו̇ת [
3]ל̇כ̇ו[

Frg. 150

1]ב̇[
2] [
3]ב̇[

Frg. 151

1] °[
2]דע̇[
3]ט̇ °[

Frg. 152

1]ם̇[
2]ג̇ °[[
3]ו̇ °[

Frg. 153

1]בר [[
2]ע ל °[[

Frg. 154

1]ל̇י[
2]נ̇י[

Frg. 155

1] כרו̇[
2]°° [

Frg. 156

1]° י[
2]שע[
3]°[

Frg. 158

1]ש̇[
2]ר ו̇ °[
3]הכ[

4] [
5]°[

Frg. 159

1]ת̇[
2]°[

Frg. 160

1]°[
2]ב °[
3]ל̇ °[

Frg. 141

1 [...]°[...]°[...]

2 [...]d h[...]

Frg. 142

1 [...]°[...]

2 [...]b[...]

Frg. 143

1 [...]°°[...]

2 [...] °[...]

3 [...]°ms°°[....]

4 [...]°[...]°°[...]

Frg. 144

1 [...]°[...]

2 ʾš°[...]

3 [...]wl[...]

Frg. 145

1 [...]° [...]

2 [...]l°[...]

Frg. 146

1 [...]h

2 [...]tynw

3 [...] to you

4 [...]°

Frg. 147

1 [...]°[...]

2 [...]°tš[...]

3 [...]ymy[...]

4 [...]wr°[...]

Frg. 148

1 [...]ʾ b[...]

2 [...] to do [...]

3 [...]wlk[...]

Frg. 150

1 [...]b[...]

2 [...]   [...]

3 [...]k[...]

Frg. 151

1 [...]°[...]

2 [...]wʿd [...]

3 [...]°ṭ[...]

Frg. 152

1 [...]m [...]

2 [...]°g°[...]

3 [...]°w[...]

Frg. 153

1 [...] rb[...]

2 [...]°l ʿ[...]

Frg. 154

1 [...]yl°[...]

2 [...]yn°[...]

Frg. 155

1 [...] arrangings of [...]

2 [...]°°[...]

Frg. 156

1 [...]°y [...]

2 [...]ʿš[...]

3 [...]°[...]

Frg. 158

1 [...]š[...]

2 [...]° wr[...]

3 [...]kh[...]

4 [...] [...]

5 [...]°[...]

Frg. 159

1 [...]t[...]

2 [...]°[...]

Frg. 160

1 [...]°[...]

2 [...]° b[...]

3 [...]° k[...]

Frg. 161

1]°°°[
2]°בׄ°°[

Frg. 162

1 ג]בׄורהׄ[

Frg. 163

1]°בׄ°[
2]°°[

Frg. 164

1]°[
2]אׄל[
3]בׄוׄכׄצׄ[
4]לׄ[

Frg. 166

1]רׄצׄ[

Frg. 167

1]וׄד[
2]לתׄ[

Frg. 168

1]פשׄ[
2]לׄ[

Frg. 169

1]יין[

Frg. 170

1]מׄא[
2]א[

Frg. 171

1]שׄ[

Frg. 172

1]°°[
2]לׄ[

Frg. 173

1]א°ג[
2]°[

Frg. 174

1]°[
2]וׄ°[

Frg. 175

1]°[
2]°[

Frg. 176

1]ם°[
2]°[

Frg. 177

1][
2]°°[

Frg. 178

1]°[

Frg. 179

1]הׄ[
2]לׄ[

Frg. 180

1]°[
2]שׄ°[

Frg. 181

1]מׄ[

Frg. 182

1]°[

Frg. 161

1 [...]°°°[...]
2 [...]°°b°[...]

Frg. 162

1 [...st]rength [...]

Frg. 163

1 [...]b°°[...]
2 [...]°°[...]

Frg. 164

1 [...]°[...]
2 [...]ʾl [...]
3 [...]bwkṣ[...]
4 [...]l[...]

Frg. 166

1 [...]rṣ[...]

Frg. 167

1 [...]wd[...]
2 [...]lt[...]

Frg. 168

1 [...] pš[...]
2 [...]l[...]

Frg. 169

1 [...]yy[...]

Frg. 170

1 [...]mʾ[...]
2 [...]ʾ[...]

Frg. 171

1 [...]š [...]

Frg. 172

1 [...]°°[...]
2 [...]l [...]

Frg. 173

1 [...]g°°[...]
2 [...]°[...]

Frg. 174

1 [...]° [...]
2 [...]° w[...]

Frg. 175

1 [...]°[...]
2 [...]°[...]

Frg. 176

1 [...]m °[...]
2 [...]°[...]

Frg. 177

1 [...]   [...]
2 [...]°°°[...]

Frg. 178

1 [...]°[...]

Frg. 179

1 [...] h[...]
2 [...]l[...]

Frg. 180

1 [...]°[...]
2 [...] š°[...]

Frg. 181

1 [...]m[...]

Frg. 182

1 [...]° [...]

153

Non-Masoretic Psalms

(4Q88=4QPs^f, 11Q5=11QPs^a, 11Q6=11QPs^b)

JAMES A. SANDERS

with J. H. CHARLESWORTH and H. W. L. RIETZ

Introduction

Four scrolls of psalms from Qumran contain non-Masoretic psalms as well as psalms familiar from the MT Psalter: 4QPs^f=4Q88, 11QPs^a=11Q5, 11QPs^b=11Q6, and the so-called 11QPsAp^a=11Q11. While others exhibit an order of MT psalms different from that of the received text, our interest here is in what we today would call non-biblical or apocryphal psalms. The Community at Qumran had many hymns and songs other than psalms (*Thanksgiving Hymns* [1QH, 1Q35, 4Q427−32], *Angelic Liturgy* [4Q400−407, 11Q17], and numerous fragments in DJD 1−7). The Community also had biblical-type psalms which, while not in the MT, were copied on scrolls of psalms along with MT psalms. It is these biblical-type psalms which concern us here.

1. Manuscripts and Texts

The Psalms Scroll from cave eleven (11Q5) is among the largest preserved from all the caves. It measures some fourteen feet (4.2 meters) in length and is comprised of five (six?) sheets of tanned goat skin which have survived. This length includes the five fragments (frgs. a to e) which belong to the first extant sheet. The scroll may have measured 24 feet originally, which would be close in size to the longest scrolls found. The scroll in its present condition is six to seven inches (15 to 17.9 cm) high, whereas it was originally nine to ten inches high. Each column preserves 14 to 17 extant lines of text, whereas each originally included 21 to 23 lines. Thirty-four columns of text survive, including the six columns on fragments a to e; but since we cannot be absolutely sure how many columns there were in the area represented by the fragments (though we know they belong somewhere before

the first continuous sheet), numbering of columns begins with the first continuous sheet. Measurements of the four or five fragments of 4Q88 (so far published) and of the six fragments of 11Q6 can be found in their respective preliminary editions.

There are nine non-Masoretic compositions in 11Q5, four known heretofore in ancient translations and five heretofore unknown. One of the latter, the "Apostrophe to Zion" on column 22, is also found in 4Q88, which has two other non-Masoretic psalms as well, an "Eschatological Hymn," and an "Apostrophe to Judah." 11Q5 (col. 19) preserves the "Plea for Deliverance" which is also found in 11Q6.

11Q6 was apparently an exact copy of 11Q5, or was another copy of the same Psalter represented by the latter, and included the "Plea for Deliverance" found on column 19 of the large scroll. The order of the biblical psalms, Psalm 141 followed by Psalm 133 and then Psalm 144, is the same as in 11Q5 (col. 23). Both 11Q5 and 11Q6 also contain a fifth heretofore unknown composition we have entitled "A Doxology."

2. Original Language

There is no reason to doubt that the original language of these compositions is Hebrew. The Syriac of Psalm 151 derives from the Greek (LXX); but that of Psalms 154 and 155 comes directly from the Hebrew.[1] Similarly, the Hebrew of Sirach is certainly closer to the original Hebrew than to either the Greek or the Syriac; a fuller Hebrew manuscript of Sirach was found in Masada.[2] There is a medieval Hebrew copy of Sirach, but it is a translation of the Greek.

---

[1] See Strugnell, "Notes on the Text and Transmission of the Apocryphal Psalms 151, 154 (= Syr. II) and 155 (= Syr. III)," *HTR* 59 (1966) 278.

[2] M. H. Segal, *Sēfer ben Sîrā' ha-šālēm* (Jerusalem: 1958 [2nd ed.]).

3. Date and Provenience

The palaeography of the manuscripts provides the *terminus ad quem* for the composition of the respective documents. The script of both 11Q5 and 11Q6 is Herodian and dates to the first half of the first century C.E.[3] The semi-cursive script of 4Q88 is Hasmonaean and dates to the first century B.C.E.[4] The heavy cursive script of 4Q448, which preserves a portion of Psalm 154 (4Q448 1.8−9; 11Q5 18.14−16), dates to the early or middle of the first century B.C.E.[5] The *terminus a quo* is more difficult to determine. The non-Masoretic psalms in these manuscripts have been variously dated back to the Persian and Hellenistic periods. Starcky dates the "Eschatological Hymn" to the latter part of the second century B.C.E. The dates of composition of Psalm 151 and Sirach 51:13ff. probably predate the second century B.C.E., since they are also preserved in Greek (LXX), which antedates that period.

Of the non-Masoretic Psalms preserved on these manuscripts, Psalm 154 is most closely aligned with the sectarian Dead Sea Scrolls. The content of the Psalm reveals three distinct groups, one which is called a "community" (יחד), and another "the simple ones" (11Q5 18.1−6). The third group, "the wicked ones" (11Q5 18.13), stands over against the other two as perpetrators of an evil time and as enemies of the 'in-group', those called into the community. The use of *yaḥad* in the instruction in 18.1, החבירו יחד ("Form a community"), is similar to the technical term at Qumran for the Community of oneness in the covenant with God (cf. 1QS; 1QH 11.10−14; 3.19−23). The phrase "form a community," however, is not found in the sectarian Dead Sea Scrolls. Other nouns that are technical terms at Qumran, but not necessarily ideas peculiar to the sectarian Dead Sea Scrolls, are "the Perfect Ones" (11Q5 18.1; cf. 1QS 4.22) and "the Poor Ones" (11Q5 18.15; cf. 1QH 2.34, 5.13f.). Other concepts reflected at Qumran include the ideas expressed in 11Q5 18.7−10 that the Most High accepts praise as equal to sacrifices and in 11Q5 18.11−12 that the righteous share in common meals and constantly study the law; these emphases, however, are not unique to Qumran. Thus, the evidence cannot prove that the Psalm was composed at Qumran. The similarity of its thought to the writings of the Qumran Community, however, cannot be dismissed. The Psalm may predate the exodus from the Temple to Qumran.

The prose insertion entitled "David's Compositions" indicates a 52-week, 364-day year. In contrast to the lunar 354-day year of the establishment in the Temple, a 364-day solar-lunar calendar, also known in various forms in *Enoch* and *Jubilees*, was probably followed by the sectarian Qumranites. While this insertion was not necessarily composed at Qumran, it was clearly compatible with their beliefs. "David's Compositions" was quite possibly composed in the first century B.C.E. or C.E., the latter if by the scribe of the scroll.

4. Presentation of the Documents[6]

Since these Psalms represent separate compositions, each document has its own brief introduction. When a composition is present on more than one manuscript, the text and translation of each manuscript version will be presented separately. Those compositions which were previously known in ancient translations are also presented with the ancient translation in parallel columns. Similarly, "A Doxology" is presented in parallel with the corresponding verses from the Masoretic Text.

5. Selected Bibliography

The sigla and abbreviations used in the texts and notes are followed by the bibliographic data of the works cited.

11Q5 (= 11QPs^a)
PAM 43.786 (col. 16), 43.787 (cols. 18−19), 43.788 (col. 21), 43.787A and 43.789A (col. 22), 43.790 and 43.790A (col. 24), 43.791 (cols. 26−27), 43.792 and 43.792A (col. 28).
Sanders, J. A., ed. *The Psalms Scroll of Qumran Cave 11*. DJD 4, 1965.
Sanders, J. A. *The Dead Sea Psalms Scroll*. Ithaca, 1967.

11Q6 (= 11QPs^b)
PAM 42.177 and 44.003 (frgs. a, b, c), 42.176 and 44.005 (frg. f).
van der Ploeg, J. P. M. "Fragments d'un manuscrit de Psaumes de Qumran (11QPs^b)," *RB* 74 (1967) 408−13; and Pl. XVIII.

11Q11 (= 11QPsAp^a)
PAM 43.982−43.988 (cols. 1−5), 44.003 (frg. a), 44.004 (frgs. b, c).
van der Ploeg, J. P. M. "Un petit rouleau de psaumes apocryphes (11QPsAp^a)." In *Tradition und Glaube* (K. Kuhn Festgabe), edited by G. Jeremias, *et al.* Göttingen, 1971, pp. 128−39; and Pls. II-VII.

4Q88 (= 4QPs^f)
PAM 43.603.
Starcky, J. "Psaumes apocryphes de la grotte 4 de Qumrân (4QPs^f VII–X)," *RB* 73 (1966) 353−71; and Pl. XIII.

General
Barton, J. *Oracles of God*. Oxford, 1986, p. 86.
Charlesworth, J. H. with J. A. Sanders, "More Psalms of David." In *Old Testament Pseudepigrapha*, edited by J. H. Charlesworth. Garden City, 1985; vol. 2, pp. 609−24.
Flint, P. W. *The Dead Sea Psalms and the Book of Psalms*. STDJ 17; Leiden, 1997.
Meyer, R. "Die Septuaginta-Fassung von Psalm 151 als Ergebnis einer dogmatischen Korrektur." In *Das Ferne und Nahe Wort* (Leonard Rost Festschrift), edited by F. Maass. Berlin, 1967, pp. 164−72.

---

[3] J. van der Ploeg, *RB* 74 (1967) 408.
[4] J. Starcky, *RB* 73 (1966) 354−55.
[5] E. Eshel, H. Eshel, and A. Yardeni, "A Qumran Composition Containing Part of Ps 154 and a Prayer for the Welfare of King Jonathan and his Kingdom," *IEJ* 42 (1992) 199−229. See Sanders in *Biblische Theologie*, pp. 297−304.
[6] This section is by Charlesworth and Rietz.

Sanders, J. A. "Cave 11 Surprises and the Question of Canon," first published in *McCormick Quarterly* 21 (1968) 284−98; republished in *New Directions in Biblical Archaeology*, edited by D. N. Freedman and J. Greenfield. Garden City, 1969, pp. 101−16.

Sanders, J. A. "The Qumran Psalms Scroll (11QPsᵃ) Reviewed." In *On Language, Culture, And Religion: In Honor of Eugene A. Nida*, edited by M. Black and W. Smalley. The Hague, 1974, pp. 79−99.

Sanders, J. A. "A Multivalent Text: Psalm 151:3−4 Revisited." *HAR* 8 (1984) 167−84.

Sanders, J. A. "Psalm 154 Revisited." In *Biblische Theologie und gesellschaftlicher Wandel* (Norbert Lohfink Festschrift), edited by G. Braulik, *et al.* Freiburg, 1993, pp. 296−306.

"A Doxology" (11Q5 Col. 16; 11Q6 Frg. f)

"A Doxology" (11Q5 16.1–6)

Col. 16

1   כי לעולם חסדו' הודו ל𐤉𐤄𐤅𐤄 כי טוב כי לעולם חסדו קול²

2   רנה וישועה באהלי צדיקים ימין 𐤉𐤄𐤅𐤄 עשה חיל ימין³

3   𐤉𐤄𐤅𐤄 רוממה ימין 𐤉𐤄𐤅𐤄 עשתה גבורה טוב לבטוח

4   ב𐤉𐤄𐤅𐤄 מבטוח באדם טוב לחסות ב𐤉𐤄𐤅𐤄 מבטוב⁴

5   בנדיבים טוב לבטוב⁵ ב𐤉𐤄𐤅𐤄 מבטוח באלף עם הודו

6   ל𐤉𐤄𐤅𐤄 כי טוב כי לעולם חסדו הללויה⁶

"A Doxology" (11Q6 Frg. f)

Frg. f

1   לעול]ם֯ חסדו ק֯[ול⁷

2   ע[ש]ה חיל ימ֯[ין⁸

---

¹ This concludes Ps 136:1-16 which began on the previous column.

² 11Q6 frg. f line 1: [ם֯ חסדו ק֯].

³ 11Q6 frg. f line 2: [שׁה חיל ימ֯].

⁴ Read מבטוח.

⁵ Read לבטוח.

⁶ Lines 7-16 preserve Ps 145:1-7.

⁷ 11Q5 16.1-2: כי לעולם חסדו פול רנה.

⁸ 11Q5 16.2-3: וישועה באהלי צדיקים ימין יהוה עשה חיל ימין יהוה רוממה.

"A Doxology" (11Q5 Col. 16; 11Q6 Frg. f)

Introduction

"A Doxology," made up of familiar phrases of liturgical material known also in Psalms 118, 136 and elsewhere, is preserved in 11Q5 column 16 and 11Q6 fragment f. This doxology is rather like the psalm in 1 Chronicles 16:8–36 which is made up of phrases familiar from Psalms 96, 105, and 106. Many composers construct such anthologies in varying combinations of familiar liturgical phrases, particularly in doxologies. It is found in what appears to be its entirety in the first six lines of 11Q5 column 16, immediately following Psalm 136 and just before Psalm 145. Only a few words of it are extant in 11Q6, and they are on an isolated fragment so that it is not certain how the little doxology on that scroll related to either the three Masoretic psalms or to the "Plea for Deliverance"; but they clearly indicate that the whole of the doxology was originally also in 11Q6.

"A Doxology" (11Q5 16.1–6)

Col. 16

1 for his mercy (endures) forever.[1] Give thanks[2] to Yahweh for (he is) good, for his mercy (endures) forever.[3] The sound of

2 a shout and of salvation (is heard) in the tents of the Righteous Ones. The right hand of Yahweh acts valiantly,[4] the right hand of

3 Yahweh is exalted, the right hand of Yahweh acts (in) power.[5] (It is) better to trust

4 in Yahweh than to trust in a human.[6] (It is) better to take refuge in Yahweh than to trust

5 in nobles.[7] (It is) better to trust in Yahweh than to trust in a thousand people.[8] Give thanks

6 to Yahweh for (he is) good, for his mercy (endures) forever.[9] Hallelujah.

"A Doxology" (11Q6 Frg. f)

Frg. f

1 […] his mercy (endures) [forev]er. The so[und of…]

2 [… a]cts valiantly, the rig[ht] ha[nd of …]

---

[1] This concludes Ps 136:1–16 which began on the previous column.
[2] Cf. P. Ackroyd, *JTS* 17 (1966) 396–99.
[3] Cf. Ps 118:1, 19; 136:1.
[4] Cf. Ps 118:15.
[5] Cf. Ps 118:16.
[6] Cf. Ps 118:8.
[7] Cf. Ps 118:9.
[8] Or "an army."
[9] Cf. Ps 118:1, 19; 136:1. Lines 7–16 preserve Ps 145:1–7.

11Q5 and 11Q6 compared with the Masoretic Text

MT Psalm 118 (rearranged)	*11Q5 and 11Q6*
(1,29) הודו ליהוה כי טוב	(1) הודו ל𐤉𐤄𐤅𐤄 כי טוב
כי לעולם חסדו[1]	כי לעולם חסדו
(15) קול רנה וישועה	(2) קול רנה וישועה
באהלי צדיקים	באהלי צדיקים
ימין יהוה עשה חיל	ימין 𐤉𐤄𐤅𐤄 עשה חיל
(16) ימין יהוה רוממה	(3) ימין 𐤉𐤄𐤅𐤄 רוממה
ימין יהוה עשה חיל	ימין 𐤉𐤄𐤅𐤄 עשתה גבורה
(8) טוב לחסות ביהוה	(4) טוב לבטוח ב𐤉𐤄𐤅𐤄
מבטח באדם[2]	מבטוח באדם
(9) טוב לחסות ביהוה	טוב לחסות ב𐤉𐤄𐤅𐤄
מבטח בנדיבים[3]	(5) מבטוב בנדיבים
	טוב לבטוב ב𐤉𐤄𐤅𐤄
	מבטוח באלף עם
(1,29) הודו ליהוה כי טוב	(6) הודו ל𐤉𐤄𐤅𐤄 כי טוב
כי לעולם חסדו[1]	כי לעולם חסדו
	הללויה

---

1 4Q84 col. 34: הֹ[כי טוב כי לעולם חסדו] (PAM 42.025; Cf. Starcky *CBQ* 26 [1964] 213-22).

2 4Q84 col. 34: טוב לבטח ביהוה מבטח בא[ֹ] (PAM 42.025; Cf. Starcky *CBQ* 26 [1964] 213-22).

3 4Q84 col. 34: טוב לחסות ביהוה מבטֹח בֹ[ן] (PAM 42.025; Cf. Starcky *CBQ* 26 [1964] 213-22).

11Q5 and 11Q6 compared with the Masoretic Text[10]

11Q5 and 11Q6

[1]Give thanks to Yahweh for (he is) good,
for his mercy (endures) forever.
The sound of [2]a shout and of salvation (is heard)
in the tents of the righteous.
The right hand of Yahweh acts valiantly,
the right hand of [3]Yahweh is exalted,
the right hand of Yahweh acts (in) power.
(It is) better to trust [4]in Yahweh
than to trust in a human.
(It is) better to take refuge in Yahweh
than to trust [5]in nobles.
(It is) better to trust in Yahweh
than to trust in a thousand people.
Give thanks [6] to Yahweh for (he is) good,
for his mercy (endures) forever.
Hallelujah.

MT Psalm 118 (rearranged)

[1,29] 11 Give thanks to Yahweh for (he is) good,
for his mercy (endures) forever.
[15]The sound of a shout and of salvation (is heard)
in the tents of the righteous.
The right hand of Yahweh acts valiantly,
[16]the right hand of Yahweh is exalted,
the right hand of Yahweh acts valiantly.
[8](It is) better to take refuge 12 in Yahweh
than to trust in a human.
[9](It is) better to take refuge in Yahweh
than to trust 13 in nobles.

[1,29]Give thanks to Yahweh for (he is) good,
for his mercy (endures) forever.

---

[10] Superscripted numbers in parentheses indicate line numbers
    for 11Q5 col. 16 and verse numbers for the MT, respectively.
[11] Cf. Ps 136:1.

[12] 4Q84 col. 34 reads "to trust."
[13] 4Q84 col. 34 also reads "than to trust."

Psalms Known In Ancient Translations

Psalm 151 A and B (11Q5 28.3−14)

Psalm 151 A and B (11Q5 28.3−14)

Col. 28[1]

3   הללויה לדויד בן ישי קטן הייתי מאחי[2] וצעיר מבני אבי וישימני

4   רועה לצונו ומושל בגדיותיו ידי עשו עוגב ואצבעותי כנור

5   ואשימה ל~~צצצ~~ כבוד אמרתי אני בנפשי ההרים לוא יעידו

---

[1]   The first two lines of this column contain Psalm 134:1-3.
There is a wide space between lines 2 and 3.   [2]   **Read** מן אחי.

Psalms Known In Ancient Translations

Psalms 151 A and B, 154, 155, and the canticle known previously in Sirach 51:13ff. are all found in 11Q5 in what are apparently their original Hebrew forms, or close to them, granting errors in transmission from composition to their appearance on the scroll. Heretofore, they were known in Greek (Ps 151), Syriac (Pss 151, 154, 155), or both (Ps 151), and in the case of Sirach in medieval Hebrew texts closer to the Greek of Sirach than to what we now have. These documents are presented here in two different formats. First, the document is presented as it is attested at Qumran, with each manuscript witness presented separately. A second transcription presents the Qumran text in one column with the corresponding text of the ancient translation in a second column. The facing page contains English translations. In translating the Syriac versions, cognates of the Hebrew are translated consistently whenever possible.

Psalm 151 A and B (11Q5 28.3−14)

Introduction

Psalm 151 has been known through the centuries as the supernumerary psalm at the end of the Septuagint Psalter, and in the Syro-Hexaplar, Codex Ambrosianus. Psalms 151, 154, and 155 have been known since the eighteenth century as three of the five Syriac apocryphal psalms, numbers I, II and III, found first in a tenth-century non-biblical document. More recently the five psalms have been found in medieval Syriac copies of the Psalter and numbered Pss 151 to 155 with Psalms II and III numbered Psalms 154 and 155.[1] Psalm 151 has been dated as early as the sixth century B.C.E.; it is difficult to discern the century in which it was composed, but it probably antedates the third century because of its appearance in the LXX.[2]

Psalm 151 A and B (11Q5 28.3−14)

Col. 28

3 A Hallelujah of David the Son of Jesse.   Smaller[3] was I than my brothers and the youngest[4] of the sons of my father when he made me

4 shepherd of his flock[5] and ruler[6] over his kids.   My hands have made a (musical) instrument and my fingers a lyre;

5 and (so) have I rendered[7] glory to Yahweh, said I[8] within my soul.[9]   The mountains do not witness

---

[1] Cf. DJD 4, pp. 53−76; *DSPS*, pp. 93−112, 141−42; *OTP* 2:609−67.

[2] See A. Hurvitz in *Eretz Israel* 8 (1967) 82−87.

[3] Said of David in 1Sam 16:11 and 17:14, and of Solomon in 1Kgs 3:7.

[4] Cf. Judg 6:15 and Ps 119:141 (11Q5 12.14); see also Pseudo-Philo's *Liber Antiquitatum Biblicarum* 62:5; and D. Flusser and S. Safrai, *Shirê Zikaron Le Yehoshua Grintz* (Tel Aviv, 1982) pp. 84−92.

[5] Cf. 1Sam 16:11.

[6] Cf. Ps 105:21.

[7] Cf. Isa 42:12. The conjunctive ו means "then" or "so" frequently in Qohelet.

[8] Cf. Ex 2:14.

[9] Or "to myself" (cf. Qoh 2:1, 15, 3:17, 18). The expression normally precedes the thought expressed and has a negative connotation (see the variant translations noted in *DSPS*, pp. 100−103 and *HAR* 8 [1984] 167−84), but the context indicates David's intention of rendering God glory which God would have seen in David's heart or soul (1Sam 16:7). The words "heart" and "soul" were used interchangeably at Qumran, as several times in 1QH 4.

6   לו והגבעות לוא יגידו עלֹ העצים את דברֹי והצואן את מעשׂי

7   כי מי יגיד ומי ידבר ומי יספר את מעשׂי[3] אדון הכול ראה (וֹ)אלוהֹי

8   הכול הוא שמע והוא האזין שלח נביאו למושחני את שמואל

9   לגדלני יצאו אחי לקראתו יפי התור ויפי המראה הגבהים בקומתם

10   היפים[5]   בשערם לוא בחר ‎𝒮ℬ𝒳𝒷 אלוהים בם וישלח ויקחני
                                  ומושל

11   מאחר הצואן וימשחני בשמן הקודש וישימני נגיד לעמו בבני

12   בריתו

13   תחלת גב[ו]רֹה[6] ל[דו]יד משמשחו נביא אלוהים אזי רֹא[י]תי[7] פלשתי

14   מֹחֹרֹף[8] ממ[ערכות האיוב] אנוכי[את]

---

[3] The macron above the י or ו of the words עלו ,דברי, and
מעשי *bis* in lines 6-7 indicates that some scholars have read
the other letter, rather than that which is transcribed.

[4] A ו with a scribal correction dot over it has been erased just
before the word אלוה.

[5] Space between היפים and בשערם is due to scar-tissue. See
photograph.

[6] The first two letters are without question and the last two are
clear enough to evoke confidence. The space in the lacuna
indicates the ו supplied.

[7] The reading reflects well the events recorded in 1 Sam
17:23-25.

[8] The top tracings of מֹחֹרֹף are clear enough to warrant
confidence.

6 to him, nor do the hills proclaim;[10] the trees have cherished[11] my words and the flock my works.[12]

7 For who can proclaim and who can bespeak and who can recount[13] the works of the Lord?   Everything[14] has God seen,[15]

8 everything has he heard and he has heeded.[16]   He sent his prophet, Samuel, to anoint me,

9 to make me great.   My brothers went out to meet him, handsome of figure[17] and handsome of appearance.[18]   (Though) they were tall of stature

10 (and) handsome by their hair, Yahweh chose them not.[19]   But he sent and took me

11 from behind the flock[20] and anointed me with holy oil,[21] and made me leader[22] to his people and ruler over the sons of

12 his covenant.[23]

13 At the beginning of [Dav]id's p[ow]er after the prophet of God had anointed him.[24]   Then I s[a]w[25] a Philistine

14 uttering defiances[26] from the r[anks of the enemy].   I [...]'t[.,.]

[10] Contrast Micah 6:1–2; Isa 44:23, 55:12; etc. The principal reason the later Hebrew recensionist, or the Greek translator, omitted ll. 5 and 6 and parts of ll. 7–8 (vv. 2b-3; see DJD 4, p. 55, and *DSPS*, p. 97) was that they express thoughts contrary to biblical teaching, despite the beautiful piety they in themselves express as David's own private and solitary musing while watching his flock. God had given David the very special gifts of making musical instruments and composing music for them; mountains and hills apparently do neither, though they were in the shepherd's lonely vigil apparently an appreciative audience. See the some sixteen variant translations of these lines compiled in *HAR* 8 (1984) 167–84, none of them alike.

[11] Read as עָלוּ as in CD 3.2, and 5.5. Others have read עָלָי or עָלֵי. Again see the variant translations in *DSPS*, pp. 100–103 and *HAR* 8 (1984) 167–84.

[12] "My words" and "my works" have also been read as "his word (or, words)" and "his work/deed (or, works/deeds)"; *DSPS*, pp. 100–103 and *HAR* 8 (1984) 167–84.

[13] In the spirit of Isa 40:12–13, Sir 16:20, *et passim*, as opposed to the assertion in Ps 118:17.

[14] As emended in Ps 114:7. The noun is construct only to "all the earth/land" in the Bible, never to "everything/universe," nor in Qumran literature. Cf. 1QH 10.8. Again see the variant translations.

[15] See similar constructions with the direct object preceeding verb and subject in 1Sam 30:19, 2Chr, 36:17 and Qoh 7:15; cf. 1QH 16.8. The point the poet celebrates here is the same made in 1Sam 16:7; specifically, that God sees everything, not merely externals but even and especially what was going on in David's lonely shepherd heart or soul; see 1Sam 13:14 and Ps 78:72 where similar ideas are expressed concerning David. Against reading "God of the universe," as some have proposed, see P. W. Skehan in *CBQ* 25 (1963) 407–08.

[16] Most ancient versions read simply "he hears," while others (LXX, Sinaiticus, and some Old Latin witnesses) read "he hears everything," a very good understanding of the Hebrew as translated above. For other understandings, see *HAR* 8 (1984) 167–84. Lines 8 to 10 retell in poetry the story in 1Sam 16:4–10.

[17] The same defective spelling (without א) of התואר in Cant 2:12 and 1Chron 17:17 as well as in 1QIs^b (= 1Q8) 52.14 and 11Q5 21.11.

[18] The very words used to describe Rachel (Gen 29:17) and Joseph (Gen 39:6).

[19] Words taken directly from 1Sam 16:8–10.

[20] Cf. 2Sam 7:8, 1Chron 17:7, Ps 78:70–71.

[21] Cf. Ps 89:21.

[22] The word used in 2Sam 7:8 and 1Chron 17:7.

[23] Cf. 1QM 17.8; 2Chr 7:18; and Micah 5:1. These lines form an *inclusio* with line 4 (v. 1b of the poem; see *DSPS*, p. 97).

[24] Drawn from 1Sam 16:13, 18.

[25] Drawn from 1Sam 17:23–25. David witnessed the humiliation of all Israel before Goliath and the Philistines.

[26] The verb חרף occurs five times in 1Sam 17 including 17:25 from which the verb "saw" was also drawn. Cf. 1Sam 17:10, 25, 26, 36, 45.

11Q5 compared with the Septuagint and Peshiṭta
Psalm 151 A

Peshiṭta[1]	*LXX*[3]	*11Q5*
ܕܕܘܝܕ ܟܕ ܒܠܚܘܕܘܗܝ, ܐܬܟܬܫ ܥܡ ܓܘܠܝܕ.	Οὗτος ὁ ψαλμὸς ἰδιόγραφος εἰς Δαυιδ καὶ ἔξωθεν τοῦ ἀριθμοῦ· ὅτε ἐμονομάχησεν τῷ Γολιαδ.	(3) הללויה לדויד בן ישי
(1) ܙܥܘܪܐ ܗܘܝܬ ܒܐܚܝ. ܘܛܠܝܐ ܒܒܝܬܗ ܕܐܒܝ. ܪܥܐ ܗܘܝܬ ܥܢܐ ܕܐܒܝ.	(1)Μικρὸς ἤμην ἐν τοῖς ἀδελφοῖς μου καὶ νεώτερος ἐν τῷ οἴκῳ τοῦ πατρός μου· ἐποίμαινον τὰ πρόβατα τοῦ πατρός μου.	קטן הייתי ומן אחי וצעיר מבני אבי
(2) ܐܝܕܝ, ܥܒܕ̈ܝ ܐܘܪܓܢܘܢ.[2] ܘܨܒ̈ܥܬܝ, ܛܩ̈ܢ ܟܢܪܐ.	(2)αἱ χεῖρές μου ἐποίησαν ὄργανον, οἱ δάκτυλοί μου ἥρμοσαν ψαλτήριον.	וישימני (4) רועה לצונו ומושל בגדיותיו ידי עשו עוגב ואצבעותי כנור (5) ואשימה ל𐤉𐤄𐤅𐤄 כבוד אמרתי אני בנפשי ההרים לוא יעידו (6) לו והגבעות לוא יגידו עלו֯ העצים את דברי֯ והצואן את מעשי֯
(3) ܘܡܢܘ ܢܚܘܐ ܠܡܪܝ, ܗܘܝܘ ܡܪܝܐ ܗܘܝܘ ܐܠܗܐ ܫܡܥ.	(3)καὶ τίς ἀναγγελεῖ τῷ κυρίῳ μου; αὐτὸς κύριος, αὐτὸς πάντων[4] εἰσακούει.	(7) כי מי יגיד ומי ידבר ומי יספר את מעשי֯ אדון הכול ראה אלוה (8) הכול הוא שמע והוא האזין

1 Syriac text of MS 12t4 is adapted with permission of E. J. Brill from W. Baars, ed., "Apocryphal Psalms," in *The Old Testament in Syriac* (Leiden, 1972) pp. 2-4.

2 From Gk. ὄργανον.

3 Greek text is adapted with permission of Vandenhoeck and Ruprecht from A. Rahlfs, ed., *Septuaginta,* vol. 10 *Psalmi cum Odis* (Göttingen: 1931) pp. 339–40.

4 Most ancient versions read simply, *αὐτὸς εἰσακούει,* while others (LXX[ℵ] Ol[Y] Gali) read, *αὐτὸς πάντων εἰσακούει*, a very good translation of the Hebrew as presented in this volume.

11Q5 compared with the Septuagint and Peshiṭta[27]
Psalm 151 A

11Q5	*LXX*[28]	*Peshiṭta*[31]
[3]A Hallelujah of David the Son of Jesse.	This psalm (is) truly written by David, though supernumery, when he singlehandedly fought Goliath.	By David, when he alone fought against Goliath.
Smaller was I than my brothers and the youngest of the sons of my father	[1]Small was I among my brothers and the youngest in the house of my father.	[1]The smallest was I among[32] my brothers and youngest in the house of my father.
when he made me [4]shepherd of his flock and ruler over his kids.	I tended the sheep of my father.	I was tending the flocks of my father.
My hands have made a (musical) instrument and my fingers a lyre;	[2]My hands made a (musical) instrument; my fingers fashioned a lyre.	[2]My hands made a (musical) instrument, and my fingers fashioned[33] a lyre.[34]
[5]and (so) have I rendered glory to Yahweh, said I within my soul.		
The mountains do not witness [6]to him, nor do the hills proclaim; the trees have cherished my words and the flock my works.		
[7]For who can proclaim and who can bespeak and who can recount the works of the Lord? Everything has God seen, [8]everything has he heard and he has heeded.	[3]And who shall proclaim for[29] my Lord? The Lord himself, he hears everything.[30]	[3]And who will declare to my Lord, that is the Lord, that is my God?

---

[27] Superscripted numbers in parentheses indicate line numbers for 11Q5 col. 28 and verse numbers for the LXX and the Peshiṭta, respectively. For further discussion of the textual issues and detailed comparisons of LXX and Syriac Psalm 151 with 11Q5 151 see DJD 4, pp. 54–64 and *DSPS*, pp. 96–100; cf. *OTP* 2:612–15.

[28] Translation by Charlesworth and Rietz.

[29] Or "to."

[30] Most ancient versions read simply "he hears," while others (LXX, Sinaiticus, and some Old Latin witnesses) read "he hears everything," a very good understanding of the Hebrew as translated above. For other understandings again see *HAR* 8 (1984) 167–84.

[31] Translation by Charlesworth and Rietz.

[32] The Beth here and in the next line indicate the superlative.

[33] Lit. "fitted."

[34] Lit. "lyres."

(4a) ܗܘ ܓܝܪ ܠܡܠܐܟܗ	(4a)αὐτὸς ἐξαπέστειλεν τὸν ἄγγελον αὐτοῦ	שלח נביאו למושחני‸את שמואל
		(9)לגדלני
		יצאו אחי לקראתו
		יפי התור ויפי המראה
(5) ܐܚܝ ܫܦܝܪܐ ܘܪܘܪܒܐ.	(5)οἱ ἀδελφοί μου καλοὶ καὶ μεγάλοι,	הגבהים בקומתם
		(10)היפים בשערם
(5) ܘܠܐ ܐܨܛܒܝ ܒܗܘܢ ܡܪܝܐ.	καὶ οὐκ εὐδόκησεν ἐν αὐτοῖς κύριος.	לוא בחר ‸‸‸‸ אלוהים בם
(4b) ܘܫܕܪ ܢܣܒܢܝ ܡܢ ܒܬܪ ܥܢܐ.	(4b)καὶ ἦρέν με ἐκ τῶν προβάτων τοῦ πατρός μου	וישלח ויקחני(11)מאחר הצואן
(4c) ܘܡܫܚܢܝ ܒܡܫܚܐ ܕܩܘܕܫܗ.	(4c)καὶ ἔχρισέν με ἐν τῷ ἐλαίῳ τῆς χρίσεως αὐτοῦ.	וימשחני בשמן הקודש
		וישימני נגיד לעמו
		ומושל בבני בריתו(12)

Psalm 151 B

(13)תחלת גב[ו]רה לד[ו]יד משמשחו נביא אלוהים

(6) ܢܦܩܬ ܠܐܘܪܥܗ ܕܦܠܫܬܝܐ. ܘܠܛܢܝ ܒܦܬܟܪܘܗܝ,	(6)ἐξῆλθον εἰς συνάντησιν τῷ ἀλλοφύλῳ, καὶ ἐπικατηράσατό με ἐν τοῖς εἰδώλοις αὐτοῦ·	אזי ר[א]י]תי פלשתי
		(14)מחרף ממ[ערכות האיוב
(7) ܐܢܐ ܕܝܢ ܟܕ ܫܡܛܬ ܡܢܗ ܣܝܦܗ ܘܣܚܦܬ. ܘܐܪܝܡܬ ܚܣܕܐ ܡܢ ܒܢܝ ܕܝܣܪܐܝܠ.	(7)ἐγὼ δὲ σπασάμενος τὴν παρ᾽ αὐτοῦ μάχαιραν ἀπεκεφάλισα αὐτὸν καὶ ἦρα ὄνειδος ἐξ υἱῶν Ισραηλ.	אנכי[[את]

He sent his prophet, Samuel, to anoint me,
(9)to make me great.
My brothers went out to meet him, handsome of figure and handsome of appearance.
(Though) they were tall of stature (10)(and) handsome by their hair, Yahweh God chose them not.

But he sent and took me (11)from behind the flock
and anointed me with holy oil, and made me leader to his people and ruler over the sons of(12) his covenant.

(4a)He sent his messenger.

(5)My brothers (were) handsome and tall,
but the Lord did not take pleasure in them.
(4b)And he took me from the sheep of my father,
(4c)and anointed me with the oil of his anointing.

(4a)He sent his messenger.

(5)My brothers (were) handsome[36] and tall,[37]
but the Lord did not choose them.[38]
(4b)And he removed me from the sheep of my father,
(4c)and anointed me with the ointment of his anointing.

Psalm 151 B

(13)At the beginning of David's power after the prophet of God had anointed him.
Then I s[a]w a Philistine

(14)uttering defiances from the r[anks of the enemy].
I [...]'t[...]

(6)I went out to meet the foreigner,[35]
and he cursed me by his idols.
(7)But I, drawing his sword from him, beheaded him
and removed shame from the sons of Israel.

(6)I went out[39] to attack the Philistine, and he cursed me by his idols.
(7)But I, when I had drawn his sword, cut off his head
and removed the shame from the sons of Israel.

---

35 Or "Philistine," since ἀλλοφύλος in the LXX often translates פלשתי.

36 The Syr. and Heb. are not cognate, and the Syr. is a literal translation of the Gr.

37 Not "old," "grown up."

38 Or "did not take pleasure in them." N. B. that the Syriac can represent either the Heb. or the Gk. – and that the Heb. and Gk. are within the same semantic range.

39 Forms of the verb, *npq*, are often used to denote a military attack.

Psalm 154 (11Q5 18.1−16)

Psalm 154 (11Q5 18.1−16)

Col. 18

1   לטובים נפשתכמה ולתמימים לפאר עליון החבירו יחד

2   להודיע ישעו ואל תתעצלו להודיע עוזו ותפארתו

3   לכול פותאים כי להודיע כבוד 𐤉𐤄𐤅𐤄 נתנה חוכמה ולספר

4   רוב מעשיו נודעה לאדם להודיע לפותאים עוזו

5   להשכיל לחסרי לבב גדולתו הרחוקים מפתחיה

6   הנדחים'   (ג)ממבואיה כי עליון הואה אדון

7   יעקוב ותפארתו על כול מעשיו ואדם מפאר עליון

8   ירצה כמגיש מנחה כמקריב עתודים ובני בקר

---

[1] Space between הנדחים and ממבואיה in line 6 is due to the rough and poorly prepared surface of the leather, probably scar tissue. This caused the scribe to make an erasure (ג̇) in line 6 and to leave the following two ruled lines blank; see photograph.

Psalm 154 (11Q5 18.1−16)

Introduction

The following text is probably the Vorlage of Syriac Psalm II, which in turn may be called a formal equivalence translation of the Hebrew; the Syriac translation corresponds to the Hebrew text at about 95 percent (or better). The first two verses of the Hebrew text and the last are not preserved on the scroll: the first two were probably at the bottom of column 17, and the psalm would have been completed in the missing lines at the bottom of column 18. Recall that the last six or seven lines of each column of 11Q5 are lost due to the decomposition of the scroll in the cave through the centuries. The missing portions are, however, easily supplied by retroversion from the Syriac. The psalm may have been composed in the third or second century B.C.E.

Psalm 154 (11Q5 18.1−16)

Col. 18

1 your souls with the good ones[1] and with the perfect ones to glorify[2] the Most High.   Form a community[3]

2 to make known[4] his salvation, and be not lax in making known his might and his glorious-beauty

3 to all the simple ones.[5]   For to make known the glory of Yahweh is Wisdom given, and to recount

4 his many works she is made known to humanity: to make known to the simple ones his might,

5 to instruct the senseless ones[6] (in) his greatness, those far from her openings,

6 those who stray from her portals.[7]   For the Most High is the Lord of

7 Jacob, and his glorious-beauty is over all his works.   And a person who glorifies the Most High

8 he accepts[8] as one who brings a meal offering, as one who presents he-goats and sons of bulls,

---

[1] An appellative (see l. 14) for members of the community or congregation; see "the perfect ones" (l. 1), "those who glorify him" (l. 14), and "the poor ones" (l. 15); cf. 1QS 3.3, *et passim*; 1QM 14.7; 1QH 1.36; etc.

[2] The Heb. verb is from the root פאר which appears in verbal forms in lines 1, 7, 14 ("glorify") and in noun forms in lines 2 and 7 ("glorious beauty"). Those who join the community are those who glorify the Most High, an expression unattested elsewhere at Qumran.

[3] Lines 1 to 3 (vv. 3 and 4) with their three imperatives form a call to constitute a congregation, assembly, or community, common terms in Qumran literature referring to the Qumran Community itself, and an admonition to be diligent in its mission.

[4] Or "to proclaim." The infinitive "to make known" appears twice in this line (v. 4) and again in ll. 3 (v. 5), 4 (v. 7), and 12 (v. 14); these along with two others, "recounting" in l. 3 (v. 6) and "to instruct" in l. 5 (v. 7), express the mission and purpose of forming the community. Cf. 1QH 6.10−13, 11.9−12, 13.12−15, 15.19−21; CD 13.7−8; and elsewhere.

[5] "Simple ones" here and in l. 4 (v. 7) means senseless ones or fools, as in 1QH 2, l. 9, etc. See the parallel "senseless ones" in l. 5 (v. 7). Elsewhere in Qumran literature it may refer to the humble or pious members of the community, but not in this psalm.

[6] Lit. "ones deficient (with respect to) the heart."

[7] Both "openings" and "portals" refer to the doors of Wisdom; cf. Prov 8:34, 9:1ff., 14:1; Sir 1:15, 14:23, 24:8ff., etc.

[8] Cf. 2Sam 24:23; Hos 8:13; Jer 14:10, 12; Ezek 20:40−41; 43:27. God accepts the person who glorifies God as favorably as one who offers many sacrifices: see ll. 8−10 (v. 11); 1QS 9.4−5.

9   כמדשן מזבח ברוב עולות כקטורת (ריֿחֿ)[2] ניחוח מיד

10   צדיקים מפתחי צדיקים נשמע קולה ומקהל חסידים

11   זמרתה על אוכלמה בשבע נאמרה ועל שתותמה בחבר

12   יחדיו שיחתם בתורת עליון אמריהמה להודיע עוזו

13   כמה רחקה מרשעים אמרה מכול זדים לדעתה הנה

14   עיני[3] 𝓪𝓪𝓪𝓪 על טובים תחמל ועל מפאריו יגדל[4] חסדו

15   מעת רעה יציל נפש[ם ברוך]𝓪𝓪𝓪[5] גואל עני מיד

16   צר[ים[6] ומצי]ל [ ]   מיע[קוֿב ושופט[7]

---

2   Note the erasure of ריֿחֿ; cf. the Syriac text.

3   עיני, the plural construct, is clear on the leather. Emend to the singular with the Syriac, or understand the second י as *ḥireq compaginis*.

4   4Q448 1.8: [ועל מפארו.

5   Or restore נפש[נם ברכו את].

6   4Q448 1.9: [עני מיד צרים. The first word of the line should be restored, with 4Q448, as צרים, instead of the earlier conjectured restorations זר]ים or זֹד]ים. See Sanders, "Psalm 154 Revisited."

7   4Q448 1.10 preserves a portion of the next line: משכנו בציון ב[.

9 as one who fattens the altar with many burnt offerings, as a sweet-smelling fragrance from the hand of

10 the righteous ones.   From the openings of the righteous ones is heard her voice, and from the assembly of the pious ones

11 her praise-song.[9]   When they eat with satiety[10] she is cited, and when they drink in fellowship

12 together, their meditation is on the Torah of the Most High, their words are to make known his might.

13 How far from the wicked ones (is) her word, from all the haughty ones to know her.[11]   Behold,

14 the eyes of Yahweh upon the good ones will have pity, and upon those who glorify him he increases his mercy;

15 from an evil time[12] will he deliver [their] soul.   [Bless] Yahweh who redeems the poor ones from the hand of

16 enem[ies and delive]rs [. . . of Ja]cob and judges

---

[9] "Her voice . . . her praise-song" apparently refers to the conviviality of the common meal at which Wisdom was celebrated in recitation and singing (l. 11), and at which study and teaching were pursued (l. 12).

[10] Probably an attempt to express how deeply satisfying the spiritual life of Wisdom, praise, prayer, study, and meditation were for members. See the equally strong expression, using another metaphor for appetite or human eros dedicated to the pursuit of Wisdom, in 21.11–17 (the Sir 51 canticle).

[11] Wisdom's word or speech is far from the wicked and haughty (cf. 1QH 6.35).

[12] A biblical expression (Amos 5:13, Micah 2:3) of a time of suffering, but without the eschatological dimension of much of Qumran literature. Nothing in this psalm, and little in the whole scroll, has that dimension.

11Q5 compared with the Peshiṭta[1]
Psalm 154

Peshiṭta[1]

ܨܠܘܬܗ ܕܚܙܩܝܐ ܟܕ ܚܕܝܪܝܢ ܗܘܘ ܠܗ ܐܬܘܪܝܐ.
ܘܫܐܠ ܗܘܐ ܡܢ ܐܠܗܐ. ܦܘܪܩܢܐ ܕܡܢܗܘܢ.
ܐܡܬܝ ܕܫܐܠ ܥܡܐ ܡܦܣܢܘܬܐ ܡܢ ܟܘܪܫ
ܕܢܗܦܟܘܢ ܠܐܬܪܗܘܢ. ܘܫܐܠܝܢ ܡܢ ܐܠܗܐ
ܕܢܬܡܠܐ ܣܘܒܪܗܘܢ.

(1) ܒܩܠܐ ܪܒܐ ܫܒܚܘ ܠܐܠܗܐ.
ܒܟܢܫܬܐ ܕܣܓܝܐܐ ܐܫܬܒܚܘ ܫܘܒܚܗ.
(2) ܘܒܣܘܓܐܐ ܕܬܪ̈ܝܨܐ ܫܒܚܘ ܩܘܠܣܗ.
ܘܥܡ ܓܒ̈ܝܐ ܐܫܬܒܚܘ ܬܫܒܘܚܬܗ.
(3) ܫܘܬܦܘ ܠܛܒ̈ܐ ܢܦܫܟܘܢ.
ܘܠܬܡ̈ܝܡܐ ܠܡܫܒܚܘ ܠܥܠܝܐ.

(4) ܐܬܟܢܫܘ ܐܟܚܕܐ ܠܡܘܕܥܘ ܥܘܫܢܗ.
ܘܠܐ ܬܬܡܗܠܘܢ ܠܡܚܘܝܘ ܦܘܪܩܢܗ.
ܘܫܘܒܚܗ ܠܟܠܗܘܢ ܥܡ̈ܡܐ.

(5) ܡܛܠ ܕܐܬܝܕܥ ܐܝܩܪܗ ܕܡܪܝܐ
ܐܬܝܗܒܬ ܚܟܡܬܐ.

(6) ܘܠܡܫܬܥܝܘ ܥܒ̈ܕܘܗܝ,
ܐܬܝܕܥܬ ܠܐܢܫܐ.

(7) ܠܡܘܕܥܘ ܠܫܒ̈ܪܐ ܥܘܫܢܗ.
ܘܠܡܣܟܠܘ ܠܚܣܝܪ̈ܝ ܠܒܐ ܬܫܒܘܚܬܗ.

(8) ܕܪ̈ܚܝܩܝܢ ܡܢ ܡ̈ܥܠܢܘܗܝ
ܘܡ̈ܒܕܪܝܢ ܡܢ ܬܪ̈ܥܘܗܝ.

(9) ܡܛܠ ܕܡܪܝܐ ܗܘ ܡܪܗ ܕܝܥܩܘܒ.
ܘܫܘܒܚܗ ܥܠ ܟܠ ܥܒ̈ܕܘܗܝ,

11Q5

[חברו][2] [(1)]לטובים נפשתכמה
ולתמימים לפאר עליון
החבירו יחד [(2)]להודיע ישעו
ואל תתעצלו להודיע עוזו
ותפארתו [(3)]לכול פותאים
כי להודיע כבוד 𐤉𐤄𐤅𐤄
נתנה חוכמה
ולספר [(4)]רוב מעשיו
נודעה לאדם
להודיע לפותאים עוזו
להשכיל[(5)] לחסרי לבב גדולתו
הרחוקים מפתחיה
הנדחים[(6)] (ג̊)ממבואיה
כי עליון הואה אדון [(7)]יעקוב
ותפארתו על כול מעשיו

1 Syriac text of MS 12t4 is adapted with permission of E. J. Brill from W. Baars, ed., "Apocryphal Psalms," in *The Old Testament in Syriac* (Leiden, 1972) pp. 7-8.

2 חברו is retroverted from the Syriac and probably would have appeared on the scroll as the last word on col. 17 with the first two verses of the psalm. It is supplied here for sense.

11Q5 compared with the Peshiṭta[13]
Psalm 154

11Q5

Peshiṭta[15]

A prayer of Hezekiah when the Assyrians were surrounding him and he was asking God's deliverance from them so that the people might receive permission from Cyrus to return to their land. And they asked God to fulfill their expectation.[16]

(1)In a great voice glorify[17] God;
in the congregation of the many ones proclaim
his glory.

(2)And in the multitude of the upright ones glorify
his excellence;
and with the faithful ones narrate his gloriousness.

[Bind][14] (1)your souls with the good ones
and with the perfect ones to glorify the Most High.

(3)Associate your souls[18] with the good ones
and with the innocent ones[19] to glorify the Most High.

Form a community (2)to make known his salvation,
and be not lax in making known his might
and his majesty (3)to all the simple ones.

(4)Gather together to make known his power,
and do not neglect to declare his (act of) rescue
and his glory to all children.[20]

For to make known the glory of Yahweh
is Wisdom given,

(5)So that the honor of the Lord be made known,
wisdom has been granted[21]

and to recount (4)his many works
she is made known to humanity:

(6)and to narrate his deeds,
she was made known[22] to humanity:

to make known to the simple ones his might,
(5)to instruct the senseless ones (in) his greatness,

(7)to make known to children his power,
and to instruct the senseless ones[23] his gloriousness,

those far from her openings,
(6)those who stray from her portals.

(8)those far[24] from her entrances,
and are dispersed from her gate.

For the Most High is the Lord of (7)Jacob,
and his majesty is over all his works.

(9)Because the Most High is the Lord of Jacob,
and his pride is over all his deeds.[25]

---

13 Superscripted numbers in parentheses indicate line numbers for 11Q5 col. 18 and verse numbers for the Pershiṭta, respectively. 4Q448 supplies portions of vss. 18 and 20. For a discussion of the possible citation of Ps 154:19−20 in 4Q448, see Sanders, "Psalm 154 Revisited," in *Biblische Theologie und gesellschaftlicher Wandel für Norbert Lohfink S.J.*, edited by G. Braulik, W. Gross, and S. McEvenue (Freiburg, 1993) pp. 296−306.

14 The verb is retroverted from the Syriac and probably would have appeared on the scroll as the last word on col. 17. "Associate yourselves" (*OTP* 2:620) would be a correct translation of the putative Hebrew, but in the mode of piety expressed in the Hebrew psalm the stronger expression is indicated. Note the occurrence of the root חבר in the first line of col. 18.

15 Translation is by Charlesworth and Rietz.

16 The title is from MS 12t4, but it is very late and has little relation to the content of the psalm.

17 Or "praise." The root *šbḥ* or its cognates appear in vss 1 (*bis*), 2 (*bis*), 3, 4, 7, 10, and 17. The masculine noun, *šwbḥ*, is translated "glory"; the feminine noun with the same meaning, *tšbwḥt'*, is distinguished as "gloriousness."

18 An emendation to *npštkwn* is not necessary, since *npškwn* means "your souls."

19 Or "perfect ones." The Heb. and Syr. are cognate, but the senses may be slightly different.

20 Or "infants"; the noun frequently refers to children under five years of age.

21 The scribe of MS 12t4 incorrectly added the Nestorian vocalization for the first-person-singular pronoun.

22 The scribe of MS 12t4 incorrectly added the Nestorian vocalization for the first-person common singular.

23 Lit. "ones deficient (with respect to) the heart." See the Heb.

24 Both verbs in this vs. appear to be passive participles.

25 Or "his servants"; but see vs. 6.

ואדם מפאר עליון

[8]ירצה כמגיש מנחה

כמקריב עתודים ובני בקר

[9]כמדשן מזבח ברוב עולות

כקטורת (ריח) ניחוח מיד[10] צדיקים

מפתחי צדיקים נשמע קולה

ומקהל חסידים[11] זמרתה

על אוכלמה בשבע נאמרה

ועל שתותמה בחבר[12] יחדיו

שיחתם בתורת עליון

אמריהמה להודיע עוזו

[13]כמה רחקה מרשעים אמרה

מכול זדים לדעתה

הנה[14] עיני יהוה

על טובים תחמל

ועל מפאריו יגדל חסדו

[15]מעת רעה יציל נפש[ם]

[ברוך] יהוה גואל עני מיד[16] צרים

[ומצי]ל [תמימים מיד רשעים]

[מקים קרן מיע]קוב

ושופט [עמים מישראל]

[נוטה] משכנו בציון

ב[וחר לנצח בירושלים]

---

(10) ...

(11) ...

(12) ...

(13) ...

(14) ... ³ ...

(15) ...

(16) ...

(17) ...

(18) ...

(19) ...

(20) ...

---

³ From Gk. νόμος.

And a person who glorifies the Most High
(8)he accepts as one who brings a meal offering,

as one who presents he-goats and sons of bulls,
(9)as one who fattens the altar with many burnt offerings,

as a sweet-smelling fragrance from the hand of (10)the righteous ones.

From the openings of the righteous ones is heard her voice,

and from the assembly of the pious ones (11)her praise-song.

When they eat with satiety she is cited,
and when they drink in fellowship(12)together,

their meditation is on the Torah of the Most High,
their words are to make known his might.

How far from the wicked ones (is) her word,
from all the haughty ones to know her.

Behold, (14)the eyes of Yahweh
upon the good ones will have pity,

and upon those who glorify him he increases his mercy;
(15)from an evil time will he deliver [their] soul.

[Bless] Yahweh who redeems the poor ones from the hand of (16)enemies

[and delive]rs [the perfect ones from the hand of the wicked,]

[who raises up the horn of Ja]cob,
and judges [the peoples of Israel;]

[(so that) he may prolong] his sojourn[26] in Zion,
ch[oosing Jerusalem forever.]

(10)And a person who glorifies the Most High
he receives[27] as one who presents a meal offering,

(11)and as one who presents he-goats and sons of bulls,
and as one who fattens the altar with an abundance of burnt offerings,[28]

and as the scent of incense from the hand of the righteous ones.

(12)From the gates of the just ones is heard her[29] voice,
and from the voice of the just ones her[30] admonition.

(13)And concerning their food fullness (is) in truth,
and concerning their feast their portions[31] (are) together,

(14)their discussions (are) on the Law of the Most High, and their word is to make known his power.

(15)How far from the wicked ones (is) her[32] word,
and from all evil ones to know her.[33]

(16)Behold, the eye(s) of the Lord will have pity[34]
upon the good ones,

(17)and upon those who glorify him he will multiply compassions;

and from an evil time[35] will he ransom their souls.

(18)Blessed be the Lord who saves the unfortunate[36]
from the hand of strangers

and ransoms the innocent ones[26] from the hand of the impious,

(19)who raises up[38] the horn of Jacob,
and the judge of the peoples of Israel;

(20)so that he may prolong[39] his sojourn[40] in Zion,
and may cause adornment[41] forever in Jerusalem.

---

26 Or "tabernacle."

27 In Ps 151:5 ṣbʾ with bᵉ means "choose"; cf. *Ode* 3:9.

28 While the Heb. and Syr. of this verse are not comprised of cognates, the sense is the same.

29 Or "his."

30 Or "his."

31 All other MSS: "in fellowship." This vs. is difficult to understand.

32 Or "his."

33 Or "him."

34 While the Heb. and Syr. are not cognate, the sense is the same.

35 While the Heb. and Syr. are not cognate, the sense is the same.

36 Not "evil ones."

37 Or "perfect ones."

38 Or "rouses up," "appoints," "promises."

39 Or "he may continue."

40 Or "tabernacle."

41 According to the extant lexicons, ṣbt is not attested in the ʾAphel; but the meaning, form, and Nestorian vocalization indicate that here it is an ʾAphel.

Psalm 155 (11Q5 24.3−17)

Psalm 155 (11Q5 24.3−17)

Col. 24[1]

3 *ᵞᵞᵹᵹᵹ* קראתי אליכה הקשיבה אלי פרשתי כפי

4 למעון קודשכה הט אוזנכה ותן לי את שאלתי ובקשתי

5 אל תמנע ממני בנה נפשי ואל תמגרה ואל תפרע לפני

6 רשעים גמולי הרע ישיב ממני דין האמת *ᵞᵞᵹᵹᵹ*

7 אל תשפטני כחטאתי כי לוא יצדק לפניכה כול חי

8 הבינני *ᵞᵞᵹᵹᵹ* בתורתכה ואת משפטיכה למדני

9 וישמעו רבים מעשיכה ועמים יהדרו את כבודכה

10 זכורני ואל תשכחני ואל תביאני בקשות ממני

11 חטאת נעורי הרחק ממני ופשעי אל יזכרו לי

12 טהרני *ᵞᵞᵹᵹᵹ* מנגע רע [ו]אל[2] יוסף לשוב אל יבש

13 שרשיו ממני ואל ינצו על[י]ו בי כבוד אתה *ᵞᵞᵹᵹᵹ*

---

1 The first two lines of this column contain Psalm 144:15.
2 There is a deep fissure in the leather running from the extant bottom of the column up through line 12; but with improved

film images there is less doubt of what is on the extant skin, and reconstruction is aided by the Syriac (see DJD 4, p. 71; *DSPS*, p. 111; *OTP*, 2:623-24).

Psalm 155 (11Q5 24.3−17)

Introduction

The following text is most likely the Vorlage of Syriac Psalm III, which in turn may be called a formal equivalence translation of the Hebrew; the Syriac corresponds to the Hebrew text at 95 percent (or better). Like Psalm 154 this psalm has no reflection of events or figures in David's life or reign as do Psalms 151−53 (Syriac Pss I, IV and V); nor, indeed, does either Psalm 154 or 155 relate in any way to events in Hezekiah's life or reign, despite the superscriptions in some Syriac MSS to them both.[1] But whereas Psalm 154 might easily be thought to have been composed as a poetic expression of the vocation and mission of the Qumran covenanters, or at least easily adapted as such, Psalm 155 has no such expression. On the contrary, it is a very fine exemplar of biblical psalms of thanksgiving with a plea for deliverance embedded in it. It brings to mind Psalms 22 and 51; it may date so early as the Persian period, but it is perhaps later.

Psalm 155 is a broken alphabetic acrostic beginning either with the supposed א of a pious pronunciation of the tetragrammaton which opens the psalm, 'ădônai, in line 3, and continuing with uneven meter through the letter ד,[2] or beginning with the letter ה in line 8.[3] In either case the acrostic ends with the letter פ beginning the final verse in what was line 19 of the original scroll. This reconstruction is indicated by the Syriac translation.[4] If one understands the acrostic to begin with ה, the first seven verses (ll. 3−6) stand as a staccato plea for deliverance in 2/2 meter which is then repeated in verse 17 (beginning of l. 16): "I cried 'O Yahweh,' and he answered me, [and he healed] my broken heart." The reference to the cry is made all the more poignant in that the first word of the poem, at the beginning of line 3, stands in anacrusis (out of meter), in service to the whole poem, as the word referred to in verse 17, "O Yahweh."

Psalm 155 is as biblical and beautiful as many Masoretic psalms. The phrase in verse 11 (l. 10), "lead me not into (that which is) too hard for me," reminds one of the similar phrase in the Lord's Prayer (Matt 6:13), as perhaps does another in verses 13 and 14 (ll. 12−13), "Purify me, O Yahweh, from (the) evil scourge, [and] let it not turn again upon me. Dry up its roots from me, and let its leaves not flourish within me."

Psalm 155 (11Q5 24.3−17)

Col. 24

3 O Yahweh,[5] I cried unto you, give heed to me. I spread forth my palms

4 toward your holy dwelling. Incline your ear and grant me my petition, and my request

5 withhold not from me. Build up my soul and do not cast it down,[6] and do not abandon (it) before

6 the wicked ones. The rewards of evil may the Judge of Truth remove from me.[7] O Yahweh,

7 judge me not according to my sins; for no one living is righteous before you.[8]

8 Grant me discernment, O Yahweh, in your Torah and from your precepts teach me,

9 that many may hear of your works, and peoples may honor your glory.

10 Remember me and do not forget me, and lead me not into (that which is) too hard for me.[9]

11 The sins of my youth cast far from me, and may my transgressions not be remembered against me.

12 Purify me, O Yahweh, from (the) evil scourge, [and] let it not turn again upon me. Dry up

13 its roots from me, and let its le[av]es not flourish[10] within me. You (are) glory, O Yahweh,[11]

---

[1] See *OTP*, 2:623.

[2] See P. W. Skehan, *CBQ* 27 (1965) 1−5.

[3] See DJD 4, pp. 70−76; *DSPS*, pp. 109−12.

[4] See DJD 4, p. 71; *DSPS*, p. 110.

[5] A vocative plea in anacrusis to the first verse serving the first strophe and indeed the whole poem. It is referred to directly in l. 16 (v. 17) and indirectly in l. 17 (v. 19); note the same vocative in lines 3, 6, 8, 12, 13, 15, and 16 (vss. 1, 8, 9, 13, 15, 17[*bis*], 19; and see v. 21).

[6] Or, with J. Strugnell, "let it not be denuded" (DJD 4, p. 72).

[7] These six lines in the one view form a seven-verse staccato plea in 2/2 meter, closing in a prayer in 2/2/2 with third person reference to the "Judge of Truth."

[8] Cf. Ps 143:2.

[9] Cf. Matt 6:13.

[10] Cf. Ezek 17:7−9; Ps 32:5; and 11Q5 19.15−16, the "Plea for Deliverance."

[11] Cf. Ps 3:4; Isa 60:19; and 1QH 4.40.

14 על כן שאלתי מלפניכה שלמה למי אזעקה ויתן לי

15 ובני אדם מה יוסיף אומֹ[צם]מֹלפֹ[נ]יכה *ܡܠܐ* מבטחי

16 קראתי *ܡܠܐ* ויענני [   ]שבר לבי נמתי

17 [ואי]שנה חלמתי גם[ ]   *ܡܠܐ*

14 therefore is my petition fulfilled before you.   To whom may I cry and he would grant (it) me?

15 And (mere) humans,[12] what more can [their] pow[er] do? Befo[r]e you, O Yahweh, (is) my trust.[13]

16 I cried "O Yahweh," and he answered me, [...] my broken heart.   I slumbered

17 [and sl]ept, I dreamt; indeed [... Yahwe]h

---

[12] Lit. "sons of humanity" or "sons of Adam."
[13] The psalmist's request and trust are both before or in the presence of God.

11Q5 compared with the Peshiṭta
Psalm 155

Peshiṭta[1]   *11Q5*

	Peshiṭta	11Q5
	(ܠܟܠܗܘܢ ܕܣܘܡܐ. ܕܟ ܡܬܘܡ ܠܟܐ ܐܡܪܝܬܐ. ܕܟܪܐ ܐܠܨܐ ܓܝ ܐܠܗܐ ܠܐܠܗܐ ܘܚܕܒܐ ܘܩܘܡܢ)	
(1)		עבג קראתי אליכה [3]
		הקשיבה אלי
		פרשתי כפי
(2)		למעון קודשכה [4]
		הט אוזנכה
(3)		ותן לי את שאלתי
		ובקשתי
(4)		אל תמנע ממני [5]
		בנה נפשי
(5)		ואל תמגרה
		ואל תפרע
(6)		לפני רשעים [6]
		גמולי הרע
(7)		ישיב ממני דין האמת
(8)		עבג אל תשפטני כחטאתי [7]
		כי לוא יצדק לפניכה כול חי
(9)		הביננני עבג בתורתכה [8]
		ואת משפטיכה למדני

---

1. Syriac text of MS 12t4 is adapted with permission of E. J. Brill from W. Baars, ed., "Apocryphal Psalms," in *The Old Testament in Syriac* (Leiden, 1972) pp. 9-10.
2. MS 12t4 is corrupt; read ܚܣܝܢܐ which is attested in the margin of 12t4 and all other extant Syriac MSS. Cf. Heb.
3. From Gk. νόμος.
4. Read ܐܠܦܢܝ.

11Q5 compared with the Peshiṭta[14]
Psalm 155

11Q5	*Peshiṭta*[16]
	A prayer of Hezekiah when the Assyrians surrounded him and he asked from God deliverance from them.

[3]O Yahweh, I cried unto you,
give heed to me.

I spread forth my palms
[4]toward your holy dwelling.

Incline your ear
and grant me my petition,

and my request
[5]withhold not from me.

Build up my soul
and do not cast it down,

and do not abandon (it)
before [6]the wicked ones.

The rewards of evil
may the Judge of Truth remove from me.[15]

O Yahweh, [7]judge me not according to my sins;
for no one living is righteous before you.

[8]Grant me discernment, O Yahweh, in your Torah
and from your precepts teach me,

[1]O Lord, I cried to you,
hearken to me.

[2]I stretched out my hands
to your holy habitations.

[3]Incline your ear[17]
and give me my petitions;

[4]my plea
do not hold back from me.

[5]Build up my soul
and do not destroy it,

[6]and do not uncover it[18]
before[19] the wicked ones.

[7]The rewards of evil[20] turn from me,
O Judge of Truth.[21]

[8]O Lord, do not judge[22] me according to my sins;
because every life (is) guilty[23] before you.

[9]Explain to me, O Lord, your Law
and your judgments teach me,[24]

---

14 Superscripted numbers in parentheses indicate line numbers for 11Q5 col. 24 and verse numbers for the Peshiṭta, respectively.

15 These six lines in the one view form a seven-verse staccato plea in 2/2 metre, closing in a prayer in 2/2/2 with third person reference to the "Judge of Truth."

16 Translation is by Charlesworth and Rietz.

17 While the Heb. and Syr. of this line are not cognate, the sense is the same.

18 I.e. "my soul."

19 While the Heb. and Syr. are not cognate, the sense is the same.

20 While the Heb. and Syr. are not cognate, the sense is the same.

21 While the Heb. and Syr. of this line are not cognate, the sense is the same.

22 While the Heb. and Syr. are not cognate, the sense is the same.

23 Lit. "not free from guilt."

24 While the Heb. and Syr. are not cognate, the sense is the same.

Syriac (Peshiṭta)	Hebrew (11Q5)
(10)	⁽⁹⁾וישמעו רבים מעשיכה
	ועמים יהדרו את כבודכה
(11)	⁽¹⁰⁾זכורני ואל תשכחני
	ואל תביאני בקשות ממני
(12)	⁽¹¹⁾חטאת נעורי הרחק ממני
	ופשעי אל יזכרו לי
(13)	⁽¹²⁾טהרני יהוה מנגע רע
	[ו]אל יוסף לשוב אלי
(14)	⁽¹³⁾יבש שורשיו ממני
	ואל ינצו על[י]ו בי
(15)	כבוד אתה יהוה
	⁽¹⁴⁾על כן שאלתי מלפניכה שלמה
(16)	למי אזעקה ויתן לי
	⁽¹⁵⁾ובני אדם מה יוסיף אומ[צם]
(17)	מלפ[נ]יכה יהוה מבטחי
	⁽¹⁶⁾קראתי יהוה ויענני
	[וירפא את] שבר לבי
(18)	⁽¹⁷⁾נמתי [ואי]שנה
	חלמתי גם [הקיצותי]
(19)	[סמכתני יהוה]
(20)	[ואקרא יהוה] [מפלטי]
(21)	

5　Read ܟܘܬܐ which is attested in the margin of 12t4.

6　Read ܬܠܠ which is supplied in the margin of MS 12t4 for ܡܢ.

(9)that many may hear of your works,
and peoples may honor your glory.

(10)Remember me and do not forget me,
and lead me not into (that which is) too hard for me.

(11)The sins of my youth cast far from me,
and may my transgressions not be remembered against me.

(12)Purify me, O Yahweh, from (the) evil scourge,
[and] let it not turn again upon me.

Dry up (13)its roots from me,
and let its le[av]es not flourish within me.

You (are) glory, O Yahweh,
(14)therefore is my petition fulfilled before you.

To whom may I cry and he would grant (it) me?
(15)And (mere) humans, what more can [their] pow[er] do?

Befo[r]e you, O Yahweh, (is) my trust.
(16)I cried "O Yahweh," and he answered me,
[and he healed] my broken heart.

I slumbered (17)[and sl]ept,
I dreamt; indeed [I awoke.]

[You supported me, O Yahweh,]
[when I invoked Yahwe]h [my deliverer.]

(10)so that many[25] may hear of your deeds,
and the peoples may give thanks for your honor.[26]

(11)Remember me and do not forget me,[27]
and do not allow me to enter (that which is) too difficult for me.

(12)The sins of my childhood remove from me,
and my insolence do not remember[28] against me.

(13)Cleanse me, O Lord, from the evil leprosy,
and do not let it again return to me.

(14)Dry up its roots[29] from me,
and do not let its leaves[30] bud in me.

(15)Powerful and great (are) you, O Lord,
hence, my petition will be fulfilled from before you.

(16)To whom may I complain and he would give to me?
And (mere) humans,[31] what can their strength add (for me)?

(17)From before you, O Lord, (is) my confidence.
I cried to the Lord, and he answered me,
and healed[32] my broken heart.

(18)I slumbered and slept,[33]
I dreamt, nevertheless I was aroused.

(19)And you supported me, O Lord,
and I shall render (thanks) because the Lord has delivered me.

(20)Now I shall behold their shame;
I trusted in you and shall not be ashamed.
Give honor (to the Lord) for ever and ever.

(21)Save Israel, your elect one,
and (those) of the house of Jacob, your chosen one.

---

25 While the Heb. and Syr. are not cognate, the sense is the same.

26 The Syr. ʼyqr is not cognate with Heb. hdr.

27 While the Heb. and Syr. are not cognate, the sense is the same.

28 While the Heb. and Syr. are not cognate, the sense is the same.

29 While the Heb. and Syr. are not cognate, the sense is the same.

30 While the Heb. and Syr. are not cognate, the sense is the same.

31 Lit. "sons of man."

32 While the Heb. and Syr. are not cognate, the sense is the same.

33 While the Heb. and Syr. are not cognate, the sense is the same.

Sirach 51:13ff. (11Q5 21.11−17 and 22.1)

Introduction

The large Psalms Scroll from Cave 11 contains the earliest Hebrew text to date of a portion of the second canticle in the last chapter of Sirach. Sirach has been known for centuries in Greek (Latin, Armenian, Slavonic, Ethiopic, and Sahidic) and Syriac (Arabic), but in 1897 fragments of a medieval Hebrew text of Sirach in Cairo were identified. They were published in 1899.[1] Ancient fragments were found at Masada and first published in 1965, but they do not contain our canticle.[2]

As in the case of Psalm 151, the Qumran Hebrew text, while identifiable as the original or very close to it, is considerably distinct both from the medieval Hebrew and from the ancient Greek and Syriac, all of which represent the same recension of the canticle. As with Psalm 151 and its non-biblical imagery, it is not certain whether there was an intervening recension in Hebrew as Vorlage to the versions and medieval text, or if it was the Greek translator, the earliest, who expunged the erotic overtones of the original Sirach canticle as represented by the 11Q text. Just as in the case of Psalm 151, it is precisely the portions which have somewhat offended some modern scholars[3] which the Greek editor (and translators dependent on the Gk.) has managed to blot out. And yet, even the Cairo Hebrew text at the מ verse (v. 13) continues the erotic metaphor: "My bowels are astir like a firepot for her, to gaze upon her, that I may own her, a pleasant possession."[4]

It may seem curious that the same canticle, though in its unexpurgated recension, should appear both as a coda to Sirach, and hence apparently attributed to its known author, Jesus ben Sira, and as a psalm in a Davidic Psalter. It is claimed in column 27 of the Psalms Scroll that David wrote 4,050 psalms and songs with the clear implication that all the poetic compositions in it were "Davidic." This would indicate that perhaps the original canticle was independent of both David and Sirach authorship, but was moving and popular enough to become attached to both. The fact that the canticle celebrates how a celibate young man can by spiritual discipline dedicate bodily drives and appetites to a pursuit of Wisdom instead of to a pursuit of sexual pleasure makes it indeed a very biblical theme as stated in Genesis, Proverbs, and the Song of Songs (see notes). The fact that it would appear to relate experiences of such dedication on the part of the young David makes it also quite compatible with biblical statements about David's pursuit of Wisdom in 1 and 2 Samuel (again see the notes). Like Psalm 151, the 11Q canticle pictures the young shepherd and king as totally dedicated to praise of God whether by his music or by his ardor in pursuit of Wisdom. It dates perhaps to the third or second century B.C.E.

---

[1] C. Taylor, *Wisdom of Ben Sira* (Cambridge, 1899).
[2] See DJD 4, pp. 79−80; *DSPS*, pp. 112−13.

[3] See Sanders, in *On Language*, pp. 84−95; *HAR* 8 (1984) 176.
[4] DJD 4, p. 84; *DSPS*, p. 117.

Sirach 51:13ff. (11Q5 21.11−17 and 22.1)

Col. 21[1]

11 אני נער בטרם תעיתי ובקשתיה באה לי בתרה ועד

12 סופה אדורשנה גם גרע נץ בבשול ענבים ישמחו לב

13 דרכה רגלי במישור כי מנעורי ידעתיה הטיתי כמעט

14 אוזני והרבה מצאתי לקח ועלה היתה לי למלמדי אתן

15 הודי זמותי ואשחקה קנאתי בטוב ולוא אשוב חריתי

16 נפשי בה ופני לוא השיבותי טרתי[2] נפשי בה וברומיה לוא

17 אשלה ידי פתֿחֿ[תי]   [   ][3] מערמיה אתבונן כפי הברותי אל

18 [   ][4]

Col. 22

1 שכרכם בעתו[5]   אזכורך לברכה ציון בכול מודי

---

[1] Lines 1-10 contain Psalm 137:9 and 138:1-8.
[2] Probably read טרדתי.
[3] פתחתי seems to be the only likely reading. What followed probably corresponded to Greek πρὸς ὕψος, but one can only conjecture what it might have been; see וברומיה in the previous stichos, line 16.

[4] The bottom of column 22 is lost.
[5] The medieval Hebrew MS from the Cairo Genizah reads: מעשיכה עשו בצדקה והוא נותן לכם שכרכם בעתו (C. Taylor, 1899). After a vacat, 11Q5 22.1 continues with the "Apostrophe to Zion."

Sirach 51:13ff. (11Q5 21.11−17 and 22.1)

Col. 21

11 I was a young man before I had erred[5] when I looked for her.   She came to me in her beauty[6] when

12 finally[7] I sought[8] her out.   Even (as) a blossom drops in the ripening of grapes,[9] making glad the heart,[10]

13 (so) my foot[11] trod in uprightness;[12] for from my young manhood have I known[13] her.   I inclined my ear

14 a little and great was the persuasion[14] I found.   And she became for me a nurse;[15] to my teacher I give

15 my ardor.[16]   I purposed to make sport:[17] I was zealous for pleasure[18] and would not turn away.   I kindled

16 my desire[19] for her[20] and would not turn away my face.   I bestirred[21] my desire for her, and on her heights[22] I would not

17 waver.[23]   [I] spread my hand[24] [. . .] and discerned[25] her unseen parts.[26]   I cleansed my palms 'l [. . .][27]

18 [. . .]

Col. 22

1 your reward in his time.[28]   I remember you for blessing, O Zion; with all my might . . . .

[5] "Erred" may be translated "wandered." Both the Greek and the Hebrew (Syr.) verbs mean both "travel" and "err"; indeed, the English "err" means not only to make a mistake but also to travel, as in the expression, "knight errant."

[6] The spelling תֹרָה lacks the א and is defective as in 1Q8 (1QIs[b]) 52:14 and in 11Q5 28.9 (Ps 151:5); cf. Wisdom 7:10, 29; 8:2. An alternative reading suggested is "in her searches" or perhaps "in search of her" (DJD 4, p. 12); cf. Qoh 1:13, 7:25. The ambiguity or multivalency may have been intended as with numerous other terms in the 11Q canticle.

[7] "When finally" might also be understood as "unto her depths (or, end)"; cf. Qoh 3:11, 12:13. Probably another multivalent term.

[8] A term which can also mean "exegete"; cf. Qoh 1:13, 1Chr 26:31, Ezek 20:3. The word is used in the Bible of seeking an oracle from God; it is also used to mean seeking guidance from Scripture ("midrash").

[9] A figure derived from Gen 40:10 meaning the maturing of young manhood.

[10] Cf. Ps 104:15.

[11] "Foot" as well as "hand" may also refer to the phallus: cf. Judg 3:24, 2Kgs 18:27, Isa 7:20, Ezek 16:25.

[12] Or "smoothness"; cf. 1QH 8.25.

[13] In biblical Hebrew the verb may indicate sexual intimacy; the metaphoric multivalency of terms continues.

[14] Or "seductive speech" as in Prov 7:21, 16:21.

[15] Literally "one who gives suck" (see the plural form in 1Sam 6:7, 10; Ps 78:71; Isa 40:11) indicating a mother or nurse figure. Wisdom is both mother and bride in Sir 15:2; cf. Prov 5:18−19, 8:30, 9:1−6; Sir 24:20−21; WisSol 7:12, 8:2. Zion is viewed as a mother who gives suck in Isa 66:7−11 and in the "Apostrophe to Zion" (11Q5 22.4−5). The corresponding term in the Greek recension means "profit" and fits the unambiguous yet pious reading of the Greek.

[16] The term may also mean "manhood" or "virility"; cf. Prov 5:9.

[17] Wisdom danced before God at creation (Prov 8:30). By using this term the poet calls to mind both sexual dalliance and the traditions of the pre-existence of Wisdom and Wisdom's relation to the Creator and to creation.

[18] Or simply "the good."

[19] Here and later in the same line the term may mean "myself" or, piously, "my soul."

[20] Or "in her," or possibly "with her."

[21] Probably טרדתי – *tărăttî* (cf. Sir 32:9).

[22] Probably "breasts" (cf. Prov 8:2; 9:3,14).

[23] Or "relax"; the figure is borrowed from Prov 9:3−14. The three negative expressions in lines 15−17 build in parallelism to an affirmation of passionate concentration and dedication to the pursuit of Wisdom.

[24] Again, "hand," as well as "foot," can be a euphemism for phallus.

[25] The Hebrew can also mean "pierce."

[26] Or "nakedness." The Greek understood "the unknown things about her."

[27] Lost are the several lines at the bottom of the column which would have provided the context for אל (prob. the negative adverb).

[28] The last (23d) verse of Sirach 51 reads in the medieval Hebrew MS: "Work your works in righteousness; and he shall give you your reward in his season." There would have been the right amount of space at the bottom of 11Q5 col. 21 to complete vss. 11 to 23 of the canticle, with these last words of the last verse appearing in place at the top of col. 22. For a translation of the second half of the canticle from the medieval Hebrew text, see *DSPS*, p. 117. After a vacat 11Q5 22.1 continues with the beginning of the "Apostrophe to Zion."

11Q5 compared with the Septuagint[29]
Sirach 51:13ff.

LXX[1]

(13)Ἔτι ὢν νεώτερος πρὶν ἢ πλανηθῆναί με
ἐζήτησα σοφίαν προφανῶς ἐν προσευχῇ μου.

(14)ἔναντι ναοῦ ἠξίουν περὶ αὐτῆς
καὶ ἕως ἐσχάτων ἐκζητήσω αὐτήν.

(15a)ἐξανθούσης ὡς περκαζούσης σταφυλῆς
εὐφράνθη ἡ καρδία μου ἐν αὐτῇ.

(15b)ἐπέβη ὁ πούς μου ἐν εὐθύτητι,
ἐκ νεότητός μου ἴχνευον αὐτήν.

(16)ἔκλινα ὀλίγον τὸ οὖς μου καὶ ἐδεξάμην
καὶ πολλὴν εὗρον ἐμαυτῷ παιδείαν.

(17)προκοπὴ ἐγένετό μοι ἐν αὐτῇ·
τῷ διδόντι μοι σοφίαν δώσω δόξαν.

(18)διενοήθην γὰρ τοῦ ποιῆσαι αὐτήν
καὶ ἐζήτησα τὸ ἀγαθόν
καὶ οὐ μὴ αἰσχυνθῶ.

(19aα)διαμεμάχισται ἡ ψυχή μου ἐν αὐτῇ

(20aα)τὴν ψυχήν μου κατεύθυνα εἰς αὐτήν

(19b)τὰς χεῖράς μου εξεπέτασα πρὸς ὕψος
καὶ τὰ ἀγνοήματα αὐτῆς ἐπενόησα.

(30)καὶ δώσει τὸν μισθὸν ὑμῶν ἐν καιρῷ αὐτοῦ.

11Q5

(21.11)אני נער בטרם תעיתי

ובקשתיה

באה לי בתרה

(12)ועד סופה אדורשנה

גם גרע נץ בבשול ענבים

ישמחו לב

(13)דרכה רגלי במישור

כי מנעורי ידעתיה

(14)הטיתי כמעט אוזני

והרבה מצאתי לקח

ועלה היתה לי

(15)למלמדי אתן הודי

זמותי ואשחקה

קנאתי בטוב

ולוא אשוב

(16)חריתי נפשי בה

ופני לוא השיבותי

טרתי נפשי בה

(17)וברומיה לוא אשלה

ידי פתח[ת]תי

מערמיה אתבונן

כפי הברותי אל]

]

(22.1)שכרכם בעתו

---

[1] Greek text is adapted with permission of Vandenhoeck and
Ruprecht from J. Ziegler, ed., *Septuaginta*, vol. 12, 2 *Sapientia
Iesu Filii Sirach* (Göttingen: 1965), pp. 364-68.

11Q5 compared with the Septuagint[29]

11Q5

[21.11]I was a young man before I had erred when I looked for her.

She came to me in her beauty
when [12]finally I sought her out.

Even (as) a blossom drops in the ripening of grapes,
making glad the heart,

[13](So) my foot trod in uprightness;
for from my young manhood have I known her.

I inclined my ear [14]a little
and great was the persuasion I found.

And she became for me a nurse;
to my teacher I give [15]my ardor.

I purposed to make sport:
I was zealous for pleasure
and would not turn away.

I kindled [16]my desire for her
and would not turn away my face.

I bestirred my desire for her,
and on her heights I would not [17]waver.

I spread my hand(s) [. . .]
and discerned her unseen parts.

I cleansed my palms ʾl [. . .]
[. . .]
[22.1]your reward in his time.

LXX[30]

[13]When I was young before I had wandered
I sought Wisdom openly in my prayer.

[14]I prayed for her before the temple
and finally[31] will I seek her out.

[15a]Blooming as the ripening of a grape
my heart has delighted in her.

[15b]My foot trod in uprightness;
from my youth have I hunted her.

[16]I inclined my ear (but) a little and received (her),
and great (was) the learning I found for myself.

[17]There was profit for me in her;
to the one who gives me Wisdom will I give glory.

[18]For I proposed to act (after) her:
and I sought good,
and I shall not be ashamed.

[19aα]My soul has wrestled with her.

[20aα]My soul I directed toward her.

[19b]My hands I stretched on high
and her secrets I perceived.

[30]and he will give your reward in his season.

---

[29] Superscripted numbers in parentheses indicate line numbers
for 11Q5 cols. 21−22 and verse numbers for the LXX, respectively. For further discussion of the textual problems including detailed comparisons with the Greek, Syriac, and
medieval Hebrew forms of the canticle, see DJD 4, pp. 79−85
and *DSPS*, pp. 112−17.

[30] Translation is by Charlesworth, Rietz, and Sanders.
[31] Lit. "to the last."

Psalms Heretofore Unknown
Plea for Deliverance (11Q5 19.1–18; 11Q6 Frgs. a, b)

Plea for Deliverance (11Q5 19.1–18)

Col. 19

1 כי לוא רמה תודה לכה' ולוא תספר חסדכה תולעה

2 חי חי (הוא)² יודה לכה יודו³ לכה כול מוטטי רגל בהודיעכה

3 חסדכה להמה וצדקתכה⁴ תשכילם כי בידכה נפש כול

4 חי נשמת כול⁵   בשר אתה⁶ נתתה עשה עמנו ꜣꜣ

5 כטובכה כרוב רחמיכה וכרוב צדקותיכה⁷ שמע

6 ꜣꜣ בקול אוהבי שמו ולוא עזב חסדו מהמה

7 ברוך⁸ ꜣꜣ עושה צדקות מעטר חסידיו

           את

8 חסד ורחמים שאגה⁹ נפשי להלל שמכה להודות ברנה

---

1 11Q6 frg. a lines 1-2: לֹ[לוא רמה תורה] כי֯[אנוכי ורל] .

2 The pronoun הוא of the similar phrase in Isa 38:19 was written after הי הי, then erased. 11Q6 does not have it, indicating that the scribe of 11Q5 included it from memory of the Isaiah passage but knew it did not belong in the psalm and then erased it. The scribe of 11Q6 put a second person masculine singular suffix on the verb and still kept the prepositional phrase following it.

3 11Q6 frg. a line 3:]יוד֯ לכה יודכה חי[.

4 11Q6 frg. a line 4: וצדקתֿב֯ להם חסדכה.

5 The scribe left a space of ca. 5 mm. after the third word (כול) due to scar tissue in the skin.

6 11Q6 frg. a line 5:]אתה בשר כול נשכית י[.

7 11Q6 frg. a line 6:]צדקותיכ וכרוב יכה[.

8 11Q6 frg. a line 7:]בר מהם חסדו זב[.

9 11Q6 frg. a line 8: שאג ורחמים חסד .

Psalms Heretofore Unknown
Plea for Deliverance (11Q5 19.1−18; 11Q6 Frgs. a, b)
Introduction

Column 19 of 11Q5 contains seventeen two-colon verses and two three-colon verses (in lines 4−5 and lines 10−11)[1] of a psalm unknown before the unrolling of the scroll in 1961. It may originally have had twenty-four or twenty-five verses, with perhaps five or six lines at the bottom of the preceding column and another line or so at the bottom of column 19 before the first line of Psalm 139 which followed it. Since we have neither the beginning nor the end of the poem, it is nearly impossible to determine its exact strophic structure.

Fragments a and b of 11Q6 contain parts of some twelve lines of the same psalm. In fact, 11Q6 is apparently an exact copy of 11Q5, according to its editor, J. van der Ploeg.[2] He indicates clearly the point, noted above on the basis of 11Q5 itself, that there was at least one line preceding the first line of our column 19. There are three more fragments of 11Q6 which contain Psalms 141, 133, and 144 (in that order), precisely the order of those psalms in 11Q5, col. 23. While the five fragments of 11Q6 are apparently all that remain of it, it is clear that the scroll was another copy of the same Psalter, containing both Masoretic and non-Masoretic psalms with the order of the psalms at variance with the MT Psalter.[3]

The "Plea" is a prayer for deliverance from sin and Satan with a praise of thanksgiving for past experiences of salvation embedded within the prayer. It is mostly biblical in vocabulary, style, form, and ideas. The oft-stated argument that God should spare human life because in death no one can thank God is poignantly made using familiar phrases, especially from Isaiah 38:18−19 and Psalm 6:4−5. While there are words and ideas known from early rabbinic literature in lines 15 ff., it is difficult to date the composition of the psalm. While a term like "evil inclination" (ll. 15−16) is used, vocabulary peculiar to Qumran, such as Belial, is not preserved in the extant lines.

It is interesting to note that while the tetragrammaton in 11Q5 is consistently written in palaeo-Hebrew script and quite distinct from the block script (*miktab 'ashur*) in which the rest of the scroll is written, in 11Q6, and 4Q88 − as well as in the so-called 11QApPs[a] (11Q11) − the tetragrammaton is written in the regular block script.[4] 11Q6 is otherwise almost *literatim*, as well as *verbatim*, an exact copy − where it is extant − of 11Q5.[5]

Plea for Deliverance (11Q5 19.1−18)

Col. 19

1 Surely a maggot cannot thank you[6] nor a grave-worm recount your mercy.

2 (But) the living can thank you, (even) all those who stumble can thank you, when you make known

3 your mercy to them and your righteousness you teach them.   For in your hand (is) the soul of every

4 living thing;[7] the breath of all flesh have you given.   Deal with us, O Yahweh,

5 according to your goodness, according to your great compassions, and according to your many righteous (deeds).   Yahweh

6 has heard the voice of those who love his name[8] and has not deprived them of his mercy.

7 Blessed be Yahweh, who does righteous deeds, crowning his pious ones

8 (with) mercy and compassions.[9]   My soul cries out to praise your name, to give thanks with a shout

---

[1] Cf. DJD 4, p. 77 and *DSPS*, p. 120.

[2] *RB* 74 (1967) 408−12; and Pl. XVIII.

[3] See the introduction to "Apostrophe to Zion" for data on another Qumran scroll of psalms, 4Q88, containing both Masoretic and non-Masoretic psalms.

[4] See Sanders, in *New Directions in Biblical Archaeology*, p. 105, n. 10.

[5] See *RB* 74 (1967) 410, and the transcription notes below.

[6] The theme that the dead cannot give thanks to God is found in Isa 38:18−19, Ps 6:4−5 and elsewhere; cf. Isa 14:11; Job

17:13, 24:20. See D. Flusser, "Qumran and Jewish 'Apotropaic' Prayers," *IEJ* 16 (1966) 194−205; and the comments of J. van der Ploeg concerning the four presumed apotropaic psalms in 11Q11 (J. van der Ploeg, "Un petit rouleau de psaumes apocryphes [11QPsAp[a]]," pp. 128−29).

[7] See Job 12:10: "In his hand is the life of every living thing and the breath of every human."

[8] Cf. Pss 5:12, 69:37, 119:132.

[9] Cf. Ps 103:4.

9   חסדיכה להגיד[10] אמונתכה לתהלתכה אין חקר למות

10   הייתי בחטאי ועוונותי לשאול מכרוני ותצילני

11   יהוה כרוב רחמיכה וכרוב צדקותיכה גם אני את

12   שמכה אהבתי ובצלכה חסיתי בזוכרי[11] עוזכה יתקף

13   לבי ועל חסדיכה אני נסמכתי סלחה יהוה לחטאתי[12]

14   וטהרני מעווני רוח אמונה ודעת חונני אל אתקלה

15   בעוֺוֹה[13] אל תשלט בי שטן ורוח טמאה מכאוב ויצר

16   רע אל ירשו בעצמי כי אתה יהוה שבחי ולכה קויתי

17   כול היום ישמֿחו אחי עמי ובית אבי השוממים בחונכה

18 [14]   עו]לם אשמחה בכה

---

[10] 11Q6 frg. a line 9: ברנה חסדיכה לה] .

[11] 11Q6 frg. b line 1: חסיתי בזוכֿ] .

[12] 11Q6 frg. b line 2: י סלחה יהוה לחֿ] .

[13] 11Q6 frg. b line 3:]ֵֵֵ֯֯֯י אל אתקלה בעֺ] .

[14] There appear to be ink markings near the beginning of the line, but they are unclear.

9 (for) your merciful (deeds), to proclaim your faithfulness — of praise of you there is no end. [10] (Near) to death

10 was I for my sins, and my iniquities had sold me to Sheol; but you delivered me,

11 O Yahweh, according to your great compassions, and according to your many righteous (deeds). Indeed have I

12 loved your name, and in your protection [11] have I found refuge.   When I remember your might my heart

13 is brave, and upon your merciful (deeds) do I lean.   Forgive my sin(s), O Yahweh,

14 and purify me [12] from my iniquity.   Vouchsafe me a spirit of faith and knowledge, (and) let me not be dishonored

15 in ruin. [13]   Let not Satan rule over me, nor an unclean spirit; neither let pain nor the evil

16 inclination take possession of my bones.   For you, O Yahweh, are my laud, and in you do I hope

17 all the day.   Let my brothers rejoice with me and the house of my father, who are astonished by your grace [14]

18 [. . . .   For e]ver will I rejoice in you.

---

[10] Or "…of your praise (or, praiseworthy act) there is no searching out."

[11] Or "shade," "shadow."

[12] Cf. Ps 51:4, Jer 33:8.

[13] The first word may be read either "in ruin" (בעווה) with Ezek 21:32, or "in iniquity" (בעויה) with Dan 4:24. 11Q6 has only the first two letters which could indicate either reading.

[14] Or "appalled by your grace (or, graciousness)" — a rare if not unique phrase.

Plea for Deliverance (11Q6 Frgs. a and b)

Frg. a

1   [כי אנוכי ודל]

2   ¹[כה]ל תודה רמה לוא]

3   ²[ודו יודכה לכה יודכה חי]

4   ³[ה]צדקתו להם חסדכה

5   ⁴[אתה בשר כול נשכית י]ח

6   ⁵[ה]צדקותיכן וכרוב [יכה]רחמ

7   ⁶[וך]מהם חסדו ב]ר[זב]ע

8   ⁷[ה]שאג ורחמים חסד

9   ⁸[גיד]ה חסדיכה ברנה

Frg. b

1   ⁹[רי]ו[חסיתי בזוכ]

2   ¹⁰[טאתי]ח לה סלחה יהוה [כת]נסמ

3   ¹¹[ויה]ע[אתקלה ב]נ[נ]ו[ח]

4   [° ° °]

1 11Q5 19.1: כי לוא רמה תודה לכה ולוא תספר חסדכה תולעה.

2 11Q5 19.2: חי חי(הוא) יודה לכה יודו לכה כול מוטטי רגל.

3 11Q5 19.2-3: בהודיעכה חסדכה להמה וצדקתכה תשכילם.

4 11Q5 19.3-4: כי בידכה נפש כול חי נשמת כול בשר אתה נתתה.

5 11Q5 19.4-6: עשה עמנו יהוה כטובכה כרוב רחמיכה וכרוב צדקותיכה שמע יהוה בקול אוהבי שמו.

6 11Q5 19.6-7: ולוא עזב חסדו מהמה ברוך יהוה.

7 11Q5 19.7-8: עושה צדקות מעטר חסידיו חסד ורחמים שאגה נפשי להלל /את\ שמכה.

8 11Q5 19.8-9: להודות ברנה חסדיכה להגיד אמונתכה לתהלתכה אין חקר.

9 11Q5 19.12-13: ובצלכה חסיתי בזוכרי עוזכה יתקף לבי.

10 11Q5 19.13-14: ועל חסדיכה אני נסמכתי סלחה יהוה לחטאתי וטהרני מעווני.

11 11Q5 19.14-15: רוח אמונה ודעת חונני אל אתקלה בעווה.

Plea for Deliverance (11Q6 Frgs. a and b)

Frg. a

1 [...] and weak (am) I, for [...]

2 [...] a maggot cannot thank [you...]

3 [...] the living can thank you, [...] can thank you. [...]

4 your mercy to them and yo[ur] righteousness [...]

5 [liv]ing thing; the breath of all flesh you [...]

6 your [compassion]s, and according to yo[ur] many righteous (deeds). [...]

7 [depr]ived them of his mercy. Bles[sed be...]

8 (with) mercy and compassions. [...] crie[s out ...]

9 with a shout (for) your merciful (deeds), to pr[oclaim...]

Frg. b

1 [...] have I found refuge. When [I re]mem[ber...]

2 [...] do I [lean.] Forgive [my] s[in(s),] O Yahweh, [...]

3 [. . . Vo]uchsafe me [...] (and) let me not be dishonored in r[uin....]

4 [...]°°°[...]

Hymn to the Creator (11Q5 26.9—15)

Hymn to the Creator (11Q5 26.9—15)

Col. 26[1]

9   גדול וקדוש 𝒶𝒷𝒶𝓰 קדוש קדושים לדור ודור לפניו הדר

10   ילך ואחריו המון מים רבים חסד ואמת סביב פניו אמת

11   ומשפט וצדק מכון כסאו מבדיל אור מאפלה שחר הכין בדעת

12   לבו אזראו[2] כול מלאכיו וירננו כי (ו)הראם[3] את אשר לוא ידעו

13   מעטר הרים תנובות   אוכל טוב לכול חי ברוך עושה

14   ארץ בכוחו מכין תבל בחוכמתו בתבונתו נטה שמים ויוצא

15   [רוח] מאו[צרותיו ברקים למט]ר[4] עשה ויעל נׁשׁיאׁ[ים מ]קׁצׁה [הארץ[5]

---

[1]   Lines 1-3 contain Ps 149:7-9 and lines 4-8 contain Ps 150:1-6.

[2]   Read או ראו. Scribe failed to leave a space between these two words; cf. Ps 89:20.

[3]   Note that a ו has been erased.

[4]   [רוח מאו]צרותיו] is reconstructed from Jer 10:13bα

[ברקים למט]ר (51:16bA); cf. Ps 135:7b. is reconstructed from Jer 10:13bα; cf. Ps 135:7aβ.

[5]   נׁשׁיאׁ[ים מ]קׁצׁה [הארץ is reconstructed from Jer 10:13aβ (51:16a); cf. Ps 135:7aα.

Hymn to the Creator (11Q5 26.9−15)

Introduction

Nine bi-cola or verses survive on 11Q5 column 26 of a wisdom psalm praising God as creator. It has affinities with the *Thanksgiving Hymns* (1QH and 4QH), but the seventh to ninth bi-cola are made up of phrases which are found in Jeremiah 10:12−13 (= 51:15−16) and Psalm 135:7 (11Q5 14.14−15). Like Psalm 154 and the Sirach 51 canticle (cols. 18 and 21), it is a Jewish sapiential poem, but unlike them it is rather pedestrian. In biblical terms, the imagery and vocabulary are late.

Hymn to the Creator (11Q5 26.9−15)

Col. 26

9 Great and holy (is) Yahweh, the holiest of the Holy Ones[1] from generation to generation.   Splendor precedes

10 him and following him (is) the rush of many waters.[2]   Mercy and truth surround his presence; truth

11 and justice, and righteousness (are) the foundation of his throne.[3]   Separating light from deep darkness, he established the dawn[4] by the knowledge

12 of his heart.[5]   When all his angels had witnessed it they sang aloud; for he showed them what they had not known:[6]

13 crowning the hills with fruits, good food for every living being.   Blessed be he[7] who makes

14 the earth by his power, establishing the world in his wisdom.   In his discernment he stretched out the heavens, and brought forth

15 [wind] from [his] st[orehouses].   He made [lightning for the rai]n, and caused mist[s] to rise [from] the end of [the earth.]

---

[1] Literally, "holy one of (the) Holy Ones"; cf. Ps 89:6−8, Hos 12:1, Zech 14:5, Isa 6:3, and e.g., 1QH 3.22, 35; 4Q400 frg. 1 cols. 1 & 2; *et passim* in Qumran literature. The expression is rhetorically comparable to "king of kings" and is probably a reference to the heavenly council (cf. Ps 82:1, 89:8; Zech 14:5).

[2] Cf. Jer 10:13a' (= 51:16a'), 1QH 2.16.

[3] Cf. Pss 85:11, 89:15, 97:2.

[4] Cf. Hos 6:3, 1QH 4.6.

[5] Or "mind." Rare and possibly unique in reference to God; but see 1QH 4, where the thought, way, and purpose of the heart of God are frequently mentioned.

[6] Almost verbatim in 1QH 13.11.

[7] This phrase is unique to the Qumran Scrolls, but all the phrases that follow are taken, though not in precise order, from Jer 10:12−13 = Jer 51:15−16; cf. Ps 135:7 (11Q5 14.15); cf. DJD 4, p. 91, the note to "Hymn to the Creator" vss. 7−9.

Apostrophe to Zion (11Q5 22.1–15; 4Q88 7.14–8.15)

Apostrophe to Zion (11Q5 22.1–15)

Col. 22[1]

1   אזכורך לברכה[3] ציון בכול מודי[4]   שכרכם בעתו[2]

2   ציון תקותך[6] גדולה זכרך לעולמים ברוך[5] אני אהבתיך

3   ודורות חסידים בך ידורו דור ודור לבוא ישועתך ותוחלת[7]

4   זיז   כבודך ברוב וישישו ישעך ליום המתאוים תפארתך

5   נביאיך חסדי יעכסו תפארתך וברחובות יינקו כבודך

---

[1] Lines 16-17 contain Psalm 93:1-3.
[2] After a blank space of four centimeters following the last words of the Sirach 51 canticle is the beginning of the "Apostrophe to Zion," which follows.
[3] 4Q88 7.14: .[לֿבֿרכֿהֿ כֿרך]

[4] Read מאודי; see DJD 4, pp. 12 and 88, and 4Q88 8.10.
[5] 4Q88 7.15: .[אהבתיֿ לֿ]
[6] 4Q88 7.16: .[תֿקֿ דֿוֹלֿה]
[7] 4Q88 7.17: .[לֿ] [חֿלֿ] .[לֿ]

Apostrophe to Zion (11Q5 22.1−15; 4Q88 7.14−8.15)
Introduction

It is very fortunate that all the non-biblical psalms in 11Q5 are apparently contained almost entirely on the extant leather of the scroll, but only two of the eight non-Masoretic compositions are complete; these are the prose paragraph on column 27 and the "Apostrophe to Zion." Tradition holds that Zion is in the prayers of all who love her; but the "Apostrophe to Zion" is not a prayer addressed to God. Rather, it is a love poem addressed to Zion in the style of the three biblical apostrophes to Zion in Isaiah 54:1−8, 60:1−22, and 62:1−8. The vocabulary and imagery, however, are drawn largely from Isaiah 66:10−11, a little poem addressed to all who love Jerusalem, bidding them to rejoice with and for Jerusalem and feast upon her consoling breasts and her abundant glory.

Soon after 11Q5 was first published, another copy of the "Apostrophe to Zion" was identified in another Qumran Psalter manuscript containing both Masoretic and non-Masoretic psalms, 4Q88.[1] The fragment of 4Q88 in question contains por-

tions of Psalms 107 to 109, in that order, followed by our "Apostrophe" and two other non-Masoretic psalms, an "Apostrophe to Judah" and an "Eschatological Hymn." The fragment contains about a third of the actual text of the "Apostrophe to Zion," largely in the last half of it, though portions of the first three lines are also present. It offers about twenty variants none of which alters the sense of the poem but a few of which bring some improvements.

The poem has three strophes. The first and last verses are tri-cola while the rest of the poem is in bi-cola verses. The first six assure Zion of her future with generations of children who will play in her parks and faithful citizens in whom she will be proud. The second strophe, vss. 7−13 (in ll. 6−11), refers to Zion's sorrow and plight and the men of violence and iniquity whom God will surely banish from her midst. The third strophe resumes the opening theme of prayers and praise for Zion. It is difficult to determine the precise date of composition.

Apostrophe to Zion (11Q5 22.1−15)

Col. 22

1 your reward in his time.[2] I remember you[3] for blessing, O Zion; with all my might[4]

2 have I loved you.[5] May your memory be blessed forever! Great (is) your hope, O Zion, that peace

3 and your longed-for salvation will come. Generation (after) generation will dwell in you and generations of pious ones (will be)

4 your glorious-beauty:[6] those who yearn[7] for the day of your salvation, that they may exult in the greatness of your glory.[8] (On the) abundance of

5 your glory they are nourished[9] and in your beautiful squares will they toddle.[10] The pious (deeds)[11] of your prophets

---

[1] *RB* 73 (1966) 353−66.
[2] This concludes Sir 51:30 which began on the previous column.
[3] Cf. Ps 137:5−6, Isa 62:6−7.
[4] Cf. Deut 6:5, 2Kgs 23:25.
[5] Cf. Isa 65:18−19, 66:10; Ps 122:6.
[6] Cf. Isa 60:19, 62:3.
[7] Cf. Ps 132:13−14.
[8] Cf. Isa 65:18−19, 66:10.

[9] Literally, "(On the) teat of your glory they suck" (from Isa 66:11).
[10] A rare word perhaps meaning "hopple" in reference to a camel (so Arabic), but used here to refer to the idyllic scene of innocent, vulnerable children safely at play; cf. Isa 3:16 for a different use of the same verb.
[11] Or "merits," or even perhaps, "sure promises" (cf. 2Chr 6:42, 32:32, 35:26; Isa 55:3).

‎6   תזכורי ובמעשי חסידיך תתפארי טהר חמס מגוך שקר

‎7   ועול נכרתו ממך יגילו[8]   בניך בקרבך וידידיך אליך נלוו

‎8   כמה קוו לישועתך   ויתאבלו עליך תמיך לוא תובד[9] תקותך

‎9   ציון ולוא תשכח תוחלתך מי זה[10] אבד צדק או מי זה מלט[11]

‎10 בעולו נבחן אדם כדרכו[12] א יש[13] כמעשיו ישתלמ(ה)[14]   סביב נכרתו

‎11 צריך ציון[15] ויתפזרו כול משנאיך[16] ערבה באף תשבחתך[17] ציון

‎12 מעלה[18] לכול תבל[19] פעמים רבות אזכורך לברכה[20] בכול לבבי אברכך[21]

‎13 צדק עולמים תשיגי[22] וברכות נכבדים תקבלי[23] קחי חזון

‎14 דוברי[24] עליך וחלמות נביאים תתבעך[25] רומי ורחבי ציון[26]

‎15 שבחי עליון פודך תשמח נפשי בכבודך

Apostrophe to Zion (4Q88 7.14–8.15)

Col. 7

‎14 אז[כ]רך לֿבֿרכהֿ [27]

‎15 א[נ]י אהבתי[ך 28]

‎16 ג[ד]ולה תק[נ]ותך 29

‎17 וש[ל]ום ותו[ח]ל[נ]ת 30

---

8 Space after יגילו is due to scar-tissue. See photograph.
9 Note the assimilation of an א: read תואבד.
10 4Q88 8.2: הֿ ˚[.
11 4Q88 8.3-4: [הֿוא זנה מלט].
12 4Q88 8.4: בֿ כדרכו.
13 Space after א of אֿישֿ is perhaps due to scar tissue, but the original seems to be אנוש, as in 4Q88 8.5. See photograph.
14 4Q88 8.5: אנוש כמֿ [יֿשֿתֿלם. Note the erasure of ה or ו after ישתלם.
15 4Q88 8.6: סביב נכרתו צריך ציון.
16 4Q88 8.7: התפזרו כול מסנאיך.
17 Read תֻשבחתך or תֻשבחתך with Starcky.
18 מעלה may be read either as a *hophal* participle, מָעֳלָה, or as an adverb, מַעְלָה.
19 4Q88 8.7-9: ערבה באף תשבוחתך ציון מֿעל כל תֿבל.
20 4Q88 8.9-10: פעמים רבות אזכרך [הֿ ציון.
21 4Q88 8.10-11: בכול מודי אני [בֿתֿיך.

22 4Q88 8.11: צדק עולמים תסיגי.
23 4Q88 8.12: בֿרֿכֿוֿתֿ נכבדים תקבלי [ ] ˚[ ].
24 Read דובר (cf. Ps 87:3), or possibly דֹבֶר with Starcky.
25 4Q88 8.13-14: קחי חֿזֿוֿןֿ [ ]וֿבֿ עליכי חלמת [בֿאֿוֿם תחבעֿ. Read תתבָעֵך from בעה with the dative of reference (cf. Isa 21:12, and Starcky in *RB* 73 [1966], 365).
26 4Q88 8.14: רומי ורחבי.
27 11Q5 22.1: אזכורך לברכה ציון. The first word lacks the *ḥōlem* that is present in 11Q5 7.1, 12 (and in 11Q5 8.9); cf. *DSPS*, p. 125, n. 8. There was probably a blank space at the beginning of the line marking the beginning of a new composition, as in 11Q5 (cf. DJD 4, p. 14).
28 11Q5 22.1-2: בכול מודי אני אהבתיך.
29 11Q5 22.2: ברוך לעולמים זכרך גדולה תקוותך ציון.
30 11Q5 22.2-3: ושלום ותוחלת ישועתך לבוא. The ל of [וש]לֿ[ום] is visible, *pace* Starcky.

6 will you remember, and in the works of your pious ones will you glory.[12]   Purged[13] be violence from your midst, falsehood

7 and deceit cut off from you.   Your children will rejoice in your midst and your precious ones will be joined to you.

8 How they have hoped for your salvation, your perfect ones have mourned for you.[14]   Your hope does not perish,

9 O Zion, nor is your longing forgotten.   Who has (ever) perished (in) righteousness, or who has (ever) survived[15]

10 in his deceit? A person is tested according to his way; a man is requited[16] according to his works; all about are your enemies

11 cut off, O Zion, and all your foes have been scattered.   Laud of you is pleasing,[17] O Zion,

12 cherished through all the world.   Many times do I remember you for blessing; with all my heart I bless you.[18]

13 Everlasting righteousness may you attain, and blessings of the glorious ones may you receive.   Accept a vision

14 bespoken of you, and dreams of[19] prophets sought for you.[20]   Be exalted and spread wide, O Zion;[21]

15 laud the Most High, your redeemer: let my soul rejoice in your glory.

Apostrophe to Zion (4Q88 7.14−8.15)

Col. 7

14 [. . . . I re]member you for blessing, [. . .]

15 [. . .] have I loved [you. . . .]

16 [. . . . G]reat (is) [your] ho[pe, . . .]

17 [. . .p]ea[ce and long]ed-f[or . . .]

---

[12] From the root פאר. In Ps 154:3 (l. 1), 10 (l. 7) and 17 (l. 14) the verb is used of those who glorify God; in Ps 154:4 (l. 2) and 9 (l. 7) the noun of the same root is used of God's glorious-beauty (see Zion's "beautiful squares" in "Apostrophe," l. 5).

[13] If read as *pu'al* perfect. In DJD 4 and *DSPS* I read it as a *pi'el* infinitive with imperative force, but it probably should be read in synonymous parallelism with "cut off" in the next colon.

[14] Cf. Isa 65:18−19, 66:10.

[15] Rare use of the verb מלט; cf. DJD 4, p. 88.

[16] From שלם; perhaps derived from the Aramaic *ithpe'il*.

[17] Perhaps an allusion to the odor of sacrifices pleasing to God, cf. Ps 154:10−11 (11Q5 18.7−10); or perhaps a more general reference (cf. Starcky in *RB* 73 [1966] 363).

[18] 4Q88 (8.9−11) reads: "Many times do I remember you for blessing, O Zion; with all my might have I loved you." The 4Q88 scribe's memory of v. 1 misguided him; but see Starcky in *RB* 73 (1966) 363.

[19] 4Q88 reads "a dream of," perhaps in better parallelism to "a vision" in the previous phrase.

[20] The last two verbal forms in this verse are rare, but render good sense in the context.

[21] Cf. Isa 51:17, 52:2, 54:2, 60:1; and Micah 4:13.

Col. 8

]	1
ה̇[31	2
הוא זנה]	3
מלט [בעולו נבחן אד]ם̇ כדרכו32	4
אנוש כמ[עשיו]י̇שׁתֿלם33	5
סביב נכרתו צריך ציון34	6
התפזרו כול מסנאיך35 ערבה	7
באף תשבוחתך ציון מ̇על כל	8
תֿבל36 פעמים רבות אזכרך	9
[לברכ]ה̇ ציון37 בכול מודי אני	10
[אה]בׄתֿיך38 צדק עולמים תסיגי39	11
[ ]˚[ ] בׄרׄכׄוׄת̇ נכבדים תקבלי40	12
קחי חזון [ד]וׄבׄר̇ עליכי חלמת	13
[נ]בׄיאׄיׄם̇ תתבעד41 רומי ורחבי42	14
[ו]ל̇]	15

---

31 Perhaps restore ה̇[ז], or more probably ה̇[זנ], as in line 3, paralleling 11Q5 22.9: מי זה אבד צדק. The top left bar of a ה is more likely than the keraia of an א, *pace* Starcky.

32 11Q5 22.9-10: או מי זה מלט בעולו נבחן אדם כדרכו.

33 11Q5 22.10: אנוש כמעשיו ישתלם א יש̇. Note אנוש, which may also have been the original reading in 11Q5. The י of י̇שׁתֿלם[ ] is visible enough to place outside the bracket. The trace following the final ם in 11Q5 may have been a ה or a ו but was erased (cf. DJD 4, p. 14).

34 11Q5 22.10-11: סביב נכרתו צריך ציון.

35 11Q5 22.11: ויתפזרו כול משנאיך.

36 11Q5 22.11-12: ערבה באף תשבחתך ציון מעלה לכול תבל.

37 11Q5 22.12: פעמים רבות אזכורך לברכה.

38 11Q5 22.12: בכול לבבי אברכך.

39 11Q5 22.13: צדק עולמים תשיגי.

40 11Q5 22.13: וברכות נכבדים תקבלי. There is room at the beginning of the line for תשיגי to correct תסיגי, as Strugnell suggested to Starcky (*RB* 73 [1966] 359); or, possibly there is scar tissue which the scribe had to skip (cf. DJD 4, p. 14). There is no conjunction on ברכות.

41 11Q5 22.13-14: קחי חזון דובר עליך וחלמות נביאים תתבער. ד]ובר[as in 11Q5 22.14, *pace* Strugnell and Starcky in *RB* 73 (1966) 359. The א of נ]בׄיאׄיׄם̇[is clear enough to place outside the brackets, but not the initial נ, *pace* Starcky.

42 11Q5 22.14: רומי ורחבי ציון.

Col. 8

1 [...]

2 [...]*h*

3 [...] who

4 has (ever) survived [in his iniquity? A pers]on [is tested] according to his way;

5 a human is requited[22] according to [his] w[orks;]

6 all about are your enemies cut off, O Zion,

7 all your foes have been scattered.   Laud of you

8 is pleasing, O Zion, cherished through all

9 the world.   Many times do I remember you

10 [for blessin]g, O Zion; with all my might have I

11 [love]d you.[23]   Everlasting righteousness may you attain,

12 [...]°[...] blessings of the glorious ones may you receive.

13 Accept a vision [be]spoken of you, a dream of[24]

14 [pr]ophets sought for you.   Be exalted and spread wide,

15 [...]*l*[...]

---

[22] From שלם; perhaps derived from the Aramaic *ithpeʿil*.

[23] 11Q5 22.12: "Many times do I remember you for blessing; with all my heart I blessed you." The 4Q88 scribe's memory of v. 1 misguided him; but see Starcky in *RB* 73 (1966) 363.

[24] 11Q5 22.14 reads "and dreams of," perhaps in better parallelism to "a vision" in the previous phrase.

Eschatological Hymn (4Q88 9.1–15)

Eschatological Hymn (4Q88 9.1–15)

Col. 9

1	]˚ ˚
2	מל[
3	]˚ ˚ [ ]˚ ˚ ˚ [
4	ויהללו אֿת [ ] ˚ רבים [
5	שם יהוה [כ]ֿי בא' לשפט אֿת
6	כל מעֿ[ש]ֿהֿ² להשבית רשעים
7	מן הארץֿ [ובני]עֿולה³ לוֿא
8	ימצאו⁴ [ויתנו שֿמֿ]יֿ[ם⁵ טלם
9	ואין שח[ת⁶ בגבו]ֿליהם⁷ והארץ
10	פריה [תתן⁸]בעתה ולוֿא
11	תכחש[תב]אֿותיה⁹ עצי
12	פרי בֿ ˚ ˚ גֿפֿנֿיֿהֿם ולוֿא¹⁰
13	יבֿזֿ[וֿ¹¹ זרים¹² תבאו]תיה יוכלו¹³
14	ענוים וישבעוֿ [י]ֿרֿאי יהֿוֿה¹⁴
15	[לֿ]

---

1 Restore בֿא [כ]ֿי with Starcky.
2 Restore מעֿ[ש]ֿהֿ with Starcky.
3 Restore ובני] עֿולה with Strugnell and Starcky. There is room for one or two other letters before the expression.
4 Read either יֿמֿצאו or יֿמצאו with Starcky. There is room for some five letters to follow.
5 Restore [ויתנו שֿמֿ]יֿם with Starcky (cf. Zech 8:12).
6 Probably restore שח[ת. Starcky thought also of the possibility of שחפת (*RB* 73 [1966] 367).
7 Restore בגבו]ליהם with Starcky.
8 Restore [תתן] with Starcky (cf. Ps 1:3 and Zech 8:12).
9 Restore תב]אֿותיה with Starcky. Cf. Hos 9:2 and Hab 3:17.

10 See Starcky's discussion of the problems with reconstructing this line (*RB* 73 [1966] 367); they seem intractible.
11 Restore יֿבֿזֿ[וֿ], not יכזב[ו, *pace* Starcky. Both the negative and the positive films provided me indicate a ז after the initial יֿ. The ו seems probable, but there is no ink mark whatever after the ו before the break in the leather.
12 Ps 109:11 suggests זרים ("strangers") for the lacuna.
13 The last word in line 13 lacks the א as in Ezek 42:5; cf. 1QS 5.16, and DJD 4, p. 12.
14 Restore [י]ֿרֿאי יהוה with Starcky (despite the printing error in his transcription).

Eschatological Hymn (4Q88 9.1–15)

Introduction

The second non-Masoretic psalm in 4Q88, following Psalms 107–109 (in that order) and also its form of the "Apostrophe to Zion," may be given the title, "Eschatological Hymn." It is very fragmentary and only about 36 words on eleven of the fifteen lines of column 9 survive. The following, and last, psalm on the 4Q88 fragments is the "Apostrophe to Judah" (col. 10). As Starcky noted, the hymn seems to be of the category of the hallel or hallelujah psalms in the Bible but with an eschatological mode. Starcky dates it in the latter part of the second century B.C.E.[1]

Eschatological Hymn (4Q88 9.1–15)

Col. 9

1 $^{\circ\circ}$[…]

2 *ml*[…]

3 $^{\circ\circ}$[…]$^{\circ}$ $^{\circ\circ}$[…]

4 many[2] $^{\circ}$[…] and let them praise the

5 name of Yahweh.[3] [Fo]r he is coming to judge[4]

6 every d[ee]d, to cause the wicked ones to cease

7 from the earth[5] [(so that) children of] iniquity[6] not

8 be found.   And the he[av]ens [will give][7] their dew

9 and no destru[ction] will be [in] their [bord]ers.   And the earth

10 [will yield] its fruit in its time and

11 its [pro]duce will not deceive.[8] Fruit

12 trees *b*$^{\circ\circ\circ}$[9] their figs and

13 [strangers] will not plund[er] their [produ]ce.[10]   Let the

14 oppressed ones[11] eat and [those who f]ear Yahweh be satisfied.

15 […]*l*[…]

---

[1] For an earlier translation in English, see Sanders, in *New Directions in Biblical Archaeology*, p. 116.

[2] The word "many" (רבים) may have the technical meaning it sometimes does at Qumran and mean "the Many."

[3] Cf. Pss 74:21, 148:5, 13; 149:3.

[4] This indicates God's eschatological judgment often affirmed in Qumran literature (cf. Pss 96:13, 98:9, 82:8, 94:2).

[5] Cf. Joel 4:12; Ps 119:119.

[6] Cf. Ps 89:23; 1QH 5.8.

[7] Reading with Starcky ם[י]שמ [ויתנו] (cf. Zech 8:12; Deut 33:28).

[8] The singular verb with subject following in the plural is not unusual in biblical Hebrew (cf. Starcky *RB* 73 [1966] 367).

[9] The text is illegible; the sense expected by the context is "will offer."

[10] The reconstruction and translation are suggested by Ps 109:11, which would have been on col. 6 of the same scroll (cf. *RB* 73 [1966] 354).

[11] Cf. אביונים, which at Qumran was a technical term, "the Poor Ones."

Apostrophe to Judah (4Q88 10.4−15)

Introduction

Like the "Eschatological Hymn" in column 9 of the same collection, the "Apostrophe to Judah" has a possible eschatological dimension, but it is not as pronounced. Like most poetry, or indeed prose peculiar to Qumran, it is highly anthological, made up of phrases adapted from earlier poetry we know from the Bible. But then most pre-exilic biblical poetry drew upon even earlier biblical traditions and from standard liturgical phrases adaptable to new cultural, musical, and cultic settings. What is clear is that composers and writers were free, like modern hymn and sermon writers, to adapt earlier material. Such adaptation occurred with that which had become somehow authoritative through the relative stability of phrasing. This intertextuality and related changes echoed the already familiar. Most Early Jewish and Christian literature is intertextual in the same sense, but these observations do not address and certainly do not solve the question of canonicity.

Whether either of these two poems was addressed to a specific occasion of or desire for the scattering of enemies and celebration of victory over evil is not certain. Here Belial, so prominent in hymns strictly peculiar to Qumran as a personification of evil, is mentioned in contrast to any composition in 11Q5−6 or in 4Q88 to this point. While *bĕliya'al* occurs in the Bible largely meaning worthlessness (without worth, without high value), at Qumran, where dualism lies barely below the surface of monotheism, Belial often stood for Satan. Only in Nahum 2:1 (Eng 1:15) might Belial be understood as personified evil (cf. Nah 1:11), but not all scholars agree on this point. Even in our "Apostrophe to Judah," where celebration is called for because Belial is no longer around, "Belial" might mean no more than is meant in such passages as Isa 33:18ff., in which the departure of oppressive conquerors is celebrated. Whatever its original meaning it would certainly have been adaptable to later views of Belial at Qumran and congenial to their thinking. The date of the "Apostrophe to Judah" is uncertain.

In lines 10−11 the author calls on Judah that his, or their, arm be lifted up and right hand be strong; such words reflect the call in early biblical passages to the beleaguered to draw upon their faith in God and upon divine strength to repel much larger and more powerful enemy forces (cf. e.g., Judg 7:11, 2Sam 2:7, Micah 4:9; *et passim* in the Bible). In contrast to the documents of the New Testament, nowhere at Qumran is Belial or Satan said to have been conquered despite many assurances that he, or it, will be when God and the heavenly armies act decisively in the final days yet to come. Here the celebration is simply that Belial, who or whatever that was, is now no longer in the midst of the faithful, on whatever occasion called for the celebration.[1]

---

[1] For an earlier translation in English see Sanders, in *New Directions in Biblical Archaeology*, p. 116.

Apostrophe to Judah (4Q88 10.4−15)

Col. 10

4	[שה'
5	הם[2] ° ° ° אז יהללו שמים וארץ
6	נא יחד יהללו ֯ כל כוכבי נשף
7	שמחה יהודה שמחתכה
8	שמחה שמחתכה וגילה גילך
9	חג חגיך נד[ר]יך[3] שלם כי אין
10	בקרֿבך בֿלֿיֿעל תרם ידך
11	תגברֿ ימינֿך הֿנֿא אואבים[4]
12	יובדו ויֿתֿפֿרדו כולן ֯ פוע[לי[5]
13	און ואתה יהוה לעו[לם]
14	תהיה כבוֿדֿכֿה לעוֿלֿ[ם וע]ד
15	[ה]לל[ו]ויה

---

[1] While the last two letters of the line are quite clear, it is difficult to reconstruct what preceded them.

[2] As Starcky notes (*RB* 73 [1966] 368), the second letter in line 5 might have been a כ, a מ, or a נ. The possibility of a ל to its left, as Starcky also suggests, seems less likely; it looks like the bottom of the right leg of the ה, which is otherwise quite clear. The first letter might have been a י or a ו, but it is far from certain.

[3] Though nothing of the ר remains, Starcky was surely right

that the third word is נד[ר]יך. The י is quite clear.

[4] הנא for הנה is found elsewhere in 4Q texts. אואבים for אויבים: cf. M. Goshen-Gottstein, *Scripta Hierosolymitana* 4, 133f.; J.T. Milik, *Biblica* 31 (1950) 205f.; Starcky, *RB* 73 (1966) 370; and J.D. Amoussine, *RQ* 7 (1971) 534.

[5] For the last word, פוע[לי], Starcky read פועלי, which may mean that a fragment was found to fit the lacuna in the film I was given, or that it has fallen out. The word, like the whole phrase, is taken from Ps 92:10 and is clear enough.

Apostrophe to Judah (4Q88 10.4–15)

Col. 10

4 [...]*šh*

5 °°°*hm*. Let then the heavens and the earth give praise[2]

6 together; let all the stars of twilight[3] give praises!

7 Rejoice, O Judah, your rejoicing;[4]

8 rejoice your rejoicing and exult your exultation![5]

9 Celebrate your festivities, fulfill your v[ow]s; for no longer

10 is Belial in your midst. May your hand be lifted up,[6]

11 and your right hand be strong. Behold enemies

12 will perish and all [worke]rs of wickedness will be scattered.[7]

13 But you, O Yahweh, (are) for[ever,]

14 your glory will be forev[er and ay]e.[8]

15 [Ha]llel[ujah!...]

---

[2] The call to heaven and earth, indeed all creation, to join in praising God is typical of numerous poetic forms in the Bible and prominent in the Great Hallel (cf. Pss 136, 148, *et al.*).

[3] נשף may be either the "twilight" of dusk (Job 3:9) or of dawn (Job 7:4); it is more often that of evening.

[4] The use of the cognate accusative intensifies the sense of celebration. Judah is here addressed in the masculine gender (see, however, Lam 1:3). The scribe of 4Q88, or his predecessors, uses either the כה- second masculine singular suffix, or the ך-. The latter does not necessarily indicate the feminine as it consistently does, e.g., in the "Apostrophe to Zion," and elsewhere at Qumran; see DJD 4, p. 12 and 4Q88 8.13.

[5] Cognate accusatives with שמח are found in Jonah 4:6 and 2Chr 29:9; with גיל are found in Isa 35:2 and Prov 23:24; cf. Pss 48:12, 97:8 and Isa 66:10. For חג, see Nah 2:1, which is also the only biblical passage where some say "Belial" means evil personified; but see introduction.

[6] Cf. Ps 89:14 and Zeph 3:14–18.

[7] The word "evil" is actually the first in l. 13. The whole phrase is adapted very nearly *verbatim* from Ps 92:10.

[8] Cf., e.g., Ps 104:31.

David's Compositions (11Q5 27.2−11)

Introduction

The prose composition in column 27 is too long to be called a superscription or subscription to a psalm, and it was not positioned by the scribe in either isolated position. It is similar to the subscription to Book II of the MT Psalter (after 72:20). The apparent subscription to 11QPs 145 (11Q5 17.17f?) may or may not have been as substantial. It is difficult to know what was in lines 18 to 21 or so of column 17 before the space necessary for the beginning of Psalm 154; it would in any case not have been as long as "David's Compositions." This work seems, therefore, to stand as unique in Psalter MSS and seems to support claims that 11Q5 (11Q6) and the other Qumran MSS containing both Masoretic and non-Masoretic psalms were liturgical collections and do not represent variant Psalters at Qumran. As is evident in reading it, however, it does not function as directions for liturgical use of specific psalms or groups of psalms in the scroll but rather serves to affirm Davidic authorship of 4,050 psalms and songs and to indicate the broadly general purposes for which David composed them. No guidance is given for liturgical usage of any of the categories of psalms and songs mentioned.

The emphasis rather is on David and his psalms in general: David was wise, literate, and a perfect instrument for God to use through prophecy to compose the Psalter, and indeed a Psalter considerably more extensive than a mere 150 or 151 Psalms. Instead of being directed to those, at Qumran or elsewhere, who might use the scroll, and how they should use the psalms in it, "David's Compositions" is directed rather patently to those who might doubt the Davidic authorship of the Psalter, of whatever size, so that those who would limit the Psalter might be persuaded otherwise. For the historian of the Psalter today, therefore, it is interesting in terms of beliefs in the first centuries B.C.E. and C.E. concerning David as Israel's great psalmist and the implications of that for the history of formation of the Psalter.[1]

It is also interesting indirectly in terms of the calendars of Early Judaism and of Jewish liturgies of the period. Both David and Solomon wrote "songs," and it is the number of songs that varies in the traditions about Solomon (1Kgs 5:12). The paragraph mentions songs for daily offering (364, in l. 6), for sabbath offerings (52, in l. 7), for festivals and holy days (30, in l. 8), and for "the stricken" (4, in l. 10).[2] The total number of songs attributed to David, therefore, would have been 450, whereas 1,005 were claimed for Solomon.[3]

More interesting perhaps to students of Early Jewish calendars are the figures relating to the number of songs David wrote and for what purpose. They indicate a 52-week, 364-day year. The lunar calendar of early rabbinic literature and indeed modern Judaism has 354 days requiring an intercalated month seven years out of nineteen in order to adjust the calendar to the earth's movements in its solar orbit. A modified 364-day solar-lunar calendar was already known from *1 Enoch* and *Jubilees* as well as somewhat indirectly surmised as the case at Qumran.[4] While 11Q5 was not necessarily composed at Qumran, it was clearly compatible with the Community's beliefs, as evidenced by the second copy of it (11Q6). If it was not composed there, their beliefs about it would have apparently been shared by other Jews as well.

David is credited in the paragraph with both prophecy and wisdom in composing his psalms and songs. Some of the attributes of David listed in lines 2−4 are noted also in 1 Samuel 16 and 2 Samuel 14 but especially in 2 Samuel 23:1−7, "The last words of David," which immediately preceded the prose paragraph as may be seen by the presence of 2 Samuel 23:7 in 27.1. There David is called the "sweet psalmist of Israel" and one "who dawns on [his subjects] like the morning light, like the sun shining forth upon a cloudless morning." Many times is David said to have the spirit of God upon him (e.g., 1Sam 16−17). The Bible itself does not, therefore, stress David's wisdom; but it was manifestly important in this scroll. Psalm 154 (col. 18), the Sirach 51 canticle (col. 21), the "Hymn to the Creator" (col. 26), and our prose composition stress the role of Wisdom in David's life and musical gifts.

---

[1] See R. Meyer, in *Das Ferne* and J. Barton, *Oracles of God.*

[2] See also the four apparently apotropaic psalms of 11Q11.

[3] Note also the mention of songs in 2Sam 22:1 (= Ps 18:1); Amos 6:5; 1Chr 6:16, 16:7−42; 2Chr 7:6, 29:26−30.

[4] See *DSPS*, p. 91, n. 1.

David's Compositions (11Q5 27.2−11)

Col. 27[1]

ו

2   ויהי דויד בן ישי חכם ואור כאור השמש סופר[2]

3   ונבון ותמים בכול דרכיו לפני אל ואנשים ויתן

4   לו יהוה רוח נבונה ואורה ויכתוב תהלים

5   שלושת אלפים ושש מאות ושיר לשורר לפני המזבח על עולת

6   התמיד לכול יום ויום לכול ימי השנה ארבעה וששים ושלוש

7   מאות ולקורבן השבתות שנים וחמשים שיר ולקורבן ראשי

8   החודשים ולכול ימי המועדות ולי ם[3] הכפורים שלושים שיר

9   ויהי כול השיר אשר דבר ששה ואבעים[4] וארבע מאות ושיר

10   לנגן על הפגועים ארבעה ויהי הכול ארבעת אלפים וחמשים

11   כול אלה דבר בנבואה אשר נתן לו מלפני העליון

---

[1] Line 1 contains 2Sam 23:7; lines 12-15 contain Ps 140:1-5.
Lines 2-4 are indented by the scribe three centimeters from
the right margin, due to rough skin surface (scar tissue?) in
the leather (cf. DJD 4, p. 14).

[2] Read וסופר.
[3] Read ליום; there is space available for the lacking ו in ולי ם.
[4] Read וארבעים for ואבעים.

214

David's Composition (11Q5 27.2−11)

Col. 27

2 And David, the son of Jesse, was wise, and a light like the light of the sun, and literate,[5]

3 and discerning and perfect in all his ways[6] before God and men.   And the Yahweh gave

4 him a discerning and enlightened spirit.[7]   And he wrote

5 3,600 psalms, and songs[8] to sing before the altar over the whole-burnt

6 perpetual offering day (after) day, for all the days of the year, 364;

7 and for the offering of the Sabbaths, 52 songs; and for the offering of the New

8 Moons and for all the days of the festivals and for the Day of Atonement, 30 songs.[9]

9 And all the songs that he composed[10] were 446, and songs

10 for making music over the stricken, 4.[11] And the total was 4,050.

11 All these he composed[12] through prophecy[13] which was given him from before the Most High.

---

[5] Lit. "and a scribe" (cf. 1Chr 27:32; b.Ber 45b).

[6] Drawn from 2Sam 22:24, 26, and 33 (// Ps 18).

[7] Cf. 1Sam 16:12−23; 2Sam 23:2 (and Isa 11:2). Elements in these first lines are drawn also from 2Sam 14:20 (cf. 11Q5 27.1) and 1Sam 16:18 (cf. 1Kgs 3:12 of Solomon).

[8] The word שיר and the instruments of "song" in biblical references to David include 2Sam 23:1 (Ps 18:1); Amos 6:5; 1Chr 6:16, 16:7−42; 2Chr 7:6, 29:26−30.

[9] See *DSPS*, p. 137, n. 3; and see the references in the first paragraph of the general introduction to this section to several documents from Caves 4 and 11 (and Masada) which relate to Sabbath liturgy poetry.

[10] Lit. "he spoke."

[11] Ps 91 is noted in rabbinic literature as a psalm to be recited over those stricken by demons or evil spirits (cf. DJD 4, p. 93). Qumran texts of Ps 91 are in 4Q88 and 11Q11 (cf. bibliography).

[12] Lit. "he spoke."

[13] Cf. 2Chr 9:29, 15:8; Neh 6:12; Acts 2:30−35.

A Liturgy for Healing the Stricken

(11QPsApª = 11Q11)

JAMES A. SANDERS

Introduction

1. Contents

Among the surprises emanating from Qumran Cave 11[1] was a fragmentary scroll which apparently contained four psalms originally, only one of which was known before the discovery (a variant form of MT Psalm 91).[2] Psalm 91 appears as the last of the psalms, all four of which seem to have been psalms designed to be recited in a liturgy for healing "the stricken" (הפגועים). This term means demon-possessed or mentally ill, and was known both at Qumran and in later rabbinic literature in which Psalm 91 is specifically mentioned as such a psalm.[3] J. van der Ploeg, the original editor, suggested that 11Q11 may preserve the four psalms which 11Q5 27.9–10 claims David composed to be recited over "the stricken."[4]

2. Original Language, Date, and Provenience

The script of 11Q11 is Herodian and dates to the early decades of the first century C.E. The date of composition, however, may be much earlier. There is no reason to doubt it was composed in Hebrew. Since 1988 E. Puech has pursued van der Ploeg's hypothesis that 11Q11 contains the four "psalms for the stricken" mentioned in 11Q5 27.9–10, and has developed it into a very interesting thesis.[5] Puech's argument, following van der Ploeg's lead, is that the four psalms identified in 11Q11 constituted a discreet ritual of exorcism which went back to pre-Qumranic Judaism, maybe even the "hassidéen" movement which gave rise to the Essenes. By contrast, the similar poems in 4Q510–511, according to Puech, are probably later in date, leaving the real

---

[1] J. A. Sanders, "Cave Eleven Surprises and the Question of Canon," *McCormick Quarterly* 21 (1968) 296–97, reprinted in *New Directions in Biblical Archaeology*, edited by D. N. Freedman and J. C. Greenfield (Garden City, 1969) pp. 113–15.

[2] J. van der Ploeg, "Le Psaume XCI dans une recension de Qumran," *RB* 72 (1965) 210–17, Pls. 8–9, followed by a comment on the text of Ps 91 (as a "Bekehrungspsalm") by O. Eissfeldt, "Eine Qumran-Textform des 91. Psalms" in *Bibel und Qumran: Beiträge zur Erforschung der Beziehungen zwischen Bibel- und Qumranwissenschaft, Hans Bardtke zum 22.9.1966* (Berlin, 1968) pp. 82–85. Van der Ploeg then published the rest of the scroll in *Tradition und Glaube: Das frühe Christentum in seiner Umwelt, Festgabe für Karl Georg Kuhn zum 65. Geburtstag*, edited by G. Jeremiah, H.-W. Kuhn and H. Stegemann (Göttingen, 1971) pp. 128–39; Pls. 2–7.

[3] See Sanders, DJD 4, p. 93.

[4] See van der Ploeg in *RB* 72 (1965) 216, and in *Tradition und Glaube*, p. 129. The *editio princeps* of 11Q5 and the preliminary edition of 11Q11 in *RB* 72 (1965) appeared at approxi-

mately the same time in 1965 without prior consultation by the two editors on these points.

[5] Puech's work in this regard is found in two studies, the publication dates of which can be confusing. The earlier of the two actually appeared after the second. Puech's first effort was presented at the Haifa conference on the Scrolls in 1988 but was not published until four years later in the compendium volume of the conference, *The Dead Sea Scrolls: Forty Years of Research*, edited by D. Dimant and U. Rappaport (STDJ 10; Leiden, 1992) pp. 64–89. The second appeared, in the meantime, in *RQ* 14 (1990) 377–408. In the Haifa volume Puech dealt with only the third and fourth (Ps 91) of the four psalms; in the later *RQ* 14 study (published earlier) he dealt with all four of the psalms in the scroll and further elaborated his thesis. One is left to assume that, given the differences in minutiae in reading the last two psalms on the scroll and in the statement of his thesis, priority should be given to the fuller *RQ* 14 (1990) treatment, even though it actually appeared two years earlier than the first, Haifa treatment.

possibility, if not probability, that the four "Davidic" psalms of 11Q11 constituted the essence of the apotropaic ritual suggested by column 27 of 11Q5.

3. Relation to Other Jewish Writings

D. Flusser suggested shortly after 11Q5 was published that the "Plea for Deliverance" in column 19 would fit the category of an apotropaic prayer.[6] In 1974 van der Ploeg published the five fragments of 11Q6 which also contains the "Plea for Deliverance" along with portions of Psalms 141, 133, and 144.[7] In 1985 B. Nitzan began to publish studies on the "power of the song," or hymn, in dealing with the supernatural by "the Master" (משכיל), or "sage," at Qumran, centering in 4Q510–4Q511, earlier published by M. Baillet in DJD 7.[8] Then in 1994 D. L. Penney and M. O. Wise published a study of 4Q560, previously thought to contain proverbs, in which they argue that the two fragments constituting 4Q560 provide a mid-term between earlier texts such as the above, and later Jewish texts of magical incantations.[9]

4. Selected Bibliography

Nitzan, B. *Qumran Prayer and Religious Poetry*. STDJ 12; Leiden, 1994.

Puech, E. "11QPsApᵃ: Un rituel d'exorcismes. Essai de reconstruction." *RQ* 14 (1990) 377–408.

Puech, E. "Les deux derniers Psaumes davidiques du rituel d'exorcisme, 11QPsApᵃ IV 4-V 14." In *The Dead Sea Scrolls: Forty Years of Research*, edited by D. Dimant and U. Rappaport. STDJ 10; Leiden, 1992, pp. 64–89.

Tov, E. *The Dead Sea Scrolls on Microfiche*. Leiden, 1995 [PAM 42.177, 43.981–88, 44.003–4, 44.113; for the previously unpublished fragments B and C, see PAM 44.004].

van der Ploeg, J. "Le Psaume XCI dans une recension de Qumran." *RB* 72 (1965) 210–17; Pls. 8–9.

van der Ploeg, J. "Un petit rouleau de psaumes apocryphes (11QPsApᵃ)." In *Tradition und Glaube: Das frühe Christentum in seiner Umwelt, Festgabe für Karl Georg Kuhn zum 65. Geburtstag*, edited by G. Jeremiah, H.-W. Kuhn, and H. Stegemann. Göttingen, 1971, pp. 128–39; Pls. 2–7.

---

[6] D. Flusser, "Qumran and Jewish 'Apotropaic' Prayers," *IEJ* 16 (1966) 194–205 (republished in *Judaism and the Origins of Christianity* [Jerusalem, 1988] pp. 214–25).

[7] Neither van der Ploeg nor Puech has addressed Flusser's suggestion. Clarity is needed on the number of apotropaic psalms at Qumran, including the four of 11Q11, 4Q510–511, "Plea for Deliverance" in 11Q5–6, and 4Q560, before one can be sure of Puech's thesis. y. Shabbat 7:2 lists Ps 3:2–9 and Ps 91:1–9 as apotropaic prayers. Ps 91:1–9 is the most stable part of Ps IV in 11Q11. The implication of Job 5:21 (if שֹׁד ["destruction"] is repointed to שֵׁד ["demon"]) could be that such prayers and practices were in place at the time of the composition of Job, or earlier.

[8] M. Baillet, DJD 7, pp. 215–62; B. Nitzan, "Hymns from Qumran to Frighten and Repel Evil Spirits," *Tarbiz* 55 (1985) 19–46 (in Hebrew with complementary notes by Y. Ta-Shma

and J. Baumgarten, 440–45); B. Nitzan, "Hymns from Qumran -- 4Q510–511," in *The Dead Sea Scrolls: Forty Years of Research*, pp. 53–63; and B. Nitzan, *Qumran Prayer and Religious Poetry* (STDJ 12; Leiden, 1994) pp. 227–72.

[9] "4Q560 preserves for us the partial resources of a Jewish magician" –by clear implication not just the Master, or "sage," at Qumran as in Nitzan's thesis concerning 4Q510–4Q511. (D. L. Penney and M. O. Wise, "By the Power of Beelzebub: An Aramaic Incantation Formula from Qumran," *JBL* 113 [1994] 627–50 [quotation from p. 650]). For information on 4Q560 see S. Reed, *et al.*, *The Dead Sea Scrolls Catalogue: Documents, Photographs and Museum Inventory Numbers*, SBL Resources for Biblical Study 32 (Atlanta, 1994) p. 144. A preliminary study of 4Q560 has appeared in R. H. Eisenman and M. O. Wise, *The Dead Sea Scrolls Uncovered* (New York, 1992) pp. 265–67.

A Liturgy for Healing the Stricken (11QPsAp[a] = 11Q11)

Frg. C		*Frg. B*		*Frg. A (Psalm I)*	
‏[יה]‏	1	‏[ ]ׄ‏	1	‏[ובוכהו]‏	1
‏[כֿב]‏	2	‏[ה]‏	2	‏[שבועֿה]‏	2
‏[ה]‏	3	‏[נ]‏	3	‏[בֿיהוה]‏	3
‏[ם ע]‏	4	‏[ויד]‏	4	‏[תנין]‏	4
‏[ׄםׄ]‏	5	‏[ ]ׄ [ ]‏	5	‏את השמים וא[ֿת האר]ֿץ‏	5
‏[תוכות]‏	6	‏[ ]ׄׄת[ן]‏	6	‏[משבֿ]יע‏	6
‏[לם]‏	7	‏[שבעים]‏	7	‏[את]ֿ‏	7
		‏[ל]‏	8	‏[הזואֿת]²‏	8
				‏[ֿאת השד]ים‏	9
				‏[וֿיֿשבֿ]³‏	10

---

[1] Cf. Puech *RQ* 55 (1990) 406, fig. 3.

[2] Perhaps restore ‏המכה הגדולה‎.‏

[3] Puech conjectures Ps I concluded with ‏אמן אמן סלה‎; cf. *RQ* 55 (1990) 398.

A Liturgy for Healing the Stricken (11QPsAp^a = 11Q11)

Frg. A (Psalm I)[1]

1 [. . .] and he who laments it[2]

2 [. . .] an oath[3]

3 [. . .] by Yahweh[4][. . .]

4 [. . .] the sea monster[5][. . .]

5 [. . . heavens and][6] eart[h. . .]

6 [. . .]adjur[ing[7]. . .]

7 [. . .]'t °[. . .]

8 [. . .] this [[8]. . .]

9 [. . .] the demon[s[9]. . .]

10 [. . . and] he will dwell[10] [. . .]

Frg. B

1 [. . .]°[. . .]

2 [. . .]h[. . .]

3 [. . .] n[. . .]

4 [. . .] and a hand [. . .]

5 [. . .] °[. . .]

6 [. . .] °°t[. . .]

7 [. . .]seventy[11][. . .]

8 [. . .]l [. . .]

Frg. C

1 [. . .]yh[. . .]

2 [. . .]kb[. . .]

3 [. . .] h[. . .]

4 [. . .]m ʿ[. . .]

5 [. . .]°m °[. . .]

6 [. . .]twkwt [. . .]

7 [. . .]lm[12] [. . .]

---

[1] Fragments A, B, and C were found among numerous fragments of other manuscripts; their shape and script identify them as belonging to 11Q11. Since column 5 is followed by the remnants of an uninscribed column, fragments A, B, and C probably preceded column 1. Unfortunately, their relative position cannot clearly be determined. [Editors]

[2] Or, "one who weeps."

[3] Cf. Num 5:19–22 for a possible meaning of the term here.

[4] Note the appearance of the divine name here and in the other psalms of 11Q11. See the discussion by Puech in *The Dead Sea Scrolls: Forty Years of Research,* pp. 80–88 and in *RQ* 14 (1990) 401–03.

[5] See 5.1 and 12, in Pss III and IV, as well as Ps 91:13.

[6] Reconstruction with Puech.

[7] See 2.5 and 3.1.

[8] Perhaps restore "mighty blow"; see 2.11 in Ps II, and cf. Puech in *RQ* 14 (1990) 399.

[9] See 1.3–4 in Ps II.

[10] With Puech, *RQ* 14 (1990) 399; cf. van der Ploeg in *Tradition und Glaube,* p. 130. Puech conjectures that Ps I concluded with "Amen. Amen. Selah" with which Pss II, III, and IV also would have concluded. "Selah" does occur at 5.3 and 14, at the ends of Pss III and IV.

[11] Or "ones satiated."

[12] Possibly "to them."

Col. 1 (Psalm II)

[בשֹׁםׁ]⁴	**1**
מעש]ֹה שלומה ויקר]א בשם יהו]⁵	**2**
הר]וחות והשדים]	**3**
[אלהֹן] הש]דים וֹ ̇ ̇שׂ]ר המשט]מה⁶	**4**
[הואה בליעל א]שרן מושל [עֹל תֹהוֹ]ם חושֹך	**5**
[לֹגדֹ]יל אל]והי [לשן ל]	**6**
[עמֹ תמֹוֹ⁷ רפואה	**7**
על] שמך נשען וקר]א]⁸	**8**
יש]ראל החזק	**9**
[את השמים	**10**
א]שר הבדיל]	**11**
[עדֹ]°	**12**

---

4 Puech reconstructs the line to read לחש לדויד על דברי ל
יהוה [בשם]; cf. *RQ* 55 (1990) 389; cf. 4.4.

5 Reconstructed with Puech; cf. van der Ploeg, *Tradition und Glaube*, p. 130.

6 Puech reconstructs lines 3-4 to read לפלט מכול נגע הר]וחות
והשדים] והלילית והאחים והציים[.

7 Van der Ploeg in *Tradition und Glaube* reads עמי ת[.

8 Puech reconstructs lines 8b-12a to read וקר]א אל השמים
ובטח על שומל יש]ראל החזק [ביהוה אלוהי אלים אשר עשה
את השמים [ואת הארץ ואת כול אשר בם א]שר הבדיל] בין
האור ובין החושך.

Col. 1 (Psalm II)

1 [...] in the name of [¹³...]

2 [... the ac]t of Solomon when he invok[ed the name of Yahweh¹⁴...]

3 [... the sp]irits and the demons [...]

4 [...]these (are) [the de]mons.¹⁵   And the pr[ince of hosti]lity,

5 [he (is) Belial w]ho [rules] over the dept[hs of dark]ness¹⁶

6 [...]*lš*[... to] magni[fy the Go]d of¹⁷

7 [...] his people accomplish healing

8 [... upon]your name finds support.¹⁸   And invok[e]

9 [... Is]rael.   Take strength

10 [...] the heavens

11 [... w]ho separated [...]

12 [...]° ‘*d*°[...]¹⁹

---

¹³ Puech (*RQ* 14 [1990] 389) plausibly reconstructs the line to read, "To David. Concerning the words of incantation] in the name of [Yahweh." Cf. 4.4.

¹⁴ Reading ויקרא as past tense describing "the act of Solomon." See 2Kgs 5:9–14 and 2Chr 6:28–31 for formulae for healing and incantation; and see Josephus' *Ant* viii 45–47 for further developments of the Solomonic reputation in this regard. See also Charlesworth, "Solomon and Jesus: The Son of David in Ante-Markan Traditions (Mk 10:47)," in *Biblical and Humane: A Festschrift for John F. Priest,* edited by L. B. Elder, D. L. Barr, and E. S. Malbon (Atlanta, 1996) pp. 125–51.

¹⁵ Cf. Deut 32:17, Ps 106:37. Puech reconstructs lines 3–4 to read, "[to deliver from every affliction of the s]pirits and the demons, [the liliths, owls, and wildcats]."

¹⁶ Puech's elaborate reconstruction of lines 4–5 is based on his prior study of evil spirits, angels, and demons in Early Judaism; cf. *RQ* 14 (1990) 390–91. For categories and names of evil spirits and demons see 4Q510 and 4Q511; 1QM 13.4, 11; 1QS 3.23; CD 16.5; *Jub* 10:8 *et passim*.

¹⁷ See similar expressions in 4Q510–511.

¹⁸ Cf. Isa 10:20, 50:10; 2Chr 13:18, 14:10, 16:7–8.

¹⁹ Puech (*RQ* 14 [1990] 388, 392), based in part on van der Ploeg (*Tradition und Glaube,* pp.131–32), reconstructs lines 8–12 thus: "And invok[e the heavens(?) and trust in the guardian of Is]rael. Take strength [in Yahweh, the God of divine beings who made] the heavens [and the earth and all which (is) in them, wh]o separated [light from darkness... ." Line 9 can also be read as "the guardian of Is]rael, the Mighty One" (cf. Isa 40:10).

Col. 2

1	[ ] [מי	
2	[א]תה[	[תהומו]ת
3	האר]ץ וב[ול]י⁹	[ארץ מי ע]שה
4	ואת המופ]תים	[ארץ]¹⁰ יהוה הוא[ה] אשר
5	עשה את ה[ ]כול	[תו משביע לכול מ]לאכים
6	את כול זר[ע	[אשר הת]ן[י]צבו לפני[ו	]ת
7	ש[מים ו[את כול] הארץ	[אשר יש]ו[ל]ח[ו]י על
8	אר]ץ חטא ועל כול א[ד]ם	[הם]¹² יודעים
9	[מעשי פל]או אשר אינם]	יחו[ה]¹³ אם לוא
10	[מלפני יהוה ל]ן	[להרוג נפש
11	[יהוה וייראו	ה]גדולה הזוא[ת]¹⁴
12	א[ח]ד מבם א[ל]ף	[מעבדי יהו]ה
13	מכה ג[ד]ולה ו[ ]¹⁵	[ר¹⁶ ת]

---

9 *Apud* Puech; van der Ploeg reads וחארץ ר].

10 Puech reconstructs lines 1b-4a to read [ואמרתה אליו מי
א[תה] העשיתה השמים ו[התהומות] וכול אשר בם [הארץ וכ]ול
אשר על ה[ארץ מי ע]שה את האותות ואת המופ]תים האלה
ב[ארץ.

11 *Apud* Puech.

12 *Apud* Puech; van der Ploeg reads א[תם.

13 Puech reconstructs lines 4b-9a to read עשה יהוה הוא[ה אשר
את ה[כול בגבור]תו משביע לכול מ[לאך לעזור] את כול זר[ע
הקודש [אשר הת]י[צבו לפני]ו וידי[ן(?) א[ת בני הש]מים ו[את

כול] הארץ [בעדם [אשר יש]ו[ל]ח[ו] [על [כול האר]ץ חטא ועל
כול א[דם רשע ו]הם יודעים [מעשי פל]או אשר אינם [עושים
לפני יהו]ה.

14 Puech reconstructs lines 9b-11 to read [מלפני] יפחדו [
יהוה ל]אסור אדם ו[להרוג נפש [וישפוט [יהוה וייראו את
המכה ה[גדולה הזוא]ת.

15 Puech reconstructs lines 12-13a to read וירדוף א[ח]ד מכם
א[לף ושר הצבא [מעבדי יהו]ה יכה מכה ג[דולה ו[ ]

16 Van der Ploeg reads a ד instead of a ר.

Col. 2

1 [...] [.... Who are]

2 [y]ou? [...] the deep[s...]

3 the earth and a[ll...] earth.   Who m[ade...]

4 and the port[ents...] earth?[20]   Yahweh (is) the on[e who]

5 made ev[erything...] his [...]*t* [...] adjuring all the an[gels...]

6 all the proge[ny...] who st[a]nd in service before [him...]*t*

7 [... he]avens and [all] the earth [...] who se[n]d upon

8 [... ear]th sin and upon every hu[man...]*hm* they know

9 his wondr[ous works] which they cannot [... Yahw]eh.[21]   If [they] do not

10 [...] from before Yahweh *l*[...] to kill a soul

11 [...] Yahweh and the[y] will fear tha[t] great [...][22]

12 [... o]ne among you [...] a th[ousand...]from the servants of Yahw[eh]

13 [... g]reat [blow] and °[...]*r t*[[23]...]

[20] Puech (*RQ* 14 [1990] 388, 393; cf. van der Ploeg, *Tradition und Glaube*, p. 132) reconstructs 2.1–4 thus: "[...and you shall say to him, 'Who are you? Did you make the heavens and] the deep[s and all that is in them,] the earth and a[ll that is upon the] earth? Who ma[de the signs] and the port[ents that (are) on the] earth?'" The question, "Who are you?" occurs frequently in the *Testament of Solomon* (Puech, *RQ* 14 [1990] 393). See the similar questions in Isa 40 and Job 38; here the questions, however, would be directed at a demon or spirit to be exorcised.

[21] Puech (*RQ* 14 [1990] 393–94; cf. van der Ploeg, *Tradition und Glaube*, pp. 132–33) thus: "Yahweh (is) the on[e who] made ev[erything by] his [might] adjuring all the an[gels to help] all the proge[ny of holiness] who st[a]nd in service before [him;

and he will judge the sons of the he]avens and [all] the earth [because of those] who se[n]d upon [all the ear]th sin and upon every hu[man evil, yet] they know his wondr[ous works] which they cannot [do before Yahw]eh."

[22] Puech (*RQ* 14 [1990] 387, 394; cf. van der Ploeg, *Tradition und Glaube*, p. 131) reconstructs the end of line 9 through line 11 so: "If [they] do not [tremble] before Yahweh while [binding a person or] killing a soul, [then] Yahweh [will render judgment], and the[y] will fear tha[t] great [blow...]."

[23] Puech (*RQ* 14 [1990] 388, 394; cf. van der Ploeg, *Tradition und Glaube*, pp. 132–133) reconstructs lines 12–13 thus: "[Then o]ne among you [will be able to pursue] a th[ousand, and the Commander of the Army(?)] from among the servants of Yahw[eh will strike a great blow and [...]."

Col. 3

1	[ו]גֿדולֿ]	[מֿשביעֿ]
2	והגדול ב]	[תקיֿף ור]דפ
3	כול הארץ]¹⁷	אֿ]לֿ השמים ו]
4	יככה יהוה מֿ]בה גדולֿ]הֿ אשר לאבדֿן]¹⁸	
5	ובחרון אפוֿ] ישלח]עליך מלאך תקיֿף]	
6	[כו]לֿ] דב]רֿו אשר] רחמיֿם עליך אֿשֿ]ר	
7	[עֿל כול אלה אשרֿ] ישֿ]לֿ]חֿך לתהום רבה	
8	[ולשאול]התחתיה וממֿ]עוןֿ]¹⁹ [שֿכב וחשך	
9	תהום רֿ]בֿה²⁰ מואדה [ֿ]²¹ עֿ]וֿד בארץ	
10	[עֿד עולם ו]ֿ²² [בֿקללת האבֿ]דוןֿ]	
11	בֿ]חֿרון אף יֿ]הוה [חושך בכֿ]וֿל	
12	[תֿעניותֿ] [מתנתך	
13	[לֿ°°] המֿ]כֿה הגֿ]דולהֿ]²³	

---

17 Puech reconstructs lines 2b-3a to read תקיֿף] מלאך וישלח / ור]דֿף אותֿך מֿ(?)ֿעֿל] כול הארץ.

18 Puech reconstructs lines 3b-4 to read אֿ]לֿ השמים א]שר יקרא / ו]על הארץ[יככה יהוה מֿ]כה גדולֿ]הֿ אשר לאבדֿן[לעולם.

19 Van der Ploeg reads ומֿי].

20 Van der Ploeg reads בֿה]; Puech רֿ]בֿה.

21 Puech reconstructs lines 5-9a to read עליך] ישלח אפוֿ] ובחרון / מלאך תקיֿתֿ] לעשותֿ] [כו]לֿ] דב]רֿו אשר] בלוא[רחמים עליך / אשֿ]ר שליטֿ] [הואה]עֿל כול אלה אשרֿ] ישֿ]לֿ]חֿך לתהום רבה

[ולשאול]התחתיה וממֿ]עון אור (?) תֿ]שֿכב וחשך [בתהום / רֿ]בֿה מואדה.

22 Puech reads ואֿ]תה.

23 Puech reconstructs lines 9b-14a to read עֿ]וֿד תשלט לוא[/ בארץ [ותאסר]עֿד עולם ואֿ]תה תקלל]בֿקללת האבֿ]דון / ותבהל בֿ]חרון אף יֿ]הוה ותמשול בֿ]חושך בכֿ]וֿל תעודות / [תֿעניותֿ] ותתן לעובדיֿך] מתנתך [ו]לֿ°°] המֿ] כֿה הגֿ]דולה / הזואת.

Col. 3

1 [and] great [. . .] adjuring [. . .]

2 and the great by[. . .] a mighty one and he will pur[sue . . .]

3 the whole earth.[24] [. . . the G]od of the heavens then [. . .]

4 Yahweh will smite you (with) a [might]y bl[ow] in order to destroy you [. . . .][25]

5 And by his burning wrath [he will send] against you a mighty angel[. . .]

6 [al]l [his co]mmand(s) which [. . .] pity against you, wh[o[26] . . .]

7 [. . .] over all those who [will s]e[nd] you to the great pit

8 [and to] deepest [Sheol], and (far) from the ab[ode . . .] will lie down, and darkness

9 [. . .] extremely [gr]eat [pit.[27] . . . l]onger on the earth,

10 [. . .] forever, and °[. . .] with the curse of Aba[ddon]

11 [. . . by] the burning wrath of Y[ahweh. . .] darkness in a[ll. . .]

12 [. . .] tribulations, [. . .] your gift

13 [. . .]*l*°°[. . . the mi]ghty b[low][28]

[24] Puech (*RQ* 14 [1990] 388, 394–95; cf. van der Ploeg, *Tradition und Glaube,* p. 133) reconstructs the end of line 2 and the beginning of line 3 of col. 3, as: "[. . . and he will send] a mighty [angel] who will pur[sue you from off] the whole earth."

[25] Puech (*RQ* 14 [1990] 388, 395; cf. van der Ploeg, *Tradition und Glaube,* p. 134) reconstructs 3.3–4 thus: "[When one invokes the G]od of the heavens then [upon the earth] Yahweh will smite you (with) a [might]y bl[ow] in order to destroy you [forever]." See the curse formula in Deut 28:22 which was probably the source for the phrasing here.

[26] Or "which."

[27] Puech (*RQ* 14 [1990] 387, 395–96; cf. van der Ploeg, *Tradition und Glaube,* pp. 134–35) reconstructs lines 5–9a so: "And by his burning wrath [he will send] against you a mighty angel [to execute al]l [his com]mand(s) which [(will be) without] pity against you, (an angel) wh[o will have dominion, indeed,] over all those who [will s]e[nd] you to the great pit [and to] deepest [Sheol], and (far) from the ab[ode of light you] will lie down and (there will be) darkness [in the] extremely [gr]eat [pit. . .]."

[28] Puech (*RQ* 14 [1990] 387, 396–97; cf. van der Ploeg, *Tradition und Glaube,* p. 135) reconstructs lines 9b–14a thus: "You will no l]onger [have dominion] on the earth, [but you will be bound] forever, and y[ou will be cursed] with the curse of Aba[ddon, and you will be terrified by] the burning wrath of Y[ahweh, and you will rule in] darkness in a[ll the fixed times of] tribulations, [and you will give your servants] your gift [. . . and . . .]*l*°°[. . .this mi]ghty b[low. . .]."

Col. 4

1	]וֹ[	צ]דֹקֹ[	]בֹ
2	אשר]	[הֹפגועֹ]ים[24]	
3	נדבי אֹ[	ר]פֹאל שלמֹ[25]	

(Psalm III)

4 לדויד עֹ]ל דברי ל[חֹש בשם יהוֹ]ה קרא בכו]ל[26] עת

5 אל הֹשמֹ]ים   ]יֹבוא אליך בלֹי]על וא]מֹרתה אליו

6 מֹי אתה]   ]אדם ומזרע הקדֹ]ושי[27]ֹם[פניך פני

7 [שוֹ]וֹ[28] וקרנֹי]ך קרני חלֹ]וֹ[םֹ חושך אתֹה ולוא אור

8]עוֹ]ל ולוא צדקהֹ[   ]שׂר הצבֹא יהוה]   ]ךֹ

9 [בשאוֹ]ל תחתית]   דֹ]לֹתֹי נחושת בֹ[29]   ]אֹ

10] אור ולוֹא]ר   ]שמש אשֹ]ר

11 הֹ]צדיק לה]אור[30]   ]וֹ]אֹמרתה הֹ]

12 צֹ]דיק לבוֹאֹ[   ]הֹרע לו שֹ]טן[31]

13 אֹ]מת מחוֹ]שֹך[32]   הצֹ]דקה לוֹ]ן[33]   ] לוֹאֹ[

14]וֹ[34]ֹ[   ]לֹ לֹ[   ]הֹ

---

24 Van der Ploeg reads [ופגוע].

25 Puech reconstructs lines 1-3 to read [ו[צֹ]דֹק[ ]בֹ[°]ׂ (?) אשר](ומזרע) [הֹפגועֹ]ים ויתהלכו עם כול] נדבי אֹ]מתו כאשר ר]פֹאל שלמֹ[[אמן אמן סלה].

26 The reconstruction indicated is Puech's. However, the psalm may have begun with בשם י. For word order see Ps 116:4, 13, 17.

27 Puech reconstructs lines 4-6a to read לדויד עֹ]ל דברי ל[חֹש בשם יהוֹ]ה קרא בכו]ל עת אל הֹשמ]ים אשר]יֹבוא אליך בלֹי]על וא]מֹרתה אליו מֹי אתה]אֹרור מֹ]אדם ומזרע הקדֹ]ושי[ם.

28 *Apud* Puech; van der Ploeg reads וֹתוה.

29 Puech reconstructs lines 8b-9a to read]שׂר הצבֹא יהוה נגדך[ ]יאֹסר]ך [בשאוֹ]ל תחתית]ויֹסגור דֹ]לֹתֹי נחושת בֹ]אלה.

30 Puech reconstructs lines 9b-11a to read]אֹ[ו]ר]יֹעבור לו]אֹ[ולוֹא יאיר אור הֹ]שמש אשֹ]ר יזרח על הֹ]צדיק להֹ]איר את פֹניו.

31 Puech reconstructs lines 11b-12a to read]וֹ]אֹמרתה הֹ]לוֹא מלאך עם הצֹ]דיק לבוֹאֹ[במשפט כי]הֹרע לו שֹ]טן.

32 Van der Ploeg reads מדֹ].

33 Puech reconstructs lines 12b-13 to read]וֹיצילהו רוח אֹ]מֹת מחוֹ]שֹך אשר הצֹ]דקה לוֹ]ן לקום במשפט.

34 With Puech there seems to be a supralinear insertion or correction (his 14a) above line 14.

Col. 4

1 [...]*w*[... ri]ghteousness [...]*b*

2 who [...] the strick[en...]

3 volunteers of '[... Ra]phael will make them whole [....][29]

(Psalm III)

4 To David.[30] Conce[rning the words of inc]antation in the name of Yahw[eh. Invoke on eve]ry occasion

5 the heave[ns...] Beli[al] shall come to you, [and] you shall [s]ay to him,

6 "Who (are) you, [...] human(s) and among the progeny of the Hol[y On]es?"[31] Your presence (is) the presence of

7 [emptin]ess and your horns (are) horns of a dre[a]m. Darkness (are) you and not light,

8 [dece]it and not righteousness.[32] [...] Commander of the Army.[33] Yahweh [...] you

9 [in] deepest [Sheo]l [... the g]ates of bronze with [...]'[34]

10 [...] light [...], nor [...] sun whi[ch...]

11 [...the] righteous to il[lumine....[35] And] you will say, "*h*[...]

12 [... ri]ghteous when he enters [...] Sa[tan] has done him wrong?"[36] [...]

13 [... tr]uth [...] from dar[kness... rig]hteousness [...] for him [...][37]

14 [...] not [...]*w* °[...]*l l*[...]*h*

---

[29] Puech (*RQ* 14 [1990] 387, 397; cf. van der Ploeg, *Tradition und Glaube*, p. 135) reconstructs 4.1–3 thus: "[...]*w*[... ri]ghteousness [...]*b*° who [...] the strick[en, and they will walk with all] the volunteers of [his] tr[uth when Ra]phael will make them whole." Following his overall thesis Puech conjectures that the second psalm concluded with "Amen. Amen. Selah" (see 5.14; and Num 5:22; Ps 41:14, 72:19, 89:53; Neh 8:6).

[30] This is the only psalm of the four that has an extant attribution to David, which Puech ascribes to all four psalms; see *The Dead Sea Scrolls: Forty Years of Research*, pp. 78–89; *RQ* 14 (1990) 399–403 for his argument that this scroll contained the four psalms to be recited over "the stricken" noted in 11Q5 27.9–10.

[31] Puech (*RQ* 14 [1990] 382; *The Dead Sea Scrolls: Forty Years of Research*, pp. 69–71; cf. van der Ploeg, *Tradition und Glaube*, pp. 135–37) reconstructs 4.4–6 thus: "To David. Conce[rning the words of inc]antation in the name of Yahw[eh. Invoke on eve]ry occasion the heave[ns. Whenever] Beli[al] shall come to you, you shall [s]ay to him, 'Who (are) you, [accursed among] human(s) and among the progeny of the Hol[y On]es?'" See 2.1–2 and Ps 54:3, 20:2, 118:10; Gen 3:14; cf. J. Naveh-Sh. Shaked, *Amulets and Magic Bowls, Aramaic Incantations of Late Antiquity* (Jerusalem, 1985), esp. amulets 7, 11, 13.

[32] The text at this point is relatively well preserved. "[Dece]it" is the reconstruction of van der Ploeg (*Tradition und Glaube*, pp. 137–38), as typical contrast to "righteousness."

[33] For "Commander of the Army" see 1QM 13.10, 17.5 and the other references in Puech (*pace* van der Ploeg).

[34] Puech (*The Dead Sea Scrolls: Forty Years of Research*, pp. 68–73; *RQ* 14 [1990] 84; cf. van der Ploeg, *Tradition und Glaube*, p. 138) reconstructs lines 8b–9a thus: "[Opposing you is] the Commander of the Army. Yahweh [will imprison] you [in] deepest [Sheo]l [and he will close the g]ates of bronze with [an oath]." Cf. Job 3:10. For "deepest Sheol," see Deut 32:22.

[35] Puech (*The Dead Sea Scrolls: Forty Years of Research*, p. 73; *RQ* 14 [1990] 384–85) reconstructs lines 9b–11a so: "Light [will no]t [pass (through it),] nor [will the light of the] sun [shine] (there) whi[ch will dawn on the] righteous to il[lumine their faces]." See Ps 97:11, 112:4.

[36] Puech (*The Dead Sea Scrolls: Forty Years of Research*, pp. 73–74; *RQ* 14 [1990] 385) reconstructs lines 11b–12a thus: "And] you will say, ['Is not an angel with the ri]ghteous when he enters [into judgment, when] Sa[tan] has done him wrong?'" See Ps 34:8, 35:4–6; Job 33:23; *1En* 20; Matt 18:10; Acts 12:7; Lk 16:22 for expressions of guardian or accompanying angels. For expressions of the confrontation of Satan by an angel of Yahweh, see Job 1:6ff., Zach 3:1ff., *1En* 40:7, *Jub* 23:29. See also the plea in "Plea for Deliverance" in 11Q5 19.15.

[37] Puech (*The Dead Sea Scrolls: Forty Years of Research*, p.74; *RQ* 14 [1990] 385) reconstructs lines 12b–13 thus: "[And the spirit of tr]uth [will rescue him] from dar[kness because rig]hteousness [will stand] for him [at the judgment...]." See 1QS 4.21–23. e.g., for "the spirit of truth," and *Visions of Amram*[b] (4Q544) for comparable theological views.

Col. 5

ת[נין	ל[ ]̊	]ד[	]ג[	1
]יהו[ה ל[עולם	]יה[	]תו[		2

(Psalm IV)

בסתר [בצ]ל שדי	] סלה[	בני בל]יעל[35]		3
] בו	] מבטח[י36]	ומצודת[י]	האומר [ ]	4
הו]אה יצילך מ[פח יקו]ש מדבר הו[ו]ת ב]אברתו יסך[ ] לך[ו]תחת				5
[כנפ]יו תשכון חסד[ו ע]ליך צנה וסוחרה אמתו סלה לוא תׄירא				6
מ̇פ̇חד לילה מחץ יעו̇ף יומ̇ם מ̇קטב ישוד [צ]הרים מדבר [באפ]ל				7
יהלך יפ̇ו̇ל מצדך אלף ור̇[בבה מי]מׄינך אל[ ]יך לו[א] יגע רק[ ]				8
בעיני[ך ותרא[ה] שלום רשע[י]ם קר[את מח]סך ש[מ]ת מחמד[ך] לוא[ ]				9
תרא[ה] ו[ל]וא יגע [ ] בא[ה]ל[י]ך כי[ ] [י]צוה ל[ך]				10
לשומ]רך בדרכי[ך] על כפי̇ם̇ ישאונ[ך] פן תגוף בא[בן רגל]ך[ ]				11
[פ]תֿן[ ] תד]רׄוך תרמו]ס כפיר [ותנו]ן[ ] ח[שקתה ̊]				12
[ ]̊ ̊ ̊ ויר[א]ך בישו̇ע[ת]ו				13
ויע[נ]נו אמן אמן[37] סלה[ ]				14

---

35 Puech supplies אמן אמן in the rest of the lacuna.
36 Van der Ploeg and Eissfeldt restore the י with MT on מבטח,

whereas Puech omits it: "il serait trop petit."
37 See note to 5.3.

Col. 5

1 [...]g[...]d[...]°l[...se]a monster

2 [...]tw[...]yh[...]Yahw[eh... for] ever

3 [...] the sons of Bel[ial....] Selah.[38]

(Psalm IV)[39]

[...] in the shelter of [... in the sha]dow of the Almighty

4 [....] Whoever says[40] [...] and [my] fortress, [... my] security[41] in whom [....]

5 [...h]e will deliver you from [the snare of the fowl]er, from dea[dly] pestilence. [In] his pinions he will cover [you,] and under

6 his [wing]s you will reside. [His] grace (will be) [fo]r you a shield and his truth a buckler.[42] Selah. You will not be afraid

7 of the terror of the night (or) the arrow that flies (by) day, the plague that rages at [n]oon, (or) the pestilence (which) [in darkn]ess

8 stalks. A thousand may fall at your side, or te[n thousand at] your [ri]ght, (but) y[ou] it will n[ot] touch. Only [...]

9 with your eyes [and you will se]e the retribution of the wick[ed]. You have [inv]oked [your] ref[uge,] you have [ma]de (him) your delight.[43]

10 You will [not] se[e... n]or shall [...] touch your [te]nts.[44] Fo[r] he has commanded [...] for you

11 to gua[rd you on] your [ways], upon (their) palms [they will lift] you up lest [... your] foot [on a st]one,

12 (and upon) a serpent[45] [... you will t]read, you will tramp[le...] and sea monster.[46] You have [he]ld fast °[....]

13 °°[... he will sh]ow you [his] salvatio[n....][47]

14 And th[ey] shall resp[ond Amen, Amen.] Selah.

---

[38] Van der Ploeg (*Tradition und Glaube*, p. 138) saw that the third psalm ends at the top of 5.1—3, after which Ps 91 immediately follows in a modified form. The word "[dra]gon" seems to end line 1. Line 2 has only two fairly clear words, "Yahweh" and "forever." Line 3 clearly has "sons of Bel[ial]." Puech (*The Dead Sea Scrolls: Forty Years of Research*, pp. 74—75; *RQ* 14 [1990] 385), as expected, conjectures "Amen. Amen." before the "Selah" which concludes the third psalm just before Ps 91 begins on the same line 3.

[39] y.Shabbat 6:2 includes Ps 91:1—9 with Ps 3:2—9 as canticles to be recited against misfortune. This was the first psalm published of the four in 11Q11, by J. van der Ploeg in *RB* 72 (1965) 210—17. O. Eissfeldt published a study of the text soon thereafter in *Bibel und Qumran* (1968); see above note 2 to the introduction. E. Puech included his study of the 11Q11 fourth psalm both in *The Dead Sea Scrolls: Forty Years of Research*, pp. 75—78, and in *RQ* 14 (1990) 378—79. Ps 91 is the best preserved of the four psalms in 11Q11. Even so, the

variants in this adapted form of the psalm are very important for understanding the whole document and for understanding apotropaic prayers in Early Judaism generally.

[40] MT reads "I will say."

[41] MLacking in the MT.

[42] Cf. MT 91:4, "... and under his wings you will find refuge. A shield and a buckler (are) his truth."

[43] MT Ps 91:9, with difficulty, reads, "For you, O Yahweh, (are surely) my refuge; the most high you have made your dwelling place."

[44] MT Ps 91:10 reads, "Evil shall not befall you, misfortune shall not draw near to your tents."

[45] Or "cobra."

[46] MT Ps 91:13 reads, "On a jackal and a serpent you will tread; you will trample a lion cub and a sea monster."

[47] MT Ps 91:14 reads, "For to me he has held fast, and I will deliver him; I will raise him up, for he knows my name."

11Q11 Ps IV Compared with Masoretic Text

MT Ps 91	*11Q11 Ps IV*
(1) ישב בסתר עליון	[ישב] בסתר [עליון]
בצל שדי יתלונן	[בצ]ל שדי[(4) יתלונן]
(2) אמר ליהוה	האומר [ליהוה]
מחסי ומצודתי	[מחסי] ומצודת[נ]י
אלהי אבטח־בו	[אלהי] מבטחי אבטח] בו
(3) כי הוא יצילך	[כי הו]אה יצילך (5)
מפח יקוש	מ[פח יקו]ש
מדבר הוות	מדבר הו[ות]
(4) באברתו יסך לך	ב[אברתו יסך] לך
ותחת־כנפיו תחסה	ותחת [כנפ]יו תשכון (6)
צנה וסחרה אמתו	חסדו ע]ליך צנה וסוחרה אמתו סלה
(5) לא־תירא מפחד לילה	לוא תירא מפחד לילה (7)
מחץ יעוף יומם	מחץ יעוף[38] יומם
(6) מדבר באפל יהלך	מקטב ישוד [צ]הרים[39]
מקטב ישוד צהרים	מדבר [באפ]ל יהלך[40] (8)
(7) יפל מצדך אלף	יפול מצדך אלף[41]
ורבבה מימינך	ור[בבה מי]מינ[ך][42]
אליך לא יגש	אל[יך לו]א יגע[43]
(8) רק בעיניך תביט	רק [תביט] בעיניך (9)
ושלמת רשעים תראה	[ותרא]ה שלום רשע[ים]
(9) כי־אתה יהוה מחסי	[קר]את מח[סך]
עליון שמת מעונך	[ש]מת מחמדך
(10) לא־תאנה אליך רעה	[לוא] תרא[ה] (10)
ונגע לא־יקרב באהלך	[ו]לוא נגע [באה]ליך

---

38 4Q84 1.10: [ועף].

39 4Q84 1.12: מק[ ] [צ]הרים.

40 4Q84 1.11: [פל יהלך].

41 4Q84 1.13: יפל [ך אל].

42 4Q84 1.14: [ב]בה [מ] [ך].

43 4Q84 1.15: גש[ ]. 4Q84 1.16 preserves a portion of Ps 91:8 not extant in 11Q11: [ ]ביט.

11Q11 Ps IV Compared with Masoretic Text*

11Q11 Ps IV

[One who dwells] in the shelter of [the Most High]
[in the sha]dow of the Almighty [(4)][he lodges.]
Whoever says[48] [to Yahweh,]
["My refuge] and [my] fortress,
[my God (is) my] security[49] in whom [I trust."]
[(5)][For h]e will deliver you
from [the snare of the fowl]er,
from dea[dly] pestilence.
[In] his pinions he will cover [you,]
and under [(6)]his [wing]s you will reside.
[His] grace (will be) [fo]r you a shield and his truth a
buckler.[50]   Selah.
You will not be afraid [(7)]of the terror of the night
(or) the arrow that flies (by) day,
the plague that rages at [n]oon,
(or) the pestilence (which) [in darkn]ess [(8)]stalks.[51]
A thousand may fall at your side,
or te[n thousand at] your [ri]ght,
(but) y[ou] it will n[ot] touch.[52]
Only [look] [(9)]with your eyes
[and you will se]e the retribution of the wick[ed].[53]
You have [inv]oked [your] ref[uge,]
you have [ma]de (him) your delight.[54]
[(10)]You will [not] se[e . . .]
[n]or shall [misfortune] touch your [te]nts.[55]

MT Ps 91

[(1)]One who dwells in the shelter of the Most High
in the shadow of the Almighty he lodges.
[(2)]I will say to Yahweh,
"My refuge and my fortress,
my God in whom I trust."
[(3)]For he will deliver you
from the snare of the fowler,
from deadly pestilence.
[(4)]In his pinions he will cover you,
and under his wings you will find refuge.
A shield and a buckler (are) his truth.

[(5)]You will not be afraid of the terror of the night
(or) the arrow that flies (by) day,
[(6)]the pestilence (which) in darkness stalks,
(or) the plague that rages at noon.
[(7)]A thousand may fall at your side,
or ten thousand at your right,
(but) you it will not approach.
[(8)]With your eyes only look
and the retribution of the wicked you will see.
[(9)]"For you, O Yahweh, (are surely) my refuge;
the most high you have made your dwelling place."
[(10)]Evil shall not befall you,
misfortune shall not draw near to your tents.

---

* Superscripted numbers in parentheses indicate line numbers for 11Q11 and verse numbers for the MT, respectively.

48 Whereas MT has "I will say," 11Q11 has the force of "Whoever says," which fits the context of a psalm to be recited by or for whoever needs divine protection against demons or evil spirits. Cf. LXX verb in third person singular. Eissfeldt accepted the 11Q11 reading (*Bibel und Qumran*, pp. 83, 85).

49 Puech reads without the suffix ', supplied by van der Ploeg and Eissfeldt, making it an unarticulated noun, lacking in the MT in any case.

50 Eissfelt accepted the 11Q11 reading in his reconstruction of MT Ps 91:4 (*Bibel und Qumran*, pp. 83, 85), disagreeing with van der Ploeg who considered the verb, "you will find refuge" secondary since the verb is never used in MT with "under his wings" (*RB* 72 [1965] 212–13). Puech agreed with Eissfelt that the verb in 11Q11 may be primitive (*RQ* 14 [1990] 379) and even suggested that the whole of Ps 91:4 in 11Q11 (5.5–6) might be primitive to the MT psalm.

51 Note the inversion of the two colons of MT Ps 91:6; 4Q84 1.11–12 supports the reading of the MT here.

52 "Touch" fits the context for which Ps 91 was adapted better than MT "approach."

53 11Q11 reverses the parallelism of the verbs from the order in MT Ps 91:8, putting the verbs at the beginning of each colon instead of at the end.

54 Since the LXX, translations have struggled with the apparent change of address between the two colons of the verse in the MT. Van der Ploeg (*RB* 72 [1965] 213) views MT as corrupt or reworked, and suggests the restoration here offered, followed by Puech; the latter, however, omits "the Most High" for lack of space on the leather. Eissfeldt (*Bibel und Qumran*, p. 85), whose interest was in recovering a primitive form of MT Ps 91, kept both divine epithets, while Puech's reconstruction of 11Q11 lacks both.

55 Van der Ploeg reads 11Q11 thus, "You will [not] se[e evil,] nor will [misfortune] touch [. . .] your tents" —leaving the lacuna after "touch." Eissfeldt (*Bibel und Qumran*, pp. 84–85) reads, "You will [not] se[e evil,. . .] nor will [misfortune] touch [you in your te]nts." Puech (*RQ* 14 [1990] 378, 380) reads, "You will [not] see [on you(?) evil,] nor will [misfortune] touch (you) [in your te]nts." 11Q11 appears to be derivative.

כ]י מלאכיו]יצוה לך	⁽¹¹⁾כי מלאכיו יצוה־לך
⁽¹¹⁾לשומ]רך בדרכי]ך	לשמרך בכל־דרכיך
על כפים] ישאונ]ך	⁽¹²⁾על־כפים ישאונך
פן] תגוף בא]בן רגל]ך[	פן־תגף באבן רגלך
⁽¹²⁾פתן [תד]רוך	⁽¹³⁾על־שחל ופתן תדרך
תרמו]ס [ותנון]	תרמס כפיר ותנין
[ח]שקתה [ ]	⁽¹⁴⁾כי בי חשק ואפלטהו
	אשגבהו כי־ידע שמי
	⁽¹⁵⁾יקראני ואענהו
	עמו־אנכי בצרה
	אחלצהו ואכבדהו
⁽¹³⁾[ויר]אך בישוע]תו	⁽¹⁶⁾ארך ימים אשביעהו
⁽¹⁴⁾ויע]נו אמן אמן] סלה	ואראהו בישועתי

Fo[r] he has commanded [his angels] for you
(11)to gua[rd you on] your [ways],[56]
upon (their) palms [they will lift] you up
lest [you strike your] foot [on a st]one,
(12)(and upon) a serpent [. . . you will t]read,
you will tramp[le . . .] and sea monster.[57]
You have [he]ld fast °[. . . .]

(13)°°[. . . he will sh]ow you [his] salvatio[n. . . .][58]
(14)And th[ey] shall resp[ond Amen, Amen.]   Selah.[59]

(11)For he has commanded his angels for you
to guard you on all your ways,
(12)upon (their) palms they will lift you up
lest you strike your foot on a stone.
(13)On a jackel and a serpent[60] you will tread;
you will trample a lion cub and a sea monster.
(14)For to me he has held fast, and I will deliver him;
I will raise him up, for he knows my name.
(15)He will invoke me and I will answer him,
I (will be) with him in trouble,
I will rescue him and I will glorify him;
(16)(With) long days I will satisfy him,
and I will show him my salvation.

56   Van der Ploeg and Eissfeldt restore the MT to the lacunae of 91:11 (11Q11 lines 10–11), while Puech omits "all" before "your [ways]."

57   Van der Ploeg (*RB* 72 [1965] 211, 214) restores 91:13 thus: "(On) a serpent [and a viper you will t]read, you will tramp[le a lion cub. . .] and a sea monster." Eissfeldt (*Bibel und Qumran*, pp. 84–85) reads, "On a serpent [and a jackal you will t]read, you will tramp[le a lion cub and a lion] and a sea monster." Puech (*RQ* 14 [1990] 378, 380; *The Dead Sea Scrolls: Forty Years of Research*, pp. 75–78) reads, "and(?) the serpent [and the viper you will t]read, you will tramp[le the lion cub] and the sea monster."

58   The last strophe of MT Ps 91 (vv. 14–16) is a Yahweh speech, a response of divine assurance in the first person for one who adheres to the affirmations of trust in God the psalm extols. Ps 91 in 11Q11 considerably modifies v. 14 and omits vv. 15 and 16. Van der Ploeg (*RB* 72 [1965] 215) cautiously supplied only the first and last words as they appear on the leather, "You have [he]ld fast, and [. . .] °° [. . . sh]ow you [my] salvatio[n]." Eissfeldt (*Bibel und Qumran*, p. 85) reconstructed it to read, "[For in Yahweh you have he]ld fast, and [he delivered you;

. . . and he glorified you and sh]owed you [his] salvatio[n]." Puech at first (*The Dead Sea Scrolls: Forty Years of Research*, pp. 75, 77–78) read, "[To Yahweh] you have [he]ld fast, and [he will deliver you] from [all misfortune, and sh]ow you [his] salvatio[n. Selah.]" Then (in *RQ* 14 [1990] 378, 380–81) Puech reads, "[To Yahweh] you have [he]ld fast, and [he will deliver you.] Also [he will raise you up/reassure you(?), and he will sh]ow you [his] salvatio[n. Selah.]"

59   Van der Ploeg (*RB* 72 [1965] 211) restored little of the last verse in 11Q11 but (*RB* 72 [1965] 215) suggests "Amen" as object of the verb, citing Neh 8:6. Eissfeldt (*Bibel und Qumran*, p. 85), whose interest was essentially text critical with regard to MT Ps 91, did not include the verse in his restoration of the psalm, except to suggest that it was probably derived from Ps 3:5. (Note that Ps 3 is the other apotropaic prayer in the MT Psalter noted in y. Shabbat 6:2). Puech pursues his thesis to the end with the double Amen (*The Dead Sea Scrolls: Forty Years of Research*, p. 78; *RQ* 14 [1990] 381), also citing Neh 8:6.

60   Or "cobra."

Daily Prayers

(4Q503=4QPrQuot)

Dennis T. Olson[1]

Introduction

1. Contents

4Q503 contains a fragmentary collection of morning and evening prayers. The prayers are in the form of blessings to be said in the evening, which is the start of each new day, and at the rising of the sun each morning with one pair of blessings for each day. The order of the blessings follows the sequence of the days of the month. The days which are specifically mentioned in the preserved fragments are days 4, 5, 6, 7, 9, 12, 16, 17, 18, and 26. A mood of joy and rejoicing predominate throughout the blessings, reflecting an attitude of praise in daily worship. The nature of the prayers for the fifteenth and the twenty-first days points to these as festival days. Thus, the month in question may be either the first or the seventh month of the year which would contain festivals on these days. A confession of sin appears only once, in fragment 81: "we have [s]inned against [you]."[2] The blessings are for the most part very formulaic and follow precisely fixed models which recur throughout the collection. The blessings are cleary intended for corporate worship rather than personal devotional practice. This corporate character of the prayers is reflected in the recurring responsorial formula, "they will bless and they will answer and they will say" which is extant thirty times throughout the collection.

The collection of 225 fragments in 4Q503 was first published by M. Baillet in 1982.[3] The arrangement of the sequence of fragments and the distribution of the text into columns by Baillet and C. H. Hunzinger appear fairly reliable, although some fragments are difficult to place.[4] J.M. Baumgarten speculates that the reconstruction of column 3 is "highly problematic" resulting in the repositioning of fragments 2 and 3.[5]

The structure of the individual evening and morning prayers is quite regular.[6] Each prayer contains a heading specifying the time of the prayer ("On the... of the month in the evening"; "And when the sun rises to shine over the earth") followed by the formula "they will bless and they will answer and they will say." Each prayer begins with a blessing ("Blessed be the God of Israel who does" or "has done"). Apparently the blessings are followed by references to the night ("And the night...at the beginning ...of the revolutions of the vessels of light...") or to the day ("And this day he has renewed... for us dominion..."). The prayers conclude with a blessing to God ("Blessed be you, God of Israel" or "Blessed be your name, God of Israel") and the formula "Peace (be) upon you, O Israel." Divisions between the prayers are often indicated by a mark in the margin or a vacat or both. The repetitive formulae allow restorations when they are anchored by at least one consonant.

2. Date and Original Language

The Hebrew script is Hasmonaean and appears to date to 100−75 B.C.E.[7] There is no indication that the original language was not Hebrew.

---

[1] I am grateful to C. Bowman whose unpublished paper, "A Theological Analysis of the Prayers from Qumran: The Daily Prayers (4Q503)," provided helpful insights and bibliography in preparation of this introduction; and to J.B.F. Miller for checking the Hebrew text.

[2] Since the day of the month is not specified on this fragment containing the confession of sin, we are unable to determine the particular day in the liturgical calendar when the confession was to be used. It may be that this confession of sin was part of the Qumran ritual on the Day of Atonement (see 1Q34−1Q34[bis]) or that it was associated with a ritual of confession preceding the Sabbath (4Q504−506).

[3] M. Baillet, DJD 7, pp. 104−36.

[4] M. Baillet, DJD 7, p. 105.

[5] J. M. Baumgarten, "4Q503 (Daily Prayers) and the Lunar Calendar," *RQ* 12 (1987) 399−407.

[6] See B. Nitzan, *Qumran Prayer and Religious Poetry* (STDJ 12; Leiden, 1994) esp. the summary on p. 70.

[7] M. Baillet, DJD 7, p. 105. A similar dating is suggested by Baumgarten, *RQ* 12 (1987) 399 and by L. H. Schiffman, "The Dead Sea Scrolls and the Early History of the Jewish Liturgy," in *The Synagogue in Late Antiquity,* edited by L. I. Levine (Philadelphia, 1987) p. 33.

3. Provenience

Although 4Q503 does not use specifically sectarian terminology, its vocabulary bears some affinities with Qumran sectarian documents. While such *termini technici* as בית קודש, בני אור, and מורה הצדק are conspicuously absent, there are the following terms, words, or concepts which are so prevalent in the documents composed at Qumran (in the order of their appearance): light contrasted with darkness, "we, his holy people," "for our knowledge," "the sons of your covenant," the frequent references to "standards" especially "standards of light," "God of lights," "Holy Ones," "the holy one of Holy Ones," "the Sons of Righteousness," "the lots of light," "the priesthood," "the armies of divine beings," "his wondrous works," and "lots of dark[ness]."[8]

If 4Q503 is a sectarian document, then it raises two central issues associated with the Community's liturgical time: 1) the kind of monthly calendar used at Qumran (probably solar-lunar), and 2) the understanding of when the day began in Qumranic liturgical practice (at sunset or sunrise). As is well known, the Qumran Community differed from many of its Jewish contemporaries in adhering to a solar-lunar calendar rather than a lunar calendar based on the various phases of the moon.[9] A Hasmonaean text in *Jubilees* 6:32−38 rejects the use of the lunar calendar, arguing that those who divide the days of the year by studying the phases of the moon will corrupt the liturgical schedule: "They will set awry the months and the appointed times and the sabbaths and the feasts."[10]

It is wrong to conclude that the calendar at Qumran was a purely solar calendar. Baumgarten has carefully demonstrated that the writer of *Jubilees* was alone in resorting to the extreme of rejecting the lunar calendar entirely.[11] The "Book of the Heavenly Luminaries" (*1 Enoch* 72−82) and Sirach 43:6−7, both of which predate *Jubilees*, integrate a solar and a lunar calendar.[12] The sequence of daily blessings in 4Q503 clearly reflects this integrated use of both lunar and solar calendars.[13] Moreover, although *1 Enoch* does not indicate whether its care-ful lunar calculations serve scientific or religious purposes, 4Q503 emphasizes the specifically religious significance of the lunar aspect of its calendar. The series of daily prayers assigns a blessing for each successive phase of the moon. Hence, Qumran's liturgical calendar probably followed the practice of intercalating lunar and solar calendars. *Jubilees'* outright rejection of the lunar calendar apparently was not shared by all Qumranites, at least in so far as their beliefs are reflected in 4Q503.

A second issue connected with the reckoning of liturgical time is the designation of the beginning of the day. Since prayers are assigned both for the evening and for the light of day in 4Q503, scholars have raised the question of when the day began for the Community. Some have argued that the Qumran Community understood the day to begin with the rising of the sun in contrast to the rest of Judaism which held that the day began with the setting of the sun.[14] However, a careful study of 4Q503 indicates that the day clearly is seen to begin with sunset in the evening. Throughout 4Q503, the formula for the new day of the month is always introduced with the formula, "on such and such day of the month *in the evening.*" The evening prayer is the first prayer of the day and is followed by the morning prayer at sunrise which is designated for the same day as the preceding evening prayer. Thus, the prayers in 4Q503 conform to standard practice in Early Judaism which understands the liturgical day to begin with the evening setting of the sun.[15]

4. Theology

The theology of these fragmentary prayers reflects the praise of God who is characterized as "holy" (Frgs. 15−16 ll. 5, 13, 18; Frg. 26 l. 3) and who has made known to the Community the mysteries of the divinely appointed times in which the Community plays a part (Frg. 33 l.4, 21; Frgs. 51−55 l. 18; Frgs. 64, 69, 70−71, 76). The deity is praised as the God of lights who creates and regulates all that is (Frg. 13 l. 1; Frgs. 21−22 l. 1; Frgs. 29−32 l. 8). The Community understands itself in these

---

8 This paragraph is added by the Editor.
9 Y. Yadin, *The Temple Scroll,* vol. 1 (Jerusalem, 1983) pp. 269−70; S. Talmon, "The Calendar Reckoning of the Sect from the Judaean Desert," *Scripta Hierosolymitana* 4 (1958) 162−99; S. Zeitlin, "On the Beginning of the Day in the Calendar of the Jubilees," *JBL* 78 (1959) 153−156; and J. T. Milik, *Ten Years of Discovery in the Wilderness of Judaea* (London, 1959) p. 152.
10 *OTP* 2:68.
11 Baumgarten, *RQ* 12 (1987) 406. Cf. Schürer, *The History of the Jewish People in the Age of Jesus Christ,* rev. ed., vol. 2 (Edinburgh, 1986) p. 581; and B. Wacholder, "The Calendar of Sabbatical Cycles during the Second Temple and the Early Rabbinic Period," *HUCA* 44 (1973) 153−96.
12 Cf. especially *1 Enoch* 74; *OTP* 1:53.
13 In addition to days that are numbered, 4Q503 mentions different numbers of "gates of light" and "standards of light"

which presumably refer to the setting and rising of the sun. The number of gates seems to correspond to the number of the day; for example, the sixth day has six gates of light. The "standards," on the other hand, may refer to the amount of light reflected by the moon on that given day. The number of flags does not exceed fourteen which would correspond to the number of phases of the moon. Cf. Baumgarten, *RQ* 12 (1987) 400, and *1 Enoch* 72−82.
14 See esp. 1QS 10.10 ("As the day and night enters I will enter into the covenant of God,... ."). Citing this passage, Talmon argues that the "Covenanters' order of prayer... begins with the morning benedictions..." (Talmon, *World,* p. 175).
15 Cf. Baumgarten, *RQ* 12 (1987) 403−404. Contrast 4Q408, possibly a sectarian document, which refers to the morning before the evening (see A. Steudel, "4Q408: A Liturgy on Morning and Evening Prayer Preliminary Edition," *RQ* 16 [1994] 313−34).

prayers as a chosen and holy people (Frgs. 1−6 l. 20; Frg. 11 l. 3; Frgs. 37−38 l. 5). As the Community praises God, it also confesses its sin before God (Frg. 81). The Community claims special, revelatory knowledge of "the psalms of glory" (Frgs. 51−55 l. 9) and of God's great design (Frgs. 51−55 l. 13). Overall, the theology of the prayers seems consistent with an early stage in the development of Qumranic theology.[16]

5. Relation to the Hebrew Bible

These prayers of Qumran are remarkably similar to prose prayers in the Hebrew Bible. Their syntactical structure and cultic setting closely correspond to the genre of biblical prayers identified as the "indirect cultic blessing of God" which features a passive participial form of the verb "to bless" followed by the deity's name and a predicative clause giving the basis for the praise of God.[17] The typical form in 4Q503 is "Blessed be the God of Israel who... ." The only significant deviation between the prayers in 4Q503 and similar prayers in the Hebrew Bible is not so much in the form or content as in the timing of the prayers. While the rising of the sun is rarely seen as a reminder to praise God in the Hebrew Bible,[18] it is the prevalent motif in these Qumran prayers. The morning prayers are tied to the rise of the sun in the frequent formula, "When the sun comes forth to shine upon the earth." This juxtaposition of sunrise and prayer echoes the observations of Josephus on the Essene custom of morning prayer:

And as for their piety toward God, it is very extraordinary; for before sunrising they speak not a word about profane matters, but put up certain prayers which they have received from their forefathers, as if they made a supplication for its rising (*War* 2.8.5).

As Josephus indicates, the spirituality of the Qumran Community was disciplined and regularized in daily corporate worship. The fragments of 4Q503 provide faint glimpses into that spirituality and life of prayer. Overall in terms of liturgical practice, these fragmentary glimpses suggest stronger continuities with other forms of Judaism prevalent at the time than scholars have sometimes admitted in the past.

6. Selected Bibliography

Baillet, M. "Prières quotidiennes." DJD 7, pp. 105−36; and Pls. XXXV, XXXVII, XXXIX, XLI, XLIII, XLV, XLVII.

Baumgarten, J. M. "4Q503 (Daily Prayers) and the Lunar Calendar," *RQ* 12 (1987) 399−407.

Nitzan, B. *Qumran Prayer and Religious Poetry*. STDJ 12; Leiden, 1994.

Tov, E. *The Dead Sea Scrolls on Microfiche*. Leiden, 1993 [PAM 40.628, 40.629, 40.636, 40.980, 41.832, 41.834, 41.836, 41.838, 41.840, 41.842, 41.844, 41.994, 42.476, 42.478, 42.480, 42.482, 42.484, 42.486, 42.487, 42.488, 43.640, 43.659, 43.861].

[16] Baumgarten, *RQ* 12 (1987) 402−403.

[17] An example of a biblical prayer in this form is Solomon's prayer of dedication of the first Temple in 1Kgs 8:56. Cf. W. S. Towner, "'Blessed be YHWH' and 'Blessed art Thou, YHWH': The Modulation of a Biblical Formula," *CBQ* 30 (1968) 386−99. Other helpful studies include H. Mowvley,

"The Concept and Content of 'Blessing' in the Old Testament," *Bible Translator* 16 (1965) 74−80; C. Westermann, *Praise and Lament in the Psalms* (Atlanta, 1981); and J. Scharbert, "brk," *TDOT*, 2, pp. 279−308.

[18] Cf. Ps. 113:3, 118:24; and Mal 1:11.

4Q503

Frgs. 1 and 4,[1] *Col. 1* [*Col. 2*][2]

ות ˚ [	4
[	5
ר ˚ [	6
[	7
[	8
[	9
[	10
[	11
[	12
[	13
ו ˚ [	14
תיו]	15
[	16
[	17
[	18
˚ [	19
[	20
˚ [	21

---

[1] Fragment 1 supplies lines 4-6; fragment 4 supplies lines 14, 15, 19, and 21.

[2] Numbers in brackets indicate columns of the scroll as proposed by Baillet, DJD 7.

4Q503

Frgs. 1 and 4, Col. 1 [Col. 2][1]

4 [...]°*wt*

5 [...]

6 [...]°*r*

7 [...]

8 [...]

9 [...]

10 [...]

11 [...]

12 [...]

13 [...]

14 [...]°*w*

15 [...]*tyw*

16 [...]

17 [...]

18 [...]

19 [...]°

20 [...]

21 [...]°

[1] Numbers in brackets indicate columns of the scroll as proposed by Baillet, DJD 7.

Frgs. 1–6, Col. 2[3] [Col. 3]

1　ובצאת֞] השמש　　ה]רקיע השמ[י]ם יברכו וענ]ו ואמרו

2　ברוך א]ל ישראל　[ל]]ו והי]ו[ם' [[הזה חד֞ש֞]

3　בארבע]ה　　[לנו ממשל]

4　עשר דג]לי　[וא חום ה]

5　בפוסחו] 　[ח יד גבורת] שלום עליכה
　　　　　ישראל]

6　בחמשֿה֞] לחודש בע]רב יברכו וענו [וא]מר֞ו ברוך א]ל ישראל

7　הסותֿם֞]　　[ח לפניו בכול מפלג כבודו והלילה]

8　ע]ולֿם ולהודות לו]]פדותנו בראשי]ת

9　ת֞סובת כלי אור] 　[ה֞יום ארבעה ע]שר

10　[אור ה]ומם ש]לום עלי]כֿה ישראל

11　　　　[　　　]

12　[וב]צֿא֞]ת השמש 　[להאיר על הארץ יברכו וע֞ו]נו ואמרו

13　המספֿר]　　[שר לחגי שמחה ומועדי כ]בוד'

14　כיא ה]יו[ם֞]　　[ח]משה עשר שע]רֿי

15　מועדי כֿב֞]וד 　[בֿגורלות לילה]

16　ישלם כב]וד 　　[[ע]ו֞לם]

17　ישראל]　　　[　　]

18　ובששה ל֞ח֞ו]דש בערב יברכו וענו וא]מֿרו בֿר]וך אל] ישראל

19　לילה אשר הו]　[שן לפניו] [˚ם עדן]

20　אנו עם קודשו] 　[בו חמש֞]ה

21　חמש]ה 　[ל] 　　[ל]

22　ומֿח֞]

23　וב]צאת השמש

---

[3] Fragment 1 supplies the right hand portion of lines 1-7; fragment 4 supplies the right hand portion of lines 12-23; fragment 2 is situated to the left of fragments 1 and 4, supplying lines 1-15; fragment 3 is situated to the left of fragment 2, supplying the left hand portion of lines 1-2; fragment 5 is situated to the left of fragment 4, supplying lines 18-21; fragment 6 is situated to the left of fragment 5, supplying lines 16-19.

[4] This lacuna indicates an area where the ink is smeared; there is no physical break in the papyrus.

[5] For restoration, cf. line 15 and CD 3.14-15.

240

Frgs. 1–6, Col. 2 [Col. 3]

1 And when [the sun] rises [...the] firmament of the heav[en]s, they will bless and [they] will answer [...]

2 "Blessed be the Go[d of Israel ...]*l*[...]*w* and this d[a]y he has renewed [....]

3 In the fourt[h...] for us dominion [...]

4 ten standa[rds of...]*w'* the warmth *h*[....]

5 When he passed over [...]*ḥ* hand of might [.... "Peace (be) upon you,] O Israel."[2]

6 On the fifth [of the month in the ev]ening they will bless and they will answer [and] they [will s]ay, "Blessed be the G[od of Israel ...]

7 their garments [...]*ḥ* before him in each division of his glory and the night [...]

8 [... f]orever and to give thanks to him [...] our redemption in the beginnin[g...]

9 [...] revolutions of the objects of light [...] today four[teen...]

10 [...] the light of the day, "Pe[ace (be) upon] you, O Israel."

11 [...] (vacat) [...]

12 [And when the sun r]is[es...] to shine upon the earth, they will bless and [they] will answe[r and they will say ...]

13 the numbe[r...]*šr* to the pilgrimage-feasts of joy and the festivals of gl[ory.]

14 Because the [da]y [... f]ifteen gate[s....]

15 Festivals of glo[ry...] in the lots of night [...]

16 he will complete the glo[ry of...] [f]orever [...]

17 Israel [....] (vacat) [...]

18 And on the sixth of the mon[th in the evening they will bless and they will answer and] they will [s]ay, "Bless[ed be the God of] Israel [...."]

19 A night which *hw*[...]*šn* before him [...]°*m* '*dn*[....]

20 We (are) his holy people [...] in him five [....]

21 Five [...]*l*[...]*l*[....]

22 And *mḥ* [....]

23 And when [the sun rises ...]

[2] Restoration based upon the observation that each prayer ends with the formula "Peace (be) upon you, O Israel," that the next line begins a new prayer, and that the supralinear correction in line 6 – "O Israel [...]" – supplies the end of the formula.

Frgs. 7–9[6] [Col. 4]

1   ש[[אור היומם לדעתנו] [

2   [בששה שערי או]ר ˚ [

3   [בני בריתכה נהלל]ה

4   [עם כול דגלי [[ל לשוני דעת ברך   ב]

5   [אור שלום [[ו]ר   ]

6   בשבעה ל[חודש בערב יברכו וענו ואמר]ו ברוך אל יש[ר]אל

7   [צדק [[ל]לה ידענו ב[[ל]

8   [אש]ר[[[ברוך א]ל[ישראל

Frg. 10 [Col. 5]

1   [ובצאת] השמש להאיר על האר[ץ

2   [עם דגלי אור ו]היו[ם ˚ [

3   [היומם תשעה [

Frg. 11 [Col. 5]

1   [ים   ]

2   בשני]ם עשר לחודש בערם [

3   [ים ואנו עם קודשו מרוממים הל[י]ל[ה]

4   א]נו ועדים עמנו במעמד (ב̇מ̇ע̇) יומם[

5   [ל] [ל]   [   ]

Frg. 12 [lost?]

---

[6] Fragment 7 supplies the beginning of line 1; fragment 8 supplies the beginning portions of lines 4-8; fragment 9 is situated to the left of fragments 7 and 8.

Frgs. 7–9 [Col. 4]

1 *š*[...] light of the day for our knowledge [...]

2 [...]° in the sixth of the gates of ligh[t...]

3 [...] the sons of your covenant, we prais[e... .]

4 With all the standards of [...]*l* the tongues of knowledge, "Bless *k*[...]

5 light, peace [...]*wr*. (vacat) [...]

6 On the seventh of [the month in the evening they will bless and they will answer and] they [will say,] "Blessed be the God of Is[rael..."]

7 righteousness [...]*l*[...]*lh* we know *b*[...]

8 [...] which [...] "Blessed be [the G]od [of Israel ..."]

Frg. 10 [Col. 5]

1 [And when] the sun [rises] to shine upon the ear[th...]

2 [...] with the standards of light, and today °[...]

3 [...] the ninth day [...]

Frg. 11 [Col. 5]

1 [...]*ym*. (vacat) [...]

2 [On the twelft]h of the month in the evening [...]

3 [...]*ym*. And we, his holy people, are exalting tonight [...]

4 [... w]e and witnesses with us in service of the day [...]

5 [..]*l*[...]*l*[... .] (vacat) [...]

Frg. 12 [lost?]

Frg. 13 [*Col. 6*]

1   [אלוהי אורים]

2   [י' אור ועד]ים

Frg. 14 [*Col. 6*]

1   [או]ר היומם [

2   ש]סכה אל ישראל בכֹ[

3   [   ]

4   [˚ ˚ קֹ ˚] הֹ[˚ ˚ ˚]

Frgs. 15—16[7] [*Col. 6*]

1   [ו]ֹש כֹ]

2   ק]דשים במרומ]ים

3   ע]ֹם[8] קודשו [

4   ו וכבוד בקוד]ש [ ] [˚ ˚] וֹ ˚ ˚ [

5   או]ֹר ועדים לנו בקוד[9] קודשים]

6   [בֹממשל אור היומם בֹרֹוֹך [

7   ש]לום עליכהֹ] ישראל

8   ברו]ֹך אל ישרֹאֹל המפלֹ]אות

9   [אֹרץ והלילה שמ]

10   [להוֹסֹיֹף לנו]

11   [כֹול מפלגו לו [

12   [אל ישרא]ל

13   [קודשכה [

14   [בשלו]שה [עשר

15   [שנים עשר]

16   י]שראל [

17   י]שראל [

18   קוד]שֹכֹהֹ]

---

7   Fragment 15 supplies lines 1-7; fragment 16 supplies lines
    8-18.

8   Or ש[ֹם.

9   Read בקודש or בקודשי.

Frg. 13 [*Col. 6*]

1 [. . .] God of lights [. . .]

2 [. . .]*y* of light and witness[es . . .]

Frg. 14 [*Col. 6*]

1 [. . . lig]ht of the day [. . .]

2 [. . .] your [na]me, O God of Israel in *k*[. . .]

3 [. . . .] (vacat) [. . .]

4 [. . .]° °*q*°[. . .]*h*°°°[. . .]

Frgs. 15−16 [*Col. 6*]

1 [. . .]*wš k*[. . .]

2 [. . . Ho]ly Ones in the height[s . . .]

3 [. . .] his holy peo[ple³ . . .]

4 [. . .]°[. . .]° °*w* and glory in the holy on[e . . .]

5 [. . . ligh]t and witnesses for us in the holy one of Holy Ones [. . .]

6 [. . .] in the dominion of the light of the day.   Blessed be [. . .]

7 [. . . "P]eace (be) upon you, [O Israel"]

8 [. . . "Bless]ed be the God of Israel who does wond[ers . . ."]

9 [. . .] earth.   And tonight *šm*[. . .]

10 [. . .] to add for us [. . .]

11 [. . .] all his division(s) to him [. . .]

12 [. . .] God of Israe[l . . .]

13 [. . .] your holiness [. . .]

14 [. . .] in the th[i]r[teenth . . .]

15 [. . .] twelve [. . .]

16 [. . . I]srael [. . .]

17 [. . .] Israel [. . .]

18 [. . . your] holiness [. . .]

³ Or "his holy na[me]."

Frg. 17 [Col. 6]

1   יבר]כו וענו [ואמרו

2   [תֹ֯ולדות ה]

3   ש]נֹ֯ים עשר]

Frg. 18 [Col. 6]

1   [לֹ֯יֹלֹ֯ה]

2   [השמש צֹ֯]

3   [רֹ֯ גדול מֹ֯]

Frg. 19 [Col. 6]

1   יברכו וענו וא]מֹ֯רוֹ֯ בֹ֯רֹ֯וֹ֯ךֹ֯] אל ישראל

2   ע]שֹ֯ר שערי אור]

Frg. 20 [Col. 6]

1   [כֹ֯בֹ֯ו]דֹ֯מֹ֯]

2   מֹ֯]שרתים]

3   [˚]ם מֹ֯עוֹ֯נֹ֯וֹ֯]

Frgs. 21–22[10] [Col. 7]

1   ]באור ⟦ כ⟧בֹ֯ודו וישמחנֹ֯ו

2   [לֹ֯⟧ ⟦לֹ֯⟧ ⟦ לֹ֯אֹ֯מֹ֯רֹ֯ לנו]

Frg. 23 [Col. 7]

1   [קודשֹ֯יֹ֯םֹ֯]

2   [[ ]

3   [˚ ˚ [ ]

---

10   Fragment 22 is situated to the left of fragment 21.

Frg. 17 [*Col. 6*]

1 [. . .] they [will ble]ss and they will answer [and they will say . . .]

2 [. . .] generations of the [. . .]

3 [. . . t]welve [. . .]

Frg. 18 [*Col. 6*]

1 [. . .] night [. . .]

2 [. . .] the sun *ṣ*[. . .]

3 [. . .]*r* great *m*[. . .]

Frg. 19 [*Col. 6*]

1 [. . . they will bless and they will answer and] they will [s]ay, "Blessed be [the God of Israel . . ."]

2 [. . . t]en gates of light [. . .]

Frg. 20 [*Col. 6*]

1 [. . .] their gl[o]ry [. . .]

2 [. . .] serving [. . .]

3 [. . .]°[. . .]*m* his fortress [. . .]

Frgs. 21–22 [*Col. 7*]

1 [. . .] in his [gl]orious light and he will allow u[s] to rejoice [. . .]

2 [. . .]*l*[. . .] saying for us [. . .]

Frg. 23 [*Col. 7*]

1 [. . .] Holy Ones [. . .]

2 [. . . .] (vacat) [. . .]

3 [. . .]° °[. . .]

Frgs. 24—25[11] *[Col. 7]*

1   [ק̇ ש̇]

2   [ו̇[ד̇ו]ב̇כ̇]

3   ובצאת השמש להאיר]על הארץ [[יברכו] וענו ואמרו ברוך

4   אל ישראל א[שר בח]ר[בנו מכול]ב̇ גוים [ה]בנו]ר̇[חב א[שר ישראל אל

5   [ותענוג̇ו] [ ] מנוח[עד[למו ץ]

6   [ ]ל חים[

7   [ם̇ י̇ר[או

Frg. 26 [Col. 7]

1   [ת̇א̇]

2   [ם̇ישע̇]מ

3   [ש̇ד]קו

4   [ל]

Frg. 27 [Col. 7]

1   [˚]

2   [ו שמים [ ]

3   [ו]ל חשב ר̇[

4   [את וכרבי]

5   דשים קו[ש קוד]ש

Frg. 28 [Col. 7]

1   [ון רשו[ ] [˚]

2   ב]ראם ערב ו[בקר

3   [עולמים]

4   [ישראל וכ]ן

5   [˚ אנו]

[11] Fragment 25 is situated to the right of fragment 24, supplying the right hand portion of lines 4-7; fragment 24 comprises 2 pieces.

Frgs. 24—25 [Col. 7]

1 [. .]š q[. . .]

2 [. . .] his g[lo]ry. [. . .]

3 [And when the sun rises to shine] upon the earth [. . .] they will bless [and they will answer and they will say, "Blessed be]

4 [the God of Israel w]ho cho[se] us from all [the] nations b[. . . ."]

5 [. . .]ṣ for a fest[ival of] rest and of delight [. . .]

6 [. . .]ḥym l°[. . .]

7 [. . .ligh]ts[. . .]

Frg. 26 [Col. 7]

1 [. . .]ʾt[. . .]

2 [. . . w]orks [. . .]

3 [. . .] his [holi]ness [. . .]

4 [. . .]l[. . .]

Frg. 27 [Col. 7]

1 [. . .]°[. . .]

2 [. . .] heavens and [. . .]

3 [. . .]r to plan for him [. . .]

4 [. . .] they will bless the[. . .]

5 [. . . the holy o]ne of Hol[y Ones . . .]

Frg. 28 [Col. 7]

1 [. . .]° [. . .] first [. . .]

2 [. . . he cr]eated them, evening and [morning. . .]

3 [. . .] ages [. . .]

4 [. . .] Israel and k[. . .]

5 [. . .] we °[. . .]

Frgs. 29–32[12] [*Col. 8*]

1 ‫ושל̊ו̊ם [עליכה ישראל‬

2 ‫בששה] עשר‬[13]

3 ‫קדש לו̊]‬

4 ‫והלילה̊]   ‬[‫ל̊ עם ז̊ב̊]‬

5 ‫[° ת̊]   ‬‫י̊]ק̊יר לנו של̊ו̊]ם̊]‬

6 ‫א̊]ל יברך ישו̊רו̊]ן‬

7 ‫ובצאת השמש להאיר ע]ל] הא̊]רץ יברב̊ו̊] וענו ואמרו‬

8 ‫[ב̊]   ‬‫[אור ישמחו ב̊]‬

9 ‫[מהל]ל̊ים שמכה אל אור̊]י̊]ם אשר חדשתה]‬

10 ‫[ ]   ‬‫[שערי אור ו̊עמנ̊]ו̊] ברנות‬[14]‫ כבודכה ב̊]‬

11 ‫[ד̊]ג̊לי לילה שלום אל̊]   ע̊]ליכה ישראל בצא]ת השמש‬

12 ‫[בש]בעה עשר לחו̊]דש   ב̊]ערב יברכו וענ̊ו] ואמרו‬

13 ‫[ל]ה̊]ללו̊] א̊]ל]‬

14 ‫]‬

15 ‫]‬

16 ‫]‬

17 ‫]‬

18 ‫ש]מ̊ח̊ת̊]‬

19 ‫ד̊]ג̊לי לילה̊]‬

20 ‫[אנו היו̊]ם‬

21 ‫יש]ר̊אל בכול מו̊]עדי‬

22 ‫בש̊]מונה עשר‬[15]‫ לחודש בערב י̊]ברכו וענו ואמרו ב̊]רוך‬

23 ‫ל]ב̊]   ‬‫קו̊]דשים והלילה̊]‬

24 ‫[ש ° ל̊]ן‬

---

[12] Fragment 29 supplies the beginning of lines 1-5; fragment 30, comprising two pieces, is situated below and to the left of fragment 29, supplying portions of lines 4-13; fragment 31 supplies the beginning of lines 21-23; fragment 32 is situated to the left of fragment 31, supplying portions of lines 18-24.

[13] The restoration is indicated by line 12.
[14] A scribe corrected ברנוד to ברנות.
[15] The restoration is indicated by line 12.

Frgs. 29–32 [Col. 8]

1 and peace [(be) upon you, O Israel . . . .]

2 On the six[teenth . . .]

3 holy for him [. . .]

4 and tonight [. . .]*l* people[4] *zk*[. . .]

5 [. . .]°*t* [. . . pr]ecious to us pe[a]ce [. . .]

6 [. . . G]od will bless Yeshuru[n[5] . . . .]

7 [. . . And when the sun rises to shine up]on [the ea]rth, they will bless [and they will answer and they will say . . .]

8 [. . .]*m*[. . .] light, they will rejoice in [. . .]

9 [prai]sing your name, O God of li[gh]ts, who renews [. . .]

10 [. . .] gates of light and with us in the proclamations of your glory *b*[. . .]

11 [st]andards of the night.   May the peace of God (be) [up]on you, O Israel, at the ris[ing of the sun . . . .]

12 [On the s]eventeenth of the mo[nth in] the evening, they will bless and they will answer [and they will say . . .]

13 [. . .] to [pr]aise [the Go]d of [. . .]

14 [. . .]

15 [. . .]

16 [. . .]

17 [. . .]

18 [. . . j]oy of [. . .]

19 [. . .] standards of the night [. . .]

20 [. . .] we toda[y . . .]

21 [. . . Is]rael in all the fes[tivals of . . . .]

22 On the e[ighteenth of the month in the evening] they [will] bless and they will answer and they will say, "Bl[essed be the God of Israel . . ."]

23 *l*[. . . Ho]ly Ones and tonight [. . .]

24 [. . .] *š*°*l*[. . .]

---

[4] Or "with."

[5] A poetic name for Israel, possibly from the root ישר ("straight" or "upright"), also occurring in Deut 32:15, 33:5, Isa 44:2.

Frgs. 33–34, Col. 1[16] *[Col. 10]*

1	או]ר היומם
2	מרו]ממים
3	קודש [
4	מועדי [
5	ך[ ]ּ ּ [
6	אל ישר]אֿל אשר
7	כ]בוד והלילה
8	ל]ֿממלכות
9	ב]מסב
10	של]ו[ם]ּ[17]
11	]
12	]
13	]
14	]
15	]
16	וע]מדנו לגו[ן]
17	שלום עליכה ישר]אֿל]
18	ל]חודש ב[ע]רֿב יברכו וענו ואמר[
19	[ ]ּ[ ]וֿהלילה לנו רוש ממשל חֿ[ו]שך
20	ברו]ך אתה אל ישראל אשר העמדת[
21	בכול מועד]י[ן] לילה יֿן [

---

[16] Fragment 33 supplies portions of lines 1-10; fragment 34 supplies portions of lines 16-21.

[17] Letter is abraded; there is no physical break in the papyrus.

Frgs. 33–34, Col. 1 [Col. 10 (Col. 9 cannot be identified)]

1 [...li]ght of the day

2 [... exa]lting

3 [...] holiness

4 [...] festivals of[6]

5 [...]°°[...]*k*

6 [... God of Isr]ael who

7 [... gl]ory and tonight

8 [...] to the kingdoms

9 [...] in the circle

10 [...] pea[c]e

11 [...]

12 [...]

13 [...]

14 [...]

15 [...]

16 [... and we (will) st]and to *gw*[...]

17 [... "Peace (be) upon you, O Isra]el." (vacat) [...]

18 [...of] the month in the e[ve]ning they will bless and they will answer and they will say, [...]

19 [...]°[...] and tonight (is) for us the beginning of the dominion of da[rkness...]

20 [... "Bless]ed are you, O God of Israel, who has established [..."]

21 [...] in all the appointed time[s of] night.[7] (vacat) [...]

---

[6] Or "appointed times of"; see line 21.

[7] See the special untranslatable character in the text (a Nabatean Qoph?).

Frgs. 33 and 35—36, Col. 2[18] *[Col. 11]*

1   ובצ[א]ת השמש על ה[ארץ

2   חדש[תה] שמחתנו באו֯ר[ן

3   שמ[   ]ג֯ו ח֯ ˚ [   ]כ֯יום[

4   בש[מ]חתו ע[מ]ד֯ים [

5   שֿל[ום]עליכֿה֯]ישראל֯[

6   [ביום שני]ם ועֿ]שרים]ל]חודש בערב יברכו וענו ואמרו ברוך

7   א[ל ישרא]ל אש֯]ר

8   ל ˚ [   ]   [[   ]   ˚ ˚ ˚ [   ]   [˚ ה ל ˚]

9   ל ˚ [   ]   [[   ]   ˚ ˚   ישר]אל

10   [ובצאת הש[מ֯ש על ה[ארץ

11   [בר]ו֯ך אל א[שר

12   [בשנים ועֿ]שרים ש]ערי אור

13   [שלום] עליכה י֯]שראל

14   [ביום שלושה ו]עשים לחודש בערב

15   [

16   [

17   [

18   [

19   [

20   יו[ם ששי

21   צ]דק

22   ב֯רוך אל[

23   בחג כבוד֯[

24   [˚ ˚ ˚

---

[18] Fragment 33 supplies the beginning of lines 1-7; fragment 35 supplies portions of lines 7-14; fragment 36 supplies lines 20-24.

Frgs. 33 and 35—36, Col. 2 [Col. 11]

1 And when the sun ri[se]s upon the [earth . . .]

2 renew[ing] our joy with light [. . .]

3 *šm*[. . .]*nw ḥ*°[. . .] as the day [. . .]

4 in his joy, st[an]ding [. . . .]

5 "Pea[ce] (be) upon you, O Israel."   [. . .]

6 [On the] tw[enty-sec]ond [day] of [the month in the evening they will bless and they will answer and they will say, "Blessed be]

7 the Go[d of Israe]l wh[o . . ."]

8 *l*°[. . .]° °°[. . .][8]

9 *l*°[. . .]° Isra[el . . . .]

10 [And when the s]un [rises] upon the [earth . . .]

11 [. . . "Ble]ssed be God w[ho . . . ."]

12 [In the tw]enty-[secondth] (of) the g[ates of light . . .]

13 [. . . "Peace (be)] upon you, O I[srael . . . ."]

14 [On the] twe[nty-third day of the month in the evening . . .]

15 [. . .]

16 [. . .]

17 [. . .]

18 [. . .]

19 [. . .]

20 [. . .] sixth [da]y

21 [. . . ri]ghteousness

22 [. . .] "Blessed be God

23 [. . ."] in the pilgrimage-feast of glory

24 [. . .]°°°

---

[8] Note the interlinear correction: "[. . .]°*h l*°[. . .]."

Frgs. 37−38[19] [*Col. 12*]

1   [ע](ו)לם]

2   בִּיום חמשה ו[עשרים

3   אֱלוהי כול קודשׁ[ים

4   קּודש ומנוח לנֹנֹו

5   מֹגורל ממשלתֹו[ן

6   [˚ ˚ ˚ ˚ ˚]

7   ]

8   [ק]דשים ˚ ˚ מֹ[

9   [בחמשה]עֹשרים שערי[ן אור

10   [מ]הללים עמנו]

11   לֹבֹודנו שלום [עליכה ישראל

12   ובִיום ששה ו[עשרים

13   [לנ]דֹן צֹדֹ[ק

---

[19] Fragment 37 supplies lines 1-6; fragment 38 supplies lines
8-13.

Frgs. 37–38 [*Col. 12*]

1 [fo]rever. [. . .]

2 On the [twenty-]fifth day [. . .]

3 the God of all the Holy On[es . . .]

4 holy and rested for u[s . . .]

5 from the lot of his dominion [. . .]

6 [. . .]°°°°°[. . .]

7 [. . .]

8 [the H]oly Ones °°*m*[. . . .]

9 [In the] twenty-[fifth] (of) the gates of [light . . .]

10 [pr]aising with us [. . .]

11 our glory, "Peace [(be) upon you, O Israel, ..."]

12 And on the [twenty]-sixth day [. . .]

13 [. . .]*l*[. . .]*dn* righteous[ness . . .]

Frg. 39 [*Col. 13*]

1   ˹ה˺ ˚ ˚ ˚ ˚ ˚ ˚ ˚ ל˹ו˺]   [ם]

   ˚ו˚ ˚ אֿתֿחֿבֿ עֿדֿ וֿלֿעֿו   ]הֿ[הואה לֿיֿלֿהֿ]

2   [גורלות חושך   עש]ר שלושה כיא   ו ˚ [

3   ישראל עליכ]ה שלום שלומנו [מֿלֿ ובוקר ערב לי]דֿג

Frg. 40, Col. 1

3   ]הֿ

4   ]הֿתֿ[

5   [˚ ˚

6   ]הֿ[

7   ]לֿ[

Frgs. 40—41, Col. 2[20]

1   [ואותו

2   ל[וממשב

3   ]] אל [21]שמֿ   ועדי מ]בכול ישראל[י

4   השמש [[ובצאת]]   [˚ לר השלישית]]הֿ[[

5   [[כבודנו]]   [קודש מנוח]]

6   [[ל והללו]]   [שם ומהולל ל]]

7   שים]דֿק כול   [˚ י קודש]]

8   [[כבוד   [[בֿ˚] [˚]

---

[20] Fragment 40 is situated on the right and fragment 41 is on the left.

[21] ש is corrected from ג.

Frg. 39 [Col. 13]

1 [...]*m* [...]*wl*° °°°°°° *h*[...]

2 [...]°*w*.⁹ Because thirt[y] lots of darkness [...]

3 [stan]ards of the evening and of the morning *ml*[...] our peace, "Peace (be) upon you, [O Israel ... .."]

Frg. 40, Col. 1

3 [...]*h*

4 [...]*th*

5 [...]°°

6 [...]*h*

7 [...]*l*

Frgs. 40–41, Col. 2

1 and him [...]

2 and in the domini[on of ...]

3 the name of God [... I]srael in all the fe[stivals of ... .]

4 And when [the sun] rises [...] the third of *lr*°[...]

5 our glory [...] rest of holiness [...]

6 and they will praise *l*[...]*l* and he shall be praising the name of [...]

7 all the Hol[y Ones ...] the Holy Ones *y*°[...]

8 glory [...]°[...]*b*°[...]

---

⁹ Note the interlinear correction: "this (is) the night of [...]*h*
and *l*ʿ*w* until ʾ*thb* °°*w*°."

Frgs. 42–44[22]

1   [° ם] [° °מב]

2   [ואל הליל י]

3   שלו[ם עלי[כ]ה̇ ישרא]ל בפי כול לש[וני

4   ל[חודש ב[ערב יבר[כ]ו וענו ואמ[רו

5   [נו ת ° ° [[ש̇בו̇עו̇ת̇ [[כבודו ו[ה]ל[י]לה לנו[

6   ל[י]לה ° ° [[[אשר̇ י[ן [[אל[ן [° [ן]

7   [לן]

Frgs. 45–47[23]

1   [ם[ן] ° ° [ ]

2   [ב̇מועדי]

3   [ו̇ע̇ינ[י ° כ ° [ ]

4   [ש̇י כבוד]

5   [[[ ] ° [[

6   ישראל אל[[ב̇ר̇ו̇ך[[ואמרו [[וענו]יברכו

7   [[מ̇]

Frgs. 48–50[24]

1   [ב̇ א י]

2   [ ]שלום עליכה יש[ראל

3   אש̇ר ישראל אל [ברוך

4   [שמחתנו וש]

5   [ואתה חתנו[שם עדי[מ̇ו]שלישי ב]

6   [ ]ישראל י[ליכה ע]שלום ת̇ב̇ה ע[ן[ו]יש[

7   ישראל[אל ברוך [[ואמ[רו]וענו יברכו]ה̇א̇רץ ה[על]איר[ובצאת השמש לה

8   כו̇ן̇ל על אל[[ו̇צדק̇[בני צדק]ע[[ם̇]י̇ם אשר̇ ע[[

---

[22] Fragment 44 is situated on the right, supplying portions of lines 5-7; fragment 43 is situated to the left of fragment 44; fragment 42 is situated to the left of fragment 43.

[23] Fragment 45 supplies portions of lines 1-4; fragments 46-47 supply portions of lines 5-7 with fragment 46 situated to the right of fragment 47.

[24] Fragment 48 supplies portions of lines 1-8; fragment 49 is situated to the right of fragment 48; fragment 50 is situated to the right of fragment 49.

Frgs. 42–44

1 [...]*bm*ᶜ°[...]*m* °[...]

2 [...]of the night for '*w*[...]

3 [... . "Peac]e (be) upon [yo]u, [O Israe]l, by the mouth of all the ton[gues of ... ."]

4 [... of the] month [in] the evening they will ble[ss] and they will answer and they will sa[y...]

5 [...] us *t*°[...] the oaths of his glory and [to]n[i]ght (is) for us [...]

6 [... n]ight °°[...] which *y*[...]*l*[...]*l*[...]° [...]

7 [...]*l*[...]

Frgs. 45–47

1 [...]° °[...]*m*[...]

2 [...] in the appointed times of[10] [...]

3 [...]° *k*° and the eyes of [...]

4 [...]*šy* glory [...]

5 [...] [...]° [...]

6 [... they will bless] and they will answer [and they will say,] "Blessed be [the God of Israel ..."]

7 [...]*m*[...]

Frgs. 48–50

1 [...]*y*' *b*[...]

2 [... "Peace (be) upon you, O Is]rael. [... ."]

3 [... "Blessed be] the God of Israel wh[o...]

4 [...] our joy and *š*[...]

5 [...] the third of our fest[ivals of j]oy. And you [...]

6 [...] your salva[ti]on. "Peace (be) u[pon you, O I]srael." [...]

7 [And when the sun rises to s]hine upon [the] earth they will bless and they will answer and they will s[ay,] "Blessed be the God of Is[rael]

8 [..."]*ym* who [wi]th the Sons of Righteousness and righteousness [...] God upon al[l...]

[10] Or "in the festivals of."

Frgs. 51—55[25]

1	‏[ם]‏ ‏[ ] ̊ ̊[ ]‏
2	‏[עֹֽד]‏ ‏[ ] א גורלות [ ] ̊ [‏
3	‏[ע]ולמים‏ ‏[אחות הֹודֹוֹתֹ]‏ ‏[‏
4	‏[תֹנֹוֹ]‏
5	‏[עֹשֹׂר שערי כבֹו]ד‏
	‏[אֹור הֹיֹומם שלום עֹלֹ]יכה ישראל‏
6	‏יברכו וענו וא[מֹרֹו ברוך אל יש]ראל‏
7	‏[ ] ̊ [ ]‏ ‏[ ] ̊ ̊ [‏
8	‏[ ] ̊ [רֹ אֹוֹר 26‏ ‏לֹ דקליֹ]‏
9	‏[כבודכה בתהלי עֹתנו‏ ‏הוד]‏
10	‏[ישראל עליכה שלום לילה מועדי]‏
11	‏[ ]‏
12	‏[ישראל אל ברוך ואמֹרֹו וענֹ]ו יברכו‏
13	‏[ולה הגֹד]בינתו במחשבת נֹ[ודיעו ה]‏
14	‏[באותֹו]ת נֹדע למען אור גורלות [‏
15	‏[מרחֹ] ̊ [ ]רֹ אשֹ[אל ישר]אל‏
16	‏[ ]‏
17	‏[וענו אל[ישר]‏
18	‏[בודו]כֹ‏
19	‏[מֹֿישֹי]חֹ‏

[25] Fragment 51 supplies the right hand portion of lines 1-3; fragment 52 is situated to the left of fragment 51; fragment 53 is situated below fragment 52, supplying lines 4-7; fragment 54 is situated to the right of fragment 53 in line 7, supplying portions of lines 7-15; fragment 55 is situated to the left of fragment 54 in line 15, supplying lines 15-19.
[26] Read דגלי.

262

Frgs. 51–55

1 [...]*m* [...]° [...]

2 [...]° ' lots of [...] until [...]

3 [...] explanations of [11] thanksgivings [... a]ges [...]

4 [...]*tnw* [...]

5 [...]-teenth of the gates of glor[y...]

6 [... they will bless and they will answer and] they [will s]ay, "Blessed be the God of Is[rael..."] [12]

7 [...]°[...]°° [...]

8 [...]*l* standards of lig[ht ...]° [...]

9 [...] you [have made kn]own to us the psalms of your glory [...]

10 [...] the appointed times of the night, "Peace (be) upon you, [O Israel."]

11 [...] (vacat) [...]

12 [... they will bless and] they [will answer] and they will say, "Blessed be the God of Israel [... ."]

13 [... . He has made] known to us the gr[eat] design of his discernment [...]

14 [...] the lots of light in order that we may know the sign[s of...]

15 [... the God of Isra]el wh[o...]° *mrt*[...]

16 [... .] (vacat) [...]

17 [... Isra]el and they will answer [...]

18 [...] his [gl]ory [...]

19 [... fi]fth [...]

---

[11] Probably an Aramaic from of the root חוה; see Job 13:17 and cf. Dan. 5:12.

[12] Note the interlinear correction: "[...] the light of day. 'Peace (be) upon [you, O Israel ... .']."

Frgs. 56–58, Col. 1

3	[֯ ֯י מועדים
4	ש[מחתנו
5	[לילה אשר
6	]
7	שמ֯ונת[
8	ב[֯משרתי ֯]
9	[ ]
10	]
11	ו[לברך
12	[שלום עליכֿה
13	[ישראל

Frg. 56, Col. 2

1	[֯ ֯ ֯]
2	אור[֗
3	ובצ[את השמש
4	וכול[
5	[מ]֯ה֯ל[ל]ים

Frg. 59 [lost?]

Frgs. 56–58, Col. 1

3 [...]°*y* appointed times[13]

4 [...] our [j]oy

5 [...] night which

6 [...]

7 [...] eight

8 [...] among those who serve °[...]

9 [... .]   (vacat) [...]

10 [...]

11 [...] and to bless

12 [...] "Peace (be) upon you,

13 [O Israel ... ."]

Frg. 56, Col. 2

1 °°°[...]

2 light [... .]

3 And when [the sun] r[ises...]

4 and all [...]

5 [...pr]ai[sing...]

Frg. 59 [lost?]

---

[13] Or "festivals."

Frg. 60

1   [˚ ˚ ˚ ˚]

2   [ומל הֹזֹה]

3   [ודורֹ ו ˚]

4   [שמ 27תֹ]

Frg. 61

1   [היום]

2   [ולילה]

3   [˚ ˚]

Frg. 62

1   אל יש[ראל]

2   [בשבתות]

3   [ל קודש ˚]

Frg. 63 [*lost?*]

Frg. 64

1   [בערב]

2   [עדנו]

3   [˚ כהונת]

4   ד[מוֹע בֹ לילה לנו אוֹת]

5   [מהללים]
     [עמנו עֹמנו להיות לילה]

6   [˚]

7   יברכ[ו הארץ על [להאיר השמש ובצאת

8   והיום עֹולמים י[ד]עֹ[ו]מֹ[

9   [דֹגֹל]

---

27 A scribe probably corrected a שׁ to a ת.

Frg. 60

1 [...]°°°°[...]

2 [...] this and *ml*[...]

3 [...]°*w* and generation [...]

4 [...]*t šm*[...]

Frg. 61

1 [...] today [...]

2 [...] and night [...]

3 [...]°°[...]

Frg. 62

1 [...] the God of Is[rael...]

2 [...] when the sabbaths [...]

3 [...]° holiness *l*[...]

Frg. 63 [lost?]

Frg. 64

1 [...] in the evening [...]

2 [...] ʿ*dnw* [...]

3 [...] priesthood of °[...]

4 [...] a sign to us for the night at the appointed t[ime...]

5 [...] a night to be praising[14] with us

6 [...]°. (vacat) [...]

7 [And when the sun rises to shine] upon the earth they will bless [...]

8 [...] the app[oin]ted t[ime]s of the ages and to[day...]

9 [...] standard [...]

---

[14] The word "praising" is supplied by the interlinear correction.

Frg. 65

1 יברכו]וֿענו ואמרו בֿ[רוך אל ישראל

2 [צבאות אלים]

3 [אֿוֿר ועדים עמֿ]נו

4 הש[מש ברוך אל]ישראל

5 שלום ע[ליכה] ישרא[ל]

Frg. 68   *Frg. 67*   *Frg. 66*

1 [ֿ נֿו בֿ]   1 אל יש]ראל אשר [1 [ם עמנו הֿ[יֿ]וֿם]

2 [ה אל יש]ראל   2 [דגל שמיני]   2 ש[מכה אל ישרא]ל

3 [חקו מר]   3 [לֿילה להגבירן]   3 שלום עלי[כה ישראל]

4 יב]רכו וֿ[ענו ואמרו   4 יברכו וענו וא[ֿמֿרֿו]

5 [קודש]

6 [ל]

Frg. 72   *Frgs. 70–71*   *Frg. 69*

1 [ ]   1 ⟦ ֿ ֿ ֿ   1 [שלות שלֿ[ט[28]

2 [ֿ ֿ אל ֿ ֿ ֿ]   2 [יֿם ⟧ ⟦ראשֿיֿ]   2 [מֿו ברוך אל ישר]אל

3 [הקוראֿ]   3 [ֿ ֿ מוֿעֿ⟦⟧ֿדים וקודֿ]ש 3 [ֿ מועד]

4 [י הֿיוֿם]   4 [היום ⟦⟧ֿהֿזֿה לנו ֿ]

5 [ֿ ארֿץ ֿ]

6 [כֿהונֿתֿ ֿ]

7 [אל בֿ ֿ ֿ ֿ]

8 [בערֿב]

9 [ה ל ֿ ֿ ֿ]

10 [ֿ ֿ ֿ]

---

28 Cf. Ezek 16:49.

Frg. 65

1 [they will bless] and they will answer and they will say, "Bl[essed be the God of Israel . . ."]

2 [. . .] the hosts of divine beings [. . .]

3 [. . .] light and witnesses with [us . . .]

4 [. . . the su]n, "Blessed be the God of [Israel . . ."]

5 [. . . "Peace (be) up]on you, [O Israe]l [. . . "]

Frg. 66

1 [. . .]*m* with us to[d]ay [. . .]

2 [. . .] your na[me,] O God of Israe[l . . .]

3 [. . . "Peace (be) upon] you, O Israel [. . ."]

4 [they will bless and they will answer and they will s]ay [. . .]

Frg. 67

1 [. . . God of Is]rael who [. . .]

2 [. . .] eighth standard [. . .]

3 [. . .] night to be strong [. . .]

Frg. 68

1 [. . .]°*nw b*[. . .]

2 [. . .]*h* the God of Is[rael . . .]

3 [. . .]*ḥqw mr*[. . .]

4 [. . . they will b]less and [they will answer and they will say . . .]

5 [. . .] holiness [. . .]

6 [. . .]*l*[. . .]

Frg. 69

1 [. . .] quiet unconc[ern . . .]

2 [. . .]*mw*, "Blessed be the God of Isra[el . . ."]

3 [. . .]° appointed time [. . .]

Frgs. 70–71

1 [. . .]° °[. . .]

2 [. . .]° *ym* [. . .] the beginning of °[. . .]

3 [. . .]° appointed times and holine[ss . . .]

4 [. . .] this day for us °[. . .]

Frg. 72

1 [. . . .] [. . .]

2 [. . .]°° God °°°[. . .]

3 [. . .] who is calling [. . .]

4 [. . .] of the day [. . .]

5 [. . .]° earth °[. . .]

6 [. . .] priesthood of °[. . .]

7 [. . .]'*l b*°°°[. . .]

8 [. . .] in the evening [. . .]

9 [. . .]*h l*°°°[. . .]

10 [. . .]°°[. . .]

Frg. 75		*Frg. 74*		*Frg. 73*	
הֿסֿתם[	1	] בֿחֿ[	1	]מ[	1
] אֿ ֯ [	2	]ֿֿלקֿ ֯ [	2	]וֿדוֿרֿ[ ] ֯ [	2
] שֿוֿ ֯ [	3	ברוֿ]ך אל יֿ[שראל	3	] באחד [	3
] בשֿמֿ[	4	]יֿ קודֿ[ש	4	]וֿן בֿ֯יֿוֿ ֯ ֯ [	4
		יש]רֿאל וע[נ]נו	5	]אלֿ[	5

Frg. 77, Col. 2		*Frg. 77, Col. 1*		*Frg. 76*	
]֯	1	[֯	1	בע]רֿב יבֿרֿכֿ[ו	1
]בֿ	2	[	2	] אשרֿ הודיעֿנוֿ[	2
]	3	]ש	3	]הלילה הזה לנו [	3
]לֿ	4	] וניחוח	4	גֿ]ורלי חושךֿ[	4

Frg. 80		*Frg. 79*		*Frg. 78*	
]לֿ[	1	] ֯ ֯ [	1	]כבֿ]וד	1
] ברוֿ[ן	2	] ֯ ֯ [	2	]עמנוֿ[	2
]מכוֿ [	3	]נֿהֿ ֯ וֿ[	3	]מֿהֿ ֯ [	3
		בֿ]ני ישֿ]ראל	4	]להאֿיר	4

Frg. 83		*Frg. 82*		*Frg. 81*	
]שלוֿ [	1	] ֯ ֯ ֯ ֯ ֯ ֯ [	1	]זֿ[	1
] שמֿ[	2	]יֿם וקדושֿ]ים	2	]כהונתֿ[	2
] שֿ ֯ [	3	] היוםֿ[	3	הֿ]טֿאֿנֿוֿ לֿ[כה	3

Frg. 86		*Frg. 85*		*Frg. 84*	
] ֯ [	1	]לֿהֿאֿיֿר [	1	] ֯ [	1
]וֿע [	2	] ֯ יכה נשֿ[	2	] [	2
]מֿעוֿ]ד	3	]לֿ[	3	יברכו וענֿ]וֿ ואמרו[	3
]הֿלֿיֿלֿ[ה	4			] שלישי [	4
				] בֿרֿ]וך	5

Frg. 73

1 [. . .]*m*[. . .]

2 [. . .]°[. . .] and generation [. . .]

3 [. . .] in one [. . .]

4 [. . .]*wn* in *yw*°°[. . .]

5 [. . .] God [. . .]

Frg. 74

1 [. . .]*bḥ*[. . .]

2 [. . .]*wlq*°[. . .]

3 [. . . "Bles]sed be the God of I[srael . . ."]

4 [. . .] of holine[ss . . .]

5 [. . . Is]rael and [they] will ans[wer . . .]

Frg. 75

1 [. . .] to be closed [. . .]

2 [. . .]°° [. . .]

3 [. . .]° *šw* [. . .]

4 [. . .] in *šm*[. . .]

Frg. 76

1 [. . . in the ev]ening [they] will bless [. . .]

2 [. . .] who has made known to us [. . .]

3 [. . .] this night for us [. . .]

4 [. . . l]ots of darkness [. . .]

Frg. 77, Col. 1

1 [. . .]°

2 [. . .]

3 [. . .]*š*

4 [. . .] and a soothing odor

Frg. 77, Col. 2

1 [. . .]

2 *b*[. . .]

3 [. . .]

4 *q*[. . .]

Frg. 78

1 [. . .] glo[ry]

2 [. . .] with us [. . .]

3 [. . .]*mh*°[. . .]

4 [. . .] to shi[ne . . .]

Frg. 79

1 [. . .]° °[. . .]

2 [. . . .]°°[. . .]

3 [. . .]*nh w*[. . .]

4 [. . . so]ns of Is[rael . . .]

Frg. 80

1 [. . .]*k*[. . .]

2 [. . .] "Blessed be [. . ."]

3 [. . .]*mkw* [. . .]

Frg 81

1 [. . .]*n*[. . .]

2 [. . .] priesthood of [. . .]

3 [. . .] we have [s]inned against [you . . .]

Frg. 82

1 [. . .]°°°°°°[. . .]

2 [. . .]*ym* and Holy On[es . . .]

3 [. . .] today [. . .]

Frg. 83

1 [. . .]*šlw* [. . .]

2 [. . .] *šm*[. . .]

3 [. . .]°*š* [. . .]

Frg. 84

1 [. . .]°[. . .]

2 [. . . .] [. . .]

3 [. . . they will bless and] they will [ans]wer and they will say [. . .]

4 [. . .] third [. . .]

5 [. . .] bles[sed . . .]

Frg. 85

1 [. . .] to shine [. . .]

2 [. . .]°*y* you *nš*[. . .]

3 [. . .]*l*[. . .]

Frg. 86

1 [. . .]°[. . .]

2 [. . .]*wˤ* [. . .]

3 [. . .] appointed ti[me[15] . . .]

4 [. . .] the nigh[t . . .][16]

---

[15] Or "festiv[al."

[16] Note the interlinear correction: "[. . .] the nigh[t . . .]."

Frg. 87

1] [
2] ה [
3 יב]רכו[
4 [אתה]

Frg. 88

1 [מ]
2] [
3 [למען]
4] ת ד [
5] י ב [

Frg. 89

1] [
2] כ]בודו ב [
3 [מאו ה]
4 [שלום]
5] [

Frg. 90

1 [כל מֹ]
2 [אל יש]ראל
3 [שלום]

Frg. 91

1] [
2 [בשמחת]
3 [ו להם]

Frg. 92

1 בצ]את השמש
2 יש]ראל
3 וב]

Frg. 93

1 [הֹ] [ ]
2 מו]עדי[
3] [
4 [אֹ]

Frg. 94

1] [
2 [חם]
3] ל [

Frg. 95

1] [
2 לה]איר [
3] ו מ[
4 [וש]

Frg. 96

1 [וֹ]
2 [ם שֹ]
3 [שיֹ]

Frg. 97 [lost?]

Frg. 98

1 [עמנֹ]ו
2 [מי]
3 [עלי]כה

Frg. 99

1 [29] °
2 [בֹ]
3 [שֹ]
4 [יֹ]

Frg. 100

1 [בֹ]
2 [° ו עם דג]לי
3 [לֹח]

Frg. 101

1] ° ° [
2] ° ° ° ° [
3] ° [

Frg. 102

1 [שֹ]
2 [ל °]
3 [פֹ]

Frg. 103

1 [ש]
2 [ע]
3 [ר]

Frg. 104

1] ° [
2 [בחוֹ]
3 [שֹר]

---

29 The first line of this fragment is now lost.

Frg. 87

1 [. . .]°[. . .]

2 [. . .]*h*°[. . .]

3 [. . .] they [will b]less [. . .]

4 [. . .] you [. . .]

Frg. 88

1 [. . .]*m*[. . .]

2 [. . . .] [. . .]

3 [. . .] in order that [. . .]

4 [. . .]°*t d*°[. . .]

5 [. . .]°*w b*°[. . .]

Frg. 89

1 [. . .]°[. . .]

2 [. . .] his [g]lory in °[. . .]

3 [. . .] *m'w*° *h*°[. . .]

4 [. . .] peace [. . .]

5 [. . .] °° [. . .]

Frg. 90

1 [. . .]*m kl*[. . .]

2 [. . .] God of Is[rael . . .]

3 [. . .] peace [. . .]

Frg. 91

1 [. . .]°°[. . .]

2 [. . .] in joy of [. . .]

3 [. . .]*w* to them [. . .]

Frg. 92

1 When [the sun rises . . .]

2 Is[rael . . .]

3 and *b*[. . .]

Frg. 93

1 [. . .]*k*[. . .]°[. . .]

2 [. . . appoin]ted times of[17] [. . .]

3 [. . . .] (vacat) [. . .]

4 [. . .] '°[. . .]

Frg. 94

1 [. . .]°[. . .]

2 [. . .] warm [. . .]

3 [. . .]*l*°[. . .]

Frg. 95

1 [. . .]°[. . .]

2 [. . .to s]hine [. . .]

3 [. . .]°*w m*[. . .]

4 [. . .]*wš* [. . .]

Frg. 96

1 [. . .]°*w* [. . .]

2 [. . .]*m š*[. . .]

3 [. . .]*šy* [. . .]

Frg. 97 [*lost?*]

Frg. 98

1 [. . .] with u[s . . .]

2 [. . .]*my* [. . .]

3 [. . .] upon [you . . .]

Frg. 99

1 °[. . .]

2 *b*[. . .]

3 *š*[. . .]

4 *y*[. . .]

Frg. 100

1 [. . .]° *b*[. . .]

2 [. . .]°*w* with the stand[ards of . . .]

3 [. . .]*lḥ*[. . .]

Frg. 101

1 [. . .] °° [. . .]

2 [. . .] °°°° [. . .]

3 [. . .] ° [. . .]

Frg. 102

1 [. . .]*š*[. . .]

2 [. . .]° *l*[. . .]

3 [. . .]*q* [. . .]

Frg. 103

1 [. . .]*š*[. . .]

2 [. . .]*ṣ* [. . .]

3 [. . .]*r* [. . .]

Frg. 104

1 [. . .]°[. . .]

2 [. . .] *bḥw*[. . .]

3 [. . .]*šr* [. . .]

[17] Or "festi]vals of."

273

Frg. 107	*Frg. 106*	*Frg. 105*
1] ˚ ˚ [	1] ˚ ˚ [	1] בן [
2] ב̇ [	2 כ]בוד ל̇[	2] ה ˚ [
3] ב ˚ [	3] ˚ ˚ ˚ ל ˚ [	3]חי̇ן

Frg. 110	*Frg. 109*	*Frg. 108*
1] שר ˚ [	1 ברו]ך [	1]ב̇[
2] ˚ ש̇ ˚ [	2] ˚ וה ˚ [	2]ומהללי̇ם
3] ˚ [		

Frg. 113	*Frg. 112*	*Frg. 111*
1]נ ז̇ ˚ [	1] ˚ ˚ ˚ [	1] כס̇[
2] ד̇ [	2]ברי̇ [	2] ˚ ו ל א[

Frg. 116	*Frg. 115*	*Frg. 114*
1 ש]קוד [	1] [	1]ס̇[
2]מים[	2] ˚ [	2]ה[
	3]חל[	

Frg. 119	*Frg. 118*	*Frg. 117*
1] ˚ מ̇[	1]ס̇י[	1] ˚ [
2]עם[	2]צ̇[	2] ˚ ש ד̇[

Frg. 122	*Frg. 121*	*Frg. 120*
1]ם[	1] ˚ כ ˚ [	1] ˚ [
2]מקום[	2]ב ו[	2 לנ]ו [

Frg. 125	*Frg. 124*	*Frg. 123*
1] ˚ י[	1]עד[	1]אין̇[
2] ˚ ˚ [	2] ˚ ס̇[	2] ˚ [

Frg. 128	*Frg. 127*	*Frg. 126*
1]ל̇[	1] ˚ מ ו[	1 כב]וד[
2] ר̇[	2]וש ס̇[	2]ל̇[

Frg. 105

1 [...] *b*[...]

2 [...]*ḥ*° [...]

3 [...]*ḥy* [...]

Frg. 106

1 [...]°°[...]

2 [...gl]ory *l*[...]

3 [...]°°°*l*°[...]

Frg. 107

1 [...]°°[...]

2 [...] *b*[...]

3 [...] *b*°[...]

Frg. 108

1 [...]*b*[...]

2 [...] and praisi[ng...]

Frg. 109

1 [...] "Bless[ed be...]"

2 [...]° and *ḥ*°[...]

Frg. 110

1 [...]*šr*°[...]

2 [...]° *š*°[...]

3 [...] ° [...]

Frg. 111

1 [...] *ks*[...]

2 [...]'*l* and °[...]

Frg. 112

1 [...]°°°[...]

2 [...]*y br*[...]

Frg. 113

1 [...]°*z n*[...]

2 [...]*d* [...]

Frg. 114

1 [...]*m* [...]

2 [...]*ḥ* [...]

Frg. 115

1 [...] [...]

2 [...]°[...]

3 [...]*lḥ* [...]

Frg. 116

1 [...] holine[ss...]

2 [...] water [...]

Frg. 117

1 [...]°[...]

2 [...]*dš*°[...]

Frg. 118

1 [...]*ym*[...]

2 [...]*ṣ*[...]

Frg. 119

1 [...]*q*°[...]

2 [...] with[18] [...]

Frg. 120

1 [...]°[...]

2 [...] to u[s...]

Frg. 121

1 [...]° *k*°[...]

2 [...]*w b*[...]

Frg. 122

1 [...]*m*[...]

2 [...] place [of...]

Frg. 123

1 [...] and '*y*[...]

2 [...]°[...]

Frg. 124

1 [...]ᶜ*d*[...]

2 [...]*m* °[...]

Frg. 125

1 [...]*wy*°[...]

2 [...]°°[...]

Frg. 126

1 [...]*gl*[ory...]

2 [...]*l*[...]

Frg. 127

1 [...] and *m*°[...]

2 [...]*m* and *š*[...]

Frg. 128

1 [...]*l*[...]

2 [...]*r* [...]

[18] Or "people."

Frg. 131	*Frg. 130* [*lost?*]	*Frg. 129*
1 ישר[אל]		1 [ͦמ]
		2 [ל]

Frg. 133	*Frg. 132, Col. 2*	*Frg. 132, Col. 1*
1 [היוͦם	1 וב[ן	1 [ ]
2 [אשר	2 וא[	2 מים [ ]

Frg. 136	*Frg. 135*	*Frg. 134*
1 [יͦם]	1 [ ]ͦ[ ]	1 בן
2 [לילה]	2 י[שראל הͦ[	2 [ ]ͦ ל
	3 [ ] [	

Frg. 139	*Frg. 138*	*Frg. 137*
1 [ברו]ך אל[ן ישראל	1 [ה]	1 [ה ͦ ͦ ס]
2 [נפלאותיו]	2 [קדש]	2 [בצאת] השמש

Frg. 142	*Frg. 141*	*Frg. 140*
1 [ב]ͦן	1 [י]ͦם	1 [ש ͦ]
2 [כי ͦ]	2 [בח ͦ]	2 ב]ͦן

Frg. 145	*Frg. 144*	*Frg. 143*
1 [ ] ͦ ͦ [ ]	1 [ו]ן יש[	1 [מהלך]
2 [אש ͦ]	2 [ש]ͦ[	2 ע[ר]ב [ ]

Frg. 148	*Frg. 147*	*Frg. 146*
1 [ ] [ ]	1 [ה]ͦם]	1 [בלי]ͦלי [ ]
2 [של]	2 [ͦ ד ͦ]	2 ה] ͦ [ ]
3 [ ] ͦ ͦ [ ]		

Frg. 151	*Frg. 150*	*Frg. 149*
1 [ ] ͦ ͦ [ ]	1 [ס]	1 [ͦמ]
2 [ ]ͦי	2 [צͦ ͦ]	2 [ות]ͦ

Frg. 129

1 [...]*m* [...]

2 [...] *l*[...]

Frg. 130 [*lost?*]

Frg. 131

1 [...] Isra[el...]

Frg. 132, Col. 1

1 [...]

2 [...] water

Frg. 132, Col. 2

1 And on¹⁹ [...]

2 and '[...]

Frg. 133

1 today [...]

2 who [...]

Frg. 134

1 *b*[...]

2 *l°*[...]

Frg. 135

1 [...]°[...]

2 [... I]srael *h*[...]

3 [....]   (vacat) [...]

Frg. 136

1 [...]*ym*[...]

2 [...] night [...]

Frg. 137

1 [...]*h°°m*[...]

2 [...] when [the sun] rises [...]

Frg. 138

1 [...]*h*[...]

2 [...]holy[...]

Frg. 139

1 [...]   "Blessed be the God [of Israel...]"

2 [...] his wonderous works [...]

Frg. 140

1 *š°*[...]

2 *by*[...]

Frg. 141

1 [...]*ym* [...]

2 [...]*bḥ°*[...]

Frg. 142

1 [...]*by*[...]

2 [...]*ky°*[...]

Frg. 143

1 [...] prai[sing...]

2 [... ev]ening [...]

Frg. 144

1 [...]*wn yš*[...]

2 [...]*šn* [...]

Frg. 145

1 [...]°°[...]

2 [...]° '*š*[...]

Frg. 146

1 [...] in the nights of [...]

2 [...]° *h*[...]

Frg. 147

1 [...]*hm*[...]

2 [...]° *d°*[...]

Frg. 148

1 [...] [...]

2 [...]*šl*[...]

3 [...]°°[...]

Frg. 149

1 [...]*m°*[...]

2 [...] and *t*[...]

Frg. 150

1 [...] *m*[...]

2 [...]*ṣ°*[...]

Frg. 151

1 [...]°°[...]

2 [...] *y*[...]

¹⁹ Or "And when"; the marginal tick above this line probably indicates the beginning of a new prayer.

Frg. 154	Frg. 153	Frg. 152
1 [˚ ˚ ˚]	1]כ[בודו	1 [וש]לום עלי[כה ישראל
2 [˚ לבגו˚]	2 [כ]ול ˚]	2 [ ] [
		3 יבר]כו ועננ[ו]ואמרו

Frg. 157	Frg. 156	Frg. 155
1 [הֿ]	1 [שו]ן	1 [˚ ם]
2 [ל]ילה]	2 [˚ ˚]	2 [כ]ה עלי[
		3 [ל]˚[ל]

Frg. 160	Frg. 159	Frg. 158
1 [˚]	1 [˚ ˚ ˚]	1 [ע]פֿ ˚ ˚]
2 [אֿ]	2 [ה˚ ˚ ˚]	2 [ל]
3 [ל]ֿ[		
[˚]		
4 [בֿ]		

Frg. 163	Frg. 162	Frg. 161
1 [˚]	1 [ש]דֿ[ו]קֿ]	1 [˚]
2 [ ]	2 [אֿ]	2 [˚]
3 [כו]רֿ[י		
4 [˚]		

Frg. 166	Frg. 165	Frg. 164
1 [˚ מ בֿ]	1 [כֿ ˚]	1 [אֿ ו ˚]
2 [˚ ˚ חֿ]	2 [ש]דוק]	2 [עמנ]ו עֿ]
	3 [ל][ל]	

Frg. 169	Frg. 168	Frg. 167
1 [˚]	1 [רש]	1 [ח]
2 [הם]	2 [י]הֿ]ל	2 [˚ עֿ]
3 [ל]		

Frg. 152

1 [. . .] "And peace (be) upon [you, O Israel . . ."]

2 [. . . .] (vacat) [. . .]

3 [. . .] they [will ble]ss and they will answer [and they will say . . .]

Frg. 153

1 [. . .] his [g]lory [. . .]

2 [. . .] all °[. . .]

Frg. 154

1 [. . .]°°°[. . .]

2 [. . .]*lbgw*°[. . .]

Frg. 155

1 [. . .]°*m*[. . .]

2 [. . . upon] you [. . .]

3 [. . .]°[. . .]*l*[. . .]

Frg. 156

1 [. . .]*šw*[. . .]

2 [. . .]°°[. . .]

Frg. 157

1 [. . .]*h* [. . .]

2 [. . . n]ight [. . .]

Frg. 158

1 [. . .]°°*pʿ*[. . .]

2 [. . .]*l*[. . .]

Frg. 159

1 [. . .]°°°[. . .]

2 [. . .]°°*h*[. . .]

Frg. 160

1 [. . .]°[. . .]

2 [. . .]ʼ[. . .]

3 [. . .]*d*[. . .]

4 [. . .]*b*[. . .]

Frg. 161

1 [. . .]°[. . .]

2 [. . .]°[. . .]

Frg. 162

1 [. . .] h[o]liness [. . .]

2 [. . .]ʼ[. . .]

Frg. 163

1 [. . .]° [. . .]

2 [. . .] [. . .]

3 [. . .] they [will] bless [. . .]

4 [. . .]° [. . .]

Frg. 164

1 [. . .]°*w* ʼ[. . .]

2 [. . .]*ṣ* with u[s . . .]

Frg. 165

1 [. . .]*k*°[. . .]

2 [. . .] holine[ss . . .]

3 [. . .]*l*[. . .]*l*[. . .]

Frg. 166

1 [. . .]*bm*°[. . .]

2 [. . .]*ḥw*°[. . .]

Frg. 167

1 [. . .]*t* [. . .]

2 [. . .]°°[. . .]

Frg. 168

1 [. . .]*šr* [. . .]

2 [. . .] *lhy*[. . .]

Frg. 169

1 [. . .]°[. . .]

2 [. . .]*hm*[. . .]

3 [. . .]*l*[. . .]

Frg. 172	*Frg. 171*	*Frg. 170*
1] ̊ [	1] ̊ ̊ [	1 ̊[הדש]
2 יב]ר̊כו]	2]ר̊י ̊[	2]ל[

Frg. 175	*Frg. 174*	*Frg. 173*
1] ̊ [	1]ובי]ום	1]ל מ̊[
2] לוא י ̊[	2]למ ̊[	
3] ̊ מ̊[		

Frg. 178	*Frg. 177*	*Frg. 176*
1]ר̊נות ע̊ם[	1]מ̊[	1]עטי[
	2] [	2]י̊ר̊ ̊[
	3] ̊[	

Frg. 181	*Frg. 180*	*Frg. 179*
1 וא]מ̊רו	1]ם	1] ̊ [
		2]א̊ש̊ר̊[

Frg. 184	*Frg. 183*	*Frg. 182*
1]אל יש[ראל	1]פר̊י בט̊נ̊]ה	1] ̊ ̊ [
2] ̊ [		

Frg. 187	*Frg. 186*	*Frg. 185*
1] עלי ̊[	1]אשר[	1]ש̊ר̊ ̊[

Frg. 190	*Frg. 189*	*Frg. 188*
1]שלח[	1] כב ̊[	1]כב̊ ̊[

Frg. 193	*Frg. 192*	*Frg. 191*
1]וד ̊[	1]י̊ר [	1]ר ̊ ̊ ה̊[
2] [		2]ל̊[

Frg. 196	*Frg. 195*	*Frg. 194*
1]בל ̊ ̊[	1] ̊ [	1]מש̊ ̊ [

Frg. 199	*Frg. 198*	*Frg. 197*
1]ו	1]במ[	1] מב ̊ [

Frg. 170

1 [. . .]*hdš*[. . .]

2 [. . .]*l*[. . .]

Frg. 173

1 [. . .]*l m*[. . .]

Frg. 176

1 [. . .]ʿ*ty*[. . .]

2 [. . .]*yr*°[. . .]

Frg. 179

1 [. . .]°[. . .]

2 [. . .] who [. . .]

Frg. 182

1 [. . .]°°[. . .]

Frg. 185

1 [. . .]*šr*°[. . .]

Frg. 188

1 [. . .] *kb*°[. . .]

Frg. 191

1 [. . .]*r*°°*h*[. . .]

2 [. . .]*l*[. . .]

Frg. 194

1 [. . .]° *mš*[. . .]

Frg. 197

1 [. . .] *mb*°[. . .]

Frg. 171

1 [. . .]°°[. . .]

2 [. . .]*dy*°[. . .]

Frg. 174

1 [. . .] and in the d[ay . . .]

2 [. . .]*lm*°[. . .]

Frg. 177

1 [. . .]*m*[. . .]

2 [. . .] [. . .]

3 [. . .]°[. . .]

Frg. 180

1 [. . .]*m*

Frg. 183

1 [. . .] fruit of [her] womb [. . .]

Frg. 186

1 [. . .] who [. . .]

Frg. 189

1 [. . .] *kb*°[. . .]

Frg. 192

1 [. . .]*yr* [. . .]

Frg. 195

1 [. . .]°[. . .]

Frg. 198

1 [. . .]*bm*[. . .]

Frg. 172

1 [. . .]°[. . .]

2 [. . .] they [will bl]ess [. . .]

Frg. 175

1 [. . .]°[. . .]

2 [. . .] not *y*°[. . .]

3 [. . .]° *m*[. . .]

Frg. 178

1 [. . .] shouts of joy with [. . .]

Frg. 181

1 [. . . and] they will [s]ay,

Frg. 184

1 [. . .] God of Is[rael . . .]

2 [. . .]

Frg. 187

1 [. . .] upon °[. . .]

Frg. 190

1 [. . .]*šlt*[. . .]

Frg. 193

1 [. . .]*wd*° [. . .]

2 [. . .] [. . .]

Frg. 196

1 [. . .]*bl*° °[. . .]

Frg. 199

1 [. . .]*w*

Frg. 202	*Frg. 201*	*Frg. 200*
1 [כען]	1 [לה֗ ֯◦]	1 [ה]

Frg. 205	*Frg. 204*	*Frg. 203*
1 [לולהי]	1 [בה֗]	1 [֯ו]

Frg. 208	*Frg. 207*	*Frg. 206*
1 [שה]	1 [ע֗ו ֯◦]	1 [קו֗]

Frg. 211	*Frg. 210*	*Frg. 209*
1 [שמ֗]	1 [מ ֯◦]	1 [לה]איר֗

Frg. 214	*Frg. 213*	*Frg. 212*
1 [ע ֯◦]	1 [ק֗ י ֯◦]	1 [ול ֯◦]

Frg. 215

1   [֯◦]
2   [לח]ודש
3   [מחשב֗ת
4   [גורלי ח֗ושך
5   א]ל ישראל
6   ובצא]ת מאור [
7   אורים]
8   [ושלח של]ום
9   עם תק]ופת השנה
10   [ ]
11   לחוד]ש
12   עמו [
13   [ל֗]

Frg. 216

1   [שר֗ ת ֯◦ ֯◦ו ֯◦]
2   [֯◦ השישי ומ֗]
3   [ר בינה ֯◦]
4   [֯◦ וב֗כ֗ול]

Frg. 217

1   [י יום]
2   [ל֗ אשר]
3   [֯◦ תמי֗]
4   [ו֗ שלו֗ם]
5   [ ]
6   [ל֗]

Frg. 200

1 [. . .]*h* [. . .]

Frg. 201

1 [. . .]°*lh* [. . .]

Frg. 202

1 [. . .] *k*ᶜ[. . .]

Frg. 203

1 [. . .]*w*°[. . .]

Frg. 204

1 *bh*[. . .]

Frg. 205

1 [. . .] if not [. . .]

Frg. 206

1 [. . .]*qw*[. . .]

Frg. 207

1 [. . .]° ᶜ*w*[. . .]

Frg. 208

1 [. . .]*šh*[. . .]

Frg. 209

1 [. . . to s]hine[. . .]

Frg. 210

1 [. . .]°*m*°[. . .]

Frg. 211

1 [. .]*šm*[. . .]

Frg. 212

1 [. . .]*wl*°[. . .]

Frg. 213

1 [. . .]°*yq*[. . .]

Frg. 214

1 [. . .]°°°[. . .]

Frg. 215

1 [. . .]°[. . .]

2 [. . . of the m]onth [. . .]

3 [. . .] desig[n of . . .]

4 [. . .] lots of dark[ness . . .]

5 [. . . G]od of Israel [. . . .]

6 [And when] the light [rise]s [. . .]

7 [. . .] lights [. . .]

8 [. . .] and he will send pea[ce . . .]

9 [. . .] with the turn[ning
   of the year . . .]

10 [. . . .] [. . .]

11 [. . .] of the mont[h . . .]

12 [. . .] his people[20] [. . .]

13 [. . .]*l*[. . .]

Frg. 216

1 [. . .]*šr t*°°*w* [. . .]

2 [. . .]° the sixth and *m*[. . .]

3 [. . .]*r* discernment °[. . .]

4 [. . .]° and in all [. . .]

Frg. 217

1 [. . .]*y* day [. . .]

2 [. . .]*l* who [. . .]

3 [. . .]° *tmy*[. . .]

4 [. . .]*w* peac[e . . .]

5 [. . . .] [. . .]

6 [. . .]*l*[. . .]

---

20 Or "with him."

Frg. 220 [lost?]	Frg. 219		Frg. 218	
	‏[חודש‏]‏	**1**	‏]‏ ֯ ‏[‏	**1**
	‏]‏ ֯ ‏ק מס‏	**2**	‏י‏]‏שרא‏֯ל אש‏]‏ר‏֯ ֯ ‏[‏	**2**
	‏]‏ל‏[‏	**3**	‏]‏גורל‏[‏ ‏]‏ ֯ ֯ ‏ה‏ ‏֯ה הסב‏֯‏[‏	**3**
			‏]‏֯ר לילה ויום‏[‏	**4**
			‏]‏ ‏[‏	**5**

Frg. 223		Frg. 222		Frg. 221	
‏]‏יבר‏[‏כו	**1**	‏]‏ותבר‏֯כ‏֯נ‏֯ו	**1**	יברכו ‏[‏וענו וא‏]‏מרו	**1**
				‏]‏פרי בט‏֯]‏נה	**2**

		Frg. 225[30]		Frg. 224	
		‏]‏ו‏֯ב‏[‏	**1**	‏]‏ה‏[‏ ‏[‏	**1**

---

[30] Fragments 226-232 have writing only on the reverse.

Frg. 218

1 [...]°[...]

2 [...I]srae[l wh]o °[...]

3 [...] lot [...]°*h hsb*[...]

4 [...]*yr* night and day [...]

5 [... .]   (vacat) [...]

Frg. 219

1 [...] month [...]

2 [...]*q ms*°[...]

3 [...]*l*[...]

Frg. 220 [*lost?*]

Frg. 221

1 [... they will bless] and
they will answer and
they will s[ay...]

2 [...] fruit of [her] wom[b...]

Frg. 222

1 [...] and you blessed u[s...]

Frg. 223

1 [...] they will ble[ss...]

Frg. 224

1 [...]*h*[...]

Frg. 225

1 [...]*wb*[...]

Appendix

Psalms Scrolls from the Judaean Desert

PETER W. FLINT

Psalms Scrolls from the Judaean Desert include thirty-nine Psalms scrolls or manuscripts incorporating Psalms (see Table), of which thirty-six were found at Qumran (three in Cave 1; one each in Caves 2, 3, 5, 6, and 8; twenty-three in Cave 4, and five in Cave 11). Another three scrolls were discovered further south: two at Masada and one at Naḥal Ḥever.

(a) Quantity Preserved. In decreasing order, the manuscripts with the greatest number of verses preserved are 11QPs[a], 4QPs[a], 5/6Ḥev-Se4 Ps, 4QPs[b], 4QPs[c], and 4QPs[e]. As the best preserved manuscript, the *Great Psalms Scroll* (11QPs[a]) features prominently in discussions concerning the Book of Psalms at Qumran. Copied in c. 50 CE, 11QPs[a] preserves forty-nine compositions (with Ps 120 not extant but originally included) that frequently differ from that of the Masoretic-150 (MT) Psalter in arrangement and in contents.

(b) Original Contents. Some Psalms scrolls originally contained only a few compositions or part of a Psalter (e.g. 4QPs[g], 4QPs[h], and 5QPs probably contained only Ps 119).

(c) Compositions in these manuscripts. Of the 150 Psalms found in the Masoretic Psalter, 126 are represented in the Psalms scrolls or other relevant manuscripts such as the *Pesharim* (1QpPs [1Q16], 4QpPs[a] [4Q171], 4QpPs[b] [4Q173], and 4QpPs[b] frg. 5 [4Q173 frg. 5]); the remaining twenty-four were most likely included, but are now lost due to deterioration and damage. Of Psalms 1–89, nineteen no longer survive (3–4, 20–21, 32, 41, 46, 55, 58, 61, 64–65, 70, 72–75, 80, 87), but of Psalms 90–150 only five are not extant (90, 108?, 110, 111, 117). At least fifteen "apocryphal" (that is, non-Masoretic) Psalms or compositions are distributed among five manuscripts (11QPs[a], 4QPs[f], 4Q522, 11QPs[b], 11QPsAp[a]); six of these were previously familiar to scholars (Psalms 151A, 151B, 154, 155; David's Last Words [= 2Sam 23:1–7]; Sir 51:13–30) and nine were unknown prior to the discovery of the Scrolls (the "Apostrophe to Judah," "Apostrophe to Zion," "David's Compositions," "Eschatological Hymn," "Hymn to the Creator," "Plea for Deliverance," and Psalms I–III of "A Liturgy for Healing the Stricken").

(d) Format of the Psalms Scrolls. At least ten manuscripts are arranged stichometrically (1QPs[a], 3QPs, 4QPs[b], 4QPs[c], 4QPs[g], 4QPs[h], 4QPs[l], 5QPs, 8QPs, MasPs[a]), and twenty-one in prose arrangement: (1QPs[b], 1QPs[c], 2QPs, 4QPs[a], 4QPs[e], 4QPs[f], 4QPs[j], 4QPs[k], 4QPs[m], 4QPs[n], 4QPs[o], 4QPs[p], 4QPs[q], 4QPs[r], 4QPs[s], 4QPs[w], 4Q522, pap6QPs, 11QPs[b], 11QPs[c], 11QPs[d]). One

scroll (11QPs[a]) contains a prose format with one Psalm – the acrostic 119 – arranged stichometrically.

(e) Titles or Superscriptions. The preserved superscriptions reveal little variation in comparison with the MT-Psalter; two exceptions are for Psalm 123 ("A Song of Ascents. Of David"; cf.. MT "A Song of Ascents") and Psalm 145 ("A Prayer. Of David"; cf. MT "A Song of Praise. Of David") in 11QPs[a].

(f) Comparative Datings. At least thirteen manuscripts were copied before the Common Era (see Table); the oldest two (4QPs[a] and 4QPs[w]) date to the second century BCE, and the remaining eleven to the first century BCE (1QPs[a], 4QPs[b], 4QPs[d], 4QPs[f], 4QPs[k], 4QPs[l], 4QPs[n], 4QPs[o], 4QPs[u], 4Q522, MasPs[b]). Seven scrolls are generally classified as Herodian (1QPs[c], 2QPs, 4QPs[h], 4QPs[m], 4QPs[p], 4QPs[r], 4QPs[v][?]), while four are assigned to the first century CE (1QPs[b], 3QPs, 5QPs, 8QPs). More specifically, ten are dated from the early to mid-first century CE (4QPs[e], 4QPs[g], 4QPs[j], 4QPs[q], 4QPs[t], 11QPs[a], 11QPs[b], 11QPs[c], 11QPs[d], MasPs[a]), and four from the mid-first century CE onwards (4QPs[c], 4QPs[s], 11QPsAp[a], 5/6Ḥev-Se4 Ps).

(g) Major Disagreements with the Masoretic Psalter. In comparison with the MT-150 Psalter, twelve scrolls contain major disagreements, whether in the *order* of Psalms (4QPs[a], 4QPs[b], 4QPs[d], 4QPs[e], 4QPs[k], 4QPs[n], 4QPs[q]), or in *content* (4QPs[f], 4Q522, 11QPsAp[a]), or both (11QPs[a] and 11QPs[b]).

(h) Other Disagreements. The Psalms scrolls contain hundreds of individual readings different from the MT. Several of these disagreements are significant for our understanding of the text of the Psalter: e.g., the missing Nun-verse of the acrostic Psalm 145:13 (11QPs[a] 17.2–3).

(i) Three Editions. Comparative examination shows that several collections of Psalms are found among the scrolls. While it is very likely that some manuscripts contain secondary compilations (e.g. 4Q522 and 11QPsAp[a]), others represent at least three literary editions of the Psalter: Psalms 1/2–89, the "11QPs[a]-Psalter" (= Psalms 1–89 plus the arrangement found in 11QPs[a], also represented by 4QPs[e] and 11QPs[b]), and the "MT-150 Psalter" (= Psalms 1–89 plus 90–150, attested by MasPs[b]).

Table of Psalms Scrolls from the Judaean Desert[1]

Details of the thirty-nine scrolls are summarized below. Column IV ("Includes Compositions not in MT") denotes those manu-

---

[1] Adapted from P. W. Flint, *The Dead Sea Psalms Scrolls and the Book of Psalms* (STDJ 17; Leiden, 1997) pp. 252–53.

scripts which contain "Apocryphal" compositions in addition to Psalms found in the Masoretic Text. Column V ("Range of Contents") lists the earliest and latest verses occurring in a scroll in terms of their Masoretic order. However, it must be emphasized that many manuscripts are very fragmentary, and thus contain only part of the specified content. Moreover, in several scrolls the order of preserved material differs from that of the Masoretic Psalter (cf. Col. III). Column VI ("Date or Period When Copied") indicates the approximate date of each manuscript based on palaeographical analysis.

Scroll by Siglum	Scroll by Number	Different Order from MT	Includes Compositions not in MT	Range of Contents (Using Order of MT)	Date or Period Copied	Photograph Numbers[2]
1QPs[a]	1Q10			86:5 to 119:80	50 BCE	PAM 40.481, 486−87, 492, 502, 504, 516, 547
1QPs[b]	1Q11			126:6 to 128:3	1st century CE	PAM 40.438, 446, 491, 535
1QPs[c]	1Q12			44:3 to 44:25	Herodian	PAM 40.504, 537, 141
1QpPs	1Q16		x	68:13−31	Herodian	LH 1398, 1421, 1430A, 1457; PAM 40.436, 443−44, 478, 495, 533, 535, 538, 540, 544; BNPA 88/830, 88/826
2QPs	2Q14			103:2 to 104:11	Herodian	PAM 40.639−40, 42.952
3QPs	3Q2			2:6−7	1st century CE	PAM 41.566, 42.955
4QPs[a]	4Q83	x		5:9 to 71:14	mid-2nd century BCE	PAM 43.027
4QPs[b]	4Q84	x		91:5 to 118:29	2nd half 1st century BCE	PAM 43.032, 42.025−26
4QPs[c]	4Q85			16:7 to 53:1	c. 50−68 CE	PAM 43.023, 156
4QPs[d]	4Q86	x		10.4:l to 147:20	mid-1st century BCE	PAM 43.021
4QPs[e]	4Q87	x		76:10 to 146:1(?)	mid-lst century CE	PAM 43.028
4QPs[f]	4Q88	x	x	22:15 to 109:28	c. 50 BCE	PAM 43.026, 603
4QPs[g]	4Q89			119:37 to 119:92	c. 50 CE	PAM 43.026
4QPs[h]	4Q90			119:10−21	Herodian	PAM 43.026
4QPs[j]	4Q91			48:1 to 53:5	c. 50 CE	PAM 43.030
4QPs[k]	4Q92	x		(?)99:1 to 135:16	1st century BCE	PAM 43.030
4QPs[l]	4Q93			104:3 to 104:12	2nd half 1st century BCE	PAM 43.030
4QPs[m]	4Q94			93:3 to 98:8	Herodian	PAM 43.030
4QPs[n]	4Q95	x		135:6 to 136:23	Herodian	PAM 43.030
4QPs[o]	4Q96			114:7 to 116:10	late 1st century BCE	PAM 43.030
4QPs[p]	4Q97			143:3 to 143:8	Herodian	PAM 43.030
4QPs[q]	4Q98	x		31:24 to 35:20	mid-1st century CE	Photo at Laboratoire de France, Paris
4QPs[r]	4Q98a			26:7 to 30:13	Herodian	PAM 43.030
4QPs[s]	4Q98b			5:8 to 88:17	50 CE or later	PAM 43.028−29, 156
4QPs[t]	4Q98c			42:6 only	c. 50 CE	PAM 42.081
4QPs[u]	4Q98d			99:1 only	late 1st centurv CE	PAM 43.021
4QPs[y] (?)	4Q98e (?) *olim* Mas1g/ MasPs[c]			18:26−29	Herodian	JWS 98
4QPs[w]	4Q236			89:20 to 89:31	175−125 BCE	PAM 43.399
4QpPs[a]	4Q171		x	37:7−60:9	Herodian	PAM 40.585, 614−15, 621, 992; 41.288, 303−4, 322, 515, 582, 793−94, 799, 858, 982, 999; 42.509, 623, 627−28, 640; 43.174, 341, 417−18, 421; 44.184, 189

[2] Tov, *Companion Volume*; Reed, *Catalogue*. For photographic images, see Tov, *The Dead Sea Scrolls on Microfiche*, Leiden, 1993. Abbreviations used: BNP = Bibliothèque Nationale, Paris; IAA = Israel Antiquities Authority; JWS = Jerusalem-West Semitic Research; LH = Lankester Harding; PAM = Palestine Archeological Museum [now the Rockefeller Museum]; SHR = Shrine of the Book.

Scroll by Siglum	Scroll by Number	Different Order from MT	Includes Compositions not in MT	Range of Contents (Using Order of MT)	Date or Period Copied	Photograph Numbers
4QpPs[b]	4Q173		x	118:20?−129:8	Herodian	PAM 41.312, 515, 581, 817; 43.440
4QpPs[b] frg. 5	4Q173 frg. 5		x	Ps 118:20?	Herodian	PAM 41.515, 817; 43.440
4QPs122	4Q522		x	122:1 to 122:9	2nd third of 1st century BCE	PAM 43.606
5QPs	5Q5			119:99 to 119:42	1st century CE	PAM 41.034; 42.316, 319
pap6QPs	6Q5			78:36−37	?	PAM 41.738, 42.943
8QPs	8Q2			17:5 to 18:13	1st century CE	PAM 42.357, 594, 951
11QPs[a]	11Q5	x	x	93:1 to 150:6	30−50 CE	PAM 42.177, 180; 43.757, 772−93, 795; SHR 6213−14, 6216, 6221−22
11QPs[b]	11Q6	x	x	77:18 to 144:2	1st half of 1st century CE	PAM 44.003, 005, 117; 42.176−77
11QPs[c]	11Q7			2:1 to 25:7	1st half of 1st century CE	PAM 42.176−77, 43.980, 44.005
11QPs[d]	11Q8			6:2 to 116:1	mid-1st century CE	PAM 44.005−8, 115; 43.980, 42.176−77
11QPsAp[a]	11Q11		x	91:1−16	50−70 CE	PAM 44.003−4, 113; 43.981−88; 42.177
Ḥev/Seiyal	XḤev/Se 4 (Se II, III, IV)			15:1 to 31:22	2nd half of lst century CE	PAM 42.188−90
MasPs[a]	Mas1e M1039−160			81:1 to 85:6	1st half of 1st century CE	SHR 5255, 5279A, 5289
MasPs[b]	Mas1f M1103−1742			147:18 to 150:6	2nd half of 1st century BCE	SHR 5616; IAA 302361, 302364

Selected Bibliography

Editions and Descriptions of the Psalms Scrolls

Allegro, J. M. *Qumrân Cave 4:I (4Q158−186)*. DJD 5; Oxford, 1968.

Baillet, M., J. T. Milik, and R. de Vaux, eds. *Les 'Petites Grottes' de Qumrân: Exploration de la falaise. Les grottes 2Q, 3Q, 5Q, 6Q, 7Q, à 10Q, Le rouleau de cuivre.* DJD III, Oxford, 1962.

Barthélemy, D. and J. T. Milik. *Qumran Cave I.* DJD 1; Oxford, 1955.

Flint, P. W. *The Dead Sea Psalms Scrolls and the Book of Psalms.* STDJ 17; Leiden, 1997, pp. 13−134, 243−71.

Flint, P. W. "The Biblical Scrolls from Naḥal Ḥever (including 'Wadi Seiyal')." In *Qumran Cave 4: XXVI, Miscellaneous Texts, Part 2.* DJD XXXVI; Oxford [in preparation].

García Martínez, F., E. J. C. Tigchelaar, and A. S. van der Woude. "Four Psalms Scrolls from Cave 11." In *Qumran Cave 11.* DJD XXIII; Oxford [in preparation].

Horgan, M. P. *Pesharim: Qumran Interpretations of Biblical Books.* CBQMS 8; Washington, D. C., 1979.

Milik, J. T. "Fragment d'une source du Psautier (4QPs89) et fragments des Jubilés, du Document de Damas, d'un phylactère dans la Grotte 4 de Qumran," *RB* 73 (1966) 94−106, esp. 94−104; and Pl. 1.

Puech, E. "Fragments du Psaume 122 dans un Manuscrit hébreu de la Grotte IV," *RQ* 9 (1977−78) 547−54.

Puech, E. *Textes Hebreux (4Q521−4Q528, 4Q576−4Q579)*

Qumrân Cave 4. XVIII. DJD XXV; Oxford [forthcoming, 1997].

Sanders, J. A. *The Psalms Scroll of Qumrân Cave 11* [11QPs[a]]. DJD IV; Oxford, 1965.

Sanders, J. A. *The Dead Sea Psalms Scroll.* Ithaca, NY, 1967.

Skehan, P. W. "Littérature de Qumran: A.Textes bibliques," *Supplément au Dictionnaire de la Bible* (1978) 9/10.805−22, esp. 813−17.

Skehan, P. W., E. Ulrich, and P. W. Flint. "The Cave 4 Psalms Scrolls." In *Qumran Cave 4:XI. The Writings.* DJD XVI; Oxford [in preparation].

Strugnell, J. "Notes en marge du volume V des 'Discoveries in the Judaean Desert of Jordan,'" *RQ* 7 (1970) 163−276.

Talmon, S. "The Psalms Scrolls from Masada." In *Masada: The Yigael Yadin Excavations 1963−1965, Final Reports*, edited by Y. Yadin, *et al.* Jerusalem, 1989−[forthcoming].

Talmon, S. "Hebrew Written Fragments from Masada," *DSD* 3 (1996) 168−77.

Talmon, S. "Fragments of a Psalms Scroll−MasPs[a] Ps 81:2[b]−85:6[a]," *DSD* 3 (1996) 296−314.

Talmon, S. "Unidentified Fragments of Hebrew Writings from the Estate of Yagael Yadin," *Tarbiz* 66 (1997) 113−21, esp. 113−15 [in Hebrew].

Yadin, Y. "Another Fragment (E) of the Psalms Scroll from Qumran Cave 11 (11QPs[a])," *Textus* 5 (1966) 1−10; and Pls. I−V.

Secondary Literature

Charlesworth, J.H. with J.A. Sanders, "More Psalms of David (Second Century B.C.–First Century A.D.)." In *OTP* 2:609–24.

Chyutin, M. "The Redaction of the Qumranic and the Traditional Book of Psalms as a Calendar," *RQ* 16 (1994) 367–95.

Flint, P.W. *The Dead Sea Psalms Scroll and the Book of Psalms.* STDJ 17; Leiden, 1997, pp. 135–241.

Goshen-Gottstein, M.H. "The Psalms Scroll (11QPsᵃ): A Problem of Canon and Text," *Textus* 5 (1966) 22–33.

Haran, M. "11QPsᵃ and the Canonical Book of Psalms." In *Minhah le-Nahum: Biblical and Other Studies Presented to Nahum M. Sarna in Honour of His 70th Birthday,* edited by M. Brettler and M. Fishbane. JSOTSup 154; Sheffield, 1993, pp. 93–201.

Sanders, J.A. "Variorum in the Psalms Scroll (11QPsᵃ)," *HTR* 59 (1966) 83–94.

Sanders, J.A. "Cave 11 Surprises and the Question of Canon," *McCQ* 21 (1968) 1–15. Reprinted in *New Directions in Biblical Archaeology,* edited by D.N. Freedman and J.C. Greenfield, Garden City, NY, 1969, pp. 101–116; and in *The Canon and Masorah of the Hebrew Bible: An Introductory Reader,* edited by S.Z. Leiman, New York, 1974, pp. 37–51.

Sanders, J.A. "The Qumran Psalms Scroll (11QPsᵃ) Reviewed." In *On Language, Culture, and Religion: In honor of Eugene A. Nida,* edited by M. Black and W.A. Smalley. The Hague and Paris, 1974, pp. 79–99.

Sanders, J.A. "Psalm 154 Revisited." In *Biblische Theologie und gesellschaftlicher Wandel: Für Norbert Lohfink, S.J.,* edited by G. Braulik, W. Gross, and S. McEvenue. Freiburg, 1993, pp. 296–306.

Skehan, P.W. "A Liturgical Complex in 11QPsᵃ," *CBQ* 34 (1973) 195–205.

Skehan, P.W. "Qumran and Old Testament Criticism." In *Qumran. Sa piété. Sa théologie et son milieu,* edited by M. Delcor. BETL 46; Paris and Leuven, 1978, pp. 163–82.

Skehan, P.W. "The Divine Name at Qumran, in the Masada Scroll, and in the Septuagint," *BIOSCS* 13 (1980) 14–44, esp. 42.

Talmon. S. "Aspects of the Textual Transmission of the Bible in the Light of Qumran Manuscipts," *Textus* 4 (1964) 95–132. Reprinted in *The World of Qumran from Within: Collected Studies,* Jerusalem and Leiden, 1989, pp. 71–116.

Talmon. S. "Pisqah Be'emsa' Pasuq and 11QPsᵃ," *Textus* 5 (1966) 11–21.

Talmon. S. "The Textual Study of the Bible – A New Outlook." In *Qumran and the History of the Biblical Text*, edited by F.M. Cross and S. Talmon. Cambridge, MA and London, 1975, pp. 321–400.

Tov. E. *Textual Criticism of the Hebrew Bible.* Minneapolis, 1992.

Ulrich, E. "Pluriformity in the Biblical Text, Text Groups, and Questions of Canon." In *Proceedings of the International Congress on the Dead Sea Scrolls: Madrid, 18–21 March 1991,* edited by J. Trebolle Barrera and L. Vegas Montaner. STDJ 11; Leiden and Madrid. 1992, vol. 1, pp. 23–41.

Ulrich, E. "The Bible in the Making: The Scriptures at Qumran." In *The Community of the Renewed Covenant: The Notre Dame Symposium on the Dead Sea Scrolls,* edited by E. Ulrich and J. VanderKam. Notre Dame, 1994, pp. 77–93.

Ulrich, E. "Multiple Literary Editions: Reflections toward a Theory of the History of the Biblical Text." In *Current Research and Technological Developments on the Dead Sea Scrolls: Conference on the Texts from the Judean Desert. Jerusalem, April 1995*, edited by D. Parry and S. Ricks. STDJ 20; Leiden, 1996, pp. 78–105; and Pls. I–II.

Wacholder, B.Z. "David's Eschatological Psalter: 11Q-Psalmsᵃ," *HUCA* 59 (1988) 23–72.

Wilson, G.H. "The Qumran Psalms Manuscripts and the Consecutive Arrangement of Psalms in the Hebrew Psalter," *CBQ* 45 (1983) 377–88.

Wilson, G.H. "The Qumran Psalms Scroll Reconsidered: Analysis of the Debate," *CBQ* 47 (1985) 624–42.

Wilson, G.H. *The Editing of the Hebrew Psalter.* SBLDS 76; Chico, CA, 1985.

Wilson, G.H. "The Qumran Psalms Scroll (11QPsᵃ) and the Canonical Psalter: Comparison of Canonical Shaping," *CBQ* 59 [forthcoming].

Dead Sea Scrolls[1]

List of Document Numbers, *Names of Documents,* **and Volume Numbers**
(where they will be printed)

CD *Damascus Document* **2**
Masada ShirShabb *Angelic Liturgy* **4B**

1QapGen *Genesis Apocryphon ar* **8**
1QH *Thanksgiving Hymns* **5**
1QM *War Scroll* **2**
1QpHab *Habakkuk Pesher* **6**
1QS *Rule of the Community* **1**
1Q1–13 *Biblical texts;* not included in PTSDSSP
1Q14 = 1QpMic *Micah Pesher 1* **6**
1Q15 = 1QpZeph *Zephaniah Pesher 1* **6**
1Q16 = 1QpPs68 *Psalm Pesher 1* **6**
1Q17 = 1QJub^{a} *Jubilees* **10**
1Q18 = 1QJub^{b} *Jubilees* **10**
1Q19a = 1Q19 = 1QNoah 2 *Noah Apocryphon 1* **7**
1Q19b = 1Q19bis *Noah Apocryphon 2* **7**
1Q20 = 1QapGen *Genesis Apocryphon ar* **8**
1Q21 = 1QTLevi *Testament of Levi ar* **10**
1Q22 = 1QDM *Sayings of Moses* **8**
1Q23–24 *Book of Giants?* **10**
1Q25 *Prophetic Apocryphon 2* **7**
1Q26 *A Wisdom Apocryphon* **8**
1Q27 = 1QMyst *Book of the Mysteries* **7**
1Q28a = 1QSa *Rule of the Congregation* **1**
1Q28b = 1QSb *Blessings* **1**
1Q29 *Liturgy of Three Tongues of Fire* **8**
1Q30 *Holy Messi[ah] Fragment* **5**
1Q31 *Men of the Covenant Fragment* **5**
1Q32 = 1QJN *New Jerusalem ar* **8**
1Q33 *War Scroll* **2**
1Q34–1Q34^{bis} = 1QPr Fetes *Prayers for Festivals* **4A**
1Q35 = 1QH35 *Thanksgiving Hymns* **5**
1Q36 *Liturgical Fragment 1* **5**
1Q37 *Elect of Israel Fragment* **5**
1Q38 *Liturgical Fragment 2* **5**
1Q39 *Liturgical Fragment 3* **5**
1Q40 *Liturgical Fragment 4* **5**
1Q41 *All the Land Fragment* **7**
1Q42 *Famine Fragment* **7**
1Q43 *All the Angel[s] Fragment* **7**
1Q44 *Indistinct Fragment 1* **9**
1Q45 *Poor Fragment* **7**
1Q46 *Just Weight Fragment* **7**
1Q47 *Indistinct Fragment 2* **9**
1Q48 *Indistinct Fragment 3* **9**
1Q49 *Your Strength Fragment* **7**
1Q50 *Tree Fragment* **7**
1Q51 *Eternal Fragment* **2**
1Q52 *Your Signs Fragment* **7**
1Q53 *Worm Fragment* **7**
1Q54 *The Covenant of His Glory Fragment* **7**
1Q55 *Nations Fragment* **7**
1Q56 *Resting Place Fragment* **7**
1Q57 *In Your Statutes Fragment* **7**
1Q58 *[Is]rael Fragment 1* **7**
1Q59 *Indistinct Fragment 4* **9**
1Q60 *Indistinct Fragment 5* **9**
1Q61 *Indistinct Fragment 6* **9**
1Q62 *Moses Fragment 1* **8**
1Q63 *On Their Standards Fragment ar* **7**
1Q64 *In the Bitterness Fragment ar* **7**
1Q65 *[I]srael Fragment 2 ar* **7**
1Q66 *Teacher Fragment ar* **7**
1Q67 *Your Blotting Out Fragment ar* **7**
1Q68 *Who is She? Fragment ar* **7**
1Q69 *Evil Ones Fragment ar* **7**
1Q70 = 1Q70bis *Indistinct Fragment 7* **9**
1Q71–72 *Biblical texts;* not included in PTSDSSP

2Q1–18 *Biblical texts;* not included in PTSDSSP
2Q19 = 2QJub^{a} *Jubilees* **10**
2Q20 = 2QJub^{b} *Jubilees* **10**
2Q21 = 2QapMoses *Apocryphon of Moses* **8**
2Q22 = 2QapDavid *David Apocryphon* **7**
2Q23 = 2QapProph *Prophetic Apocryphon 1* **7**
2Q24 = 2QJN *New Jerusalem ar* **8**
2Q25 *Juridical Fragment* **2**
2Q26 = 2QEn Giants *Book of Giants ar* **10**
2Q27 *Indistinct Fragment 8* **9**
2Q28 *Verdict Fragment* **2**
2Q29 *Indistinct Fragment 9* **9**
2Q30 *Indistinct Fragment 10* **9**
2Q31 *Indistinct Fragment 11* **9**
2Q32 *Indistinct Fragment 12* **9**
2Q33 *Ninev[eh] Fragment* **7**

3Q1–3 *Biblical texts;* not included in PTSDSSP
3Q4 = 3QpIsa *Isaiah Pesher 2* **6**
3Q5 = 3QJub *Jubilees* **10**
3Q6 = 3QHymn *Hymn of Praise* **5**
3Q7 = 3QTestJu? *Testament of Judah* **10**
3Q8 *Angel of Pea[ce] Fragment* **7**
3Q9 *Our Congregation Fragment* **7**
3Q10 *Indistinct Fragment 13* **9**
3Q11 *Indistinct Fragment 14* **9**
3Q12 *Indistinct Fragment 15* **9**
3Q13 *Indistinct Fragment 16* **9**
3Q14 *Indistinct Fragment 17* **9**
3Q15 *Copper Scroll* **9**

4Q1–14 *Biblical texts;* not included in PTSDSSP
4Q15–16 = 4QExod^{d-e} *Excerpted Exodus* **6**
4Q17–36 *Biblical texts;* not included in PTSDSSP
4Q37–38 = 4QDeut^{j,k1} *Excerpted Deuteronomy* **6**
4Q39–40 *Biblical texts;* not included in PTSDSSP
4Q41 = 4QDeut^{n} *Excerpted Deuteronomy* **6**
4Q42–43 *Biblical texts;* not included in PTSDSSP
4Q44 = 4QDeut^{q} *Excerpted Deuteronomy* **6**
4Q45–87 *Biblical texts;* not included in PTSDSSP

---

[1] For further information see Tov, *Companion Volume*; Reed, *Catalogue;* and Fitzmyer, *Tools*.

4Q524 *A Halakhic Text* **3**
4Q525 *Beatitudes* **5**
4Q526 *Hebrew Fragment C* **9**
4Q527 *Hebrew Fragment D* **9**
4Q528 *Hebrew Fragment E* **9**
4Q529 *Words of Michael ar* **8**
4Q530 *Book of Giants*[b] *ar* **10**
4Q531 *Book of Giants*[c] *ar* **10**
4Q532 *Book of Giants*[d] *ar* **10**
4Q533 *Giants or Pseudo-Enoch ar* **10**
4Q534 = 4QMess *Elect of God Text ar* **7**
4Q535 *Aramaic Fragment N* **9**
4Q536 *Aramaic Fragment C* **9**
4Q537 = AJa *Apocryphon of Jacob ar* **7**
4Q538 = AJu *Apocryphon of Judah ar* **7**
4Q539 = AJo *Apocryphon of Joseph ar* **7**
4Q540 = AhA bis = 4QTLevi[c]? *Testament of Levi ar* **10**
4Q541 = AhA = 4QTLevi[d]? *Testament of Levi ar* **10**
4Q542 *Testament of Qahat ar* **8**
4Q543–548 *Visions of Amram*[a-f] *ar* **8**
4Q549 *Work Mentioning Hur and Miriam* **8**
4Q550 = PrEsther[a-e+f] *Prayer of Esther ar* **5**
4Q551 *Daniel and Susannah? ar* **10**
4Q552–553 *Four Kingdoms*[a-b] *ar* **8**
4Q554 = 4QJN[a] *New Jerusalem ar* **8**
4Q555 = 4QJN[b] *New Jerusalem ar* **8**
4Q556 *Vision*[a] *ar* **8**
4Q557 *Vision*[c] *ar* **8**
4Q558 *Vision*[b] *ar* **8**
4Q559 *Biblical Chronology ar* **8**
4Q560 *Proverbs? ar* **8**
4Q561 *Physiognomy or Horoscope ar* **9**
4Q562 *Aramaic Fragment D* **9**
4Q563 *Aramaic Fragment E* **9**
4Q564 *Aramaic Fragment F* **9**
4Q565 *Aramaic Fragment G* **9**
4Q566 *Aramaic Fragment H* **9**
4Q567 *Aramaic Fragment I* **9**
4Q568 *Aramaic Fragment K* **9**
4Q569 *Aramaic Fragment L* **9**
4Q570 *Aramaic Fragment R* **9**
4Q571 *Aramaic Fragment V* **9**

4Q572 *Aramaic Fragment W* **9**
4Q573 *Aramaic Fragment X* **9**
4Q574 *Aramaic Fragment Y* **9**
4Q575 *Aramaic Fragment Z* **9**

5Q1–8 *Biblical texts;* not included in PTSDSSP
5Q9 = 5QToponyms *Toponyms* **7**
5Q10 = 5QapMal *Malachi Apocryphon* **7**
5Q11 *Possible Fragment of the Rule of the Community* **1**
5Q12 = 5QD *Damascus Document* **2**
5Q13 *Sectarian Rule* **1**
5Q14 = 5QCurses *Curses* **5**
5Q15 = 5QJN *New Jerusalem ar* **8**
5Q16 *His Couches Fragment* **7**
5Q17 *Indistinct Fragment 26* **9**
5Q18 *Indistinct Fragment 27* **9**
5Q19 *Indistinct Fragment 28* **9**
5Q20 *Lebanon Fragment* **7**
5Q21 *Indistinct Fragment 29* **9**
5Q22 *Abraha[m] Fragment* **7**
5Q23 *Land Fragment* **7**
5Q24 *Indistinct Fragment 30 ar* **9**
5Q25 *Sons of Jacob Fragment* **7**

6Q1–7 *Biblical texts;* not included in PTSDSSP
6Q8 = 6QapGen *Genesis Apocryphon ar* **8**
6Q9 = 6QapSam/Kgs *Samuel-Kings Apocryphon* **7**
6Q10 = 6QProph *Prophetic Text* **7**
6Q11 = 6QAllegory *Allegory of the Vine* **7**
6Q12 = 6QapProph *Prophetic Apocryphon 3* **7**
6Q13 = 6QPriestProph *Priestly Prophecy* **7**
6Q14 = 6QApoc *Apocalyptic Text ar* **8**
6Q15 = 6QD *Damascus Document* **2**
6Q16 = 6QBen *Benediction 2* **5**
6Q17 = 6QCal *Calendar Text* **9**
6Q18 = 6QHymn *Hymns* **5**
6Q19–20 *Biblical Paraphrases* **6**
6Q21 *Prophetic Fragment* **7**
6Q22 *Mose[s] Fragment 2* **8**

6Q23 *Indistinct Fragment 31 ar* **9**
6Q24 *Indistinct Fragment 32* **9**
6Q25 *Indistinct Fragment 33* **9**
6Q26 *M[en] of the House Fragment* **7**
6Q27 *Indistinct Fragment 34* **9**
6Q28 *Indistinct Fragment 35* **9**
6Q29 *Indistinct Fragment 36* **9**
6Q30 *[Congrega]tion of the Faithless Fragment* **7**
6Q31 *Indistinct Fragment 37* **9**

7Q1 *Biblical text;* not included in PTSDSSP
7Q2 *Letter of Jeremiah* **10**
7Q3–19 *Greek Fragments* **9**

8Q1–4 *Biblical texts;* not included in PTSDSSP
8Q5 = 8QHymn *A Hymn* **5**

9Q1 *Papyrus Fragment* **9**

10Q1 *Ostracon* **9**

11Q1–4 *Biblical texts;* not included in PTSDSSP
11Q5 = 11QPs[a] *Non-Masoretic Psalms* **4A**
11Q6 = 11QPs[b] *Non-Masoretic Psalms* **4A**
11Q7–9 *Biblical texts;* not included in PTSDSSP
11Q10 = 11QtgJob *Targum on Job* **6**
11Q11 = 11QPsAp[a] *A Liturgy for Healing the Stricken* **4A**
11Q12 = 11QJub *Jubilees* **10**
11Q13 = 11QMelch *Melchizedek* **6**
11Q14 = 11QBer *Benediction 1* **5**
11Q15–16 *11QHymns*[a-b] **5**
11Q17 = 11QShirShabb *Angelic Liturgy* **4B**
11Q18 = 11QJN *New Jerusalem ar* **8**
11Q19 = 11QTemple[a] *Temple Scroll* **7**
11Q20 = 11QTemple[b] *Temple Scroll* **7**
11Q21 *Unidentified Fragment 4 paleo* **9**
11Q22 *Unidentified Fragment 5* **9**
11Q23 *Unidentified Fragment 6* **9**

Names of Documents, (Document Numbers), and **Volume Numbers**
(where they will be printed)

Men of People Who Err (4Q306) **8**
Men of the Covenant Fragment (1Q31) **5**
M[en] of the House Fragment (6Q26) **7**
Micah Pesher 1–2 (1Q14), (4Q168) **6**
Midrash Sefer Moses (4Q249) **3**
More Precepts of the Torah (4Q394–399) **3**
Moses Apocryphon A–C (4Q374–375, 377) **8**
Moses Fragment 1–2 (1Q62), (6Q22) **8**
Mysteries^{a-c} (4Q299–301) **8**
Nabatean Letter (4Q343) **9**
Nahum Pesher (4Q169) **6**
Narrative 1–4 (4Q458, 461–463) **8**
Nations Fragment (1Q55) **7**
New Jerusalem (1Q32), (2Q24), (4Q232, 554–555), (5Q15), (11Q18) **8**
Ninev[eh] Fragment (2Q33) **7**
Noah Apocryphon 1–2 (1Q19a–b) **7**
Non-Masoretic Psalms (4Q88), (11Q5–6) **4A**
On Resurrection (4Q521) **7**
On Their Standards Fragment ar (1Q63) **7**
Ordinances (4Q159) **1**
Ordo (4Q334) **9**
Ostracon (10Q1) **9**
Otot (4Q319) **10**
Our Congregation Fragment (3Q9) **7**
Papyrus Fragment (9Q1) **9**
Papyrus Fragment of Tobit? (4Q478) **10**
Papyrus of Jubilees? (4Q482–483) **10**
Parabiblical Exodus gr (4Q127) **6**
Parabiblical Joshua paleo (4Q123) **6**
Parabiblical Kings (4Q382) **6**
Parabiblical Pentateuch (4Q368) **6**
Parable of the Tree (4Q302a) **8**
Pesher on the True Israel (4Q239) **6**
Pesher-Like Fragment (4Q183) **6**
Physiognomy or Horoscope ar (4Q561) **9**
Poetic Fragments 1–3 (4Q445–447) **5**
Polemical Fragment (4Q471a) **8**
Poor Fragment (1Q45) **7**
Possible Fragment of the Rule of the Community (5Q11) **1**
Praise of God (4Q302) **5**
Prayer for King Jonathan (4Q448) **5**
Prayer Fragment (1Q34a) **4**
Prayer of Enosh? (4Q369) **5**
Prayer of Esther ar (4Q550) **5**
Prayer of Joseph (4Q371–373) **5**
Prayer of Michael (4Q471b) **5**
Prayer of Nabonidus (4Q242) **5**
Prayers for Festivals (1Q34–1Q34^{bis}), (4Q507–509) **4A**

Priestly Prophecy (6Q13) **7**
Prophetic Apocryphon 1–3 (1Q25), (2Q23), (6Q12) **7**
Prophetic Fragment (6Q21) **7**
Prophetic Text (6Q10) **7**
Proverbs? ar (4Q560) **8**
Psalm Pesher 1–3 (1Q16), (4Q171, 173) **6**
Psalms of Joshua^{a-b} (4Q378–379) **5**
Psalter-Like Fragment (4Q237) **4**
Pseudepigraphic Work 1–3 (4Q229, 459–460) **8**
Pseudo-Daniel ar (4Q243–245) **6**
Pseudo-Ezekiel^{a-d, g} (4Q385–388, 391) **8**
Pseudo-Lamentations (4Q179) **5**
Pseudo-Moses^{a-e} (4Q385a, 387a, 388a–390) **8**
Purification Ritual (4Q512) **5**
Purification Rule (4Q514) **1**
Qumran Pseudepigraphic Psalms (4Q380–381) **4A**
Resting Place Fragment (1Q56) **7**
Reworked Pentateuch^{a-e} (4Q158, 364–367) **6**
Rule of the Community (1QS), (4Q255–264) **1**
Rule of the Congregation (1Q28a) **1**
Rules (4Q513) **1**
Sale of Land 1–2 (4Q345–346) **9**
Sale of Property (4Q349) **9**
Samuel-Kings Apocryphon (6Q9) **7**
Sapiential Fragments (4Q307–308); 1–3 (4Q485–4Q487) **8**
Sapiential Testament (4Q185) **8**
Sapiential Works (4Q408, 410–413); A^{a-e} (4Q415–418, 423); B–C (4Q419, 425); E (4Q423a); 1–6 (4Q424, 426, 472, 474–476) **8**
Sayings of Moses (1Q22) **8**
Scribbles on Papyrus (4Q361) **9**
Sectarian Rule (5Q13) **1**
Serekh Ha-Niddot (Menstrual Flow) (4Q284) **3**
So-Called Marriage Ritual (4Q502) **5**
Songs of the Master (4Q510–511) **5**
Sons of Jacob Fragment (5Q25) **7**
Tanhumim (4Q176) **6**
Targum on Job (4Q157), (11Q10) **6**
Targum on Leviticus (4Q156) **6**
Teacher Fragment ar (1Q66) **7**
Temple Scroll (11Q19–20) **7**
Testament of Judah (3Q7), (4Q484) **10**
Testament of Levi ar (1Q21), (4Q213–214, 540–541) **10**

Testament of Naphtali (4Q215) **10**
Testament of Qahat ar (4Q542) **8**
Testimonies (4Q175) **6**
Thanksgiving Hymns (1QH, 1Q35), (4Q427–432) **5**
Three Tongues of Fire (4Q376) **8**
Tobit ar (4Q196–199) **10**
Toponyms (5Q9) **7**
Treatise on Genesis and Exodus (4Q422) **6**
Tree Fragment (1Q50) **7**
Two Ways (4Q473) **8**
Unclassified Fragments 2–5 (4Q178, 311, 313, 316) **9**
Unclassified Fragments 6–7 (4Q464a–b) **6**
Unclassified Fragments 8–16 (4Q465, 479–481, 481b–f) **9**
Unidentified Fragments 1, 4–6 (4Q250), (11Q21–23) **9**
Unidentified Parabiblical Material paleo (4Q124–125) **6**
Unidentified Parabiblical Material gr (4Q126) **6**
Unidentified Pesher (4Q172) **6**
Various Prayers (4Q441–444, 449–457) **5**
Verdict Fragment (2Q28) **2**
Vision^{a-c} (4Q556–558) **8**
Vision of Samuel (4Q160) **7**
Visions of Amram^{a-f} ar (4Q543–548) **8**
War Scroll (1QM, 1Q33), (4Q491–496) **2**
War Scroll-Like Fragment (4Q497) **2**
Ways of Righteousness^{a-b} (4Q420–421) **8**
Who is She? Fragment ar (1Q68) **7**
Wicked and Holy (4Q180–181) **2**
Wisdom Apocryphon (1Q26) **8**
Words of the Lights (4Q504–506) **4A**
Words of Michael ar (4Q529) **8**
Words to the Sons of Dawn (4Q298) **8**
Work Mentioning Hur and Miriam (4Q549) **8**
Work Similar to Barki Nafshi (4Q439) **5**
Work with Citation of Jubilees (4Q228) **10**
Work with Prayers (4Q291–293) **5**
Worm Fragment (1Q53) **7**
Your Blotting Out Fragment ar (1Q67) **7**
Your Signs Fragment (1Q52) **7**
Your Strength Fragment (1Q49) **7**
Zephaniah Pesher 1–2 (1Q15), (4Q170) **6**
Zodiology and Brontology ar (4Q318) **9**